hirteen u   Stat

ne people to dissolve the political b

ture's God entitle them, a decent

to be self-evident, that all men a

That to secure these rights, Gover

these ends, it is the Right of the

hem shall seem most likely to effe

accordingly all experience hath

t when along train of abuses an

ch Government, and to provide

their former Systems of Governm

THE REVOLUTIONARY YEARS

Britannica's Book
of the
American Revolution

THE REVOLUTIONARY YEARS

*Britannica's Book
of the
American Revolution*

Mortimer J. Adler
Editor

Wayne Moquin
Associate Editor

ENCYCLOPÆDIA BRITANNICA, INC.

Chicago Toronto London Geneva Sydney Tokyo Manila Johannesburg Seoul

KEY TO SOURCE CODES

Archives   *American Archives: Fourth Series Containing a Documentary History of the English Colonies in North America from the King's Message to Parliament of March 7, 1774, to the Declaration of Independence by the United States.* Edited by Peter Force. In 6 vols. Washington, 1837-1846. The six series of this collection contain documents dating from *circa* 1600 to 1787.

C. F. Adams   *The Works of John Adams, Second President of the United States, with a Life of the Author.* Edited by Charles Francis Adams. In 10 vols. Boston, 1850-1856.

Ford   *The Writing of Thomas Jefferson.* Edited by Paul L. Ford. In 10 vols. New York and London, 1892-1899.

H. A. Washington   *The Writings of Thomas Jefferson: Being his Autobiography, Correspondence, Reports, Messages, Addresses and Other Writings, Official and Private.* Edited by H. A. Washington. In 9 vols. Washington, 1853-1854. Vol. 8, Philadelphia, 1871.

J. C. Hamilton   *The Works of Alexander Hamilton, etc., etc.* Edited by John C. Hamilton. In 7 vols. New York, 1850-1851.

Johnston   *The Correspondence and Public Papers of John Jay.* Edited by Henry P. Johnston. In 4 vols. New York, 1890-1893.

Journals   *Journals of the American Congress: from 1774 to 1788.* In 4 vols. Washington, 1823.

MHSC   *Collections, Massachusetts Historical Society.* Cambridge and Boston, 1795 *et seq.*

Niles   *Principles and Acts of the Revolution in America.* Edited by Hezekiah Niles. Centennial edition, New York, 1876 (first published Baltimore, 1822).

OSL   *Old South Leaflets.* Published by the Directors of the Old South Work, Old South Meeting House. In 8 vols. (Documents 1-200). Boston, n.d.

Sparks   *The Works of Benjamin Franklin, etc., etc.* Edited by Jared Sparks. In 10 vols. Boston, 1836-1840.

Thorpe   *The Federal and State Constitutions, Colonial Charters, and Other Organic Laws of the States, Territories, and Colonies now or Heretofore Forming the United States of America.* Edited by Francis N. Thorpe. In 7 vols. Washington, 1909.

Contents

Introduction

This book is entitled *The Revolutionary Years*. Yet the time span covered in its pages is considerably greater than the eight-year period during which the War for Independence was fought. This apparent contradiction represents an acceptance of and agreement with the view of many of the early patriots that the "Rebellion" and the "Revolution" were not the same thing. John Adams wisely observed in 1818 that the war had been only a phase of the Revolution. "The Revolution," he said, "was effected before the war commenced. The Revolution was in the minds and hearts of the people. . . ."

It was not Adams' intent to play down the crucial importance of the war by which independence was won. But he regarded the war as a transitional conflict within a larger revolutionary context. The rebellion was, first of all, the culmination of a series of politico-economic contests with Great Britain, beginning about 1763 and eventuating in the DECLARATION OF INDEPENDENCE and its accompanying war. But the war—the rebellion—was also part of a much longer evolutionary process involving the way the colonists thought about the new land they were living in, about the vast opportunities it offered, about the adapting of old-world institutions to utterly new circumstances, about the breakdown of rigid social class lines, and about the enlarged areas of economic, social, and religious freedom.

As the uniqueness of their situation coalesced with the struggle for independence, many of the colonists, now rebels and Americans, realized that what was under way involved more than an act of separation from Britain. They felt, if they did not always say it explicitly, that they were launching a new experiment as well as a new nation. The implications of this newness only slowly became apparent as war gave place to the need for a workable form of government that would not be simply a weak imitation of what they had thrown off. Very soon after the war, perceptive men in the new states announced that much remained to be done. Thinkers such as Noah Webster, Joel Barlow, Alexander Hamilton, James Madison, and James Wilson urged the completion of the task of political revolution that had really only been well started by the DECLARATION OF INDEPENDENCE. The Founding Fathers responded to this demand by framing the CONSTITUTION of 1787.

We, to whom it has been given to celebrate the Bicentennial of the Declaration, know that whatever revolution was begun by our 18th-century American ancestors was never completed by them. Even the Constitution itself was more a beginning than an ending, for it was merely a first firm step on the road to expanding opportunities and political freedom.

Widening the definition and extent of "the revolutionary years" may seem at first to obscure more than it clarifies. It is easier, if somewhat non-reflective, to celebrate a day, a specific occurrence that can be pinned down as to its place and time. The vivid image of a Paul Revere's ride, a battle at Lexington or Concord, a Valley Forge, touches our romantic sensibilities more intimately than a matrix of ideas and issues that span decades and tend to become somewhat fuzzy for those whose current concerns may be so different.

But what we really celebrate this Bicentennial Year is not just a day or a series of occurrences that went to make up a past war. What we celebrate is the Revolution—the people, the politics, the conflicts, and the resolutions—everything that worked together to make the United States what it became in 1789—and beyond. Our country is not what it was two hundred years ago. But what it is today it nevertheless owes in great measure to what was said and done in that far-off century.

This book, then, is not merely a recapitulation of the War for Independence. It is an attempt to set before the reader the "what-happened" of our Revolution in terms of the issues and conflicts that fired the colonists and prodded them to make a new nation. It is a commemoration of how the Americans worked out their political destiny by means of trial and error, success and failure, with all the vices and virtues, shortcomings, sense and nonsense that encumber every such complex undertaking. The selections in this book are meant to allow those whom we designate as Founding Fathers to speak for themselves as they once spoke to each other.

Such a procedure does not allow for a direct exchange of ideas between them and us. But it does allow us to compare the way we think about government, politics, liberty, protest, taxation, restraint, and the rest of the social apparatus with the way the people of 1763, 1776, and 1789 thought about the same matters. They did not necessarily agree with each other any more than we at present do. And we may even find that we do not agree with them on how a people ought to govern themselves. But whether we agree or disagree, at least we will be acquainted with a central portion of our heritage. A central portion of our heritage, but by no means all of it. For the American heritage stretches backward through the whole colonial era and into the stream of western European history. And it stretches forward through the 20th century and on into the 21st. "The revolutionary years" cannot be bracketed with dates, because the Revolution that began in America has never ended.

Chronology

1763

Feb. 10. Treaty of Paris ends Nine Years' Great War and breaks French power in North America. France cedes to the British all possessions in Canada and, except New Orleans, the eastern half of Louisiana (the Mississippi Valley), including navigation rights on the Mississippi River. Western half of Louisiana extending to the Rockies is granted by France to Spain along with New Orleans; this territory remains under Spanish control until 1800, when it is returned to France by secret Treaty of San Ildefonso.

May 16 - June 18. "Conspiracy of Pontiac." Indian tribes in Ohio-Great Lakes region unite in attacks on settlements and forts, now held by British. In one month all forts west of Niagara are destroyed, except Forts Pitt and Detroit; Fort Detroit is besieged by Ottawa tribe and their allies under Chief Pontiac for five months. **Oct.-Nov.** Pontiac gives up efforts to destroy Fort Detroit, but although tribes elsewhere have come to terms with British in August, he does not make peace with Indian Commissioner Sir William Johnson until July 25, 1766. Indians accept British rule, surrender white captives and some individual Indians who have been charged with personal crimes.

Oct. 7. Proclamation of 1763 is signed by George III. To conciliate Indians, end land speculation, and consolidate settlement and government on the frontier, a royal proclamation, prepared and issued in London, forbids general settlement west of the Appalachian Mountains and regulates purchases of land from Indians east of stated limits; it also orders settlers in upper Ohio country "forthwith to remove themselves." Indian territory west of the Proclamation line is put under military control. Former French territories are divided into three small provinces, East Florida, West Florida, and Quebec; and English law is established in Quebec, an unpopular move with French Catholic settlers.

1764

April 5. Sugar Act, revising Molasses Act of 1733, becomes first Parliamentary measure specifically designed to raise money in the colonies for the British Crown. The Act inaugurates the Grenville ministry policy requiring colonies to help pay costs of administering the empire, now greatly extended by the gains made in the Nine Years' Great War; the policy, never actually put in force, is calculated to make the colonies also contribute to payment of the British war debt. Actions mark the end of previous purely commercial policy of Britain toward her colonies.

A Grenville measure of the same date is designed to enforce trade laws by strengthening the poorly run customs service; another is the Currency Act, directed especially at Virginia, which had issued paper money during the war. This act prohibits the plantation colonies from issuing legal tender, a prohibition that had been in effect since 1751 in the commercial colonies of New England. The Act thus creates a bond of interest between these two regions.

May 24. Grenville measures are subject of Boston town meeting at which James Otis brings up for the first time the issue of taxation without representation and proposes a protest by all the colonies. **June 12.** Massachusetts House of Representatives forms a committee of correspondence to sound out other colonies.

July. Otis' *The Rights of the British Colonies Asserted and Proved* summarizes the taxation-without-representation argument.

August. Boston merchants agree to stop buying British luxury goods, thus beginning the policy of resistance by nonimportation that is taken up by all colonies within the year.

1765 - 1766

March 22. Stamp Act, Parliament's first direct tax imposed on the American colonies, requires purchase of tax stamps for most kinds of circulating paper, such as pamphlets, licenses, ship's papers, legal documents, insurance policies, and newspapers.

March 24. Quartering Act requires colonial authorities to provide food, lodging in barracks, and supplies for British troops. Various acts of this kind are passed, the last in 1774.

May 29. Virginia Resolutions proposed by Patrick Henry with "Treason" speech. To oppose the Stamp Act, which affects all classes and sections, Sons of Liberty are or-

ganized and use violence to force Crown collection agents to resign. **Aug. 26.** Mob attacks home of Massachusetts Chief Justice Thomas Hutchinson, at Boston. **Oct. 9-25.** Circular letter sent June 8 from Massachusetts Assembly to other colonies leads to Stamp Act Congress at New York City; 9 colonies are represented. **Oct. 19.** Congress adopts John Dickinson's moderate "Declaration of Rights and Grievances" to be submitted to British government. **Oct. 28-Dec. 9.** Further nonimportation agreements are signed by New York, Philadelphia, and Boston merchants, and by November 1, when Stamp Act goes into effect, business is almost stopped in all colonies. Business resumes by end of year without stamps in defiance of the law. **Jan. 17, 1766.** Merchants in Britain move for repeal of Act, citing business failures caused by shrinking American market for their goods.

Among colonial writings in opposition to Grenville policy are John Dickinson's *Considerations Upon the Rights of the Colonists to the Privileges of British Subjects,* Daniel Dulany's *Considerations on the Propriety of Imposing Taxes,* and John Adams' series of articles in the *Boston Gazette,* revised and republished in book form in 1768.

1765 - 1767

First professional training in medicine offered by College of Philadelphia (affiliated with University of Pennsylvania in 1791). King's College (later Columbia University) offers medical training in 1767.

1765 - 1781

Pennsylvania-born painter, Benjamin West, having moved permanently to England, teaches and influences visiting American artists; among them are Charles Willson Peale, Gilbert Stuart, John Singleton Copley, and Ralph Earl.

1766

March 18. Parliament repeals Stamp Act on argument of William Pitt that colonies should not be taxed without representation, and on testimony of Benjamin Franklin, agent for Pennsylvania, that colonies are unable to pay tax, so that enforcement by troops may lead to rebellion. Declaratory Act of same day nevertheless affirms authority of Parliament over colonies "in all cases whatsoever."

April 26. Nonimportation policy is abandoned when colonies learn of repeal of Stamp Act. **June 30.** New York Assembly votes statues to honor George III and William Pitt.

John Street Church, first colonial Methodist Church, is established in New York City, breaking away, as elsewhere, from Anglicans. Spreads, notably to Virginia, through activities of itinerant preachers sent out by English founder, John Wesley.

1766 - 1767

Aug. 11, 1766. Refusal by New York Assembly in January to support Quartering Act of 1765 increases tension and eventually leads to clashes between British soldiers and colonials when British destroy liberty pole in New York. **June 6, 1767.** Assembly finally votes appropriation for the Act, temporarily avoiding suspension ordered by Parliament in December 1766, but suspension is nevertheless put into effect on October 1.

1766. Southwark Theatre, first permanent playhouse to be built in America, erected in Philadelphia; opening performance is Vanbrugh and Cibber's *The Provoked Husband*. **1767.** First native play to be professionally produced in the colonies, *The Prince of Parthia*, by Thomas Godfrey, is shown at same theater.

1767

Philadelphia instrument maker David Rittenhouse builds first colonial apparatus (orrery) for demonstrating the phases and motions of the planets in the solar system.

1767 - 1768

June 29. Townshend Acts (named after Charles Townshend, nominally chancellor of the exchequer, actually head of the British government) impose duties on various imports and empower Crown authorities to collect payment. These duties are "external" taxes, and thus theoretically acceptable to the colonists, but as their aim is in part to pay the cost of civil administration, the taxation-without-representation issue is raised again. **Oct. 28.** Nonimportation is revived first in Boston and then (December 2-29) in other colonies. **Nov. 5, 1767-Jan. 1768.** John Dickinson's *Letters from a Farmer in Pennsylvania to the Inhabitants of the British Colonies,* 12 essays, appear in the *Pennsylvania Chronicle,* calling Acts unconstitutional and criticizing suspension of New York Assembly.

Daniel Boone, starting from North Carolina, makes his first exploration west of Appalachians; travels along present-day Kentucky-West Virginia border. Others from the colonies have visited the region since at least 1750.

"Yankee Doodle" (from an English song with an air known as early as the 16th century in Holland) mentioned in libretto of first American opera (printed but not produced), *The Disappointment, or the Force of Credulity;* unknown librettist uses the pen name "Andrew Barton."

1768

Feb. 11. Massachusetts Circular Letter drawn up by Samuel Adams denounces Townshend Acts, urges united colonial opposition to them. **March 4.** Massachusetts Governor Sir Francis Bernard dissolves General Court after condemning Letter as seditious. **May.** By this time assemblies of New Hampshire, New Jersey, and Connecticut have upheld Massachusetts, and similar letter is sent out by Virginia Assembly. **June 30.** Massachusetts Assembly votes 92-17 to defy British command to rescind letter. Minority who vote to support Crown are denounced by Sons of Liberty, and seven are defeated in election of May 1769.

March. Proclamation of 1763 modified to allow Proclamation line to be moved west as Indian treaties are negotiated and land purchased. Most important of treaties are October 14 Treaty of Hard Labor with Cherokees and November 5 Treaty of Fort Stanwix with Iroquois; these bring former Indian lands in Virginia up to the Ohio River as well as putting western New York and western Pennsylvania under British control.

June 10. Seizure by customs officials of John Hancock's sloop *Liberty* for nonpayment of duty on Madeira wine provokes assault by crowd. **Oct. 1.** Two regiments of British troops, requested by customs officials in February, March, and June, finally arrive and are stationed in Boston.

Aug. 1-28. Further and more stringent nonimportation measures taken in Boston and New York; other colonies follow suit, and by end of 1769, only New Hampshire has not joined nonimportation protest, which all but suspends trade with England.

1768 - 1775

A number of commercial corporations are formed; several fire insurance companies, a Massachusetts wharf company, water supply companies, and a Philadelphia corporation for the purpose of promoting manufactures.

1768 - 1792

Series of strikes (rare before 1768), in which New York tailors demand higher wages, and printers strike (1778) and gain $3 per week; Philadelphia seamen strike in 1779 for higher wages and better working conditions. Philadelphia printers form a union in 1786; New York shoemakers in 1792.

1769

May 16. Virginia Resolves condemn British government for tax and other policies. **May 17.** Address to Crown by Patrick Henry and Richard Henry Lee is prevented when Governor Botetourt dissolves Assembly. **May 18.** Burgesses meet in Raleigh Tavern, Williamsburg, and form Virginia Association, a stringent nonimportation agreement. **June-Nov.** Similar associations are created in Maryland, South Carolina, Georgia, and North Carolina; nonimportation agreements are drawn up in seaport towns of Delaware, Connecticut, and Rhode Island.

Dec. 27. Grand Ohio Company organized by Samuel Wharton and other Englishmen to obtain a grant of 20 million acres under Treaty of Fort Stanwix. Grant approved by Board of Trade in May 1770, with understanding that territory is to be organized as proprietary colony of Vandalia. Project is abandoned with approach of the Revolution.

1770

Jan 31. Lord North becomes head of British government. **April 12.** Townshend Acts repealed, with exception of tea duty, and Quartering Act is not renewed. In the colonies, nonimportation is abandoned a second time, except in Boston, a center of the tea trade. Associations have been disbanded in all colonies by July 1771.

March 5. The Boston Massacre. Growing tension has caused frequent clashes between citizenry and quartered soldiers in New York and Massachusetts. Belligerent crowd gathers around Boston sentry who summons aid; resulting musket volley kills five citizens. Lieutenant Governor Thomas Hutchinson averts general uprising by acceding to demand to remove troops to harbor islands. **March 6.** Captain Thomas Preston and six of his men are arrested for murder. **Oct. 24-30.** They are defended by patriot lawyers John Adams and Josiah Quincy. Preston and four soldiers are acquitted; two soldiers receive only token punishment.

1771

Uprising of group called "Regulators" in North Carolina protests discriminatory laws and under-representation of western counties in state legislature. **May 16.** Climax comes at Alamance Creek, where 2,000 rebels, many unarmed, are defeated by 1,200 soldiers under command of Governor William Tryon. Thirteen rebels are found guilty of treason; seven are executed.

Philadelphia's Southwark Theatre produces *The Rising Glory of America*, from a poem of the same name written by Philip Freneau and Hugh Henry Brackenridge and read by Brackenridge at the graduation ceremonies of the College of New Jersey in the same year. Two other plays by Brackenridge, *The Battle of Bunker's Hill* and *The Death of General Montgomery*, are produced by this theater in 1776 and 1777.

1772 - 1773

June 9. Merchant John Brown and eight boatloads of followers attack customs schooner *Gaspee* aground off Providence, Rhode Island. **Sept. 2.** Commissioners of inquiry are named to identify culprits and send them to England for trial. **June 1773.** This threat to local self-rule having been thwarted by hostility of Rhode Islanders, who make it impossible to determine guilt, commission is adjourned.

1772 - 1774

June 13. Massachusetts Governor Hutchinson announces that his salary will in future be paid by the Crown. **Sept.** Policy is also applied to Massachusetts judges, rendering these officers independent of financial control of the General Court. **Nov. 2.** New standing Committee of Correspondence, headed by James Otis, is formed in Boston by Samuel Adams in response to this threat. **March 12-Feb. 1774.** Similar committees are formed in Virginia, Rhode Island, Connecticut, New Hampshire, and South Carolina; only North Carolina and Pennsylvania do not follow suit.

1773

May 10. Tea Act, passed to save British East India Company from bankruptcy threatened by overextension, authorizes selling part of huge tea surplus duty-free in colonies. This allows company to undersell both legitimate tea merchants and colonial smugglers, who have avoided the duty by buying from the Dutch, and thus to monopolize the tea trade. Opposition to the Tea Act grows in Philadelphia, Boston, and New York. **Nov. 27.** The *Dartmouth*, first of three tea ships, arrives in Boston. **Nov. 29-30.** Huge mass meetings are held in protest. **Dec. 16.** Boston Tea Party, in which a group of men disguised as Mohawk Indians boards the *Dartmouth* and dumps entire tea cargo, 342 chests, into Boston harbor.

Benjamin Franklin writes two satirical essays, "An Edict by the King of Prussia" and "Rules by Which a Great Empire May be Reduced to a Small One"; they are published in both England and America.

1773 - 1774

June 1773. Samuel Adams reads letters from Governor Thomas Hutchinson and Lieutenant Governor Andrew Oliver in session of Massachusetts House of Representatives. Letters have been sent from England secretly by Benjamin Franklin to demonstrate that objectionable acts of Britain are often owing to poor advice from Crown agents in the colonies. House petitions Crown to remove Hutchinson and Oliver. **Jan. 30, 1774.** In ensuing scandal in England, Franklin is dismissed as deputy postmaster general for America.

1774

January. Virginia Governor John Murray, earl of Dunmore, in effort to establish control of settlement in the Ohio country, appropriates Indian lands in western Pennsylvania. This and other intrusions goad Shawnee and Ottawa Indians into what becomes "Lord Dunmore's War." **Oct. 10.** Indians are defeated, cede hunting rights in Kentucky, and agree to unhindered access to and navigation on Ohio River.

March 31. First of Coercive Acts (called "Intolerable Acts" by Americans) designed to punish Massachusetts is Boston Port Bill, which prohibits loading and unloading of ships in Boston harbor until East India Company is paid for destroyed tea. **May 20.** Administration of Justice Act allows for transfer to England of legal suits against Crown officials; such trials had previously been held in provincial courts, often hostile to Crown officers or Crown authority. Massachusetts Government Act in effect annuls Massachusetts charter by greatly increasing the powers of Crown officers and reducing those of officers elected locally.

May 30. Quebec Act extends boundary of Canada south to the Ohio River, cutting off western claims of Massachusetts, Virginia, and Connecticut; Act sets up highly centralized Crown-controlled government in Canada, gives Catholic Church many privileges, provokes fear that as colonists move west they will be governed in French way and that Catholic influence will increase in Ohio Valley. This Act is also considered one of the "Intolerable" measures.

June 2. New Quartering Act authorizes troop billetings in private dwellings as well as taverns and unoccupied buildings and extends application to all colonies.

Sept. 5. First Continental Congress, with all colonies except Georgia represented, assembles at Philadelphia to consider ways of dealing with Coercive Acts. **Sept. 17.** Congress is persuaded by radical delegates to endorse Suffolk Resolves, adopted earlier by a convention of Suffolk County, Massachusetts. Resolves urge civil disobedience, self-rule, and severe economic pressure on Britain. **Sept. 28.** In an effort to establish a milder alternative to these Resolves, conservatives endorse Joseph Galloway's "Plan of Union Between Great Britain and Her Colonies," but are defeated by vote; Plan is expunged from the record on October 22.

Oct. 14. "Declaration and Resolves" of the Congress condemn most British measures enacted since 1763. Oct. 18. Continental Association for nonimportation and other sanctions against Britain is formed, including machinery for enforcement. Oct. 26. Congress adjourns, resolving to meet again May 10, 1775, if measures voted have not been successful. Continental Association is established in all colonies by April 1775, Georgia having adopted a modified plan in January.

Loyalist argument set forth in a series of newspaper letters by Daniel Leonard using the pen name "Massachusettensis" and refuted by patriot John Adams ("Novanglus"), extends to April 1775. Also published are James Wilson's *Considerations on the Nature and Extent of the Legislative Authority of the British Parliament* and Thomas Jefferson's *A Summary View of the Rights of British America,* both of which reject Parliamentary rule in favor of royal rule.

The Shakers, a monastic Protestant sect led by "Mother" Ann Lee, start their first communal settlement at Watervliet, New York.

Population of the colonies is estimated at 2,600,000.

1775

Feb. 1. Second Massachusetts Provincial Congress (originally formed at Salem on October 7, 1774) meets to prepare the province for war. Feb. 9. Having heard Declaration of the First Provincial Congress, Parliament declares Massachusetts to be in a state of rebellion. Feb. 27. Lord North's Conciliation Plan pledges that no new revenue bills will be passed for colonies willing to tax themselves, but refuses to recognize Continental Congress. March 23. Patrick Henry, in "Liberty or Death" speech before Virginia Assembly, accurately predicts early news of "the clash of resounding arms" from New England. March 30. Parliament passes bill forbidding New England colonies to trade with any countries except Britain and British West Indies and barring New England fishermen from the North Atlantic fisheries. April 13. Britain extends provisions of this act to New Jersey, Pennsylvania, Maryland, Virginia, and South Carolina upon news of their ratification of Continental Association.

March 10. Daniel Boone is sent out by the Transylvania Company to establish a trail (the Wilderness Road) through Cumberland Gap to Kentucky bluegrass country. March 17. Strip of land through the Gap and all lands between Kentucky River and Cumberland Valley are sold by Cherokees for £10,000. April 6. Boone founds Boonesborough, and several other Kentucky settlements are established in March and April. Sept. 25. Attempt to organize Transylvania as proprietary colony is frustrated when delegates to Continental Congress are rejected because Virginia claims jurisdiction over Kentucky region.

April 14. Aware that militia arms are cached at Concord, Massachusetts, General Thomas Gage dispatches British soldiers to attempt seizure. April 18. Seven hundred troops cross Charles River from Boston to Cambridge on way to Concord in evening. Boston Committee of Safety sends Paul Revere and William Dawes by different routes to alert the countryside; Revere reaches Lexington, but he, Dawes, and Dr. Samuel Prescott, who joins them, are stopped on way to Concord. Prescott escapes and warns Concord. April 19. When British arrive at Lexington at dawn, 77 armed minutemen are drawn up to greet them. Americans have almost been persuaded to retire when unidentified shot brings spontaneous volley from British, killing eight and wounding 10 minutemen. British march to Concord, seize minor arms cache, but all along return route to Boston are set upon by American militia, 4,000 of whom inflict 273 casualties before troops reach safety of Charlestown. Boston is then laid under siege by patriots (until March 1776). **April 22.** Provincial Congress authorizes raising of 30,000 men and appeals to other colonies for aid. By May 20 Rhode Island, Connecticut, and New Hampshire have voted to send 9,500 men.

May 10. Second Continental Congress convenes at Philadelphia. **May 15.** Congress resolves to put colonies in a state of defense. **May 29.** Address to the people of Canada is written; it asks them to join colonies as "fellow sufferers." **June 14-17.** Congress resolves to raise men for New England army in Pennsylvania, Maryland, and Virginia; unanimously votes appointment of George Washington as commander in chief; adopts plan of organization for forces now known as the Continental Army. **June 22.** Congress votes $2 million fund for support of Army, the 12 "Confederated Colonies" to share the burden according to population. (Georgia is not yet officially represented at Convention.)

May 10. Benedict Arnold and Ethan Allen lead small force that captures Fort Ticonderoga with many military supplies. **May 12.** Crown Point (north of Fort Ticonderoga) is seized. **May 16.** Arnold takes St. John's in Canada. **June 17.** British capture Charlestown peninsula and north bank of Charles River above Boston after battles of Breed's Hill and Bunker Hill. British losses are enormous. **July 3.** George Washington takes command of 14,500 troops at Cambridge.

July 5. Congress adopts John Dickinson's "Olive Branch Petition" to George III, asking for peaceful settlement of differences. **July 6.** Another Dickinson resolution, "Declaration of the Causes and Necessities

of Taking Up Arms," states that colonies do not desire independence, but will not yield to enslavement. It also hints that colonies may receive foreign aid against Britain. **July 31.** Congress rejects Lord North's Conciliation Plan.

Sept. 12. Congress reconvenes with all 13 colonies represented. **Oct. 13-Nov. 10.** A navy and two battalions of marines are authorized. **Nov. 9.** Congress hears that on August 23 George III rejected "Olive Branch Petition" and declared colonies in open state of rebellion. **Nov. 29.** Committee is appointed to get in touch with "our friends abroad" and money is voted for its use. **Dec. 6.** Answer to George III affirms loyalty to Crown, but refuses allegiance to Parliament. **Dec.** French agent appears to express French interest in trade with colonies and suggest possibility of aid in war against England. **Dec. 23.** Royal proclamation closes colonies to all trade as of March 1, 1776.

Nov. 13. Expedition led by Brigadier General Richard Montgomery captures Montreal. **Dec. 11.** Governor Dunmore of Virginia is defeated by 900 Virginians and North Carolinians near Norfolk, which is ruined as a base of operations. **Dec. 31.** Benedict Arnold and 1,100 volunteers, joined by Montgomery, attack Quebec; campaign ends in disaster with Arnold wounded and Montgomery killed.

First American submarine, called *American Turtle*, constructed by David Bushnell, who in next year attempts unsuccessfully to blow up British frigate in New York Harbor.

First surgical textbook written in America is *Remarks on the Treatment of Wounds and Fractures*, by John Jones, personal physician to both Benjamin Franklin and George Washington.

Philadelphia paper, *Pennsylvania Evening Post*, published by Benjamin Towne, is first daily newspaper in America (discontinued 1784). By this year there are 37 newspapers in the colonies; political division is 23 patriot, 7 loyalist, and 7 neutral. *New York Weekly Mercury* publishes two editions during Revolution — patriot in Newark, New Jersey, and loyalist in New York City. Average weekly circulation of all papers: 3,500.

In spite of restrictions imposed by Britain in 1750, colonial iron manufacture has increased rapidly. By 1775 colonies are producing one-seventh of the world supply.

1775 - 1776

John Trumbull publishes part of his popular satire on Tories, *M'Fingal;* first complete edition is not published until 1782.

1776

Jan. 10. Thomas Paine publishes his pamphlet, *Common Sense,* anonymously; calls George III responsible for acts against colonies, thus creating sentiment for independence among colonists, who had previously opposed Parliament but remained loyal to Crown.

March 1. French Minister Vergennes suggests to Spain that Spain join France in secret measures of aid to American colonies. **March 3.** Congress, ignorant of possible French and Spanish support, sends Silas Deane to Europe to procure military assistance. **April 6.** Congress votes to open American ports to all nations except Britain. **May 2.** Louis XVI of France authorizes the sending of one million livres' worth of munitions through secret agent Pierre de Beaumarchais. Equal amount of armaments is provided by Spain. These supplies sustain Continental Army in 1776-1777.

March 17. British and Loyalists under Sir William Howe evacuate Boston on threat of siege by General Henry Knox with 55 cannon hauled from Fort Ticonderoga.

June 7. Richard Henry Lee of Virginia proposes resolution to Congress that the United Colonies "ought to be free and independent states." **June 11.** Congress appoints committee to draft a Declaration of Independence before adopting resolution. **June 28.** Declaration, written by Thomas Jefferson, is presented, and Lee's resolution is approved by July 2. **July 4.** After making some revisions in Declaration, Congress approves it without dissent. (New York abstains, but approves on July 15.)

June 28. British attack on Charleston, South Carolina, by forces under Generals Sir Henry Clinton and Sir Peter Parker thrown back, ending British campaign in South for two years. **Aug. 22.** Howe's removal to New York from Boston and gathering of 20,000 troops on Staten Island (including 9,000 German mercenaries) leads to battle with Continental troops in Brooklyn, where bloody defeat persuades Washington to withdraw to Manhattan and fortify Harlem Heights.

Sept. 11. Peace conference held on Staten Island between representatives of Congress and Admiral Lord Howe (brother of Sir William Howe) fails when Howe insists that Declaration of Independence be revoked before discussion can begin.

Sept. 15. British occupy New York City. **Sept. 21.** Unexplained fire destroys most housing, leaving British without shelter. **Sept. 22.** Nathan Hale, caught while carrying military information, executed as American spy. **Oct. 13.** Battle for Lake Champlain results in defeat of Arnold's forces, but Sir Guy Carleton lets Ticonderoga stand over the winter. **Nov.-Dec.** Washington retreats through New Jersey, crossing Delaware River into Pennsylvania on December 11. **Dec. 12.** Congress, anticipating British attack on Philadelphia, flees to Baltimore after giving Washington dictatorial powers. **Dec. 26.** Knowing that Howe has sent most of his army back to winter quarters in New York, Washington recrosses Delaware, surprises and takes Hessian garrison at Trenton, New Jersey.

Constitutions enacted by 11 of original 13 states, with Connecticut and Rhode Island continuing under colonial charters by deleting references to British Crown. Common features of constitutions are provisions for strong legislatures and weak executives, frequent elections, property qualifications for voting and office-holding, and an appointive judiciary holding office during good behavior.

Many states adopt Bills of Rights, notably bill written by George Mason for Virginia, adopted on June 12, 1776.

1776 - 1783

"Test Acts" passed by revolutionary state governments require repudiation of loyalty to British Crown. Loyalists are variously exiled, disfranchised, barred from public office and the professions, and doubly and triply taxed. One hundred thousand Loyalists flee to Canada or England; these and many remaining are deprived of property by state confiscation acts; actual amount seized is unknown, but Crown ultimately pays them £3,300,000 in compensation. Division of Loyalist estates among numerous Americans after war helps shift balance of political power from owners of large estates to owners of small or middle-sized properties.

1777

Jan. 3. Washington eludes British force under Cornwallis near Trenton, New Jersey, inflicts heavy casualties on enemy at Princeton. **Jan. 6.** He establishes his 5,000 men in winter quarters near Morristown. Victories have vastly improved morale.

March 4. Congress returns to Philadelphia to discuss ways of getting foreign aid. In next few months it recruits and commissions, among others, Marquis de Lafayette, Baron Johann de Kalb, Thaddeus Kosciuszko, and "Baron" Friedrich von Steuben.

June 14. Congress specifies design of U.S. flag: "thirteen stripes alternate red and white . . . thirteen stars of white on a blue field."

June 17. General John Burgoyne begins campaign to isolate New England, capturing various posts in northern New York and around Lake Ontario by August. **Aug. 13.** Having run out of supplies, Burgoyne sends force to seize stores at Bennington, Vermont, and is frustrated by American militia. **Oct. 7.** He fails in attempt to capture Albany, where he is defeated by Arnold and others, and is forced to retreat to Saratoga, New York. **Oct. 17.** Surrounded by superior forces, Burgoyne surrenders his army of 5,700 men, who are shipped back to England on their pledge not to serve again against Americans.

Sept. 11-26. Howe occupies Philadelphia after defeating American forces guarding the city at Brandywine Creek. **Sept. 19-30.** Congress flees first to Lancaster, Pennsylvania, and then to York. **Oct. 4.** Washington is defeated with heavy losses by Howe near Germantown, and by middle of December has established winter quarters at Valley Forge.

Nov. 15. "Articles of Confederation and Perpetual Union," originally submitted to Congress July 12, 1776, are adopted after intermittent debate and submitted to the states for ratification, which is not completed by all states until March 1, 1781.

Dec. 17. France recognizes independence of U.S. on hearing news of Burgoyne's surrender.

1778

Jan. 8. French Foreign Minister Count Vergennes, unable to induce Spain to join France and America formally in war against England, offers French alliance to American commissioners Benjamin Franklin, Silas Deane, and Arthur Lee, at Paris. They sign treaties of alliance and of amity and commerce between France and U.S. March 20. American commissioners received informally by Louis XVI, and immediate appointment of French Minister Conrad Gérard to U.S. leads to replacement of commission by a single minister to France. Sept. 14. Benjamin Franklin is elected to the post.

Feb. 17. In an effort to avert U.S. Congress ratification of the French alliance, Lord North proposes extremely wide conciliation measures, among them the appointment of a peace commission to negotiate with the Congress. March 9. The plan is voted by Parliament and commission sent to Philadelphia. June 17. Congress rejects plan with notice that only withdrawal of British troops and recognition of U.S. independence can be basis for agreement. Before leaving Philadelphia one commissioner unsuccessfully attempts to bribe three congressmen.

April 14-May 8. American privateer *Ranger,* commanded by Captain John Paul Jones, invades Irish Sea, takes two prizes, spikes guns of fort at Whitehaven, England, and captures British sloop-of-war which is taken to Brest, France. Similar raids by American privateers had taken 733 prizes by February.

June 19. Washington leaves Valley Forge in pursuit of General Sir Henry Clinton (Howe's replacement), who has marched from Philadelphia toward New York on news of approach of French fleet to America. July 4. After indecisive battle at Monmouth, New Jersey, American General Charles Lee is court-martialed for disobedience. July 29-Aug. 10. French fleet under Comte d'Estaing blockades Newport, R. I., waiting for land forces, but is forced to withdraw to Boston for repairs after battle with Admiral Howe's fleet. Nov. 4. D'Estaing leaves Boston for West Indies.

July 4-Feb. 25, 1779. Colonel George Rogers Clark leads 175 Virginians to capture Kaskaskia and Vincennes, gaining control of the Illinois country for Virginia.

Dec. 29. British capture Savannah, Georgia, in move by Sir Henry Clinton to shift theater of war and rally Loyalists of Southern colonies.

First American manual of standard drugs and medicines published (in Latin) by William Brown, surgeon general to the middle department of the Continental Army.

Jonathan Carver publishes *Travels Through the Interior Parts of North America,* containing information on Indian customs and natural history of Great Lakes and upper Mississippi region.

1779

January-June. British forces extend control of South despite American successes in South Carolina, Tennessee, and elsewhere. July 16. Clinton is thwarted in attempt to gain control of Hudson River by General Anthony Wayne's victory at Stony Point, New York. Aug. 29-Sept. 15. Successful expedition of Generals John Sullivan and James Clinton against Loyalists and Indians in northwestern New York reduces danger from Iroquois. Sept. 15-Oct. 9. Attempt to retake Savannah by D'Estaing's fleet and French and American forces under General

Benjamin Lincoln fails with heavy allied losses, among them Polish Count Casimir Pulaski, who is killed.

Feb. 23-Aug. 14. Congress debates peace proposal; terms are independence, minimum boundaries, British evacuation of U.S. territory, and right of navigation on Mississippi River. **Sept. 27.** John Adams named to negotiate treaty with Britain.

June 21. Spain, opposing American independence but anxious for her own colonial possessions, joins war against England when British refuse to give up Gibraltar as price of Spanish neutrality. **Sept. 27.** Congress President John Jay is appointed minister to Spain, but is unable to secure recognition, an alliance, or any further substantial aid during two and a half years in Madrid.

Sept. 28. John Paul Jones, in refitted French vessel renamed *Bonhomme Richard* (in honor of Benjamin Franklin's "Poor Richard"), engages British 44-gun *Serapis* off the east coast of England, captures and boards it as his own ship burns and sinks.

Despite loans from France and Spain, America is in desperate straits financially after issue of nearly $200 million in paper money ("Continentals"). In January paper currency is valued, relative to coin, at 8 to 1, but by December it has fallen to 40 to 1. At the December rate, $120 million (actually only $3 million) is accepted in payment from states in 1780, when the worthless currency is retired.

Struggle for control of West during Revolution, during which migration continues, results in various frontier clashes. Destruction of 11 Chickamauga Indian villages in the Tennessee Valley opens way to rapid expansion of settlement in Tennessee and Kentucky (whose population is 20,000 by 1780) now that settlers can move in over the Wilderness Road and down the Ohio River.

1780

May 5. Mutiny breaks out in Washington's camp at Morristown, New Jersey, after winter more severe than that at Valley Forge, but rebellious units, demanding full, instead of one-eighth rations, and five months' overdue pay, are controlled by Pennsylvania troops.

May 12. General Benjamin Lincoln surrenders Charleston, South Carolina, which has been besieged by 14,000 British for 45 days. Capture of 5,400 men and four American ships is worst defeat of the war.

Aug. 5. Benedict Arnold, having opened secret and treasonable negotiations with General Sir Henry Clinton, is placed in charge of fort at West Point on the Hudson River. **Sept. 23.** Attempt to deliver plans of the fort to the enemy through Clinton's adjutant, Major André, is frustrated by André's capture. **Sept. 25.** On hearing of this, Arnold flees to join British, with whom he campaigns until end of war. **Sept. 29.** André is convicted of spying and executed on October 2.

Aug. 16-Oct. 7. American forces suffer bloody defeat by Cornwallis at Camden, South Carolina, but partially compensate by victory of sharpshooting frontiersmen at King's Mountain, South Carolina.

Efforts of John Adams result in founding of American Academy of Arts and Sciences at Boston. Other learned societies, chiefly for promotion of agriculture, are founded in New Jersey, South Carolina, and Pennsylvania during 1781-1785.

1781

Jan. 1. Twenty-four hundred Pennsylvania Line troops in Washington's camp mutiny when unpaid veterans see new recruits being given money to enlist. **Jan. 7.** Concessions by state officials end mutiny, but 1,200 men leave the service.

Jan. 17. Americans under General Daniel Morgan defeat British force at Cowpens, South Carolina. **March 15.** British triumph at Guilford Court House, North Carolina, but Cornwallis' army is badly weakened and is forced to retire to Wilmington, North Carolina. **April 25-May 20.** Cornwallis moves north to subdue Virginia, which he raids almost at will. **June 10-19.** American reinforcements under Anthony Wayne and von Steuben arrive, and Cornwallis turns back to Yorktown to establish a base, arriving on August 7. **Sept.** Helped by other American victories in South Carolina, American forces under General Nathanael Greene succeed in narrowing area of British control of South Carolina to Charleston and vicinity.

Feb. 20. Appointment of Robert Morris as superintendent of finance begins long fight by Congress to overcome inflation. **May 21.** After taking office, Morris proposes creation of first private commerical bank in U.S. **Dec. 31.** Bank is chartered as the Bank of North America. Meanwhile, new loans from France in May and Holland in November help to restore solvency.

March 1. Articles of Confederation go into effect upon ratification by last of 13 states. Delay since adoption of Articles by Congress in November 1777 has been occasioned in part by western land question, which began with proposal by John Dickinson in July 1776 that the Articles include western state boundaries. This motion was defeated, and a subsequent attempt by the states without western claims to have such boundaries drawn was again defeated in Congress in October 1777. But land bounties granted by Congress and the states as inducements to British military deserters and American soldiers who would sign up

for the duration of the war had made the problem of organization of western territories acute, and in 1778 Maryland had refused to ratify Articles unless state claims were ceded to Congress. New York, Connecticut, and Virginia having ceded, Maryland signs Articles on February 27, but cessions by all states are not completed until 1802.

Aug. 30. French Admiral Count François de Grasse arrives off Yorktown, Virginia, with fleet that sets up blockade, disembarks troops that join forces with Lafayette, von Steuben, and Anthony Wayne, who have surrounded Yorktown by land. **Sept. 5-10.** British naval attack on French fleet fails. **Sept. 14-24.** De Grasse sends ships up Chesapeake Bay to bring Washington's army, which has been marching from New York, to Williamsburg to join the siege. **Sept. 28.** From Williamsburg 17,000 allied troops march against 7,500 British at Yorktown. **Oct. 18.** After various skirmishes and severe hammering by allied siege guns, Cornwallis decides his position is hopeless and surrenders his army, though Clinton is one week away with 7,000 reinforcements. **Oct. 19.** British troops lay down their arms while their bands play "The World Turned Upside Down."

1782

Feb. 27. Cornwallis' surrender at Yorktown, and British defeats by French in the West Indies, result in fall of the North ministry when Parliament votes against further prosecution of war in America. **March 22.** North is succeeded by Lord Rockingham, who immediately opens negotiations with American peace commissioners in Paris; commissioners are John Adams, Benjamin Franklin, John Jay, and Henry Laurens. **Nov. 30.** Preliminary articles signed, pending similar Anglo-French accord. Terms include recognition of U.S. independence, boundary stipulations, U.S. rights to North

Atlantic fisheries, validation of debts due to citizens of both countries, and cessation of hostilities, with evacuation of British land and naval forces.

Publication of *Letters From an American Farmer,* impressions of America by J. Hector St. John [de Crèvecoeur], who has traveled through Ohio Valley and Great Lakes region before settling on farm in New York. Though enthusiastic about America, he returns to France for good in 1790.

First Catholic parochial school in U.S. is erected by St. Mary's Church, Philadelphia.

1783

Jan. 20. Britain and France reach accord, thus validating Anglo-American treaty signed November 30, 1782. **Feb. 4.** British proclaim cessation of hostilities after also signing articles of peace with Spain. **April 15.** Articles of peace ratified by Congress, Treaty of Paris signed September 3; signed treaty is ratified on January 14, 1784.

April 26. Seven thousand Loyalists, fearing American vengeance after British army is evacuated, leave from New York. **June-Nov.** Continental Army disbands. **Nov. 25.** Last British forces sail from New York. **Dec. 4.** Washington says farewell to his officers at Fraunces' Tavern, New York. **Dec. 23.** He presents himself to Congress at Annapolis, resigns his commission as commander in chief and takes "leave of all the employments of public life."

End of Revolution affirms legal changes brought about in the several states since 1776. Among these are replacement of royal government by republican form; confiscation of royal lands and Loyalist property; abolition of quitrents, entail, and primogeniture; disestablishment of tax-supported Anglican Church; reform of penal codes; and

advance of public education. Slave trade is abolished or heavily taxed in 11 states by 1786, and prohibited in Northwest Territory in 1787.

Massachusetts Medical School is founded in Boston.

Benjamin Franklin invents bifocal spectacles with both reading and distance lenses in a single frame.

Noah Webster publishes his *American Spelling Book (Blue-Backed Speller)*; estimated sale by 1883 is 70 million copies.

Continental Congress poll estimates population of United States at 2,389,300; 211,000 drop from 1774 is due to war deaths and Loyalist emigration to England and Canada.

1784

Feb. 22. Captain John Greene sails the *Empress of China* from New York, reaches Canton, China, by way of Cape Horn on August 30. Cargo of tea and silks brought back in 1785 leads other U.S. merchants to send more ships to China in effort to make up for losses due to shrunken British market for U.S. goods.

March 1. Committee headed by Thomas Jefferson presents to Congress a plan for interim government of Western lands, proposing eventual division of territory into states to be admitted on equal terms with original 13. **April 23.** Plan is adopted and becomes basic idea in the Northwest Ordinance of 1787.

May 28. Superintendent of Finance Robert Morris requests that he be replaced by a board of three commissioners. **Nov. 1.** He leaves office having accumulated a precarious surplus of $21,000 (after meeting army's demobilization pay in 1783 from his own pocket). Recent foreign loans are largely responsible for the surplus, since Congress has no power of taxation under the Articles of Confederation but is dependent on requisitions from states for funds. Of an $8 million requisition voted in October 1781, only about $1,500,000 has been paid by January 1784.

Aug. 23. Convention of settlers west of Appalachian Mts. organizes independent state of Franklin in area ceded to U.S. by North Carolina. After four years of nominal statehood under John Sevier settlers accept renewed jurisdiction of North Carolina.

Dec. 23. New York City selected as temporary national capital until a federal district on the Delaware River can be set up.

Potomac Company organized with George Washington as president to build route connecting Potomac River with Ohio Valley. Canal is begun, and first water locks in U.S. built, but project proves unprofitable and is never completed.

First American theological college is established in New Brunswick, New Jersey.

John Filson publishes *The Discovery, Settlement, and Present State of Kentucke* which contains, in addition to Filson's account, an alleged autobiography of Daniel Boone.

1784 - 1797

1784. Judge Tapping Reeve establishes law school in Litchfield, Connecticut; followed by Peter Van Schaack's law school at Kinderhook, New York, in 1786; law lectures at University of Pennsylvania in 1790; and Columbia College in 1797.

1785

Jan. 24. Congress, being unable to obtain commercial concessions from foreign countries because Article IX of Articles of Confederation allows each state to set its own duties on foreign commerce, appoints committee to appeal to the states. Committee recommends amending Article IX but no action is taken by the states. Maryland, South Carolina, Pennsylvania, New York, Rhode Island, and North Carolina all have discriminatory duties on imports from Britain. **June 23.** Massachusetts and New Hampshire act to prohibit British ships from carrying their exports.

March 28. Commissioners from Virginia and Maryland meet at Mount Vernon, Virginia, to consider problems of navigation on Chesapeake Bay and Potomac River. Agreement recommends that Virginia and Maryland legislatures adopt uniform currency, uniform commercial regulations, and other measures of common commercial interest. **Dec. 5.** Maryland legislature endorses plan and proposes that Delaware and Pennsylvania be included.

Aug. 24. Beginning of a year of futile negotiations with Spain over U.S. right of navigation on the lower Mississippi River, which Spanish minister to U.S. refuses to concede, claiming title by virtue of 1763 Treaty of Paris. Issue is unresolved until Pinckney Treaty of 1795.

Automatic flour mill, invented by Oliver Evans, is put into operation in Maryland. New features, such as elevator and conveyor belt, cut labor needs in half.

Postwar dumping of British manufactures raises imports nearly to prewar level, but exports, no longer given preferential treatment in Britain, reach only 50 percent. British restrictions on trade with West Indies after 1783 further reduce American commerce which is only partly helped by opening of China trade and development of Pacific Northwest fur trade.

1785 - 1790

New York Society for Promoting Manu-mission (freeing of slaves) established with John Jay as president; similar societies established in other states, including several in the South, to 1788. Legislation to abolish slavery has been enacted in Pennsylvania in 1780, Connecticut and Rhode Island in 1784, New York in 1785, and is passed in New Jersey in 1786. Massachusetts constitution had abolished slavery in 1780. Slavery is prohibited in Northwest Territory by its ordinance. By 1790 about 93 percent of slaves in U.S. are in Southern states.

1786

Jan. 16. Virginia Assembly adopts Thomas Jefferson's Statute for Religious Freedom, model for First Amendment to the U.S. Constitution. Measure is virtually the same as one originally written and proposed in 1779 and not adopted.

Feb. 28. British notify U.S. that they will not evacuate Great Lakes posts, as promised by 1783 Treaty of Paris, until U.S. honors its debts to Britain.

June 28. Treaty with Morocco leads to suspension of Moroccan piracy on American commerce in Mediterranean Sea and off Spanish coast, but pirate raids from Algiers, Tunis, and Tripoli continue off Barbary coast until 1797.

Sept. 11-14. Following James Madison's suggestion of January 21, Virginia legislature invites all states to discuss interstate commercial problems at Annapolis, Maryland. Convention assembles at appointed time with only delegates from New York, New Jersey, Delaware, Pennsylvania, and Virginia present; those from New Hampshire, Massachusetts, Rhode Island, and North Carolina arrive too late to participate, and the rest of the states do not join

in. Meager representation frustrates aim of convention but Alexander Hamilton, in address endorsed on September 14, calls upon the states to meet at Philadelphia in May 1787 to discuss all matters necessary "to render the constitution of the federal government adequate to the exigencies of the Union."

Imports and exports drop from 1785 levels, farm wages are down 20 percent; shortage of money, insistent creditors, and high taxes contribute to general economic depression. Pressure for paper money results in $800,000 issue from seven states, alarming creditors. They are further disturbed by the outbreak of Shays's Rebellion in Massachusetts, where debt-ridden farmers in western part of state rise in arms against constituted authorities, protesting economic injustice and legal discrimination. Rebellion led by Daniel Shays is not finally put down until February 1787, after unequal struggle with state troops.

First American steamboat, invented by John Fitch, is granted franchise for use on New Jersey waters; it is launched on Delaware River in 1787.

1787

May 25. Constitutional Convention opens at Philadelphia 11 days late, after waiting for quorum of seven states; all states except Rhode Island eventually attend. George Washington is unanimously elected to preside but takes no part in debates. William Jackson is made secretary. **May 29.** Edmund Randolph offers Virginia Plan which goes beyond revision of Articles of Confederation; Plan is debated until June 13. This proposal, in which states are represented in proportion to population, is opposed by small states, who hope to retain equality of states as under Articles of Confederation, but with enlarged powers of central government. **June 15.** Delegates of small states propose New Jersey Plan, a revision of the Articles. Plan is debated for four days. **June 19.** Virginia Plan is adopted by 7 states to 3, committing Convention to frame a new basis for central government rather than merely revise Articles.

July 13. During Convention debate on proposed Constitution, Congress of the Confederation passes Northwest Ordinance. Based on Jefferson's Report of 1784, Ordinance provides for government of territory east of the Mississippi River and north of the Ohio; it includes provision for division of territory into three to five states and their admission into the Union when population is large enough.

July 16. Convention adopts Connecticut Compromise. The work of Benjamin Franklin and others and introduced by Roger Sherman, it resolves issue of state representation by providing for equal votes for states in proposed Senate but votes according to population in House. **Aug. 6 - Sept. 10.** Draft Constitution as prepared by five-member Committee of Detail is submitted to Convention and debated on all points; the debate is led by James Madison and George Mason of Virginia, Gouverneur Morris and James Wilson of Pennsylvania, Roger Sherman of Connecticut, and Elbridge Gerry of Massachusetts. Morris is assigned to prepare final draft. **Sept. 17.** After making a few changes, state delegations approve final draft, and 39 of the 42 delegates still in attendance sign (Gerry, Mason, and Randolph refusing), transmit the Constitution to Congress of the Confederation, and adjourn.

Sept. 20. Congress of the Confederation receives draft Constitution and defeats motion to censure Convention for exceeding instructions merely to revise Articles of Confederation. **Sept. 28.** Congress votes to send draft Constitution to the individual states for consideration by special ratifying conventions (ratification cannot be by legislatures or popular vote). Nine ratifications are needed for adoption.

Oct. 27. First of 85 "Federalist" papers published. Federalists, who approve the Constitution, and anti-Federalists, who oppose it, flood the states with written arguments. Most distinguished and influential are those written by "Publius" (Alexander Hamilton, James Madison, and John Jay), which appear in New York newspapers. Two-volume collection, *The Federalist,* is published in 1788.

Dec. 7. Ratification begins with convention of Delaware which ratifies unanimously.

Dec. 12. Pennsylvania convention, which has met on November 21, ratifies by vote of 46 to 23 after much delaying debate by strong anti-Federalist factions.

Dec. 18. New Jersey ratifies unanimously only a week after meeting on December 11.

Royall Tyler's comedy, *The Contrast,* is performed by a professional acting group in New York City; it is first American play with an American hero.

1788

Jan. 2. Georgia convention meets, ratifies Constitution unanimously. Debates on Constitution continue in other states.

Jan. 9. Connecticut convention, which has met on January 4, ratifies by vote of 128 to 40.

Feb. 6. Massachusetts convention, having met since January 9, ratifies by vote of 187 to 168. Opponents are persuaded to vote favorably when Samuel Adams proposes as condition of ratification that nine amendments be recommended at once to Congress and the other states. One of these is the basis for present-day Article X of the Bill of Rights, which reserves to the states powers not expressly delegated to the federal government.

March 24. Rhode Island rejects Constitution by direct vote. Federalists have refused to take part because a state convention has been rejected; thus only about half the qualified voters cast ballots, and only 237 out of about 3,000 voters favor ratification.

April 7. Marietta, Ohio, founded by settlers sent West by the Ohio Company, organized in 1786 for land speculation and development of land granted by Congress in exchange for Continental securities.

April 28. Maryland convention, which has met on April 21, ratifies by 63 to 11.

May 23. South Carolina anti-Federalists in legislature almost prevent holding ratifying convention, but resolution is passed, convention meets May 12 and ratifies 149 to 73.

June 21. New Hampshire convention, having met on February 13 and adjourned until June to see what action other states will take, ratifies by 57 to 47 after proposing 12 amendments. This ninth ratification is last needed for acceptance of Constitution among the ratifying states.

June 25. Virginia convention ratifies by vote of 89 to 79 after three weeks of heated argument led by Patrick Henry (against) and James Madison (for ratification). Convention recommends a bill of rights of 20 articles.

July 2. Congress of the Confederation accepts the new Constitution as ratified. **Sept. 13.** Congress arranges for conduct of government under new order to begin on March 4, 1789, when first Constitutional Congress will meet in New York. **Oct. 10.** Congress transacts its last official business under the Articles.

July 26. New York convention, having met on June 17, ratifies by 30 to 27. Anti-Federalists are majority, but Alexander Hamilton manages to delay vote until ninth ratification and Virginia's vote are announced, feeling correctly that this will sway convention. Additional factor is threat of New York City to secede from the state and ratify separately. Convention urges amendment to secure a federal bill of rights.

Aug. 2. North Carolina convention, meeting on July 21, refuses to ratify without a bill of rights, although Federalist feeling is strong.

Dec. 23. Maryland cedes 10 square miles on the Potomac River to Congress as site for federal capital of government under the new Constitution.

1789

Feb. 4. Presidential electors, chosen in each ratifying state as provided by new Constitution, cast ballots (counted in Senate on April 6) unanimously electing George Washington first President; John Adams, with 34 votes, becomes vice-president.

March 4. Majority of members of Congress for new government, elected in January and February, are still en route to New York and Congress does not have quorum present on date specified by Congress of the Confederacy. **April 1-8.** House of Representatives (30 of 59 members) and Senate (9 of 22 members) organize for conduct of business.

April 30. President Washington inaugurated at temporary capital in New York City on balcony of Federal Hall; he delivers inaugural address in Senate Chamber of Hall. Executive departments — War, Treasury, Foreign Affairs — continue temporarily as under Articles of Confederation.

May 5. Beginning of the French Revolution with meeting of Estates General at Versailles and formation by the third estate (commons) of the National Assembly. **July 14.** Paris mob storms the Bastille in attempt to get arms and to free political prisoners. Spontaneous uprisings all over France follow, as peasants revolt against feudal lords. **Aug. 27.** Assembly adopts the Declaration of Rights, preamble to first Constitution, which is largely based on American Declaration of Independence. Eventually most of Europe is involved and hostilities continue for 10 years.

July 4. New Congress passes first tariff bill, setting duties varying from 5 to 15 percent on various specified imports, to raise revenue for government expenses. A 10 percent reduction is allowed for goods imported in U.S.-owned and U.S.-built ships.

July 27. Organization of new executive departments begins with creation of Department of Foreign Affairs (later changed to Department of State). Thomas Jefferson is appointed secretary of state on September 26 but John Jay manages this department until Jefferson's return in March 1790 from post as minister to France. **Aug. 7.** War Department, created in 1785, is carried over intact to new government; General Henry Knox is appointed secretary of war on September 12. **Sept. 2.** Treasury Department is organized with Alexander Hamilton appointed secretary of the treasury on September 11. **Sept. 22.** Office of Postmaster General created and Samuel Osgood appointed on September 26, but Post Office is not permanently organized until 1795.

Sept. 9. House of Representatives begins action to adopt a federal bill of rights. Twelve amendments of the many proposed by various state ratifying conventions are recommended by Congress for adoption and proposed to states on September 25. Ten amendments are ratified by the necessary number of states and become part of the Constitution on December 15, 1791.

Sept. 24. Congress passes Federal Judiciary Act, setting up Supreme Court with a chief justice and five associate justices, also 13 district courts. **Sept. 26.** John Jay appointed first Chief Justice of the United States; Edmund Randolph appointed Attorney General.

Nov. 21. Submission to states by Congress of 12 amendments of a bill of rights results in second North Carolina ratifying convention which approves Constitution with amendments by vote of 194 to 77.

Georgia legislature grants to group of land companies for speculative purposes over 25 million acres in the region of the Yazoo River (Alabama and Mississippi); later grant of 35 million acres in 1795 leads eventually to Yazoo land fraud case of *Fletcher* v. *Peck* (1810), in which Supreme Court invalidates a state law for the first time.

Dr. John Jeffries, loyalist surgeon, holds first public lecture on anatomy in Boston; gathering is broken up by mob of citizens already indignant about dissection practised for study and teaching.

Protestant Episcopal Church organized independently of Church of England at first triennial convention held in Philadelphia.

Gazette of the United States, newspaper founded in New York by John Fenno and moved to Philadelphia in 1790, becomes leading Federalist weekly.

First American novel, *The Power of Sympathy*, is published; author is William Hill Brown.

University of North Carolina founded, becoming first state university to function; instruction begins in 1795.

End of Revolution and beginning of the new nation lead to a new architecture, a revival of classic Roman styles (later Greek also). Revival is inspired in part by Thomas Jefferson whose design for Virginia Capitol in Richmond is first Roman-style American building; his University of Virginia designs follow same trend. Classical influence is shown in buildings in Washington, D.C., designed by various architects, notably Benjamin Henry Latrobe, as well as a number of state capitols and commercial buildings. In spite of new style, architects such as Charles Bulfinch continue to build Adam (English) types of houses, especially in New England, for 30 years after the Revolution. Most architects of this period are not professionals but carpenter-builders.

Beginning of early period of historical, panoramic and religious painting such as "The Declaration of Independence" by John Trumbull, John Vanderlyn's "The Panorama of Versailles," and "The Bearing of the Cross" by William Dunlap.

Selections

Jonathan Mayhew: On Unlimited Submission to Rulers

*Reverend Jonathan Mayhew, whom John Adams called a "transcendent genius,"
early parted company with his Puritan heritage. On the religious side, his ideas
changed gradually from Congregationalism to Unitarianism, and politically his
thought was sufficiently radical so that he supported the American Revolution. His*
Discourse Concerning Unlimited Submission, *delivered as a sermon on
January 30, 1750, marked the anniversary of the execution of Charles I of England
a century earlier. In it he argued against the divine right of kings and any form of
royal or ecclesiastical absolutism. The sermon, Adams wrote to Hezekiah Niles
in 1818, "was read by everybody; celebrated by friends, and abused by enemies.
During the reigns of King George the First and King George the Second, the reigns
of the Stuarts — the two Jameses and the two Charleses — were in general disgrace
in England. In America they had always been held in abhorrence. The persecutions
and cruelties suffered by [the colonists'] ancestors under those reigns had been
transmitted by history and tradition, and Mayhew seemed to be raised up to revive
all their animosity against tyranny, in church and state, and at the same time to
destroy their bigotry, fanaticism, and inconsistency." Most of the discourse is
reprinted here.*

Source: *A Discourse Concerning Unlimited Submission and Non-Resistance to
the Higher Powers, etc., etc.,* Boston, 1750.

1. Let every soul be subject unto the higher powers. For there is no power but of God: the powers that be are ordained of God.

2. Whosoever therefore resisteth the power, resisteth the ordinance of God: and they that resist shall receive to themselves damnation.

3. For rulers are not a terror to good works but to the evil. Wilt thou then not be afraid of the power? Do that which is good, and thou shalt have praise of the same.

4. For he is the minister of God to thee for good. But if thou do that which is evil, be afraid; for he beareth not the sword in vain; for he is the minister of God, a revenger to execute wrath upon him that doth evil.

5. Wherefore ye must needs be subject, not only for wrath but also for conscience sake.

6. For, for this cause pay you tribute also; for they are God's ministers, attending continually upon this very thing.

7. Render therefore to all their dues: tribute to whom tribute is due; custom to whom custom; fear to whom fear; honor to whom honor.

Romans 13:1-7

IT IS EVIDENT that the affair of civil government may properly fall under a *moral* and *religious* consideration, at least so far forth as it relates to the general nature and end of magistracy and to the grounds and extent of that submission which persons of a private character ought to yield to those who are vested with authority. This must be allowed by all who acknowledge the divine original of Christianity. For although there be a sense, and a very plain and important sense, in which Christ's *kingdom is not of this world*, His inspired apostles have, nevertheless, laid down some general principles concerning the office of civil rulers and the duty of subjects, together with the reason and obligation of that duty. And from hence it follows that it is proper for all who acknowledge the authority of Jesus Christ and the inspiration of His apostles to endeavor to understand what is in fact the doctrine which they have delivered concerning this matter.

It is the duty of *Christian* magistrates to inform themselves what it is which their religion teaches concerning the nature and design of their office. And it is equally the duty of all *Christian* people to inform themselves what it is which their religion teaches concerning that subjection which they owe to *the higher powers*. It is for these reasons that I have attempted to examine into the Scripture account of this matter, in order to lay it before you with the same *freedom* which I constantly use with relation to other doctrines and precepts of Christianity; not doubting but you will *judge* upon ev-

erything offered to your consideration with the same spirit of *freedom* and *liberty* with which it is *spoken*.

The passage read is the most full and express of any in the New Testament relating to rulers and subjects; and, therefore, I thought it proper to ground upon it what I had to propose to you with reference to the authority of the civil magistrate and the subjection which is due to him. . . .

The apostle's [St. Paul] doctrine . . . may be summed up in the following observations, viz.:

That the end of magistracy is the good of civil society, as such.

That civil rulers, as such, are the ordinance and ministers of God; it being by His permission and providence that any bear rule and agreeable to His will that there should be *some persons* vested with authority in society, for the well-being of it.

That which is here said concerning civil rulers extends to all of them in common; it relates indifferently to monarchical, republican, and aristocratical government, and to all other forms which truly answer the sole end of government, the happiness of society; and to all the different degrees of authority in any particular state, to inferior officers no less than to the supreme.

That disobedience to civil rulers in the due exercise of their authority is not merely a *political sin* but a heinous *offense against God and religion*.

That the true ground and reason of our obligation to be subject to the *higher powers* is the usefulness of magistracy (when properly exercised) to human society and its subserviency to the general welfare.

That obedience to civil rulers is here equally required under all forms of government which answer the sole end of all government, the good of society; and to every degree of authority in any state, whether supreme or subordinate. (From whence it follows that if unlimited obedience and nonresistance be here required as a duty under any one form of government, it is also required as a duty under all other forms and as a duty to subordinate rulers as well as to the supreme.)

And, lastly, that those civil rulers to whom the apostle enjoins subjection are the persons *in possession; the powers that be,* those who are *actually* vested with authority.

There is one very important and interesting point which remains to be inquired into; namely, the *extent* of that subjection *to the higher powers* which is here enjoined as a duty upon all Christians. Some have thought it warrantable and glorious to disobey the civil powers in certain circumstances and, in cases of very great and general oppression when humble remonstrances fail of having any effect and when the public welfare cannot be otherwise provided for and secured, to rise unanimously even against the sovereign himself in order to redress their grievances; to vindicate their natural and legal rights; to break the yoke of tyranny and free themselves and posterity from inglorious servitude and ruin. It is upon this principle that many royal oppressors have been driven from their thrones into banishment, and many slain by the hands of their subjects. . . .

Now there does not seem to be any necessity of supposing that an absolute, unlimited obedience, whether active or passive, is here enjoined merely for this reason, that the precept is delivered in *absolute terms,* without any *exception* or *limitation* expressly mentioned. We are enjoined . . . to be *subject to the higher powers,* and . . . to be *subject for conscience sake.* . . .

Were it known that those in opposition to whom the apostle wrote allowed of civil authority in general and only asserted that there were some cases in which obedience and nonresistance were not a duty, there would then, indeed, be reason for interpreting this passage as containing the doctrine of unlimited obedience and nonresistance, as

it must, in this case, be supposed to have been leveled against such as denied that doctrine. But since it is certain that there were persons who vainly imagined that civil government in general was not to be regarded by them, it is most reasonable to suppose that the apostle designed his discourse only against them. And agreeably to this supposition we find that he argues the usefulness of civil magistracy in general, its agreeableness to the will and purpose of God who is *over all,* and so deduces from hence the obligation of submission to it. But it will not follow that because civil government is, in general, a good institution and necessary to the peace and happiness of human society, therefore, there be no supposable cases in which resistance to it can be innocent. So that the duty of unlimited obedience, whether active or passive, can be argued neither from the manner of expression here used nor from the general scope and design of the passage.

And if we attend to the nature of the argument with which the apostle here enforces the duty of submission to *the higher powers,* we shall find it to be such a one as concludes not in favor of submission to all who bear the *title* of rulers in common but only to those who *actually* perform the duty of rulers by exercising a reasonable and just authority for the good of human society. This is a point which it will be proper to enlarge upon, because the question before us turns very much upon the truth or falsehood of this position. It is obvious then, in general, that the civil rulers whom the apostle here speaks of, and obedience to whom he presses upon Christians as a duty, are *good rulers,* such as are, in the exercise of their office and power, benefactors to society. . . .

And what reason is there for submitting to that government which does by no means answer the design of government? "Wherefore ye must needs be subject not only for wrath but also for conscience sake"

(Rom. 13:5). Here the apostle argues the duty of a cheerful and conscientious submission to civil government from the nature and end of magistracy as he had before laid it down, *i.e.*, as the design of it was to punish evildoers and to support and encourage such as do well, and as it must, if so exercised, be agreeable to the will of God. But how does what he here says prove the duty of a cheerful and conscientious subjection to those who forfeit the character of rulers? — to those who encourage the bad and discourage the good? The argument here used no more proves it to be a sin to resist such rulers than it does to *resist the devil,* that he may *flee from us.* For one is as truly the minister of God as the other. "For, for this cause pay you tribute also: for they are God's ministers, attending continually upon this very thing" (Rom. 13:6). Here the apostle argues the duty of paying taxes, from this consideration, that those who perform the duty of rulers are continually attending upon the public welfare.

But how does this argument conclude for paying taxes to such princes as are continually endeavoring to ruin the public? And especially when such payment would facilitate and promote this wicked design! "Render, therefore, to all their dues; tribute to whom tribute is due; custom to whom custom; fear to whom fear; honor to whom honor" (Rom. 13:7). Here the apostle sums up what he had been saying concerning the duty of subjects to rulers. And his argument stands thus: "Since magistrates who execute their office well are common benefactors to society and may, in that respect, be properly styled the ministers and ordinance of God, and since they are constantly employed in the service of the public, it becomes you to pay them tribute and custom and to reverence, honor, and submit to them in the execution of their respective offices." This is apparently good reasoning. But does this argument conclude for the duty of paying tribute, custom, reverence,

Rev. Jonathan Mayhew, portrait by John Greenwood

honor, and obedience to such persons as (although they bear the title of rulers) use all their power to hurt and injure the public? — such as are not *God's* ministers but *Satan's?* — such as do not take care of, and attend upon, the public interest, but their own, to the ruin of the public? — that is, in short, to such as have no natural and just claim at all to tribute, custom, reverence, honor, and obedience?

It is to be hoped that those who have any regard to the apostle's character as an inspired writer, or even as a man of common understanding, will not represent him as reasoning in such a loose, incoherent manner and drawing conclusions which have not the least relation to his premises. For what can be more absurd than an argument thus framed? — "Rulers are, by their office, bound to consult the public welfare and the good of society; therefore, you are bound to pay them tribute, to honor and to submit to them, even when they destroy the public welfare and are a common pest to society by acting in direct contradiction to the nature and end of their office."

Thus, upon a careful review of the apostle's reasoning in this passage, it appears that his arguments to enforce submission are of such a nature as to conclude only in favor of submission *to such rulers as he himself describes; i.e.,* such as rule for the good of society, which is the only end of their institution. Common tyrants and public oppressors are not entitled to obedience from their subjects by virtue of anything here laid down by the inspired apostle.

I now add, further, that the apostle's argument is so far from proving it to be the duty of people to obey and submit to such rulers as act in contradiction to the public good, and so to the design of their office, that it proves *the direct contrary.* For, please to observe, that if the end of all civil government be the good of society, if this be the thing that is aimed at in constituting civil rulers, and if the motive and argument for submission to government be taken from the apparent usefulness of civil authority, it follows that when no such good end can be answered by submission there remains no argument or motive to enforce it; and if instead of this good end's being brought about by submission, a *contrary end* is brought about and the ruin and misery of society effected by it, here is a plain and positive reason against submission in all such cases, should they ever happen. And, therefore, in such cases, a regard to the public welfare ought to make us withhold from our rulers that obedience and subjection which it would, otherwise, be our duty to render to them.

If it be our duty, for example, to obey our king merely for this reason, that he rules for the public welfare (which is the only argument the apostle makes use of), it follows, by a parity of reason, that when he turns tyrant and makes his subjects his prey to devour and to destroy instead of his charge to defend and cherish, we are bound to throw off our allegiance to him and to resist, and that according to the tenor of the apostle's argument in this passage. Not to discontinue our allegiance, in this case, would be to join with the sovereign in promoting the slavery and misery of that society, the welfare of which we ourselves, as well as our sovereign, are indispensably obliged to secure and promote as far as in us lies. It is true the apostle puts no case of such a tyrannical prince; but, by his grounding his argument for submission wholly upon the good of civil society, it is plain he implicitly authorizes and even requires us to make resistance whenever this shall be necessary to the public safety and happiness. . . .

But it ought to be remembered that if the duty of universal obedience and nonresistance to our king or prince can be argued from this passage, the same unlimited submission under a republican or any other form of government, and even to all the subordinate powers in any particular state, can be proved by it as well; which is more than those who allege it for the mentioned purpose would be willing should be inferred from it. So that this passage does not answer their purpose but really overthrows and confutes it. This matter deserves to be more particularly considered.

The advocates for unlimited submission and passive obedience do, if I mistake not, always speak with reference to kingly or monarchical government, as distinguished from all other forms and with reference to submitting to the will of the king in distinction from all subordinate officers acting beyond their commission and the authority which they have received from the Crown. It is not pretended that any persons besides kings have a divine right to do what they please, so that no one may resist them without incurring the guilt of factiousness and rebellion. If any other supreme powers oppress the people, it is generally allowed that the people may get redress by resistance, if other methods prove ineffectual. And if any officers in a kingly government go beyond the limits of that power which they have derived from the Crown (the supposed original source of all power and authority in the state) and attempt, illegally, to take away the properties and lives of their fellow subjects, they may be *forcibly* resisted, at least till application be made to the Crown. But as to the sovereign himself, he may not be resisted in any case, nor any of his officers while they confine themselves within the bounds which he has prescribed to them. . . .

This is, I think, a true sketch of the principles of those who defend the doctrine of passive obedience and nonresistance. Now, there is nothing in Scripture which supports this scheme of political principles. As to the passage under consideration, the apostle here speaks of civil rulers in *general*, of all persons in *common*, vested with authority for the good of society, without any particular reference to one form of government more than to another, or to the supreme power in any particular state more than to subordinate powers. The apostle does not concern himself with the different forms of government. This he supposes is left entirely to human prudence and discretion. Now, the consequence of this is that unlimited and passive obedience is no more enjoined in this passage under monarchical government, or to the supreme power in any state, than under all other species of government which answer the end of government, or to all the subordinate degrees of civil authority, from the highest to the lowest. Those, therefore, who would from this passage infer the guilt of resisting kings in all cases whatever, though acting ever so contrary to the design of their office, must, if they will be consistent, go much farther and infer from it the guilt of resistance under all other forms of government and of resisting any petty officer in the state, though acting

beyond his commission, in the most arbitrary, illegal manner possible.

The argument holds equally strong in both cases. All civil rulers, as such, are the ordinance and ministers of God; and they are all, by the nature of their office and in their respective spheres and stations, bound to consult the public welfare. With the same reason, therefore, that any deny unlimited and passive obedience to be here enjoined under a republic or aristocracy or any other established form of civil government, or to subordinate powers acting in an illegal and oppressive manner, (with the same reason) others may deny that such obedience is enjoined to a king or monarch or any civil power whatever. For the apostle says nothing that is *peculiar to kings;* what he says extends equally to *all* other persons whatever, vested with any civil office. They are all, in exactly the same sense, the ordinance of God and the ministers of God; and obedience is equally enjoined to be paid to them all. For, as the apostle expresses it, there is *no power but of God;* and we are required to render to *all their dues,* and not *more* than their *dues.* And what these *dues* are, and to *whom* they are to be *rendered,* the apostle does not say, but leaves to the reason and consciences of men to determine.

Thus it appears that the common argument, grounded upon this passage in favor of universal and passive obedience, really overthrows itself by proving too much, if it proves anything at all; namely, that no civil officer is, in any case whatever, to be resisted, though acting in express contradiction to the design of his office; which no man in his senses ever did or can assert.

If we calmly consider the nature of the thing itself, nothing can well be imagined more directly contrary to common sense than to suppose that *millions* of people should be subjected to the arbitrary, precarious pleasure of *one single man* (who has *naturally* no superiority over them in point of authority) so that their estates, and everything that is valuable in life, and even their lives also, shall be absolutely at his disposal if he happens to be wanton and capricious enough to demand them. What unprejudiced man can think that God made *all* to be thus subservient to the lawless pleasure and frenzy of *one* so that it shall always be a sin to resist him! Nothing but the most plain and express revelation from Heaven could make a sober, impartial man believe such a monstrous, unaccountable doctrine; and, indeed, the thing itself appears so shocking, so out of all proportion, that it may be questioned whether all the miracles that ever were wrought could make it credible that this doctrine really came from God.

At present, there is not the least syllable in Scripture which gives any countenance to it. The hereditary, indefeasible divine right of kings, and the doctrine of nonresistance, which is built upon the supposition of such a right, are altogether as fabulous and chimerical as transubstantiation or any of the most absurd reveries of ancient or modern visionaries. These notions are fetched neither from divine revelation nor human reason; and if they are derived from neither of those sources, it is not much matter from whence they come, or whither they go. Only it is a pity that such doctrines should be propagated in society, to raise factions and rebellions, as we see they have, in fact, been, both in the *last* and in the *present reign*.

But, then, if unlimited submission and passive obedience to the *higher powers* in all possible cases be not a duty, it will be asked, "How far are we obliged to submit? If we may innocently disobey and resist in some cases, why not in all? Where shall we stop? What is the measure of our duty? This doctrine tends to the total dissolution of civil government and to introduce such scenes of wild anarchy and confusion as are more fatal to society than the worst of tyranny."

After this manner, some men object; and, indeed, this is the most plausible thing that can be said in favor of such an absolute submission as they plead for. But the worst (or rather the best) of it is that there is very little strength or solidity in it; for similar difficulties may be raised with respect to almost every duty of natural and revealed religion. To instance only in two, both of which are near akin and, indeed, exactly parallel to the case before us. It is unquestionably the duty of children to submit to their parents and of servants to their masters. But no one asserts that it is their duty to obey and submit to them in all supposable cases or universally a sin to resist them. Now does this tend to subvert the just authority of parents and masters? Or to introduce confusion and anarchy into private families? No. How then does the same principle tend to unhinge the government of that larger family, the body politic? We know, in general, that children and servants are obliged to obey their parents and masters respectively. We know, also, with equal certainty, that they are not obliged to submit to them in all things, without exception, but may, in some cases, reasonably and, therefore, innocently resist them. These principles are acknowledged upon all hands, whatever difficulty there may be in fixing the exact limits of submission.

Now, there is at least as much difficulty in stating the measure of duty in these two cases as in the case of rulers and subjects. So that this is really no objection, at least no reasonable one, against resistance to the *higher powers;* or, if it is one, it will hold equally against resistance in the other cases mentioned. It is indeed true that turbulent, vicious-minded men may take occasion from this principle, that their rulers may, in some cases, be lawfully resisted to raise factions and disturbances in the state and to make resistance where resistance is needless and, therefore, sinful. But is it not equally true that children and servants of turbulent, vicious minds may take occasion from this principle, that parents and masters may, in some cases, be lawfully resisted to resist when resistance is unnecessary and, therefore, criminal? Is the principle in either case false in itself merely because it may be abused and applied to legitimate disobedience and resistance in those instances to which it ought not to be applied? According to this way of arguing, there will be no true principles in the world, for there are none but what may be wrested and perverted to serve bad purposes, either through the weakness or wickedness of men.

A *people*, really oppressed to a great degree by their sovereign, cannot well be insensible when they are so oppressed. And such a people (if I may allude to an ancient fable) have, like the Hesperian fruit, a dragon for their protector and guardian; nor would they have any reason to mourn if some Hercules should appear to dispatch him. For a nation thus abused to arise unanimously and to resist their prince, even to the dethroning him, is not criminal but a reasonable way of vindicating their liberties and just rights; it is making use of the means, and the only means, which God has put into their power for mutual and self-defense. And it would be highly criminal in them not to make use of this means. It would be stupid tameness and unaccountable folly for whole nations to suffer *one* unreasonable, ambitious, and cruel man to

wanton and riot in their misery. And, in such a case, it would, of the two, be more rational to suppose that they did *not resist* than that they who did would *receive to themselves damnation.* . . .

To conclude, let us all learn to be *free* and to be *loyal.* Let us not profess ourselves vassals to the lawless pleasure of any man on earth. But let us remember, at the same time, government is *sacred* and not to be trifled with. It is our happiness to live under the government of a prince who is satisfied with ruling according to law, as every other good prince will. We enjoy under his administration all the liberty that is proper and expedient for us. It becomes us, therefore, to be contented and dutiful subjects. Let us prize our freedom but not *use our liberty for a cloak of maliciousness.* There are men who strike at liberty under the term licentiousness. There are others who aim at popularity under the disguise of patriotism. Be aware of both. *Extremes* are dangerous. There is at present amongst us, perhaps, more danger of the latter than of the former; for which reason I would exhort you to pay all due regard to the government over us, to the king and all in authority, and to lead a *quiet and peaceable life.* And while I am speaking of loyalty to our earthly prince, suffer me just to put you in mind to be loyal also to the Supreme Ruler of the universe, "by whom kings reign and princes decree justice" (Prov. 8:15). To which King eternal, immortal, invisible, even to the only wise God be all honor and praise, dominion and thanksgiving, through Jesus Christ our Lord. Amen.

JAMES OTIS: Rights of the British Colonies

The Revenue Act of 1764 was meant to replace the Sugar Act of 1733. Its purpose was to raise money for defense and improve the tax collecting system. To counteract this new act of Parliament, James Otis, a political leader of Massachusetts Bay, published in the same year The Rights of the British Colonies Asserted and Proved. *Otis discussed the constitutional position of the colonies in the Commonwealth which he believed the British empire to be. In the* Rights, *Otis developed principles he had earlier stated in 1761 in his argument against the writs of assistance.*

Source: *The Rights of the British Colonies Asserted and Proved,* 3rd edition,
London, 1766, pp. 17-22, 52-65, 70-77, 95-99.

GOVERNMENT HAVING BEEN proved to be necessary by the law of nature, it makes no difference in the thing to call it, from a certain period, *civil.* This term can only relate to form, to additions to or deviations from the substance of government: this being founded in nature, the superstructures and the whole administration should be conformed to the law of universal reason. A supreme legislative and a supreme executive power must be placed *somewhere* in every commonwealth. Where there is no other positive provision or compact to the contrary, those powers remain in the *whole body of the people.* It is also evident there can be but *one* best way of depositing those powers; but what that way is, mankind have been disputing in peace and in war more than 5,000 years. If we could suppose the individuals of a community met to deliberate whether it were best to keep those powers in their own hands or dispose of them in trust, the following questions would occur: Whether those two great powers of *legislation* and *execution* should remain united? If so, whether in the hands of the many or jointly or severally in the hands of a few, or jointly in some one individual?

If both those powers are retained in the hands of the many, where nature seems to have placed them originally, the govern-ment is a simple *democracy* or a government of all over all. This can be administered only by establishing it as a first principle that the votes of the majority shall be taken as the voice of the whole. If those powers are lodged in the hands of a few, the government is an *aristocracy* or *oligarchy.* Here too the first principle of a practicable administration is that the majority rules the whole. If those great powers are both lodged in the hands of one man, the government is a *simple monarchy,* commonly though falsely called *absolute* if by that term is meant a right to do as one pleases. *Sic volo, sic jubeo, stet pro ratione voluntas* [Thus I will it, thus I command it, let my desire serve for reason] belongs not of right to any mortal man.

The same law of nature and of reason is equally obligatory on a *democracy,* an *aristocracy,* and a *monarchy:* whenever the administrators in any of those forms deviate from truth, justice, and equity, they verge toward tyranny, and are to be opposed; and if they prove incorrigible they will be deposed by the people, if the people are not rendered too abject. Deposing the administrators of a simple democracy may sound odd, but it is done every day and in almost every vote. A, B, and C, for example, make a democracy. Today A and B are for so vile a measure as a standing army. Tomorrow B and C vote it out. This is as really deposing the former administrators as setting up and making a new king is deposing the old one. Democracy in the one case and monarchy in the other still remain; all that is done is to change the administration.

The first principle and great end of government being to provide for the best good of all the people, this can be done only by a supreme legislative and executive ultimately in the people or whole community where God has placed it; but the inconveniences, not to say impossibility, attending the consultations and operations of a large body of people have made it necessary to transfer the power of the whole to a *few*. This necessity gave rise to deputation, proxy, or a right of representation.

A power of legislation without a power of execution in the same or other hands would be futile and vain. On the other hand, a power of execution, supreme or subordinate, without an independent legislature would be perfect despotism.

The difficulties attending a universal congress, especially when society became large, have brought men to consent to a delegation of the power of all: the weak and the wicked have too often been found in the same interest, and in most nations have not only brought these powers jointly into the hands of one or some few of their number but made them hereditary in the families of despotic nobles and princes.

The wiser and more virtuous states have always provided that the representation of the people should be numerous. Nothing but life and liberty are *naturally* hereditable; this has never been considered by those who have tamely given up both into the hands of a tyrannical oligarchy or despotic monarchy.

The analogy between the natural, or material, as it is called, and the moral world is very obvious; God himself appears to us at some times to cause the intervention or combination of a number of simple principles, though never when one will answer the end; gravitation and attraction have place in the revolution of the planets, because the one would fix them to a center and the other would carry them off indefinitely; so in the moral world the first simple principle is equality and the power of the whole. This will answer in small numbers; so will a tolerably virtuous oligarchy or a monarchy. But when the society grows in bulk, none of them will answer well singly, and none worse than absolute monarchy. It becomes necessary, therefore, as numbers increase, to have those several powers properly combined, so as from the whole to produce that harmony of government so often talked of and wished for but too seldom found in ancient or modern states.

The grand political problem in all ages has been to invent the best combination or distribution of the supreme powers of legislation and execution. Those states have ever made the greatest figure, and have been most durable, in which those powers have not only been separated from each other but placed each in more hands than one or a few. The Romans are the most shining example, but they never had a balance between the Senate and the people, and the want of this is generally agreed by the few who know anything of the matter to have been the cause of their fall. The British constitution in theory and in the present administration of it in general comes nearest the idea of perfection of any that has been reduced to practice; and if the principles of it are adhered to it will, according to the infallible prediction of Harrington, always keep the Britons uppermost in Europe till their only rival nation shall either embrace that perfect model of a commonwealth given us by that author or come as near it as Great Britain is. Then indeed, and not till then, will that rival and our nation either be eternal confederates or contend in greater earnest than they have ever yet done, till one of them shall sink under the power of the other and rise no more.

Great Britain has at present most evidently the advantage and such opportunities of honest wealth and grandeur as perhaps no state ever had before, at least not since the days of Julius Caesar, the destroyer of the Roman glory and grandeur, at a time when, but for him and his adherents, both might have been rendered immortal.

We have said that the form and mode of government is to be settled by compact, as it was rightfully done by the Convention after the abdication of James II, and assented to by the first representative of the nation chosen afterward, and by every Parliament and by almost every man ever since but the bigots to the indefeasible power of tyrants, civil and ecclesiastic. There was neither time for nor occasion to call the whole people together. If they had not liked the proceedings it was in their power to control them, as it would be should the supreme legislative or executive powers ever again attempt to enslave them. The people will bear a great deal before they will even murmur against their rulers; but when once they are thoroughly roused and in earnest against those who would be glad to enslave them their power is irresistible. . . .

Every British subject born on the continent of America or in any other of the British dominions is by the law of God and nature, by the common law, and by act of Parliament (exclusive of all charters from the Crown) entitled to all the natural, essential, inherent, and inseparable rights of our fellow subjects in Great Britain. Among those rights are the following, which it is humbly conceived no man or body of men, not excepting the Parliament, justly, equitably, and consistently with their own rights and the constitution can take away.

First, that the supreme and subordinate powers of legislation should be free and sacred in the hands where the community have once rightfully placed them.

Second, the supreme national legislative cannot be altered justly till the Commonwealth is dissolved, nor a subordinate legislative taken away without forfeiture or other good cause. Nor then can the subjects in the subordinate government be reduced to a state of slavery and subject to the despotic rule of others. A state has no right to make slaves of the conquered. Even when the subordinate right of legislature is forfeited and so declared, this cannot affect the natural persons either of those who were invested with it or the inhabitants so far as to deprive them of the rights of subjects and of men. The colonists will have an equitable right, notwithstanding any such forfeiture of charter, to be represented in Parliament or to have some new subordinate legislature among themselves. It would be best if they had both.

Deprived, however, of their common rights as subjects they cannot lawfully be while they remain such. A representation in Parliament from the several colonies — since they are become so large and numerous as to be called on not to maintain provincial government, civil and military among themselves (for this they have cheerfully done) but to contribute toward the support of a national standing army, by reason of the heavy national debt, when they themselves owe a large one contracted in the common cause — can't be thought an unreasonable thing, nor if asked could it be called an immodest request. *Qui sentit commodum sentire debet et onus* [He who derives the advantage ought to sustain the burden] has been thought a maxim of equity. But that a man should bear a burden for other people as well as himself without a return never long found a place in any lawbook or decrees but those of the most despotic princes. Besides the equity of an American representation in Parliament, a thousand advantages would result from it. It would be the most effectual means of giving those of both countries a thorough knowledge of each other's interests, as well as that of the whole, which are inseparable.

Were this representation allowed, instead

of the scandalous memorials and depositions that have been sometimes, in days of old, privately cooked up in an inquisitorial manner by persons of bad minds and wicked views and sent from America to the several boards, persons of the first reputation among their countrymen might be on the spot from the several colonies truly to represent them. Future ministers need not, like some of their predecessors, have recourse for information in American affairs to every vagabond stroller that has run or rid post through America from his creditors, or to people of no kind of reputation from the colonies, some of whom, at the time of administering their sage advice, have been as ignorant of the state of this country as of the regions in Jupiter and Saturn.

No representation of the colonies in Parliament alone would, however, be equivalent to a subordinate legislative among themselves, nor so well answer the ends of increasing their prosperity and the commerce of Great Britain. It would be impossible for the Parliament to judge so well of their abilities to bear taxes, impositions on trade, and other duties and burdens, or of the local laws that might be really needful, as a legislative here.

Third, no legislative, supreme or subordinate, has a right to make itself arbitrary. It would be a most manifest contradiction for a free legislative, like that of Great Britain, to make itself arbitrary.

Fourth, the supreme legislative cannot justly assume a power of ruling by extempore arbitrary decrees, but is bound to dispense justice by known settled rules and by duly authorized independent judges.

Fifth, the supreme power cannot take from any man any part of his property, without his consent in person or by representation.

Sixth, the legislature cannot transfer the power of making laws to any other hands.

These are their bounds, which by God and nature are fixed; hitherto have they a right to come, and no further.

1. To govern by stated laws.

2. Those laws should have no other end ultimately but the good of the people.

3. Taxes are not to be laid on the people but by their consent in person or by deputation.

4. Their whole power is not transferable.

These are the first principles of law and justice, and the great barriers of a free state and of the British constitution in particular. I ask, I want, no more. Now let it be shown how 'tis reconcilable with these principles, or to many other fundamental maxims of the British constitution, as well as the natural and civil rights which by the laws of their country all British subjects are entitled to as their best inheritance and birthright, that all the northern colonies, who are without one representative in the House of Commons, should be taxed by the British Parliament.

That the colonists, black and white, born here are freeborn British subjects and entitled to all the essential civil rights of such, is a truth not only manifest from the provincial charters, from the principles of the common law, and acts of Parliament, but from the British constitution, which was reestablished at the Revolution with a professed design to secure the liberties of all the subjects to all generations.

In the 12 and 13 of William . . . the liberties of the subject are spoken of as their best birthrights. No one ever dreamed, surely, that these liberties were confined to the Realm. At that rate no British subjects in the dominions could, without a manifest contradiction, be declared entitled to all the privileges of subjects born within the Realm to all intents and purposes which are rightly given foreigners by Parliament after residing seven years. These expressions of Parliament as well as of the charters must be vain and empty sounds unless we are allowed the essential rights of our fellow subjects in Great Britain.

Now; can there be any liberty where

property is taken away without consent? Can it with any color of truth, justice, or equity be affirmed that the northern colonies are represented in Parliament? Has this whole continent of near three thousand miles in length, and in which and his other American dominions His Majesty has or very soon will have some millions of as good, loyal, and useful subjects, white and black, as any in the three kingdoms, the election of one member of the House of Commons?

Is there the least difference as to the consent of the colonists whether taxes and impositions are laid on their trade and other property by the Crown alone or by the Parliament? As it is agreed on all hands the Crown alone cannot impose them, we should be justifiable in refusing to pay them, but must and ought to yield obedience to an act of Parliament, though erroneous, till repealed.

I can see no reason to doubt but that the imposition of taxes, whether on trade, or on land, or houses, or ships, on real or personal, fixed or floating property, in the colonies is absolutely irreconcilable with the rights of the colonists as British subjects and as men. I say men, for in a state of nature no man can take my property from me without my consent; if he does, he deprives me of my liberty and makes me a slave. If such a proceeding is a breach of the law of nature, no law of society can make it just. The very act of taxing exercised over those who are not represented appears to me to be depriving them of one of their most essential rights as freemen, and if continued seems to be in effect an entire disfranchisement of every civil right. For what one civil right is worth a rush after a man's property is subject to be taken from him at pleasure without his consent? If a man is not his own assessor in person or by deputy, his liberty is gone or lies entirely at the mercy of others.

I think I have heard it said that when the Dutch are asked why they enslave their col-

onies, their answer is that the liberty of Dutchmen is confined to Holland, and that it was never intended for provincials in America or anywhere else. A sentiment, this, very worthy of modern Dutchmen; but if their brave and worthy ancestors had entertained such narrow ideas of liberty, seven poor and distressed provinces would never have asserted their rights against the whole Spanish monarchy, of which the present is but a shadow. It is to be hoped none of our fellow subjects of Britain, great or small, have borrowed this Dutch maxim of plantation politics; if they have, they had better return it from whence it came; indeed they had. Modern Dutch or French maxims of state never will suit with a British constitution.

It is a maxim that the King can do no wrong; and every good subject is bound to believe his King is not inclined to do any. We are blessed with a prince who has given abundant demonstrations that in all his actions he studies the good of his people and the true glory of his Crown, which are inseparable. It would therefore be the highest degree of impudence and disloyalty to imagine that the King, at the head of his Parliament, could have any but the most pure and perfect intentions of justice, goodness, and truth that human nature is capable of.

All this I say and believe of the King and Parliament in all their acts, even in that which so nearly affects the interest of the colonists, and that a most perfect and ready obedience is to be yielded to it while it remains in force. I will go further, and readily admit that the intention of the Ministry was not only to promote the public good by this act, but that Mr. Chancellor of the Exchequer had therein a particular view to the "ease, the quiet, and the good will of the colonies," he having made this declaration more than once. Yet I hold that 'tis possible he may have erred in his kind intentions toward the colonies, and taken away our fish and given us a stone.

With regard to the Parliament, as infallibility belongs not to mortals, 'tis possible *they* may have been misinformed and deceived. The power of Parliament is uncontrollable but by themselves, and we must obey. They only can repeal their own acts. There would be an end of all government if one or a number of subjects or subordinate provinces should take upon them so far to judge of the justice of an act of Parliament as to refuse obedience to it. If there was nothing else to restrain such a step, prudence ought to do it, for forcibly resisting the Parliament and the King's laws is high treason. Therefore let the Parliament lay what burdens they please on us, we must, it is our duty to submit and patiently bear them till they will be pleased to relieve us. And 'tis to be presumed the wisdom and justice of that august assembly always will afford us relief by repealing such acts as through mistake or other human infirmities have been suffered to pass, if they can be convinced that their proceedings are not constitutional or not for the common good.

The Parliament may be deceived, they may have been misinformed of facts, and the colonies may in many respects be misrepresented to the King, his Parliament, and his Ministry. In some instances, I am well assured the colonies have been very strangely misrepresented in England. I have now before me a pamphlet called the *Administration of the Colonies,* said to be written by a gentleman who formerly commanded in chief in one of them. I suppose this book was designed for public information and use. There are in it many good regulations proposed which no power can enforce but the Parliament. From all which I infer that if our hands are tied by the passing of an act of Parliament, our mouths are not stopped, provided we speak of that transcendent body with decency, as I have endeavored always to do; and should anything have escaped me or hereafter fall from my pen that bears the least aspect but that of obedience, duty, and loyalty to the King and Parliament, and the highest respect for the Ministry, the candid will impute it to the agony of my heart rather than to the pravity of my will.

If I have one ambitious wish, 'tis to see Great Britain at the head of the world, and to see my King, under God, the father of mankind. I pretend neither to the spirit of prophecy nor any uncommon skill in predicting a crisis, much less to tell when it begins to be "nascent" or is fairly midwived into the world. But if I were to fix a meaning to the two first paragraphs of the *Administration of the Colonies,* though I do not collect it from them, I should say the world was at the eve of the highest scene of earthly power and grandeur that has been ever yet displayed to the view of mankind. The cards are shuffling fast through all Europe. Who will win the prize is with God. This however I know, *detur digniori.* [Let it be given to the more worthy.]

The next universal monarchy will be favorable to the human race, for it must be founded on the principles of equity, moderation, and justice. No country has been more distinguished for these principles than Great Britain, since the Revolution. I take it every subject has a right to give his sentiments to the public, of the utility or inutility of any act whatsoever, even after it is passed, as well as while it is pending. The equity and justice of a bill may be questioned with perfect submission to the legislature. Reasons may be given why an act ought to be repealed, and yet obedience must be yielded to it till that repeal takes place. If the reasons that can be given against an act are such as plainly demonstrate that it is against *natural* equity, the executive courts will adjudge such act void. It may be questioned by some, though I make no doubt of it, whether they are not obliged by their oaths to adjudge such act void. If there is not a right of private judgment to be exercised, so far at least as to petition for a repeal or to determine the expediency of risking a trial at law, the Parliament might make itself arbitrary, which it is conceived it cannot by the constitution.

I think every man has a right to examine as freely into the origin, spring, and foundation of every power and measure in a commonwealth as into a piece of curious machinery or a remarkable phenomenon in nature, and that it ought to give no more offense to say the Parliament have erred or are mistaken in a matter of fact or of right than to say it of a private man, if it is true of both. If the assertion can be proved with regard to either, it is a kindness done them to show them the truth. With regard to the public, it is the duty of every good citizen to point out what he thinks erroneous in the Commonwealth.

I have waited years in hopes to see some one friend of the colonies pleading in public for them. I have waited in vain. One privilege is taken away after another, and where we shall be landed God knows, and I trust will protect and provide for us even should we be driven and persecuted into a more western wilderness on the score of liberty, civil and religious, as many of our ancestors were to these once inhospitable shores of America. I have formed great expectations from a gentleman who published his first volume in quarto on the rights of the colonies two years since; but, as he foresaw, the state of his health and affairs has prevented his further progress.

The misfortune is, gentlemen in America, the best qualified in every respect to state the rights of the colonists, have reasons that prevent them from engaging. Some of them have good ones. There are many infinitely better able to serve this cause than I pretend to be; but from indolence, from timidity, or by necessary engagements they are prevented. There has been a most profound and I think shameful silence, till it seems almost too late to assert our indisputable rights as men and as citizens. What must posterity think of us? The trade of the whole continent taxed by Parliament, stamps and other internal duties and taxes

as they are called, talked of, and not one petition to the King and Parliament for relief.

I cannot but observe here that if the Parliament have an equitable right to tax our trade, 'tis indisputable that they have as good a one to tax the lands and everything else. The taxing trade furnishes one reason why the other should be taxed, or else the burdens of the province will be unequally borne, upon a supposition that a tax on trade is not a tax on the whole. But take it either way, there is no foundation for the distinction some make in England between an internal and an external tax on the colonies. By the first is meant a tax on trade, by the latter a tax on land and the things on it.

A tax on trade is either a tax of every man in the province, or 'tis not. If 'tis not a tax on the whole, 'tis unequal and unjust that a heavy burden should be laid on the trade of the colonies to maintain an army of soldiers, customhouse officers, and fleets of guardships, all which the incomes of both trade and land would not furnish means to support so lately as the last war, when all was at stake, and the colonies were reimbursed in part by Parliament. How can it be supposed that all of a sudden the trade of the colonies alone can bear all this terrible burden? The late acquisitions in America, as glorious as they have been and as beneficial as they are to Great Britain, are only a security to these colonies against the ravages of the French and Indians. Our trade upon the whole is not, I believe, benefited by them one groat.

All the time the French islands were in our hands, the fine sugars, etc., were all shipped home. None as I have been informed were allowed to be brought to the colonies. They were too delicious a morsel for a North American palate. If it be said that a tax on the trade of the colonies is an equal and just tax on the whole of the inhabitants, what then becomes of the notable distinction between external and internal taxes? Why may not the Parliament lay stamps, land taxes, establish tithes to the Church of England, and so indefinitely? I know of no bounds. I do not mention the tithes out of any disrespect to the Church of England, which I esteem by far the best *national* church and to have had as ornaments of it many of the greatest and best men in the world. But to those colonies who in general dissent from a principle of conscience it would seem a little hard to pay toward the support of a worship whose modes they cannot conform to.

If an army must be kept up in America at the expense of the colonies, it would not seem quite so hard if after the Parliament had determined the sum to be raised, and apportioned it, to have allowed each colony to assess its quota and raise it as easily to themselves as might be. But to have the whole levied and collected without our consent is extraordinary. 'Tis allowed even to *tributaries* and those laid under *military* contribution to assess and collect the sums demanded. The case of the provinces is certainly likely to be the hardest that can be instanced in story. Will it not equal anything but downright military execution? Was there ever a tribute imposed even on the conquered? A fleet, an army of soldiers, and another of tax gatherers kept up, and not a single office either for securing or collecting the duty in the gift of the tributary state. . . .

To say the Parliament is absolute and arbitrary is a contradiction. The Parliament cannot make 2 and 2, 5: omnipotency cannot do it. The supreme power in a state is *jus dicere* [to declare the law] only: *jus dare* [to give the law], strictly speaking, belongs alone to God. Parliaments are in all cases to declare what is for the good of the whole; but it is not the declaration of Parliament that makes it so. There must be in every instance a higher authority, viz., God. Should an act of Parliament be against any of His natural laws, which are immutably true, their declaration would be contrary to eternal truth, equity, and justice, and conse-

quently void; and so it would be adjudged by the Parliament itself when convinced of their mistake. Upon this great principle, parliaments repeal such acts as soon as they find they have been mistaken in having declared them to be for the public good when in fact they were not so. When such mistake is evident and palpable, as in the instances in the appendix, the judges of the executive courts have declared the act "of a whole Parliament void." See here the grandeur of the British constitution! See the wisdom of our ancestors!

The supreme legislative and the supreme executive are a perpetual check and balance to each other. If the supreme executive errs it is informed by the supreme legislative in Parliament. If the supreme legislative errs it is informed by the supreme executive in the King's courts of law. Here the King appears, as represented by his judges, in the highest luster and majesty, as supreme executor of the Commonwealth; and he never shines brighter but on his throne, at the head of the supreme legislative. This is government! This is a constitution! to preserve which, either from foreign or domestic foes, has cost oceans of blood and treasure in every age; and the blood and the treasure have upon the whole been well spent.

British America has been bleeding in this cause from its settlement. We have spent all we could raise, and more; for, notwithstanding the parliamentary reimbursements of part, we still remain much in debt. The province of the Massachusetts, I believe, has expended more men and money in war since the year 1620, when a few families first landed at Plymouth, in proportion to their ability than the three kingdoms together. The same, I believe, may be truly affirmed of many of the other colonies; though the Massachusetts has undoubtedly had the heaviest burden. This may be thought incredible, but materials are collecting; and though some are lost, enough may remain to demonstrate it to the world. I have reason to hope at least that the public will soon see such proofs exhibited as will show that I do not speak quite at random.

Why then is it thought so heinous by the author of the *Administration of the Colonies*, and others, that the colonists should aspire after "a one whole legislative power" not independent of but subordinate to the laws and Parliament of Great Britain? It is a mistake in this author to bring so heavy a charge as high treason against some of the colonists, which he does in effect in this place by representing them as "claiming in fact or in deed the same full, free, independent, unrestrained power and legislative will in their several corporations, and under the King's commission and their respective charters, as the government and legislature of Great Britain holds by its constitution and under the great charter." No such claim was ever thought of by any of the colonists. They are all better men and better subjects; and many of them too well versed in the laws of nature and nations and the law and constitution of Great Britain to think they have a right to more than a *provincial subordinate legislative.*

All power is of God. Next and only subordinate to Him in the present state of the well-formed, beautifully constructed British monarchy, standing where I hope it ever will stand, for the pillars are fixed in judgment, righteousness, and truth, is the King and Parliament. Under these, it seems easy to conceive subordinate powers in gradation, till we descend to the legislative of a town council or even a private social club. These have each "a one whole legislative" subordinate, which, when it doesn't counteract the laws of any of its superiors, is to be indulged. Even when the laws of subordination are transgressed, the superior does not destroy the subordinate, but will negative its acts, as it may in all cases when disapproved.

This right of negative is essential, and may be enforced. But in no case are the essential rights of the subjects inhabiting the

subordinate dominions to be destroyed. This would put it in the power of the superior to reduce the inferior to a state of slavery; which cannot be rightfully done even with conquered enemies and rebels. After satisfaction and security is obtained of the former and examples are made of so many of the latter as the ends of government require, the rest are to be restored to all the essential rights of men and citizens. This is the great law of nature; and agreeable to this law is the constant practice of all good and mild governments. This lenity and humanity has nowhere been carried further than in Great Britain. The colonies have been so remarkable for loyalty that there never has been any instance of rebellion or treason in them. This loyalty is in very handsome terms acknowledged by the author of the *Administration of the Colonies:*

> It has been often suggested that care should be taken in the administration of the plantations lest, in some future time, these colonies should become independent of the mother country. But perhaps it may be proper on this occasion, nay, it is justice to say it, that if by becoming independent is meant a revolt, nothing is further from their nature, their interest, their thoughts. If a defection from the alliance of the mother country be suggested, it ought to be and can be truly said that their spirit abhors the sense of such; their attachment to the Protestant succession of the House of Hanover will ever stand unshaken; and nothing can eradicate from their hearts their natural and almost mechanical affection to Great Britain, which they conceive under no other sense nor call by any other name than that of home. Any such suggestion, therefore, is a false and unjust aspersion on their principles and affections, and can arise from nothing but an entire ignorance of their circumstances.

After all this loyalty, it is a little hard to be charged with claiming, and represented as aspiring after, independency. The inconsistency of this I leave. We have said that the loyalty of the colonies has never been suspected; this must be restricted to a just suspicion. For it seems there have long been groundless suspicions of us in the minds of individuals. And there have always been those who have endeavored to magnify these chimerical fears. I find Mr. Dummer complaining of this many years since. "There is," says he, "one thing more I have heard often urged against the charter colonies, and indeed 'tis what one meets with from people of all conditions and qualities, though with due respect to their better judgments, I can see neither reason nor color for it. 'Tis said that their increasing numbers and wealth, joined to their great distance from Britain, will give them an opportunity, in the course of some years, to throw off their dependence on the nation and declare themselves a free state if not curbed in time by being made entirely subject to the Crown."

This jealousy has been so long talked of that many seem to believe it really well grounded. Not that there is danger of a "revolt," even in the opinion of the author of the *Administration,* but that the colonists will by fraud or force avail themselves, in "fact or in deed," of an independent legislature. This, I think, would be a revolting with a vengeance. What higher revolt can there be than for a province to assume the right of an independent legislative or state? I must therefore think this a greater aspersion on the colonists than to charge them with a design to revolt in the sense in which the gentleman allows they have been abused: it is a more artful and dangerous way of attacking our liberties than to charge us with being in open rebellion. That could be confuted instantly; but this seeming indirect way of charging the colonies with a desire of throwing off their dependency requires more pains to confute it than the other; therefore it has been recurred to.

The truth is, gentlemen have had departments in America the functions of which they have not been fortunate in executing. The people have by these means been rendered uneasy at bad provincial measures.

They have been represented as factious, seditious, and inclined to democracy whenever they have refused passive obedience to provincial mandates as arbitrary as those of a Turkish bashaw: I say provincial mandates, for to the King and Parliament they have been ever submissive and obedient.

These representations of us many of the good people of England swallow with as much ease as they would a bottle bubble or any other story of a cock and a bull; and the worst of it is, among some of the most credulous have been found stars and garters. However, they may all rest assured, the colonists, who do not pretend to understand themselves so well as the people of England, though the author of the *Administration* makes them the fine compliment to say they "know their business much better," yet will never think of independency. Were they inclined to it, they know the blood and the treasure it would cost, if ever effected; and when done, it would be a thousand to one if their liberties did not fall a sacrifice to the victor.

We all think ourselves happy under Great Britain. We love, esteem, and reverence our mother country, and adore our King. And could the choice of independency be offered the colonies or subjection to Great Britain upon any terms above absolute slavery, I am convinced they would accept the latter. The Ministry in all future generations may rely on it that British America will never prove undutiful till driven to it as the last fatal resort against ministerial oppression, which will make the wisest mad, and the weakest strong. . . .

Sometimes we have been considered only as the corporations in England; and it may be urged that it is no harder upon us to be taxed by Parliament for the general cause than for them, who besides are at the expense of their corporate subordinate government. I answer: 1. Those corporations are represented in Parliament. 2. The colonies are and have been at great expense in raising men, building forts, and supporting the

King's civil government here. Now I read of no governors and other officers of His Majesty's nomination that the City of London taxes its inhabitants to support; I know of no forts and garrisons that the City of London has lately built at its own expense, or of any annual levies that they have raised for the King's service and the common cause. These are things very fitting and proper to be done by a subordinate dominion, and 'tis their duty to do all they are able; but it seems but equal they should be allowed to assess the charges of it themselves. The rules of equity and the principles of the constitution seem to require this. Those who judge of the reciprocal rights that subsist between a supreme and subordinate state or dominion by no higher rules than are applied to a corporation of buttonmakers will never have a very comprehensive view of them.

Yet sorry am I to say it, many elaborate writers on the administration of the colonies seem to me never to rise higher in their notions than what might be expected from a secretary to one of the quorum. If I should be ranked among this number I shall have this consolation, that I have fallen into what is called very good company and among some who have seen very high life below stairs. I agree with the Administrator that of whatever revenues raised in the colonies, if they must be raised without our consent, "the first and special appropriation of them ought to be the paying the governors and all the other Crown officers," for it would be hard for the colonists to be obliged to pay them after this. It was on this principle that at the last Assembly of this province I moved to stop every grant to the officers of the Crown, more especially as I know some who have built very much upon the fine salaries they shall receive from the plantation branch of the revenue. Nor can I think it "injustice to the frame of human nature" to suppose, if I did not know it, that with similar views several officers of the Crown in some of the colonies have been pushing

for such an act for many years. They have obtained their wish, and much good it will do them. But I would not give much for all that will center net in the exchequer after deducting the costs attending the execution of it and the appropriations to the several officers proposed by the Administrator.

What will be the unavoidable consequence of all this, suppose another war should happen and it should be necessary to employ as many provincials in America as in the last? Would it be possible for the colonies, after being burdened in their trade, perhaps after it is ruined, to raise men? Is it probable that they would have spirit enough to exert themselves? If 'tis said the French will never try for America, or if they should, regular troops are only to be employed, I grant our regular troops are the best in the world, and that the experience of the present officers shows that they are capable of every species of American service; yet we should guard against the worst. If another trial for Canada should take place, which from the known temper of France we may judge she will bring on the first fair opportunity, it might require 30,000 or 40,000 regulars to secure His Majesty's just rights.

If it should be said that other American duties must then be levied, besides the impossibility of our being able to pay them, the danger recurs of a large standing army so remote from home; whereas a good provincial militia, with such occasional succors from the mother country as exigencies may require, never was and never will be attended with hazard. The experience of past times will show that an army of 20,000 or 30,000 veterans, half 3,000 miles from Rome, were very apt to proclaim Caesars. The first of the name, the assassin of his country, owed his false glory to stealing the affections of an army from the commonwealth.

I hope these hints will not be taken amiss; they seem to occur from the nature of the subject I am upon; they are delivered in pure affection to my King and country, and amount to no reflection on any man. The best army and the best men we may hereafter have may be led into temptation; all I think is that a prevention of evil is much easier than a deliverance from it.

The sum of my argument is: that civil government is of God; that the administrators of it were originally the whole people; that they might have devolved it on whom they pleased; that this devolution is fiduciary, for the good of the whole; that by the British constitution this devolution is on the King, Lords, and Commons, the supreme, sacred, and uncontrollable legislative power not only in the Realm but through the dominions; that by the abdication, the original compact was broken to pieces; that by the Revolution it was renewed and more firmly established, and the rights and liberties of the subject in all parts of the dominions more fully explained and confirmed.

That in consequence of this establishment and the acts of succession and union, His Majesty George III is rightful King and sovereign, and, with his Parliament, the supreme legislative of Great Britain, France, and Ireland, and the dominions thereto belonging; that this constitution is the most free one and by far the best now existing on earth; that by this constitution every man in the dominions is a free man; that no parts of His Majesty's dominions can be taxed without their consent; that every part has a right to be represented in the supreme or some subordinate legislature; that the refusal of this would seem to be a contradiction in practice to the theory of the constitution; that the colonies are subordinate dominions and are now in such a state as to make it best for the good of the whole that they should not only be continued in the enjoyment of subordinate legislation but be also represented in some proportion to their number and estates in the grand legislature of the nation; that this would firmly unite all parts of the British empire in the greatest peace and prosperity, and render it invulnerable and perpetual.

Virginia Stamp Act Resolutions

Patrick Henry, at a meeting of the Virginia House of Burgesses, proposed seven resolutions against the Stamp Act. While only four were adopted, on May 30, 1765, all seven proposed Virginia resolves were printed in the newspapers of many of the colonies, providing a basis for popular opposition to the Stamp Act.

Source: *Journals of the House of Burgesses of Virginia 1761-1765*, John Pendleton Kennedy, ed., Richmond, 1907.

Resolved, that the first adventurers and settlers of this His Majesty's colony and dominion of Virginia brought with them and transmitted to their posterity, and all other His Majesty's subjects since inhabiting in this His Majesty's said colony, all the liberties, privileges, franchises, and immunities that have at any time been held, enjoyed, and possessed by the people of Great Britain.

Resolved, that by two royal charters, granted by King James I, the colonists aforesaid are declared entitled to all liberties, privileges, and immunities of denizens and natural subjects to all intents and purposes as if they had been abiding and born within the Realm of England.

Resolved, that the taxation of the people by themselves, or by persons chosen by themselves to represent them, who can only know what taxes the people are able to bear, or the easiest method of raising them, and must themselves be affected by every tax laid on the people, is the only security against a burdensome taxation, and the distinguishing characteristic of British freedom,

without which the ancient constitution cannot exist.

Resolved, that His Majesty's liege people of this his most ancient and loyal colony have without interruption enjoyed the inestimable right of being governed by such laws, respecting their internal polity and taxation, as are derived from their own consent, with the approbation of their sovereign, or his substitute; and that the same has never been forfeited or yielded up, but has been constantly recognized by the kings and people of Great Britain.

Francis Bernard: Boston Stamp Act Riots

Colonial resistance to the new British imperial policies was directed particularly toward the Stamp Act. The reaction of the colonies to its passage was vehement. In Boston, a radical group called the Sons of Liberty destroyed the stamps wherever they found them, tarred and feathered the stamp agents, and sacked the homes and warehouses of the rich, who could be presumed to be favorites of the royal governors. The following account of the riots by Francis Bernard, governor of Massachusetts, was prepared for the Earl of Halifax on August 31, 1765.

Source: *British Public Record Office, C.O. 5/755.*

It is with the utmost concern that I am obliged to continue the subject of my last letters of the 15th and 16th and of the 22nd instant; the disorders of the town having been carried to much greater lengths than what I have before informed Your Lordship of.

After the demolition of Mr. Oliver's house was found so practicable and easy that the government was obliged to look on without being able to take any one step to prevent it, and the principal people of the town publicly avowed and justified the act, the mob, both great and small, became

highly elated, and all kinds of ill humors were set on float. Everything that for years past had been the cause of any popular discontent was revived and private resentments against persons in office worked themselves in and endeavored to execute themselves under the mask of the public cause. Among others the affairs of the attack upon the Admiralty and Custom House above four years ago (which after a contestation of a year by the steadiness and resolution of myself I may truly say, and the other officers of the Crown, ended entirely in conclusions on the side of the Crown) was brought up again and became as fresh as if it had been a business of yesterday. One B—— H—— of this town, who was in London about two years ago, had got a sight of the depositions which were sent home on the behalf of the Crown. Upon his return to Boston he took upon him to report the substance of these with additions of his own, and concluded with an assertion that the whole body of merchants had been represented as smugglers. This occasioned some murmuring at that time but it soon passed over.

All this story has been now revived with fresh circumstances of acrimony and inflammation, and a diligent pointing out the persons who in the former contest had acted on the side of the Crown, and H——, instead of telling his story verbally, reduced it into writing, which was handed about the town. This occasioned much clamor among some of the merchants who were told, without the least foundation in truth, that they were represented at home by name; and the clamor, as usual, soon descended from the top to the bottom of the town, and several persons' houses began to be threatened. This was truly the principal if not the sole cause of the second insurrection, which has had such shocking effects.

On Monday, August 26, there was some small rumor that mischief would be done that night, but it was in general disregarded. Toward evening some boys began to light a bonfire before the Town House, which is a usual signal for a mob. Before it was quite dark a great company of people gathered together crying liberty and property, which is the usual notice of their intention to plunder and pull down a house. They first went to Mr. Paxton's house (who is marshal of the Court of Admiralty and surveyor of the port), and finding before it the owner of the house (Mr. Paxton being only a tenant), he assured them that Mr. Paxton had quitted the house with his best effects; that the house was his; that he had never injured them; and finally invited them to go to the tavern and drink a barrel of punch.

The offer was accepted and so that house was saved. As soon as they had drunk the punch, they went to the house of Mr. Story, registrar deputed of the Admiralty, broke into it and tore it all to pieces; and took out all the books and papers, among which were all the records of the Court of Admiralty, and carried them to the bonfire and there burned them. They also looked about for him with an intention to kill him. From thence they went to Mr. Hallowell's, comptroller of the customs, broke into his house and destroyed and carried off everything of value, with about £30 sterling in cash. This house was lately built by himself and fitted and furnished with great elegance. But the grand mischief of all was to come.

The lieutenant governor had been apprised that there was an evil spirit gone forth against him, but being conscious that he had not in the least deserved to be made a party in regard to the Stamp Act or the Custom House, he rested in full security that the mob would not attack him, and he was at supper with his family when he received advice that the mob were coming to him. He immediately sent away his children and determined to stay in the house himself, but happily his eldest daughter returned and declared she would not stir from the house unless he went with her; by which means she got him away, which was undoubtedly the occasion of saving his life. For as soon as the mob had got into the house, with a most irresistible fury they immediately looked about for him to murder him, and even made diligent inquiry whither he was gone. They went to work with a rage scarce to be exemplified by the most savage people. Everything movable was destroyed in the most minute manner except such things of value as were worth carrying off, among which was near £1,000 sterling in specie, besides a great quantity of family plate, etc.

But the loss to be most lamented is that there was in one room kept for that pur-

pose a large and valuable collection of man-
uscripts and original papers which he had
been gathering all his lifetime, and to which
all persons who had been in possession of
valuable papers of a public kind had been
contributing as to a public museum. As
these related to the history and policy of
the country from the time of its settlement
to the present and was the only collection
of its kind, the loss to the public is great
and irretrievable as it is to himself, the loss
of the papers of a family which had made a
figure in this province for 130 years.

As for the house, which from its structure
and inside finishing seemed to be from a
design of Inigo Jones or his successor, it appears that they were a long while resolved
to level to the ground. They worked for
three hours at the cupola before they could
get it down, and they uncovered part of the
roof; but I suppose that the thickness of the
walls which were of very fine brickwork,
adorned with Ionic pilasters worked into
the wall, prevented their completing their
purpose though they worked at it till day-
light. The next day the streets were found
scattered with money, plate, gold rings, etc.,
which had been dropped in carrying off.
The whole loss in this house only is reck-
oned at £3,000 sterling.

As soon as I received advice of this at the
Castle, I immediately sent an order to the
secretary to summon a Council at Cambridge early in the afternoon, not thinking
Boston a safe place to sit at. As I was going thither, on the road I received a letter
from the secretary desiring that I would
hold the Council in Boston; for that this
affair had given such a turn to the town
that all the gentlemen in the place were
ready to support the government in detec-
ting and punishing the actors in the last
horrid scene, and there was a town meeting
appointed to testify their abhorrence of it. I
accordingly went to the Council and there
issued orders to the colonel of the regiment
of militia, the captain of the company of
cadet guards, the captains of the batteries

and of the companies of militia in Charles
Town, Cambridge, and Roxbury to raise
their several corps and make detachments
therefrom to keep a constant guard. And I
recommended to the gentlemen of the town
who were excused from military duty to en-
roll themselves as volunteers in some of the
corps, many of which did, especially in the
cadets, which were doubled upon this occasion; to whom I assigned the guard of the
Custom House where there were several
thousand pounds of the King's money.

And these measures were but just taken
in time for otherwise a much greater mischief would have happened the second
night than the former. For, it seems, the
mob had set down no less than fifteen
houses in or near the town to be attacked
the next night, among which was the Custom House and the houses of some of the
most respectable persons in the government.
It was now becoming a war of plunder, of
general leveling and taking away the distinction of rich and poor so that those
gentlemen who had promoted and approved the cruel treatment of Mr. Oliver
became now as fearful for themselves as the
most loyal person in the town could be.
They found, as I told some of them, that
they had raised the devil and could not lay
him again. However, by means of the military guards the town was kept quiet that
night without anything happening except
that the cadets were obliged once to present
their pieces, but did not fire.

After I had established these guards,
which took up all that day, I considered
whether it would not be proper to call in
assistance from without. By an instruction I
am directed to have the advice of Council
whenever I call for military aid. I knew that
the Council would never advise me to call
in the King's troops in cases more desperate
than this. Their own situation and dependence would make them afraid of being answerable to the people for so disagreeable a
step. I therefore put the question whether it
was expedient to advertise General Gage

and Lord Colville of what had happened at Boston. But they advised in the negative, saying that such advertisement would amount to a tacit request for forces; and though they expected such forces would be ordered hither some time or other, they would not help to bring them here nor hasten them before their time.

I therefore transmitted to General Gage a copy of this resolution of Council, copies of my proclamations, with advice of the intention of lodging the stamps in the Castle, and augmenting the garrison for that purpose; from all which he will see the restraints I am under. I then acquainted the Council with the various reports I had heard of the Castle being threatened if the stamps were put in there, represented the present state of garrison, and proposed that an independent company should be raised for augmenting the garrison, which they readily came into, and I immediately dispatched orders for that purpose. I am also by all means in my power strengthening the Castle so that if I can get the reinforcement here in time, I shan't be afraid for the Castle against any number, though I cannot think that any people will be desperate enough to attack it, notwithstanding what has been given out.

When first the town took this new turn, I was in hopes that they would have disavowed all the riotous proceedings, that of the first night as well as the last. But it is no such thing: great pains are taken to separate the two riots; what was done against Mr. Oliver is still approved of as a necessary declaration of their resolution not to submit to the Stamp Act; and even the cruel treatment of him and his family is justified by its consequences — the frightening him into a resignation. And it has been publicly hinted that if a line is not drawn between the first riot and the last, the civil power will not be supported by the principal people of the town, as it is assured it shall

be now. And indeed, if the last riot had been the only one, the civil government would appear to be in full power. Many people concerned in the last riot are daily taken up and committed to jail, where a constant guard is kept by the militia, and the town cries aloud for some of them to be made examples of. And yet if one was to offer to take one of the persons concerned in the first riot only, things would again be flung into confusion and the civil power would become as weak as ever. So that the present authority of the government is only exercised upon condition and with prescribed limitations.

It seems therefore that the horror of this last affair has not at all abated the spirit of the people against the Stamp Act. I am again and again assured that this town and country about it (how far deep I can't say) are as resolute as ever to oppose the execution of the Stamp Act and to suffer the utmost extremities rather than submit to it. There are but two things which are like to produce a change in these resolutions: the one is a nearer and fuller prospect of the anarchy and confusion which must take place when the courts of justice and public offices are shut up, as they must be on November 1 unless stamps are allowed to be used. These must necessarily alarm all serious people and especially those who have much property. The other is the meeting of the Assembly, which I believe I shall be obliged to call at the time it is prorogued to, September 25, though I could have wished that it might have been postponed till I could have received orders from England.

I should have much dependence upon the prudence of the Assembly in common cases, but I know not how to expect that they will act against the voice of the people, if it is such as I am told it is. On the other hand, they must be greatly staggered when they are called upon to assist the execution of an act of Parliament which is opposed by violence. Hitherto the opposition is chargeable upon private persons only; it will then be adopted by the legislature, and if that should fail in so important a duty, they must expect that a forfeiture of their rights will be the consequence. If these two causes — the apprehension of confusion when all business shall cease, and the prudence, or what is the same, the fear of the Assembly — should cooperate together, it is possible that the act may be yet carried into execution at its day. I shall watch every opportunity and improve every incident to produce so happy an event.

I labor under many difficulties, and none more than that the Council, which I have to advise with, is composed almost wholly of gentlemen whose connections and properties are in Boston. They that live out of Boston will not come in; I have but two or three such since the last riot and I have known some that have been afraid to come to Boston. By these means nothing can pass the Council that is likely to be displeasing to Boston; expedients are thereby rendered very few and spirited measures are quite impracticable. I submitted to the Council whether it would not be best to call the Assembly at a distance from Boston, that it might sit free from intimidation or undue influence: it passed in the negative. I then asked if I should call a general council by summoning every member to meet at Cambridge, and I urged that several members, naming them, objected to coming to Boston: it passed in the negative. I then proposed calling such general council at Boston, which was approved of, and it is appointed for Thursday next, September 5. It is true that I can without advice of Council call the Assembly and the Council to what place I please, but it is the business of the Council, among other things, to guard the governor against popular odium from his taking unpopular measures necessary to

government by concurring with him and advising such measures; and when they refuse so to do, it would be dangerous as well as impolitic for the governor to expose himself solely to the resentment of the people by acting without or contrary to the advice of Council.

I must, however, add that it is become now much safer to meet at Boston than it was a week ago. The town is now become as quiet as ever it was, and the principal gentlemen have desired me, who have of late slept in the Castle, although I have been in town almost every day, and sometimes all day long, to live more at the Province House, assuring me that I shall have a guard of what number of gentlemen I please; and I shall go to the Province House on Monday and stay there some days, to show that I don't keep out of the town for fear of it. There will therefore remain only the objection to the Assembly's meeting at Boston upon account of undue influence, which I own has considerable weight with me; though perhaps it may not have so much weight with the Council, by whom I must be determined concerning the sitting of the Assembly.

P.S. — I have taken the liberty to use only initial letters in one name as the person is of no significance and has a brother who is a very faithful officer of the King.

This is the Place to affix the STAMP.

JOHN ADAMS: A Burdensome and Unconstitutional Tax

The Stamp Act gave Adams his first opportunity to enter into Massachusetts politics and into the struggle between the mother country and the colonies. He drew up a set of resolutions of protest against the act for the town of Braintree, Massachusetts, on October 14, 1765. Similar resolutions were passed by other Massachusetts townships.

Source: C. F. Adams, III: "Instructions of the Town of Braintree to Their Representatives, 1765."

Sir,

In all the calamities which have ever befallen this country, we have never felt so great a concern, or such alarming apprehensions, as on this occasion. Such is our loyalty to the King, our veneration for both houses of Parliament, and our affection for all our fellow subjects in Britain that measures which discover any unkindness in that country toward us are the more sensibly and intimately felt. And we can no longer forbear complaining that many of the measures of the late Ministry, and some of the late acts of Parliament, have a tendency, in our apprehension, to divest us of our most essential rights and liberties. We shall confine ourselves, however, chiefly to the act of Parliament, commonly called the Stamp Act, by which a very burdensome and, in our opinion, unconstitutional tax is to be laid upon us all; and we [are to be] subjected to numerous and enormous penalties, to be prosecuted, sued for, and recovered at the option of an informer in a Court of Admiralty without a jury.

We have called this a burdensome tax, because the duties are so numerous and so high, and the embarrassments to business in this infant, sparsely settled country so great,

that it would be totally impossible for the people to subsist under it, if we had no controversy at all about the right and authority of imposing it. Considering the present scarcity of money, we have reason to think the execution of that act for a short space of time would drain the country of its cash, strip multitudes of all their property, and reduce them to absolute beggary. And what the consequence would be to the peace of the province, from so sudden a shock and such a convulsive change in the whole course of our business and subsistence, we tremble to consider.

We further apprehend this tax to be unconstitutional. We have always understood it to be a grand and fundamental principle of the constitution that no freeman should be subject to any tax to which he has not given his own consent, in person or by proxy. And the maxims of the law, as we have constantly received them, are to the same effect: that no freeman can be separated from his property but by his own act or fault. . . .

But the most grievous innovation of all is the alarming extension of the power of Courts of Admiralty. In these courts one judge presides alone! No juries have any concern there! The law and the fact are both to be decided by the same single judge, whose commission is only during pleasure, and with whom, as we are told, the most mischievous of all customs has become established, that of taking commissions on all condemnations; so that he is under a pecuniary temptation always against the subject. . . . We have all along thought the acts of trade in this respect a grievance; but the Stamp Act has opened a vast number of sources of new crimes, which may be committed by any man and cannot but be committed by multitudes, and prodigious penalties are annexed, and all these are to be tried by such a judge of such a court! . . .

We cannot help asserting, therefore, that this part of the act will make an essential change in the constitution of juries, and it is directly repugnant to the Great Charter itself; for, by that charter, "no amercement shall be assessed, but by the oath of honest and lawful men of the vicinage"; and, "no freeman shall be taken, or imprisoned, or disseized of his freehold, or liberties of free customs, nor passed upon, nor condemned, but by lawful judgment of his peers, or by the law of the land." So that this act will "make such a distinction, and create such a difference between" the subjects in Great Britain and those in America as we could not have expected from the guardians of liberty in "both."

As these, sir, are our sentiments of this act, we, the freeholders and other inhabitants, legally assembled for this purpose, must enjoin it upon you to comply with no measures or proposals for countenancing the same, or assisting in the execution of it but by all lawful means consistent with our allegiance to the King and relation to Great Britain to oppose the execution of it till we can hear the success of the cries and petitions of America for relief.

We further recommend the most clear and explicit assertion and vindication of our rights and liberties to be entered on the public records, that the world may know, in the present and all future generations, that we have a clear knowledge and a just sense of them, and, with submission to Divine Providence, that we never can be slaves.

Nor can we think it advisable to agree to any steps for the protection of stamped papers or stamp officers. Good and wholesome laws we have already for the preservation of the peace; and we apprehend there is no further danger of tumult and disorder, to which we have a well-grounded aversion; and that any extraordinary and expensive exertions would tend to exasperate the people and endanger the public tranquillity, rather than the contrary. Indeed, we cannot too often inculcate upon you our desires, that all extraordinary grants and expensive measures may, upon all occasions, as much as possible, be avoided. The public money of this country is the toil and labor of the people, who are under many uncommon difficulties and distresses at this time, so that all reasonable frugality ought to be observed. And we would recommend, particularly, the strictest care and the utmost firmness to prevent all unconstitutional drafts upon the public treasury.

———◆———

The die was now cast; I had passed the Rubicon. Swim or sink, live or die, survive or perish with my country was my unalterable determination.

JOHN ADAMS. Daniel Webster, in his *Eulogy of Adams and Jefferson* (1826), paraphrased the words thus: "Sink or swim, live or die, survive or perish, I give my hand and my heart to this vote."

DANIEL DULANY: On the Propriety of Imposing Taxes in the British Colonies

In October, seven months after the passage of the Stamp Act, Daniel Dulany, a Maryland lawyer, produced a pamphlet entitled Considerations on the Propriety of Imposing Taxes in the British Colonies, for the Purpose of Raising a Revenue, by Act of Parliament. *Dulany opposed the Stamp Act, scoffing at the British idea that the colonists (like British industrial cities) were "virtually represented" in Parliament by strangers. Dulany's forceful arguments ranked foremost among political writings of the period. William Pitt supported Dulany's reasoning when he pleaded in England for the repeal of the Stamp Act.*

Source: *Considerations on the Propriety of Imposing Taxes in the British Colonies, for the Purpose of Raising a Revenue, by Act of Parliament,* London, 1766.

I SHALL UNDERTAKE to disprove the supposed similarity of situation, whence the same kind of representation is deduced of the inhabitants of the colonies, and of the British nonelectors; and, if I succeed, the notion of a virtual representation of the colonies must fail, which, in truth, is a mere cobweb spread to catch the unwary and entangle the weak. I would be understood. I am upon a question of propriety, not of power; and though some may be inclined to think it is to little purpose to discuss the one when the other is irresistible, yet are they different considerations; and, at the same time that I invalidate the claim upon which it is founded, I may very consistently recommend a submission to the law, whilst it endures. . . .

Lessees for years, copyholders, proprietors of the public funds, inhabitants of Birmingham, Leeds, Halifax, and Manchester, merchants of the City of London, or members of the corporation of the East India Company, are, as such, under no personal incapacity to be electors; for they may acquire the right of election, and there are actually not only a considerable number of electors in each of the classes of lessees for years, etc., but in many of them, if not all, even members of Parliament. The interests, therefore, of the nonelectors, the electors, and the representatives are individually the same; to say nothing of the connection among neighbors, friends, and relations. The security of the nonelectors against oppression is that their oppression will fall also upon the electors and the representatives. The one cannot be injured and the other indemnified.

Further, if the nonelectors should not be taxed by the British Parliament, they would not be taxed at all; and it would be iniquitous, as well as a solecism in the political system, that they should partake of all the benefits resulting from the imposition and application of taxes, and derive an immunity from the circumstance of not being qualified to vote. Under this constitution, then, a double or virtual representation may be reasonably supposed.

The electors, who are inseparably connected in their interests with the nonelectors, may be justly deemed to be the representatives of the nonelectors, at the same time they exercise their personal privilege in their right of election, and the members chosen, therefore, the representatives of both. This is the only rational explanation of the expression "virtual representation." None has been advanced by the assertors of it, and their meaning can only be inferred from the instances by which they endeavor to elucidate it; and no other meaning can be stated to which the instances apply. . . .

The inhabitants of the colonies are, as such, incapable of being electors, the privilege of election being exercisable only in person, and, therefore, if every inhabitant of America had the requisite freehold, not one could vote but upon the supposition of his ceasing to be an inhabitant of America and becoming a resident in Great Britain, a supposition which would be impertinent because it shifts the question — Should the colonies not be taxed by parliamentary impositions; their respective legislatures have a regular, adequate, and constitutional authority to tax them; and therefore there would not necessarily be an iniquitous and absurd exemption from their not being represented by the House of Commons?

There is not that intimate and inseparable relation between the electors of Great Britain and the inhabitants of the colonies, which must inevitably involve both in the same taxation. On the contrary, not a single actual elector in England might be immediately affected by a taxation in America, imposed by a statute which would have a general operation and effect upon the properties of the inhabitants of the colonies.

But though it has been admitted that the Stamp Act is the first statute that has imposed an internal tax upon the colonies *for the single purpose of revenue,* yet the advocates for that law contend that there are many instances of the Parliament's exercising a supreme legislative authority over the colonies and actually imposing *internal taxes* upon their properties — that the duties upon any exports or imports are internal taxes; that an impost on a foreign commodity is as much an internal tax as a duty upon any production of the plantations; that no distinction can be supported between one kind of tax and another, an authority to impose the one extending to the other.

If these things are really as represented by the advocates for the Stamp Act, why did

the chancellor of the Exchequer make it a question for the consideration of the House of Commons, whether the Parliament could impose an *internal tax* in the colonies or not for the *single purpose of revenue?*

It appears to me that there is a clear and necessary distinction between an act imposing a tax for the single purpose of revenue and those acts which have been made for the regulation of trade and have produced some revenue in consequence of their effect and operation as regulations of trade.

The colonies claim the privileges of British subjects. It has been proved to be inconsistent with those privileges to tax them without their own consent, and it has been demonstrated that a tax imposed by Parliament is a tax *without their consent.*

The subordination of the colonies and the authority of Parliament to preserve it have been fully acknowledged. Not only the welfare but perhaps the existence of the mother country, as an independent kingdom, may depend upon her trade and navigation, and these so far upon her intercourse with the colonies that if this should be neglected, there would soon be an end to that commerce, whence her greatest wealth is derived and upon which her maritime power is principally founded. From these considerations, the right of the British Parliament to regulate the trade of the colonies may be justly deduced; a denial of it would contradict the admission of the subordination and of the authority to preserve it, resulting from the nature of the relation between the mother country and her colonies. It is a common and frequently the most proper method to regulate trade by duties on imports and exports. The authority of the mother country to regulate the trade of the colonies being unquestionable, what regulations are the most proper are to be of course submitted to the determination of the Parliament; and if an incidental revenue should be produced by such regulations, these are not therefore unwarrantable.

A right to impose an internal tax on the

colonies without their consent for the single purpose of revenue is denied; a right to regulate their trade without their consent is admitted. The imposition of a duty may, in some instances, be the proper regulation. If the claims of the mother country and the colonies should seem on such an occasion to interfere and the point of right to be doubtful (which I take to be otherwise), it is easy to guess that the determination will be on the side of power and that the inferior will be constrained to submit. . . .

Not only as a friend to the colonies but as an inhabitant having my all at stake upon their welfare, I desire an exemption from taxes imposed *without my consent,* and I have reflected longer than a moment upon the consequences. I value it as one of the dearest privileges I enjoy. I acknowledge dependence on Great Britain, but I can perceive a degree of it without slavery, and I disown all other. I do not expect that the interests of the colonies will be considered by some men but in subserviency to other regards. The effects of luxury, and venality, and oppression, posterity may perhaps experience, and *sufficient for the day will be the evil thereof.*

Francis Bernard: The Growing Opposition to England

Elaborate and accurate accounts of political events in the colonies during the 1760s were written by Governor Francis Bernard of Massachusetts to the British secretaries of state and the Board of Trade. He gave a detailed account of the actions of James Otis, blaming him for most of the opposition to the Stamp Act. Bernard's letters are a valuable source for the history of Massachusetts during the time he was governor. He directed the following one to the Earl of Shelburne on December 22, 1766.

Source: *British Public Record Office,* C. O. 5/892.

I AM EXTREMELY SORRY that I am obliged to enter minutely into the civil divisions of this province and the causes and effects of the same. I should have been glad to have saved Your Lordship the trouble of reading so unpleasing a report and myself the disagreeable task of making it. I should also have been glad to have concealed the present unhappy state of the province if there was any prospect of its amendment; although in truth the disgrace arising therefrom is chargeable but to few persons, for though the driven and the led are many, the drivers and the leaders are but few. But since the faction which has raised itself upon the public calamity knows no bounds and seems determined to persist in bringing all authority down to the level of the people (preserving nevertheless the form of the government which may be made consistent with such a scheme) and to make an example of a governor who has dared to stand in the gap, and to endeavor to support the royalty of the government, I cannot any longer excuse myself laying open this system to the bottom. Not only my own defense, for that I might have safely left to a review of my general conduct since I have been governor, but my duty in discovering designs and proceedings full of danger to the King's government require it of me.

I would avoid personalities, but in the present case it is impossible. The troubles of this country take their rise from and owe their continuance to one man, so much that his history alone would contain a full account of them. This man, James Otis, Esq., was a lawyer at Boston when I came to the government. He is by nature a passionate, violent, and desperate man, which qualities sometimes work him up to an absolute frenzy. I say nothing of him which is not known to be his certain character, confirmed by frequent experience. Soon after my entrance upon the government the place of chief justice of the province became vacant. The lieutenant governor was proposed for that office by the best men in the government. Mr. Otis (the father of *the* Otis) proposed himself for a seat on the bench in case one of the judges was made chief. Both these proposals could not be complied with and there was no balancing between the two candidates. But Mr. Otis, Senior, urged his pretensions by telling me and the lieutenant governor that if he (the lieutenant governor) was appointed, we should both of us repent it. Otis, Junior, did not confine himself to hints but declared publicly, with oaths, that "if his father was not appointed judge, he would set the whole province in a flame though he perished in the attempt." This was proved by the oaths of two gentlemen of credit, whose depositions are now in the public offices at home. However, I appointed the lieutenant governor with the general approbation of the whole province and Messrs. Otis immediately proceeded to make good their promises.

In less than half a year they stirred up a persecution against the Court of Admiralty and the Custom House, promising nothing less than the abolishment of the activity of both. In this it was unavoidable, as it was intended, that I should be involved as well as the chief justice. This persecution (it may be truly called so) lasted two years. In the course of it five actions were brought against different Custom House officers, one (made bailable) against the surveyor general (not the present) for £7,500 ster-

ling, all by the advice and direction of Otis, Junior. In the course of these proceedings Otis everywhere appeared the principal. He was chief director, chamber council, counselor at the bar, popular haranguer, and Assembly orator; for the merit of this opposition to the King's officers procured him a seat in the House. However, after about two years' harassment this matter subsided with the maintenance of the King's rights, which were preserved, I may truly say, by my firmness and perseverance and by the steadiness of the chief justice and the other judges of the Superior Court. A full account of these proceedings, chiefly supported by oath, was returned to the Treasury and to the Board of Trade, and will appear further from my letters to the secretary of state and the Lords of trade, in 1761 and 1762.

When this was over he still continued in a constant opposition to government, except during an interval when his father was soliciting for two offices, which put him at the head of his county. These I gave to him, together with a good place to one of his sons, and was assured that this would wipe away all the ill humor which his former disappointment had occasioned. But no sooner were these patents sealed than Otis renewed his hostilities against government with fresh vigor; but to no purpose, as the Council and House were then filled with men of worth and ability, who greatly outweighed and outnumbered the opposers of government; and as I had at that time a credit with the province equal at least to any of my predecessors at any time. The business of the government was carried on with the utmost harmony and good humor, and I never met the Assembly without giving and receiving mutual testimonies of our satisfaction with one another. All this fair form of civil power, which had its chief foundation upon the prudence and good temper of the constituent members of the government and the confidence of the people, and had scarce any coercive power to resort to upon occasion, was at once overturned by the fatal and unfortunate Stamp Act. This let loose all the ill humors of the common people and put them into the hands of designing men to be employed not so much for the defense of their real and constitutional rights as to humble the government and bring it to the level of the very people.

I desire not to revive the disputes concerning the Stamp Act; I wish they were buried beyond the reach of memory, and they would have been buried before now if the opposition had not had further views than the defeat of the taxation. But, My Lord, the opposing [of] the Stamp Act has been made a mask for a battery, a stalking horse to take a better aim at the royalty of the government. This was apparent whilst the repeal was in suspense, but since it has passed, it is put out of all doubt. For this purpose, when the people's passions were thoroughly worked up, when their fears, jealousy, and credulity were got to such a pitch that it was dangerous as well as impracticable to reason with them, they were told that the scheme of the Stamp Act was formed in this province. The principal officers of the government and others of the first men of the province were pointed out as the contrivers of it. Otis himself said, in the House as well as out of it, that he knew the room (meaning in my house), the time, and the company when the plan was settled. All persons who had any weight or influence in the province, and had been used to exercise it in the support of the government, were branded by the name of friends to the Stamp Act; when the propagators of these calumnies knew in their conscience that there did not exist within the province a friend to the Stamp Act, not even in the stamp officer himself, who to my knowledge at no time wished for the continuance of the act.

These being the purposes of the faction, means were taken to distress the govern-ment quite foreign to the repeal of the Stamp Act, and such as if they had been known in Parliament, would have tended to prevent it. I shall mention a few particulars which will divide these matters into heads. Mr. Otis in a speech in the House directed against the government of Great Britain said that "he wished that the island was sunk in the sea so that the King and his family were saved." This proviso I suppose was to qualify the treasonableness of the wish. Of the King's governors he has said that "those who were appointed to the American governments were such as were obliged either by their crimes or their debts to fly their country." Of the Council (who had given no other offense than by assisting me to secure the stamp papers at the castle) he said in the House "it was an infernal

Courtesy, Christ Church, Oxford

Sir Francis Bernard (1712-1779); portrait by John Singleton Copley

divan and deserved to be sent to the place from whence they derived their councils." In the House it was common for him to tell a member who spoke on the side of government that he should not sit in that House the next year. And accordingly, as soon as the General Court was dissolved in order for a new election, there was published in a weekly paper conducted by Otis and his junto, a list of thirty-two members, the most respectable in the House and noted for their attachment to government, who were proscribed as enemies to their country because they had given their testimony against the violences lately committed. And of these thirty-two, nineteen lost their election.

Most of the foregoing passed whilst the event of the Stamp Act was in suspense and therefore might have well been forgotten if the party himself had desired that they should. But when the same violent measures are pursued after the repeal of the Stamp Act is made known, as before; when the King's government and all that bear office in it are persecuted with the same unrelenting acrimony as if nothing had been done for the people and they were under no obligations to the King and his Parliament; when the servant, to whom his King had forgiven 10,000 talents, takes his fellow servant by the throat for 100d., it is difficult not to connect the proceedings before and after the repeal. However, I shall draw a line between them in order to show that the repeal occasioned no relaxation in the disposition and designs of the faction which had raised itself by the Act.

It was the general opinion that Otis himself wished that the Act might not be repealed as that would answer his inflammatory purposes better. This was collected partly from a declaration he made about the time of the advice of the event being expected, that he hoped it would not be repealed; for, said he, "We will repeal it ourselves." As soon as the advice of the repeal came Otis published an advertisement which all the printers were obliged to insert under pain of mob execution. I enclose this

advertisement which Otis owned to be his till he found it to be generally reprobated, after which he would neither own it nor deny it. By the terms of this, it is plain that the repeal was to produce no remission either of the pretensions against Parliament, or the persecution of the friends of the government. The week after this came out a republication of the list of the thirty-two members who had been proscribed as friends of the Stamp Act and therefore enemies to their country, accompanied with observations, among which it was said "that a general purgation in both houses was of absolute necessity." That is, that every member of either house who professed to have a regard for the support of the government and the royal rights thereof should lose his seat.

About this time Mr. Otis began to declare that they had fixed upon fifteen councilors who were to be turned out at the next election. This threat was continued almost to the day of election. I must add one transaction more which passed in this interval, which will properly conclude this paragraph. Mr. Otis at a meeting at the town hall (which I think was to fix a time for public rejoicings for the repeal) in a set speech told the people that "the distinction between inland taxes and port duties was without foundation, for whoever had a right to impose one had a right to impose the other. And therefore as the Parliament had given up the one (for he said the act for securing the dependency had no relation to taxes), they had given up the other; and the merchants were great fools if they submitted any longer to the laws restraining their trade, which ought to be free." This speech made a great deal of noise, and it was observed by serious men that Otis had thereby made himself answerable for all the disturbances which should thereafter happen in the execution of the laws of trade. But the natural consequence, and what immediately followed, was that a common talk prevailed among the people that there should be no more seizures in this town. There have been but two seizures made in the province since, and they have been both rescued with a high hand. In that at Boston it is remarkable that the man who opposed the officers sent for Otis and he went thither as his counselor. This is the manner in which this man and his faction, after they had heard of the repeal of the Stamp Act, prepared to make a return for it on the part of this province.

John Dickinson: On the Suspension of the New York Assembly

Letters from a Farmer in Pennsylvania, written by John Dickinson, though conciliatory in tone, did much to formulate the sense of wrong in British policies that led the colonies at last to strike for independence. Published first in newspapers during 1767 and 1768, the Letters *were later brought out in a pamphlet that went rapidly through at least ten editions. In his letter of November 5, 1767, Dickinson discussed Parliament's suspension of the New York Assembly.*

Source: *Memoirs of the Historical Society of Pennsylvania,* Vol. XIV, Philadelphia, 1895, pp. 307-312.

My Dear Countrymen,

I am a farmer, settled after a variety of fortunes near the banks of the River Delaware in the province of Pennsylvania. I received a liberal education and have been engaged in the busy scenes of life; but am now convinced that a man may be as happy without bustle as with it. My farm is small; my servants are few and good; I have a little money at interest; I wish for no more; my employment in my own affairs is easy; and with a contented, grateful mind . . . I am completing the number of days allotted to me by divine goodness.

Being generally master of my time, I spend a good deal of it in a library, which I think the most valuable part of my small estate; and being acquainted with two or three gentlemen of abilities and learning who honor me with their friendship, I have acquired, I believe, a greater share of knowledge in history and the laws and constitution of my country than is generally attained by men of my class, many of them not being so fortunate as I have been in the opportunities of getting information.

From infancy I was taught to love humanity and liberty. Inquiry and experience have since confirmed my reverence for the lessons then given me by convincing me more fully of their truth and excellence. Benevolence toward mankind excites wishes for their welfare, and such wishes endear the means of fulfilling them. These can be found in liberty only, and therefore her sacred cause ought to be espoused by every man, on every occasion, to the utmost of his power. As a charitable but poor person does not withhold his mite because he cannot relieve *all* the distresses of the miserable, so should not any honest man suppress his sentiments concerning freedom, however small their influence is likely to be. Perhaps he may "touch some wheel" that will have an effect greater than he could reasonably expect.

These being my sentiments, I am encouraged to offer to you, my countrymen, my thoughts on some late transactions that appear to me to be of the utmost importance to you. Conscious of my defects, I have waited some time in expectation of seeing the subject treated by persons much better qualified for the task; but being therein disappointed, and apprehensive that longer delays will be injurious, I venture at length to request the attention of the public, praying that these lines may be read with the same zeal for the happiness of British America with which they were written.

With a good deal of surprise I have observed that little notice has been taken of an act of Parliament, as injurious in its principle to the liberties of these colonies as the Stamp Act was: I mean the act for suspending the legislation of New York.

The assembly of that government complied with a former act of Parliament, requiring certain provisions to be made for the troops in America, in every particular, I think, except the articles of salt, pepper, and vinegar. In my opinion they acted imprudently, considering all circumstances, in not complying so far as would have given satisfaction as several colonies did. But my dislike of their conduct in that instance has not blinded me so much that I cannot plainly perceive that they have been punished in a manner pernicious to American freedom and justly alarming to all the colonies.

If the British Parliament has a legal authority to issue an order that we shall furnish a single article for the troops here and to compel obedience to that order, they have the same right to issue an order for us to supply those troops with arms, clothes, and every necessary, and to compel obedience to that order also; in short, to lay any burdens they please upon us. What is this but taxing us at a certain sum and leaving to us only the manner of raising it? How is this mode more tolerable than the Stamp Act? Would that act have appeared more pleasing to Americans if, being ordered thereby to raise the sum total of the taxes, the mighty privilege had been left to them of saying how much should be paid for an instrument of writing on paper, and how much for another on parchment?

An act of Parliament commanding us to do a certain thing, if it has any validity, is a tax upon us for the expense that accrues in complying with it, and for this reason, I believe, every colony on the continent that chose to give a mark of their respect for Great Britain, in complying with the act relating to the troops, cautiously avoided the mention of that act, lest their conduct should be attributed to its supposed obligation.

The matter being thus stated, the assembly of New York either had or had not a right to refuse submission to that act. If they had, and I imagine no American will say they had not, then the Parliament had no right to compel them to execute it. If they had not that right, they had no right to punish them for not executing it; and therefore had no right to suspend their legislation, which is a punishment. In fact, if the people of New York cannot be legally taxed but by their own representatives, they cannot be legally deprived of the privilege of legislation, only for insisting on that exclusive privilege of taxation. If they may be legally deprived in such a case of the privilege of legislation, why may they not, with equal reason, be deprived of every other privilege? Or why may not every colony be treated in the same manner, when any of them shall dare to deny their assent to any impositions that shall be directed? Or what signifies the repeal of the Stamp Act, if these colonies are to lose their other privileges by not tamely surrendering that of taxation?

There is one consideration arising from the suspension which is not generally attended to but shows its importance very clearly. It was not necessary that this suspension should be caused by an act of Parliament. The Crown might have restrained the governor of New York even from calling the assembly together, by its prerogative in the royal governments. This step, I suppose, would have been taken if the conduct of the assembly of New York had been regarded as an act of disobedience to the Crown alone. But it is regarded as an act of "disobedience to the authority of the British legislature." This gives the suspension a consequence vastly more affecting. It is a parliamentary assertion of the supreme authority of the British legislature over these colonies in the point of taxation; and it is intended to compel New York into a submission to that authority. It seems therefore to me as much a violation of the liberty of the people of that province, and consequently of all these colonies, as if the Parliament had sent a number of regiments to be quartered upon them, till they should comply.

For it is evident that the suspension is meant as a compulsion; and the method of compelling is totally indifferent. It is indeed probable that the sight of red coats and the hearing of drums would have been most alarming, because people are generally more influenced by their eyes and ears than by their reason. But whoever seriously considers the matter must perceive that a dreadful stroke is aimed at the liberty of these colonies. I say of these colonies; for the cause of one is the cause of all. If the Parliament may lawfully deprive New York of any of her rights, it may deprive any or all the other colonies of their rights; and nothing can possibly so much encourage such attempts as a mutual inattention to the interest of each other. To divide and thus to destroy is the first political maxim in attacking those who are powerful by their union. He certainly is not a wise man who folds his arms and reposes himself at home, seeing with unconcern the flames that have invaded his neighbor's house without using any endeavors to extinguish them. When Mr. Hampden's ship-money cause for $3s.$ $4d.$ was tried, all the people of England, with anxious expectations, interested themselves in the important decision; and when the slightest point touching the freedom of one colony is agitated, I earnestly wish that all the rest may with equal ardor support their sister. Very much may be said on this subject, but I hope more at present is unnecessary.

With concern I have observed that two assemblies of this province have sat and adjourned without taking any notice of this act. It may perhaps be asked: What would have been proper for them to do? I am by no means fond of inflammatory measures. I detest them. I should be sorry that anything should be done which might justly displease our sovereign or our mother country. But a firm, modest exertion of a free spirit should never be wanting on public occasions. It appears to me that it would have been sufficient for the assembly to have ordered our agents to represent to the King's ministers their sense of the suspending act and to pray for its repeal. Thus we should have borne our testimony against it; and might therefore reasonably expect that on a like occasion we might receive the same assistance from the other colonies.

Small things grow great by concord.

A FARMER

Resolutions of a Boston Town Meeting Against the King

Because Boston had become the focal point of colonial opposition to British tax policies, General Gage ordered British troops to be stationed there in the spring of 1768. This news caused an immediate reaction in Massachusetts. When the Boston town meeting requested Governor Bernard to call a special session of the legislature, he refused on the grounds that he had to have permission from Britain. On September 13, the town meeting adopted resolutions stating the rights of the colonists, and proceeded to call a provincial convention to meet in Boston on September 22. These revolutionary proceedings were printed in town newspapers, and copies were circulated throughout the colony.

Source: *The Annual Register . . . for the Year 1768,* London, 1768, pp. 238-241.

THE COMMITTEE appointed to take the state of our public affairs into consideration reported the following declaration and resolves:

Whereas it is the first principle in civil society, founded in nature and reason, that no law of the society can be binding on any individual without his consent, given by himself in person or by his representative of his own free election; *and whereas* in and by an act of the British Parliament passed in the first year of the reign of King William and Queen Mary, of glorious and blessed memory, entitled "An Act declaring the Rights and Liberties of the Subject, and Settling the Succession of the Crown," the preamble of which act is in these words, viz.: "*Whereas* the late King James II, by the assistance of diverse evil councilors, judges, and ministers employed by him did endeavor to subvert and extirpate the Protestant religion, and the laws and liberties of this kingdom," it is expressly among other things declared that the levying money for the use of the Crown by pretense of prerogative, without grant of Parliament for a longer time or in other manner than the same is granted, is illegal.

And whereas in the third year of the reign of the same King William and Queen Mary, Their Majesties were graciously pleased by their royal charter to give and grant to the inhabitants of His Majesty's province all the territory therein described to be held in free and common socage; and also to ordain and grant to the said inhabitants certain rights, liberties, and privileges therein expressly mentioned, among which it is granted, established, and ordained that all and every the subjects of Them, Their Heirs, and Successors, which shall go to inhabit within said province and territory, and every of their children which shall happen to be born there, or on the seas in going thither or returning from thence, shall have and enjoy all liberties and immunities of free and natural subjects, within any of the dominions of Them, Their Heirs, and Successors, to all intents, purposes, and constructions whatever, as if they and every of them were born within the Realm of England.

And whereas by the aforesaid act of Parliament made in the first year of the said King William and Queen Mary, all and singular the premises contained therein are claimed, demanded, and insisted on as the undoubted rights and liberties of the subjects born within the Realm.

And whereas the freeholders and other inhabitants of this town, the metropolis of the province in said charter mentioned, do hold all the rights and liberties therein contained to be sacred and inviolable; at the same time publicly and solemnly acknowledging their firm and unshaken allegiance to their alone and rightful sovereign King George III, the lawful successor of the said King William and Queen Mary to the British throne: Therefore,

Resolved, that the said freeholders and other inhabitants of the town of Boston will at the utmost peril of their lives and fortunes take all legal and constitutional measures to defend and maintain the person, family, crown, and dignity of our said sovereign Lord George III; and all and singular the rights, liberties, privileges, and immunities granted in the said royal charter, as well as those which are declared to be belonging to us as British subjects by birthright, as all others therein specially mentioned.

And whereas by the said royal charter it is specially granted to the Great and General Court or assembly therein constituted to impose and levy proportionable and reasonable assessments, rates, and taxes upon the estates and persons of all and every the proprietors and inhabitants of said province or territory for the service of the King in the necessary defense and support of his government of this province and the protection and preservation of his subjects therein: Therefore:

Voted, as the opinion of this town, that the levying money within this province for the use and service of the Crown in other manner than the same is granted by the Great and General Court or assembly of this province is in violation of the said royal charter; and the same is also in violation of the undoubted natural rights of subjects, declared in the aforesaid act of Parliament, freely to give and grant their own money for the service of the Crown, with their own consent, in person or by representatives of their own free election.

And whereas in the aforesaid act of Parliament it is declared that the raising or keeping a standing army within the Kingdom in time of peace, unless it be with the consent of Parliament, is against law, it is the opinion of this town that the said declarations are founded in the indefeasible right of the subjects to be *consulted,* and to give their *free consent in person* or by representatives of their own free election to the raising and keeping a standing army among them; and the inhabitants of this town being free subjects have the same right derived from nature and confirmed by the British constitution, as well as the said royal charter; and, therefore, the raising or keeping a standing army without their consent in person or by representatives of their own free election would be an infringement of their natural, constitutional, and charter rights; and the employing such army for the enforcing of laws made without the consent of the people, in person or by their representatives, would be a grievance.

The foregoing report being diverse times distinctly read and considered by the town, the question was put whether the same shall be accepted and recorded, and passed unanimously in the affirmative.

Upon a motion made and seconded, the following vote was unanimously passed, viz.:

Whereas by an act of Parliament of the first of King William and Queen Mary, it is declared that for the redress of all grievances, and for amending, strengthening, and preserving the laws, parliaments ought to be held frequently; and inasmuch as it is the opinion of this town that the people labor under many intolerable grievances which unless speedily redressed threaten the total destruction of our invaluable natural, constitutional, and charter rights:

And furthermore as His Excellency the Governor has declared himself unable, at the request of this town, to call a General Court, which is the assembly of the states of this province for the redress of such grievances:

Voted, that this town will now make choice of a suitable number of persons to act for them as a committee in convention, with such as may be sent to join them from the several towns in this province, in order that such measures may be consulted and advised as His Majesty's service, and the peace and safety of his subjects in this province may require; whereupon the Hon. James Otis, Esq., the Hon. Thomas Cushing, Esq., Mr. Samuel Adams, and John Hancock, Esq., were appointed a committee for the said purpose, the town hereafter to take into consideration what recompense shall be made them for the service they may perform.

Voted, that the selectmen be directed to write to the selectmen of the several towns within this province informing them of the foregoing vote, and to propose that a convention be held, if they shall think proper, at Faneuil Hall, in this town, on . . . the 22nd day of September, instant, at 10 o'clock before noon.

JOSEPH WARREN: Against a British Army in the Colonies

Until some time after the Revolution, the anniversary of the Boston Massacre was the occasion for a commemorative oration. On March 5, 1772, Joseph Warren, a Revolutionary patriot, delivered an eloquent speech designed to arouse bitter feelings against the British troops and against Britain.

Source: Niles: "Oration Delivered at Boston, March 5, 1772."

WHEN WE TURN OVER the historic page and trace the rise and fall of states and empires, the mighty revolutions which have so often varied the face of the world strike our minds with solemn surprise, and we are naturally led to endeavor to search out the causes of such astonishing changes.

That man is formed for social life is an

observation which, upon our first inquiry, presents itself immediately to our view, and our reason approves that wise and generous principle which actuated the first founders of civil government; an institution which has its origin in the weakness of individuals, and has for its end the strength and security of all; and so long as the means of effecting this important end are thoroughly known, and religiously attended to, government is one of the richest blessings to mankind, and ought to be held in the highest veneration.

In young and new-formed communities, the grand design of this institution is most generally understood and the most strictly regarded; the motives which urged to the social compact cannot be at once forgotten, and that equality which is remembered to have subsisted so lately among them prevents those who are clothed with authority from attempting to invade the freedom of their brethren; or if such an attempt is made, it prevents the community from suffering the offender to go unpunished. Every member feels it to be his interest and knows it to be his duty to preserve inviolate the constitution on which the public safety depends, and he is equally ready to assist the magistrate in the execution of the laws, and the subject in defense of his right; and so long as this noble attachment to a constitution, founded on free and benevolent principles, exists in full vigor in any state, that state must be flourishing and happy. . . .

It was this attachment to a constitution founded on free and benevolent principles which inspired the first settlers of this country. They saw with grief the daring outrages committed on the free constitution of their native land; they knew nothing but a civil war could at that time restore its pristine purity. So hard was it to resolve to embrue their hands in the blood of their brethren that they chose rather to quit their fair possessions and seek another habitation in a distant clime. When they came to this New World, which they fairly purchased of the Indian natives, the only rightful proprietors, they cultivated the then barren soil by their incessant labor, and defended their dear-bought possessions with the fortitude of the Christian and the bravery of the hero.

After various struggles which, during the tyrannic reigns of the House of Stuart, were constantly kept up between right and wrong, between liberty and slavery, the connection between Great Britain and this colony was settled in the reign of King William and Queen Mary by a compact, the conditions of which were expressed in a charter by which all the liberties and immunities of British subjects were confided to this province as fully and as absolutely as they possibly could be by any human instrument which can be devised. And it is undeniably true that the greatest and most important right of a British subject is that he shall be governed by no laws but those to which he, either in person or by his representatives, has given his consent. And this, I will venture to assert, is the great basis of British freedom; it is interwoven with the constitution, and whenever this is lost, the constitution must be destroyed.

The British constitution (of which ours is a copy) is a happy compound of the three forms (under some of which all governments may be ranged), viz., monarchy, aristocracy, and democracy; of these three the British legislature is composed, and without the consent of each branch, nothing can carry with it the force of a law; but when a law is to be passed for raising a tax, that law can originate only in the democratic branch, which is the House of Commons in Britain, and the House of Representatives here. The reason is obvious: they and their constituents are to pay much the largest part of it; but as the aristocratic branch, which in Britain is the House of Lords, and in this province, the Council, are also to pay some part, their consent is necessary; and as the monarchic branch, which in Britain is the king, and with us, either the king in person or the governor whom he shall be pleased to appoint to act in his stead, is supposed to have a just sense of his own interest, which is that of all the subjects in general, his consent is also necessary, and when the consent of these three branches is obtained, the taxation is most certainly legal.

Let us now allow ourselves a few moments to examine the late acts of the British Parliament for taxing America. Let us with candor judge whether they are constitutionally binding upon us; if they are, in the name of justice let us submit to them, without one murmuring word.

First, I would ask whether the members of the British House of Commons are the democracy of this province. If they are, they are either the people of this province, or are elected by the people of this province to represent them, and have therefore a constitutional right to originate a bill for taxing them; it is most certain they are neither; and therefore nothing done by them can be said to be done by the democratic branch of our constitution. I would next ask whether the lords, who compose the aristocratic branch of the legislature, are peers of America. I never heard it was (even in those extraordinary times) so much as pretended, and if they are not, certainly no act of theirs can be said to be the act of the aristocratic branch of our constitution. The power of the monarchic branch, we with pleasure acknowledge, resides in the king, who may act either in person or by his representative; and I freely confess that I can see no reason why a proclamation for raising in America issued by the king's sole authority would not be equally consistent with our own constitution, and therefore equally binding upon us with the late acts of the British Parliament for taxing us; for it is plain that if there is any validity in those acts, it must arise altogether from the monarchical branch of the legislature. . . .

I further think that it would be at least as equitable; for I do not conceive it to be of the least importance to us by whom our property is taken away, so long as it is taken without our consent; and I am very much at a loss to know by what figure of rhetoric the inhabitants of this province can be called free subjects when they are obliged to obey implicitly such laws as are made for them by men 3,000 miles off, whom they know not, and whom they never empowered to act for them, or how they can be said to have property, when a body of men over whom they have not the least control, and who are not in any way accountable to them, shall oblige them to deliver up any part or the whole of their substance without even asking their consent. . . .

Yet whoever pretends that the late acts of the British Parliament for taxing America ought to be deemed binding upon us must admit at once that we are absolute slaves, and have no property of our own; or else that we may be freemen, and at the same time under a necessity of obeying the arbitrary commands of those over whom we have no control or influence, and that we may have property of our own which is entirely at the disposal of another. Such gross absurdities, I believe, will not be relished in this enlightened age; and it can be no matter of wonder that the people quickly perceived and seriously complained of the inroads which these acts must unavoidably make upon their liberty, and of the hazard to which their whole property is by them exposed; for, if they may be taxed without their consent, even in the smallest trifle, they may also, without their consent, be deprived of everything they possess, although never so valuable, never so dear.

Certainly it never entered the hearts of our ancestors that after so many dangers in this then desolate wilderness, their hardearned property should be at the disposal of the British Parliament; and as it was soon found that this taxation could not be supported by reason and argument, it seemed necessary that one act of oppression should be enforced by another, and therefore, contrary to our just rights as possessing, or at least having a just title to possess, all the liberties and immunities of British subjects, a standing army was established among us in time of peace; and evidently for the purpose of effecting that which it was one principal design of the founders of the constitution to prevent (when they declared a standing army in a time of peace to be against law), namely, for the enforcement of obedience to acts which, upon fair examination, appeared to be unjust and unconstitutional.

The ruinous consequences of standing armies to free communities may be seen in the histories of Syracuse, Rome, and many other once flourishing states, some of which have now scarce a name! Their baneful influence is most suddenly felt when they are placed in populous cities; for, by a corruption of morals, the public happiness is immediately affected! And that this is one of the effects of quartering troops in a populous city is a truth to which many a mourning parent, many a lost despairing child in this metropolis must bear a very melancholy testimony.

Soldiers are also taught to consider arms as the only arbiters by which every dispute is to be decided between contending states; they are instructed implicitly to obey their commanders without inquiring into the justice of the cause they are engaged to support; hence it is that they are ever to be dreaded as the ready engines of tyranny and oppression. And it is too observable that they are prone to introduce the same mode of decision in the disputes of individuals, and from thence have often arisen great animosities between them and the inhabitants, who, whilst in a naked, defenseless state, are frequently insulted and abused by an armed soldiery. And this will be more especially the case when the troops are informed that the intention of their being stationed in any city is to overawe the inhabitants. That this was the avowed design of stationing an

armed force in this town is sufficiently known; and we, my fellow citizens, have seen, we have felt the tragical effects!

The fatal 5th of March, 1770, can never be forgotten. The horrors of that dreadful night are but too deeply impressed on our hearts. Language is too feeble to paint the emotion of our souls when our streets were stained with the blood of our brethren, when our ears were wounded by the groans of the dying, and our eyes were tormented with the sight of mangled bodies of the dead.

When our alarmed imagination presented to our view our houses wrapped in flames, our children subjected to the barbarous caprice of the raging soldiery, our beauteous virgins exposed to all the insolence of unbridled passion, our virtuous wives, endeared to us by every tender tie, falling a sacrifice to worse than brutal violence, and perhaps like the famed Lucretia, distracted with anguish and despair, ending their wretched lives by their own fair hands. When we beheld the authors of our distress parading in our streets, or drawn up in a regular battalia, as though in a hostile city, our hearts beat to arms; we snatched our weapons, almost resolved by one decisive stroke to avenge the death of our slaughtered brethren, and to secure from future danger all that we held most dear. But propitious heaven forbade the bloody carnage and saved the threatened victims of our too keen resentment, not by their discipline, not by their regular array. No, it was royal George's livery that proved their shield — it was that which turned the pointed engines of destruction from their breasts. The thoughts of vengeance were soon buried in our inbred affection to Great Britain, and calm reason dictated a method of removing the troops more mild than an immediate resource to the sword. With united efforts you urged the immediate departure of the troops from the town — you urged it, with a resolution which ensured success — you obtained your wishes, and the removal of the troops was effected without one drop of their blood being shed by the inhabitants.

The immediate actors in the tragedy of that night were surrendered to justice. It is not mine to say how far they were guilty. They have been tried by the country and *acquitted* of murder! And they are not to be again arraigned at an earthly bar; but, surely the men who have promiscuously scattered death amidst the innocent inhabitants of a populous city ought to see well to it that they be prepared to stand at the bar of an omniscient judge! And all who contrived or encouraged the stationing troops in this place have reasons of eternal importance to reflect with deep contrition on their base designs, and humbly to repent of their impious machinations.

The infatuation which has seemed for a number of years to prevail in the British councils with regard to us is truly astonishing! What can be proposed by the repeated attacks made upon our freedom, I really cannot surmise, even leaving justice and humanity out of question. I do not know one single advantage which can arise to the British nation from our being enslaved. I know not of any gains which can be wrung from us by oppression which they may not obtain from us by our own consent in the smooth channel of commerce. We wish the wealth and prosperity of Britain; we contribute largely to both. Does what we contribute lose all its value because it is done voluntarily? The amazing increase of riches to Britain, the great rise of the value of her lands, the flourishing state of her Navy, are striking proofs of the advantages derived to her from her commerce with the colonies; and it is our earnest desire that she may still continue to enjoy the same emoluments, until her streets are paved with American gold; only let us have the pleasure of calling it our own whilst it is in our own hands; but this it seems is too great a favor. We are to be governed by the absolute command of others; our property is to be taken away without our consent. If we complain, our complaints are treated with contempt; if we assert our rights, that assertion is deemed insolence; if we humbly offer to submit the matter to the impartial decision of reason, the sword is judged the most proper argument to silence our murmurs!

But this cannot long be the case. Surely the British nation will not suffer the reputation of their justice and their honor to be thus sported away by a capricious ministry; no, they will in a short time open their eyes to their true interest. They nourish in their own breasts a noble love of liberty; they hold her dear, and they know that all who have once possessed her charms had rather die than suffer her to be torn from their embraces. They are also sensible that Britain is so deeply interested in the prosperity of the colonies that she must eventually feel every wound given to their freedom; they cannot be ignorant that more dependence may be placed on the affections of a brother than on the forced service of a slave; they must approve your efforts for the preservation of your rights; from a sympathy of soul they must pray for your success. And I

Joseph Warren, portrait by John Singleton Copley

doubt not but they will, ere long, exert themselves effectually to redress your grievances. Even in the dissolute reign of King Charles II, when the House of Commons impeached the earl of Clarendon of high treason, the first article on which they founded their accusation was that "he had designed a standing army to be raised, and to govern the kingdom thereby." And the eighth article was that "he had introduced an arbitrary government into His Majesty's plantation." A terrifying example to those who are now forging chains for this country.

You have, my friends and countrymen, frustrated the designs of your enemies by your unanimity and fortitude. It was your union and determined spirit which expelled those troops who polluted your streets with innocent blood. You have appointed this anniversary as a standard memorial of the bloody consequences of placing an armed force in a populous city, and of your deliverance from the dangers which then seemed to hang over your heads; and I am confident that you never will betray the least want of spirit when called upon to guard your freedom. None but they who set a just value upon the blessings of liberty are worthy to enjoy her. Your illustrious fathers were her zealous votaries. When the blasting frowns of tyranny drove her from public view they clasped her in their arms, they cherished her in their generous bosoms, they brought her safe over the rough ocean and fixed her seat in this then dreary wilderness; they nursed her infant age with the most tender care; for her sake they patiently bore the severest hardships; for her support they underwent the most rugged toils; in her defense they boldly encountered the most alarming dangers; neither the ravenous beasts that ranged the woods for prey, nor the more furious savages of the wilderness could damp ardor!

Whilst with one hand they broke the stubborn glebe [land], with the other they grasped their weapons, ever ready to protect her from danger. No sacrifice, not even their own blood, was esteemed too rich a libation for her altar! God prospered their valor, they preserved her brilliancy unsullied; they enjoyed her whilst they lived, and dying, bequeathed the dear inheritance to your care. And as they left you this glorious legacy, they have undoubtedly transmitted to you some portion of their noble spirit to inspire you with virtue to merit her and courage to preserve her. You surely cannot, with such examples before your eyes as every page of the history of this country affords, suffer your liberties to be ravished from you by lawless force, or cajoled away by flattery and fraud.

The voice of your fathers' blood cries to you from the ground: my sons, scorn to be slaves! In vain we met the frowns of tyrants. In vain we crossed the boisterous ocean, found a new world, and prepared it for the happy residence of liberty. In vain we toiled. In vain we fought. We bled in vain, if you, our offspring, want valor to repel the assaults of her invaders! Stain not the glory of your worthy ancestors, but like them resolve never to part with your birthright; be wise in your deliberations, and determined in your exertions for the preservation of your liberties. Follow not the dictates of passion, but enlist yourselves under the sacred banner of reason; use every method in your power to secure your rights; at least prevent the curses of posterity from being heaped upon your memories.

If you, with united zeal and fortitude, oppose the torrent of oppression; if you feel the true fire of patriotism burning in your breasts; if you, from your souls, despise the most gaudy dress that slavery can wear; if you really prefer the lonely cottage (whilst blessed with liberty) to gilded palaces surrounded with the ensigns of slavery, you may have the fullest assurance that tyranny, with her whole accursed train, will hide their hideous heads in confusion, shame, and despair. If you perform your part, you must have the strongest confidence that the same Almighty Being who protected your pious and venerable forefathers, who enabled them to turn a barren wilderness into a fruitful field, who so often made bare his arm for their salvation, will still be mindful of you, their offspring.

May this Almighty Being graciously preside in all our councils. May He direct us to such measures as He Himself shall approve, and be pleased to bless. May we ever be a people favored of God. May our land be a land of liberty, the seat of virtue, the asylum of the oppressed, a name and a praise in the whole earth, until the last shock of time shall bury the empires of the world in one common undistinguished ruin!

Samuel Adams: The Rights of the Colonists

On November 2, 1772, the Boston town meeting, upon Samuel Adams' motion, appointed "a committee of correspondence . . . to state the rights of the Colonists and of this Province in particular, as men, as Christians, and as subjects; and to communicate the same to the several towns and to the world." On November 20, Adams presented the declaration of rights which he, as a member of the committee, had drafted. In Adams' paper, observed William V. Wells, is "embodied the whole philosophy of human rights, condensed from the doctrines of all times, and applied to the immediate circumstances of America. Upon this paper was based all that was written or spoken on human liberty in the Congress which declared independence" (Life of Samuel Adams).

Source: OSL 173.

NATURAL RIGHTS OF THE COLONISTS AS MEN

AMONG THE NATURAL RIGHTS of the colonists are these: first, a right to life; second, to liberty; third, to property; together with the right to support and defend them in the best manner they can. These are evident branches of, rather than deductions from, the duty of self-preservation, commonly called the first law of nature.

All men have a right to remain in a state of nature as long as they please; and in case of intolerable oppression, civil or religious, to leave the society they belong to, and enter into another.

When men enter into society, it is by voluntary consent; and they have a right to demand and insist upon the performance of such conditions and previous limitations as form an equitable original compact.

Every natural right not expressly given up, or, from the nature of a social compact, necessarily ceded, remains.

All positive and civil laws should conform, as far as possible, to the law of natural reason and equity.

As neither reason requires nor religion permits the contrary, every man living in or out of a state of civil society has a right peaceably and quietly to worship God according to the dictates of his conscience.

"Just and true liberty, equal and impartial liberty," in matters spiritual and temporal, is a thing that all men are clearly entitled to by the eternal and immutable laws of God and nature, as well as by the law of nations and all well-grounded municipal laws, which must have their foundation in the former.

In regard to religion, mutual toleration in the different professions thereof is what all good and candid minds in all ages have ever practised, and, both by precept and example, inculcated on mankind. And it is now generally agreed among Christians that this spirit of toleration, in the fullest extent consistent with the being of civil society, is the chief characteristical mark of the church. Insomuch that Mr. Locke has asserted and proved, beyond the possibility of contradiction on any solid ground, that such toleration ought to be extended to all whose doctrines are not subversive of society. The only sects which he thinks ought to be, and which by all wise laws are excluded from such toleration, are those who teach doctrines subversive of the civil government under which they live. The Roman Catholics or Papists are excluded by reason of such doctrines as these: that princes excommunicated may be deposed, and those that they call heretics may be destroyed without mercy; besides their recognizing the pope in so absolute a manner, in subversion of government, by introducing, as far as possible into the states under whose protection they enjoy life, liberty, and property, that solecism in politics, *imperium in imperio*, leading directly to the worst anarchy and confusion, civil discord, war, and bloodshed.

The natural liberty of man, by entering into society, is abridged or restrained so far only as is necessary for the great end of society, the best good of the whole.

In the state of nature every man is, under God, judge and sole judge of his own rights and of the injuries done him. By entering into society he agrees to an arbiter or indifferent judge between him and his neighbors; but he no more renounces his original right than by taking a cause out of the ordinary course of law, and leaving the decision

to referees or indifferent arbitrators. In the last case, he must pay the referees for time and trouble. He should also be willing to pay his just quota for the support of government, the law, and the constitution; the end of which is to furnish indifferent and impartial judges in all cases that may happen, whether civil, ecclesiastical, marine, or military.

The *natural* liberty of man is to be free from any superior power on earth, and not to be under the will or legislative authority of man, but only to have the law of nature for his rule.

In the state of nature men may, as the patriarchs did, employ hired servants for the defense of their lives, liberties, and property; and they should pay them reasonable wages. Government was instituted for the purposes of common defense, and those who hold the reins of government have an equitable, natural right to an honorable support from the same principle that "the laborer is worthy of his hire." But then the same community which they serve ought to be the assessors of their pay. Governors have no right to seek and take what they please; by this, instead of being content with the station assigned them, that of honorable servants of the society, they would soon become absolute masters, despots, and tyrants. Hence, as a private man has a right to say what wages he will give in his private affairs, so has a community to determine what *they* will give and grant of their substance for the administration of public affairs. And, in both cases, more are ready to offer their service at the proposed and stipulated price than are able and willing to perform their duty.

In short, it is the greatest absurdity to suppose it in the power of one or any number of men, at the entering into society, to renounce their essential natural rights, or the means of preserving those rights, when the grand end of civil government, from the very nature of its institution, is for the support, protection, and defense of those very rights; the principal of which, as is before observed, are life, liberty, and property. If men, through fear, fraud, or mistake, should in terms renounce or give up any essential natural right, the eternal law of reason and the grand end of society would absolutely vacate such renunciation. The right to freedom being the gift of God Almighty, it is not in the power of man to alienate this gift and voluntarily become a slave.

THE RIGHTS OF THE COLONISTS AS CHRISTIANS

THESE MAY BE BEST understood by reading and carefully studying the institutes of the great Lawgiver and Head of the Christian Church, which are to be found clearly written and promulgated in the New Testament.

By the act of the British Parliament, commonly called the Toleration Act, every subject in England, except Papists, etc., was restored to, and reestablished in, his natural right to worship God according to the dictates of his own conscience. And, by the charter of this province, it is granted, ordained, and established (that is, declared as an original right) that there shall be liberty of conscience allowed in the worship of God to all Christians, except Papists, inhabiting, or which shall inhabit or be resident within, such province or territory. Magna Charta itself is in substance but a constrained declaration or proclamation and promulgation in the name of the King, Lords, and Commons, of the sense the latter had of their original, inherent, indefeasible natural rights as also those of free citizens equally perdurable with the other. That great author, that great jurist, and even that court writer, Mr. Justice Blackstone, holds that this recognition was justly obtained of King John, sword in hand. And peradventure it must be one day, sword in hand, again rescued and preserved from total destruction and oblivion.

THE RIGHTS OF THE COLONISTS AS SUBJECTS

A COMMONWEALTH or state is a body politic, or civil society of men, united together to promote their mutual safety and prosperity by means of their union.

The absolute rights of Englishmen and all freemen, in or out of civil society, are principally personal security, personal liberty, and private property.

All persons born in the British American colonies are, by the laws of God and nature and by the common law of England, exclusive of all charters from the Crown, well entitled, and by acts of the British Parliament are declared to be entitled, to all the natural, essential, inherent, and inseparable rights, liberties, and privileges of subjects born in Great Britain or within the Realm. Among those rights are the following, which no man, or body of men, consistently with their own rights as men and citizens, or members of society, can for themselves give up or take away from others.

First, "the first fundamental positive law of all commonwealths or states is the establishing the legislative power. As the first fundamental *natural* law, also, which is to govern even the legislative power itself, is the preservation of the society."

Second, the legislative has no right to absolute, arbitrary power over the lives and fortunes of the people; nor can mortals assume a prerogative not only too high for men, but for angels, and therefore reserved for the exercise of the Deity alone.

"The legislative cannot justly assume to itself a power to rule by extempore arbitrary decrees; but it is bound to see that justice is dispensed, and that the rights of the subjects be decided by promulgated, standing, and known laws, and authorized *independent judges*"; that is, independent, as far as possible, of prince and people. "There should be one rule of justice for rich and poor, for the favorite at court, and the countryman at the plough."

Third, the supreme power cannot justly take from any man any part of his property, without his consent in person or by his representative.

These are some of the first principles of natural law and justice, and the great barriers of all free states and of the British constitution in particular. It is utterly irreconcilable to these principles and to many other fundamental maxims of the common law, common sense, and reason that a British House of Commons should have a right at pleasure to give and grant the property of the colonists. (That the colonists are well entitled to all the essential rights, liberties, and privileges of men and freemen born in Britain is manifest not only from the colony charters in general, but acts of the British Parliament.) The statute of the 13th year of George II, chap. 7, naturalizes even foreigners after seven years' residence. The words of the Massachusetts charter are these:

> And further, our will and pleasure is, and we do hereby for Us, Our Heirs, and Successors, grant, establish, and ordain that all and every of the subjects of Us, Our Heirs, and Successors, which shall go to, and inhabit within our said province or territory, and every of their children, which shall happen to be born there or on the seas in going thither or returning from thence, shall have and enjoy all liberties and immunities of free and natural subjects within any of the dominions of Us, Our Heirs, and Successors, to all intents, constructions, and purposes whatsoever, as if they and every one of them were born within this Our Realm of England.

Now what liberty can there be where property is taken away without consent? Can it be said with any color of truth and justice that this continent of 3,000 miles in length, and of a breadth as yet unexplored, in which, however, it is supposed there are 5,000,000 people, has the least voice, vote, or influence in the British Parliament? Have they all together any more weight or power to return a single member to that House of Commons who have not inadvertently, but deliberately, assumed a power to dispose of their lives, liberties, and properties, than to choose an emperor of China? Had the colonists a right to return members to the British Parliament, it would only be hurtful; as, from their local situation and circumstances, it is impossible they should ever be truly and properly represented there.

The inhabitants of this country, in all probability, in a few years will be more numerous than those of Great Britain and Ireland together; yet it is absurdly expected by the promoters of the present measures that these, with their posterity to all generations, should be easy, while their property shall be disposed of by a House of Commons at 3,000 miles' distance from them, and who cannot be supposed to have the least care or concern for their real interest; who have not only no natural care for their interest, but must be in effect bribed against it, as every burden they lay on the colonists is so much saved or gained to themselves. Hitherto, many of the colonists have been free from quitrents; but if the breath of a British House of Commons can originate an act for taking away all our money, our lands will go next, or be subject to rack rents from haughty and relentless landlords, who will ride at ease, while we are trodden in the dirt. The colonists have been branded with the odious names of traitors and rebels only for complaining of their grievances. How long such treatment will or ought to be borne is submitted.

Benjamin Franklin: Rules by Which a Great Empire May Be Reduced to a Small One

Franklin spent the better part of the years between 1757 and 1775 in London as a sort of ambassador extraordinary from various colonial assemblies to Great Britain, attempting to bring about some alteration in its colonial policy. During these years he gradually lost faith in the wisdom of the British government, reluctantly coming to feel that America could no longer profit by its rule. Rebuffed at nearly every turn by ministers whose incivility betrayed their ignorance of American affairs, he lost heart for his mission, though he did not actually return home until he had decided that all hope for conciliation was gone. It was at the height of his difficulties that he turned to political satire as a weapon in his negotiations. An Edict by the King of Prussia, parodying the English King's arbitrary acts with respect to America, and Rules by Which a Great Empire May Be Reduced to a Small One, which is reprinted here, appeared originally in the London Public Advertiser in 1773. While tactically a mistake, since their immediate effect was only to antagonize the pro-American party in London, these pieces have long survived their occasion by virtue of their brilliant and incisive irony.

Source: Sparks, IV, pp. 387-398.

An ancient sage valued himself upon this, that though he could not fiddle, he knew how to make a great city of a little one. The science that I, a modern simpleton, am about to communicate, is the very reverse.

I address myself to all ministers who have the management of extensive dominions, which from their very greatness are become troublesome to govern, because the multiplicity of their affairs leaves no time for fiddling.

1. In the first place, gentlemen, you are to consider that a great empire, like a great cake, is most easily diminished at the edges. Turn your attention, therefore, first to your remotest provinces; that as you get rid of them, the next may follow in order.

2. That the possibility of this separation may always exist, take special care the provinces are never incorporated with the mother country; that they do not enjoy the same common rights, the same privileges in commerce; and that they are governed by severer laws, all of your enacting, without allowing them any share in the choice of the legislators. By carefully making and preserving such distinctions, you will (to keep to my simile of the cake) act like a wise gingerbread baker, who, to facilitate a division, cuts his dough half through in those places where, when baked, he would have it broken to pieces.

3. Those remote provinces have perhaps been acquired, purchased, or conquered at the sole expense of the settlers, or their ancestors, without the aid of the mother country. If this should happen to increase her strength, by their growing numbers, ready to join in her wars; her commerce, by their growing demand for her manufactures; or her naval power, by greater employment for her ships and seamen, they may probably

suppose some merit in this, and that it en-titles them to some favor; you are therefore to forget it all, or resent it, as if they had done you injury. If they happen to be zeal-ous Whigs, friends of liberty, nurtured in revolution principles, remember all that to their prejudice, and resolve to punish it; for such principles, after a revolution is thor-oughly established, are of no more use; they are even odious and abominable.

4. However peaceably your colonies have submitted to your government, shown their affection to your interests, and patient-ly borne their grievances, you are to sup-pose them always inclined to revolt, and treat them accordingly. Quarter troops among them who by their insolence may provoke the rising of mobs, and by their bullets and bayonets suppress them. By this means, like the husband who uses his wife ill from suspicion, you may in time convert your suspicions into realities.

5. Remote provinces must have gover-nors and judges to represent the royal per-son, and execute everywhere the delegated parts of his office and authority. You minis-ters know that much of the strength of gov-ernment depends on the opinion of the people; and much of that opinion on the choice of rulers placed immediately over them. If you send them wise and good men for governors, who study the interest of the colonists, and advance their prosperity, they will think their king wise and good, and that he wishes the welfare of his subjects. If you send them learned and upright men for judges, they will think him a lover of jus-tice. This may attach your provinces more to his government. You are therefore to be careful whom you recommend for those of-fices. If you can find prodigals who have ruined their fortunes, broken gamesters, or stockjobbers, these may do well as gover-nors, for they will probably be rapacious, and provoke the people by their extortions. Wrangling proctors and pettifogging law-yers, too, are not amiss, for they will be for

ever disputing and quarreling with their lit-tle parliaments. If withal they should be ig-norant, wrongheaded, and insolent, so much the better. Attorneys' clerks and Newgate solicitors will do for chief justices, especially if they hold their places during your plea-sure; and all will contribute to impress those ideas of your government that are proper for a people you would wish to re-nounce it.

6. To confirm these impressions and strike them deeper, whenever the injured come to the capital with complaints of mal-administration, oppression, or injustice, pun-ish such suitors with long delay, enormous expense, and a final judgment in favor of the oppressor. This will have an admirable effect every way. The trouble of future complaints will be prevented, and governors and judges will be encouraged to further acts of oppression and injustice; and thence the people may become more disaffected, and at length desperate.

7. When such governors have crammed their coffers and made themselves so odious to the people that they can no longer re-main among them with safety to their per-son, recall and reward them with pensions. You may make them baronets, too, if that respectable order should not think fit to re-sent it. All will contribute to encourage new governors in the same practice, and make the supreme government detestable.

8. If, when you are engaged in war, your colonies should vie in liberal aids of men and money against the common ene-my upon your simple requisition, and give far beyond their abilities, reflect that a pen-ny taken from them by your power is more honorable to you than a pound presented by their benevolence; despise therefore their voluntary grants, and resolve to harass them with novel taxes. They will probably com-plain to your Parliament, that they are taxed by a body in which they have no rep-resentative, and that this is contrary to com-mon right. They will petition for redress.

Let the parliaments flout their claims, reject their petitions, refuse even to suffer the reading of them, and treat the petitioners with the utmost contempt. Nothing can have a better effect in producing the alienation proposed; for though many can forgive injuries, none ever forgave contempt.

9. In laying these taxes, never regard the heavy burdens those remote people already undergo in defending their own frontiers, supporting their own provincial governments, making new roads, building bridges, churches, and other public edifices, which in old countries have been done to your hands by your ancestors, but which occasion constant calls and demands on the purses of a new people. Forget the restraints you lay on their trade for your own benefit, and the advantage a monopoly of this trade gives your exacting merchants. Think nothing of the wealth those merchants and your manufacturers acquire by the colony commerce; their increased ability thereby to pay taxes at home; their accumulating, in the price of their commodities, most of those taxes, and so levying them from their consuming customers; all this, and the employment and support of thousands of your poor by the colonists, you are entirely to forget. But remember to make your arbitrary tax more grievous to your provinces by public declarations importing that your power of taxing them has no limits; so that when you take from them without their consent one shilling in the pound, you have a clear right to the other nineteen. This will probably weaken every ideal of security in their property, and convince them that under such a government they have nothing they can call their own — which can scarce fail of producing the happiest consequences!

10. Possibly, indeed, some of them might still comfort themselves and say, "Though we have no property, we have yet something left that is valuable; we have constitutional liberty, both of person and of conscience. This King, these Lords, and these Commons, who it seems are too remote from us to know us and feel for us, cannot take from us our habeas corpus right, or our right of trial by a jury of our neighbors; they cannot deprive us of the exercise of our religion, alter our ecclesiastical constitution, and compel us to be Papists, if they please, or Mahometans." To annihilate this comfort, begin by laws to perplex their commerce with infinite regulations, impossible to be remembered and observed; ordain seizures of their property for every failure; take away the trial of such property by jury, and give it to arbitrary judges of your own appointing, and of the lowest characters in the country, whose salaries and emoluments are to arise out of the duties or condemnations, and whose appointments are during pleasure. Then let there be a formal declaration of both houses that opposition to your edicts is treason, and that any person suspected of treason in the provinces may, according to some obsolete law, be seized and sent to the metropolis of the empire for trial; and pass an act that those there charged with certain other offenses, shall be sent away in chains from their friends and country to be tried in the same manner for felony. Then erect a new court of inquisition among them, accompanied by an armed force, with instructions to transport all such suspected persons, to be ruined by the expense if they bring over evidences to prove their innocence, or be found guilty and hanged, if they cannot afford it.

And, lest the people should think you cannot possibly go any farther, pass another solemn declaratory act, "that King, Lords, Commons had, have, and of right ought to have, full power and authority to make statutes of sufficient force and validity to bind the unrepresented provinces in all cases whatsoever." This will include spiritual with temporal, and, taken together, must operate wonderfully to your purpose by convincing them that they are at present under a power something like that spoken of in the Scriptures, which can not only kill their bodies, but damn their souls to all eternity, by compelling them, if it pleases, to worship the devil.

11. To make your taxes more odious and more likely to procure resistance, send from the capital a board of officers to superintend the collection, composed of the most indiscreet, ill-bred, and insolent you can find. Let these have large salaries out of the extorted revenue, and live in open, grating luxury upon the sweat and blood of the industrious, whom they are to worry continually with groundless and expensive prosecutions before the above-mentioned arbitrary revenue judges — all at the cost of the party prosecuted, though acquitted, because the King is to pay no costs. Let these men, by your order, be exempted from all the common taxes and burdens of the province, though they and their property are protected by its laws. If any revenue officers are suspected of the least tenderness for the people, discard them. If others are justly complained of, protect and reward them. If any of the under officers behave so as to provoke the people to drub them, promote those to better offices. This will encourage others to procure for themselves such profitable drubbings, by multiplying and enlarging such provocations, and all will work toward the end you aim at.

12. Another way to make your tax odious is to misapply the produce of it. If it was originally appropriated for the defense of the provinces, the better support of government, and the administration of justice, where it may be necessary, then apply none of it to that defense, but bestow it where it is not necessary, in augmented salaries or pensions to every governor who had distinguished himself by his enmity to the people, and by calumniating them to their sovereign. This will make them pay it more unwillingly, and be more apt to quarrel with those that collect it and those that imposed it, who will quarrel again with them, and all shall contribute to your main purpose, of making them weary of your government.

13. If the people of any province have been accustomed to support their own governors and judges to satisfaction, you are to apprehend that such governors and judges may be thereby influenced to treat the people kindly, and to do them justice. This is another reason for applying part of that revenue in larger salaries to such governors and judges, given, as their commissions are, during your pleasure only; forbidding them to take any salaries from their provinces; that thus the people may no longer hope any kindness from their governors, or (in Crown cases) any justice from their judges. And, as the money thus misapplied in one province is extorted from all, probably all will resent the misapplication.

New York Historical Society

Sons of Liberty organized resistance to the Tea Act, which would have given the East India Co. a monopoly of tea trade

14. If the parliaments of your provinces should dare to claim rights, or complain of your administration, order them to be harassed with repeated dissolutions. If the same men are continually returned by new elections, adjourn their meetings to some country village, where they cannot be accommodated, and there keep them during pleasure; for this, you know, is your prerogative, and an excellent one it is, as you may manage it to promote discontents among the people, diminish their respect, and increase their disaffection.

15. Convert the brave, honest officers of your Navy into pimping tide-waiters and colony officers of the customs. Let those who in time of war fought gallantly in defense of the commerce of their countrymen, in peace be taught to prey upon it. Let them learn to be corrupted by great and real smugglers; but (to show their diligence) scour with armed boats every bay, harbor, river, creek, cove, or nook throughout the coast of your colonies; stop and detain every coaster, every wood boat, every fisherman, tumble their cargoes and even their ballast inside out and upside down; and, if a pennyworth of pins is found unentered, let the whole be seized and confiscated.

Thus shall the trade of your colonists suffer more from their friends in time of peace than it did from their enemies in war. Then let these boats' crews land upon every farm in their way, rob the orchards, steal the pigs and the poultry, and insult the inhabitants. If the injured and exasperated farmers, unable to procure other justice, should attack the aggressors, drub them, and burn their boats; you are to call this high treason and rebellion, order fleets and armies into their country, and threaten to carry all the offenders 3,000 miles to be hanged, drawn, and quartered. O! this will work admirably!

16. If you are told of discontents in your colonies, never believe that they are general, or that you have given occasion for them; therefore, do not think of applying any remedy, or of changing any offensive measure. Redress no grievance, lest they should be encouraged to demand the redress of some other grievance. Grant no request that is just and reasonable, lest they should make another that is unreasonable. Take all your informations of the state of the colonies from your governors and officers in enmity with them. Encourage and reward these leasing makers; secrete their lying accusations, lest they should be confuted; but act upon them as the clearest evidence; and believe nothing you hear from the friends of the people. Suppose all *their* complaints to be invented and promoted by a few factious demagogues, whom if you could catch and hang, all would be quiet. Catch and hang a few of them accordingly; and the blood of the martyrs shall work miracles in favor of your purpose.

17. If you see rival nations rejoicing at the prospect of your disunion with your provinces, and endeavoring to promote it; if they translate, publish, and applaud all the complaints of your discontented colonists, at the same time privately stimulating you to severer measures, let not that alarm or offend you. Why should it, since you all mean the same thing?

18. If any colony should at their own charge erect a fortress to secure their port against the fleets of a foreign enemy, get your governor to betray that fortress into your hands. Never think of paying what it cost the country, for that would look at least like some regard for justice; but turn it into a citadel to awe the inhabitants and curb their commerce.

If they should have lodged in such fortress the very arms they bought and used to aid you in your conquests, seize them all; it will provoke like ingratitude added to robbery. One admirable effect of these operations will be to discourage every other colony from erecting such defenses, and so your enemies may more easily invade them, to the great disgrace of your government, and of course the furtherance of your project.

19. Send armies into their country under

pretence of protecting the inhabitants; but, instead of garrisoning the forts on their frontiers with those troops, to prevent incursions, demolish those forts, and order the troops into the heart of the country, that the savages may be encouraged to attack the frontiers, and that the troops may be protected by the inhabitants. This will seem to proceed from your ill will or your ignorance, and contribute farther to produce and strengthen an opinion among them that you are no longer fit to govern them.

20. Lastly, invest the general of your army in the provinces with great and unconstitutional powers, and free him from the control of even your own civil governors. Let him have troops enough under his command, with all the fortresses in his possession; and who knows but (like some provincial generals in the Roman Empire, and encouraged by the universal discontent you have produced) he may take it into his head to set up for himself? If he should, and you have carefully practised these few excellent rules of mine, take my word for it, all the provinces will immediately join him; and you will that day (if you have not done it sooner) get rid of the trouble of governing them, and all the plagues attending their commerce and connection from henceforth and forever.

Q.E.D.

You are a member of Parliament, and one of that majority which has doomed my country to destruction. You have begun to burn our towns, and murder our people, — Look upon your hands! — They are stained with the blood of your relations! — You and I were long friends: — you are now my enemy, — and I am, Yours, B. Franklin.

BENJAMIN FRANKLIN, letter to William Strahan, July 5, 1775.
This letter, to an old friend, was never sent.

The Colonies Reduced

Design'd & Engrav'd for the Political Register.

John Carter Brown Library

RULE AND REBELLION

The successful conclusion of the French and Indian War left England with considerable debts and increased responsibilities in America. The loose control that had distinguished British colonial rule from that of the French and Spanish was tightened in an effort to ease the burden of defense and administration. Settlement west of the Alleghenies was forbidden by the Proclamation of 1763, and new taxes were established to increase revenue from the colonies.

However reasonable these measures were to Parliament, many colonists thought them a burdensome violation of their rights. Conflict between the mother country and the colonies was based on differences of principle and self-interest, but was increased by the presence in the colonies of skilled propagandists, and in England by a proud and corrupt Parliament. When the first disputes arose, few men on either side believed, or hoped, that in only a decade the united colonies would declare themselves free and independent.

(Top left) Cartoon: Americans being robbed by the King's agents; (top right) King George III; (above) George Grenville, promoter of the Stamp Act; a tax stamp and an American parody

The Stamp Act

The Stamp Act of 1765, like the Sugar Act of the previous year, brought to a head the dispute over whether Parliament, in addition to regulating and governing the American colonies, could tax them for revenue as well. Unfortunately for Parliament, the stamp tax had its most serious effects on the most articulate and influential Americans: the lawyers, publishers, and tavern keepers.

v.United,Provinces

[No *Stamped Paper* to be had.]

North-American.

YOU remember that at our laſt meeting, we agreed upon this day candidly to enquire into the juſtice as well as policy of Great-Britain, in taxing the North-Americans; and as this is a matter of the greateſt importance to both countries, I ſhall with pleaſure hear you endeavour to defend the meaſures that have been taken to the utmoſt of my power, I mean as far as is conſiſtent with truth or right reaſon: but if I ſhould differ with you in opinion, I hope you will hear me with the ſame candor that I ſhall you.

Courtier.

Upon theſe principles, Sir, I join iſſue; and firſt, as to

LONDON, Auguſt 29.

His Excellency the Earl of Hertford, Lord Lieutenant of Ireland, has appointed the Hon. Col. Cunningham, and Capt. Fleming, to be his Aids de Camp.

Very large Orders from Spain are come over for the purchaſe of corn, ſo great a ſcarcity of which has not been known there for many years.

A Letter from on board the Hardwicke Indiaman, in St. Jago road, capital of the Cape de Verd Iſlands, dated May 16, mentions, that ſhe touched there the 8th of that Month for Water, (having had a very good paſſage) where ſhe found the Hector and True Briton. The Royal Charlotte came in there for water a few days after.

and not chiming in with the *oppreſſive* Meaſures of thoſe in Power, having had many broad Hints and Overtures, to bring them over for that Purpoſe. Which they rejected with Diſdain. I ſhou'd be very ſorry to find your Paper under ſo much *undue* Influence, as to omit inſerting Things of ſo great Conſequence to the Peace, Happineſs, and Tranquility of the Public in general. I cannot in Juſtice to theſe Gentlemen's Characters, read your Papers, without making ſome Reply to ſo great a Falaſy.

I am, Sir, Your obedient Servant,

A Citizen of Montreal.

N. B. For Conveniency, we have new Comiſſion of the Peace every Quarter Seſſions; ſuppoſe it is ſo in the other Colonies.

St. Jago, (Jamaica) Auguſt 24.

Extract from the Proceedings of the Aſſembly of the 16th Auguſt.

And Colonial Resistance

Daniel Dulany

Resistance to the Stamp Act was both practical and philosophical. Men designated as stamp agents found their property and health endangered by mobs, which also burned stamped paper whenever possible. And the British argument that the colonists were "virtually represented" in Parliament was countered by the constitutional reasoning of Daniel Dulany, James Otis, and other colonial thinkers.

(Top) Cartoon: Boston and the colonies attack the Stamp Act monster, which holds English freedom in its claws; (bottom left) engraving showing rioters burning stamped paper; (center) newspaper notice following such a riot

Courtesy, the British Museum

Etching in celebration of the repeal of the Stamp Act which appeared at the head of a song entitled "The World Turned Upside Down, or, the Old Woman Taught Wisdom"

Stamp Act Repeal

While Parliament would not officially heed colonial protests against the Stamp Act, they did listen to English merchants who suffered from colonial boycotts. Important also were Parliamentary politics: a change of ministries brought in compromis-ers who soon repealed the Stamp Act. The repeal was celebrated throughout the colonies. In their triumph, the colonists failed to take note of the Declaratory Act, passed at the same time, which reaffirmed the absolute rule of Parliament over the colonies.

Lord Rockingham, rival and successor of George Grenville, who repealed the Stamp Act

Public Records Office, London

National Portrait Gallery, London

The Townshend Duties

The notion that Americans objected only to "internal" taxes, such as on newspaper printing, but not to "external" taxes on foreign trade, was dispelled by the reaction to the "Townshend Duties" on imported goods.

Named after Charles Townshend, unpredictable Chancellor of the Exchequer, the duties were unpopular even in England, and after another period of boycotts, were repealed in 1770, except for the one on tea.

(Top) 1768 engraving by Paul Revere shows British troops landing in Boston to enforce law and order; (bottom left) John Hancock, wealthy Boston merchant and backer of the Sons of Liberty, whose income was derived in part by smuggling goods in violation of British trade regulations; portrait by John Singleton Copley

To the PUBLIC.

AS I am convinced that my refusing to store my Goods, was wrong; I do promise and consent, That they shall be deposited in the public Store with other Goods which were imported contrary to the *Non-importation Agreement*;---which I hope will appease the Minds of my injured Fellow Citizens, and convince them that I do not regard sacrificing my private Interest for the *Good of the Public.*

Simeon Coley.

New-York, 21st July, 1769.
Afternoon, 2 o'Clock.

(Top left) Efforts to install a bishop in America were resisted even by Anglicans here as an unnecessary extension of British rule; (top right) Samuel Adams, the colonial agitator, shown here in 1770 demanding that Gov. Hutchinson remove British troops from Boston, in a portrait by J. S. Copley; (center right) Thomas Hutchinson, governor of Massachusetts during this troubled period; (bottom left) Green Dragon Inn in Boston, meeting place for the Sons of Liberty

The BLOODY MASSACRE perpetrated in King—Street BOSTON on March 5th 1770 by a party of the 29th REG.

Unhappy Boston! see thy Sons deplore,
Thy hallow'd Walks besmear'd with guiltless Gore.
While faithless P——n and his savage Bands,
With murd'rous Rancour stretch their bloody Hands,
Like fierce Barbarians grinning o'er their Prey,
Approve the Carnage and enjoy the Day.

If scalding drops from Rage from Anguish Wrung
If speechless Sorrows lab'ring for a Tongue,
Or if a weeping World can ought appease
The plaintive Ghosts of Victims such as these:
The Patriot's copious Tears for each are shed,
A glorious Tribute which embalms the Dead.

But know, Fate summons to that awful Goal,
Where Justice strips the Murd'rer of his Soul:
Should venal C——ts the scandal of the Land,
Snatch the relentless Villain from her Hand,
Keen Execrations on this Plate inscrib'd,
Shall reach a Judge who never can be brib'd.

The unhappy Sufferers were Mess.rs Sam.l Gray, Sam.l Maverick, Jam.s Caldwell, Crispus Attucks & Pat.k Carr
Killed. Six wounded; two of them (Christr Monk & John Clark) Mortally

Boston "Massacre"

The British soldiers stationed in Boston to preserve order found little to do: the Bostonians practised a form of passive resistance, often taunting the Redcoats, but rarely caused violence. An exception was the "Boston Massacre," in which beleaguered soldiers fired into a threatening mob. The incident was publicly attacked by Paul Revere and Samuel Adams as wanton British brutality, but the soldiers were defended by John Adams and Robert Auchmuty and acquitted.

(Top left) Robert Auchmuty, portrait attributed to Robert Feke; (center left) youthful portrait of John Adams by Joseph Badger; (top right) Paul Revere's interpretation of the incident he calls a "Bloody Massacre," in one of the most widely circulated pieces of propaganda before the Revolution; (bottom left) Paul Revere, by John Singleton Copley

A NEW METHOD OF MACARONY MAKING AS PRACTISED AT BOSTON

**Colonials torture a customs house agent
for accepting a tea shipment**

A
Party
in
Protest

The famous Tea Party was well planned, probably by Samuel Adams, the colonial master of propaganda and agitation. Dumping the tea was an illegal extension of the boycott on tea occasioned, not by a tax, but by the granting of a tea monopoly to the East India Company. This hurt colonial merchants, and seemed an ominous precedent to sellers of other goods; therefore, protest did not stop with the Tea Party.

Monday Morning, December 27, 1773.

THE Tea-Ship being arrived, every Inhabitant, who wishes to preserve the Liberty of America, is desired to meet at the STATE-HOUSE, This Morning, precisely at TEN o'Clock, to advise what is best to be done on this alarming Crisis.

General Gage, made governor of Massachusetts to enforce the Coercive Acts

The Coercive Acts Backfire

British cartoon lampoons the "Bostonians in distress"

Parliament was not amused by the Tea Party, and in retaliation passed the Coercive Acts (1774), closing Boston harbor and placing Massachusetts under close British rule. With bad timing, Parliament also passed the Quebec Act, extending the boundaries of that centrally ruled Catholic province down to the Ohio River. This made Boston a cause instead of an example, and united the Protestant colonies in her aid.

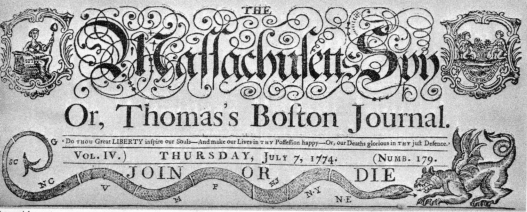

THE

Massachusetts Spy

Or, Thomas's Boston Journal.

Do THOU *Great LIBERTY inspire our Souls—And make our Lives in* THY *Possession happy—Or, our Deaths glorious in* THY *just Defence.*

VOL. IV.) THURSDAY, JULY 7, 1774. (NUMB. 179.

JOIN OR DIE

The First Continental Congress

The Coercive Acts were thought to endanger all the colonies, so a congress was convened in Philadelphia in September 1774 to decide a course of action. For many delegates the question was no longer whether Parliament could tax the colonies, but whether it could legislate for them at all. Enough radicals, such as Patrick Henry of Virginia, were present to ensure the defeat of a proposal for conciliation by Joseph Galloway of Pennsylvania. After adopting a declaration of rights, an address to the people of Great Britain, and an agreement not to buy or use English goods, the Congress resolved to meet again if their grievances were not redressed.

(Above left) Joseph Galloway; (left) Patrick Henry; (below) a portion of the "Address to the People of Great Britain," from the "Extracts," (bottom) Carpenters' Hall in Philadelphia, meeting place of the first Congress

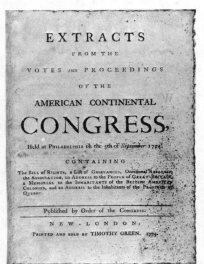

EXTRACTS

FROM THE

VOTES AND PROCEEDINGS

OF THE

AMERICAN CONTINENTAL

CONGRESS,

Held at Philadelphia on the 5th of *September* 1774.

CONTAINING

The BILL of RIGHTS, a List of GRIEVANCES, Occasional RESOLVES, the ASSOCIATION, an ADDRESS to the PEOPLE of GREAT-BRITAIN, a MEMORIAL to the INHABITANTS of the BRITISH AMERICAN COLONIES, and an ADDRESS to the Inhabitants of the Province of QUEBEC.

Published by Order of the CONGRESS.

N E W - L O N D O N :

PRINTED AND SOLD BY TIMOTHY GREEN. 1774.

To the People of GREAT-BRITAIN,

From the DELEGATES appointed by the several *English* Colonies of *New-Hampshire, Massachusetts-Bay, Rhode-Island* and *Providence Plantations, Connecticut, New-York, New-Jersey, Pennsylvania,* the *Lower Counties* on *Delaware, Maryland, Virginia, North-Carolina,* and *South-Carolina,* to consider of their Grievances in GENERAL CONGRESS, at *Philadelphia, September 5th,* 1774.

FRIENDS *and* FELLOW SUBJECTS,

WHEN a Nation, led to greatness by the hand of Liberty, and possessed of all the glory that heroism, munificence, and humanity can bestow, descends to the ungrateful task of forging chains for her Friends and Children, and instead of giving support to Freedom, turns advocate for Slavery and Oppression, there is reason to suspect she has either ceased to be virtuous, or been extremely negligent in the appointment of her rulers.

In

"A view of the south part of Lexington," engraved by Amos Dolittle from sketches by Ralph Earl

The First Shots

The first shots between provincials and British regulars were exchanged in confusion at Lexington, as soldiers marched past on their way to seize colonial military stores in Concord. On their retreat to Boston, the regulars were trailed by sharpshooting colonists firing from cover. The emboldened colonists then determined to drive the small British garrison from Boston, but failed at Bunker Hill, for lack of ammunition.

America burns while Parliament fiddles and argues; "Bunker's Hill, or America's Head-Dress"

Conciliation Fails

The second meeting of the Continental Congress began in May 1775, after the battles of Lexington and Concord. At this late date the delegates attempted conciliation — not with Parliament, but with the King as loyal subjects entitled to their own legislature — and sent the "Olive Branch Petition" to George III. But the King would not read it.

In January of 1776, an uncompromising pamphlet by Thomas Paine became a best seller and helped convince thousands of Americans that their continent should be independent of the little British island.

(Left) Signature page of the "Olive Branch Petition"; (below) Edmund Burke, supporter of the colonies in Parliament; (bottom) Thomas Paine and title page from his influential pamphlet, "Common Sense"

COMMON SENSE;

ADDRESSED TO THE

INHABITANTS

OF

AMERICA,

On the following interesting

SUBJECTS.

I. Of the Origin and Design of Government in general, with concise Remarks on the English Constitution.

II. Of Monarchy and Hereditary Succession.

III. Thoughts on the present State of American Affairs.

IV. Of the present Ability of America, with some miscellaneous Reflections.

Man knows no Master save creating HEAVEN, Or those whom choice and common good ordain.
THOMSON.

PHILADELPHIA;
Printed, and Sold, by R. BELL, in Third-Street.
MDCCLXXVI.

Declaration of Independence

Independence Hall, Philadelphia, meeting place of 2nd Continental Congress

A draft of the Declaration including a portion, later omitted, condemning the slave trade

On July 2, 1776, the Congress formally resolved for independence, and on July 4 adopted a declaration supporting that resolution. A committee had been appointed to draw up the declaration, but it was primarily the work of Thomas Jefferson. Intended to justify independence, the document blamed the colonies' troubles on the King, though all of their disputes had been with Parliament.

"Congress Voting Independence" by Robert Edge Pine and Edward Savage; (below) a sketch of Thomas Jefferson by Benjamin Latrobe and a draft of the Lee resolution for independence, June 7, 1776

The Independence of the Massachusetts Legislature

The Bay Colony was a leader in the growing resistance to royal authority. The legislature of Massachusetts attempted during 1773 to stimulate intercolonial cooperation through committees of correspondence. Governor Hutchinson contested the determination of the legislature to exercise its prerogative in appointing such committees. In reply to the governor's criticism of the Massachusetts House of Representatives, a committee consisting of Sam Adams, John Hancock, and others submitted the following report on February 5, 1774.

Source: Niles: "Extract from the Answer of the House of Representatives to the Governor, February 5, 1774."

IT AFFORDS GREAT SATISFACTION to this house to find that His Majesty has been pleased to put an end to an undue claim, heretofore made by the governors of this province, grounded upon a supposition that the consent of the chair was necessary to the validity of the judicial acts of the Governor and Council. Whereby their proceedings, when sitting as the Supreme Court of Probate, and as the court for determining in cases of marriage and divorce, have been so often impeded. The royal order, that the governor shall acquiesce in the determination of the majority of the Council, respects not the Council only but the body of the people of this province. And His Majesty has herein showed his regard to justice, as well as the interest and convenience of his subjects, in rescuing a clause in the charter from a construction which, in the opinion of this house, was repugnant to the express meaning and intent of the charter, inconsistent with the idea of a court of justice, and dangerous to the rights and property of the subject.

Your Excellency is pleased to inform the two houses that you are required to signify to them His Majesty's disapprobation of the appointment of committees of correspondence, in various instances, which sit and act during the recess of the General Court by prorogation. You are not pleased to explain to us the grounds and reasons of His Majesty's disapprobation; until we shall have such explanation laid before us, a full answer to this part of your speech will not be expected from us. We cannot, however, omit saying upon this occasion that while the common rights of the American subjects continue to be attacked in various instances, and at times when the several assemblies are not sitting, it is highly necessary that they should correspond with each other in order to unite in the most effectual means for the obtaining a redress of their grievances. And as the sitting of the general assemblies in this and most of the colonies depends upon the pleasure of the governors, who hold themselves under the direction of administration, it is to be expected that the meeting of the assemblies will be so ordered, as that the intention proposed by a correspondence between them will be impracticable but by committees to sit and act in the recess.

We would, moreover, observe that, as it has been the practice for years past for the governor and lieutenant governor of this province, and other officers of the Crown, at all times, to correspond with ministers of state and persons of influence and distinction in the nation in order to concert and carry on such measures of the British administration as have been deemed by the colonists to be grievous to them, it cannot be thought unreasonable or improper for the colonists to correspond with their agents, as well as with each other, to the end that their grievances may be so explained to His Majesty, as that, in his justice, he may afford them necessary relief. As this province has heretofore felt the great misfortune of the displeasure of our sovereign by means of misrepresentations, permit us further to say there is room to apprehend that His Majesty has, in this instance, been misinformed and that there are good grounds to suspect that those who may have misinformed him have had in meditation further measures destructive to the colonies, which they were apprehensive would be defeated by means of committees of correspondence sitting and acting in the recess of the respective assemblies.

It must be pleasing to the good people of this province to find that the heavy debt which had been incurred by their liberal aids, through the course of the late war for the subduing His Majesty's inveterate enemies and extending his territory and dominion in America, is so nearly discharged. Whenever the house of representatives shall deem it incumbent upon them to provide for any future charges, it will be done, as it ought, by such ways and means as, after due deliberation, to them shall seem meet.

In the meantime, this House will employ the powers with which they are entrusted in supporting His Majesty's just authority in the province, according to the royal charter, and in dispatching such public business as now properly lies before us. And, while we pursue such measures as tend, by God's blessing, to the redress of grievances and to the restoration and establishment of the public liberty, we persuade ourselves that we shall, at the same time, as far as in us lies, most effectually secure the tranquility and good order of the government, and the great end for which it was instituted, the safety and welfare of the people.

GOUVERNEUR MORRIS: Against Revolutionary Enthusiasm

Gouverneur Morris of New York feared the social upheaval that he thought likely to occur in the event of a "democratic" revolution. Morris was a member of the colonial aristocracy and believed "that if the disputes with Britain continue, we shall be under the worst of all possible dominions . . . the domination of a riotous mob." But when the break with England came, Morris supported the American cause. The occasion of the following letter of May 20, 1774, to [John] Penn was a meeting in New York called to consider Boston's proposals to stop all trade with Britain.

Source: *Archives*, I, pp. 342-343.

YOU HAVE HEARD, and you will hear, a great deal about politics, and in the heap of chaff you may find some grains of good sense. Believe me, sir, freedom and religion are only watchwords. We have appointed a committee, or rather we have nominated one. Let me give you the history of it. It is needless to premise that the lower orders of mankind are more easily led by specious appearances than those of a more exalted station. This, and many similar propositions, you know better than your humble servant.

The troubles in America, during Grenville's administration, put our gentry upon this finesse. They stimulated some daring coxcombs to rouse the mob into an attack upon the bounds of order and decency. These fellows became the Jack Cades of the day, the leaders in all the riots, the bellwethers of the flock. The reason of the maneuver in those who wished to keep fair with the government, and at the same time to receive the incense of popular applause, you will readily perceive. On the whole, the shepherds were not much to blame in a politic point of view. The bellwethers jingled merrily and roared out liberty, and property, and religion, and a multitude of cant terms, which everyone thought he understood and was egregiously mistaken. For you must know the shepherds kept the dictionary of the day, and, like the mysteries of the ancient mythology, it was not for profane eyes or ears. This answered many purposes; the simple flock put themselves entirely under the protection of these most excellent shepherds.

By and by, behold a great metamorphosis, without the help of Ovid or his divinities, but entirely effectuated by two modern genii — the God of Ambition and the Goddess of Faction. The first of these prompted the shepherds to shear some of their flock, and then, in conjunction with the other, converted the bellwethers into shepherds. That we have been in hot water with the British Parliament ever since everybody knows. Consequently, these new shepherds had their hands full of employment. The old ones kept themselves least in sight, and a want of confidence in each other was not the least evil which followed. The port of Boston has been shut up. These sheep, simple as they are, cannot be gulled as heretofore. In short, there is no

Gouverneur Morris, portrait by Ezra Ames

ruling them; and now, to leave the metaphor, the heads of the mobility [the mob] grow dangerous to the gentry, and how to keep them down is the question. While they correspond with the other colonies, call and dismiss popular assemblies, make resolves to bind the consciences of the rest of mankind, bully poor printers, and exert with full force all their other tribunitial powers, it is impossible to curb them.

But art sometimes goes farther than force, and, therefore, to trick them handsomely, a committee of patricians was to be nominated, and into their hands was to be committed the majesty of the people, and the highest trust was to be reposed in them by a mandate that they should take care *quod respublica non capiat injuriam* [that the republic should not suffer injury]. The tribunes, through the want of good legerdemain in the senatorial order, perceived the finesse; and, yesterday, I was present at a grand division of the city, and there I beheld my fellow citizens very accurately counting all their chickens, not only before any of them were hatched but before above one-half of the eggs were laid. In short, they fairly contended about the future forms of our government, whether it should be founded upon aristocratic or democratic principles.

I stood in the balcony, and on my right hand were ranged all the people of property, with some few poor dependents, and on the other all the tradesmen, etc., who thought it worth their while to leave daily labor for the good of the country. The spirit of the English constitution has yet a little influence left, and but a little. The remains of it, however, will give the wealthy people a superiority this time, but would they secure it they must banish all schoolmasters and confine all knowledge to themselves. This cannot be. The mob begin to think and to reason. Poor reptiles! it is with them a vernal morning; they are struggling to cast off their winter's slough, they bask in the sunshine, and ere noon they will bite, depend upon it.

The gentry begin to fear this. Their committee will be appointed; they will deceive the people and again forfeit a share of their confidence. And if these instances of what with one side is policy, with the other perfidy, shall continue to increase and become more frequent, farewell aristocracy. I see, and I see it with fear and trembling, that if the disputes with Great Britain continue, we shall be under the worst of all possible dominions; we shall be under the domination of a riotous mob.

It is the interest of all men, therefore, to seek for reunion with the parent state. A safe compact seems, in my poor opinion, to be now tendered. Internal taxation is to be left with ourselves; the right of regulating trade to be vested in Great Britain, where alone is found the power of protecting it. I trust you will agree with me, that this is the only possible mode of union. Men by nature are free as air. When they enter into society, there is, there must be, an implied compact, for there never yet was an express one, that a part of this freedom shall be given up for the security of the remainder. But what part? The answer is plain. The least possible, considering the circumstances of the society, which constitute what may be called its political necessity.

And what does this political necessity require in the present instance? Not that Britain should lay imposts upon us for the support of government, nor for its defense; not that she should regulate our internal police. These things affect us only. She can have no right to interfere. To these things we ourselves are competent. But can it be said that we are competent to the regulating of trade? The position is absurd, for this affects every part of the British Empire, every part of the habitable earth. If Great Britain, if Ireland, if America, if all of them are to make laws of trade, there must be a collision of these different authorities, and then who is to decide the *vis major*? To recur to this, if possible to be avoided, is the greatest of all great absurdities.

Political necessity, therefore, requires that this power should be placed in the hands of one part of the Empire. Is it a question which part? Let me answer by taking another. Pray, which part of the Empire protects trade? Which part of the Empire receives almost immense sums to guard the rest? And what danger is in the trust? Some men object that England will draw all the profits of our trade into her coffers. All that she can, undoubtedly. But unless a reasonable compensation for his trouble be left to the merchant here, she destroys the trade, and then she will receive no profit from it.

If I remember, in one of those kind letters with which you have honored me, you desire my thoughts on matters as they rise. How much pleasure I take in complying with your requests let my present letter convince you. If I am faulty in telling things which you know better than I do, you must excuse this fault, and a thousand others, for which I can make no apology.

A Proposal for a Continental Congress

Early in May of 1774 the Boston Committee of Correspondence sent a circular letter throughout the colonies urging a stoppage of trade with Britain. This appeal was met with a mixed response. In New York, a committee of fifty-one, dominated by merchants, drafted a reply on May 23. While this committee had no desire to halt trade, it was determined to maintain control of the anti-British sentiments of the populace. The reply, therefore, sympathized with Boston's situation, but implied that only a continental congress could suitably handle the matter.

Source: *Archives*, I, pp. 297-298.

THE ALARMING MEASURES of the British Parliament relative to your ancient and respectable town, which has so long been the seat of freedom, fill the inhabitants of this city with inexpressible concern. As a sister colony, suffering in defense of the rights of America, we consider your injuries as a common cause, to the redress of which it is equally our duty and our interest to contribute. But what ought to be done in a situation so truly critical, while it employs the anxious thoughts of every generous mind, is very hard to be determined.

Our citizens have thought it necessary to appoint a large committee, consisting of fifty-one persons, to correspond with our sister colonies on this and every other matter of public moment, and at ten o'clock this forenoon we were first assembled. Your letter, enclosing the vote of the town of Boston, and the letter of your Committee of Correspondence were immediately taken into consideration.

While we think you justly entitled to the thanks of your sister colonies for asking their advice on a case of such extensive consequences, we lament our inability to relieve your anxiety by a decisive opinion. The cause is general, and concerns a whole continent, who are equally interested with you and us; and we foresee that no remedy can

be of avail unless it proceeds from the joint act and approbation of all; from a virtuous and spirited union which may be expected while the feeble efforts of a few will only be attended with mischief and disappointment to themselves and triumph to the adversaries of our liberty.

Upon these reasons we conclude that a congress of deputies from the colonies in general is of the utmost moment; that it ought to be assembled without delay, and some unanimous resolution formed in this fatal emergency, not only respecting your deplorable circumstances, but for the security of our common rights. Such being our sentiments, it must be premature to pronounce any judgment on the expedient which you have suggested. We beg, however, that you will do us the justice to believe that we shall continue to act with a firm and becoming regard to American freedom, and to cooperate with our sister colonies in every measure which shall be thought salutary and conducive to the public good.

We have nothing to add, but that we sincerely condole with you in your unexampled distress, and to request your speedy opinion of the proposed congress, that if it should meet with your approbation, we may exert our utmost endeavors to carry it into execution.

Thomas Jefferson: A Summary View of the Rights of British America

News of the Boston Port Bill, closing and otherwise punishing Boston until it apologized for the Tea Party of the previous December, reached Williamsburg, Virginia, in May 1774. In response, certain younger members of the Virginia House of Burgesses, among them Thomas Jefferson, submitted a resolution calling for June 1 to be set aside as a day of fasting and humiliation for this and "every injury to American rights." Lord Dunmore, the royal governor of the province, promptly dissolved the House. Under the leadership of Patrick Henry, the members adjourned to the Raleigh Tavern, where they resolved to call for a general congress of the colonies to consider "those measures which the united interests of America may from time to time require." They also summoned a special Virginia revolutionary convention for August 1, to decide what might be done to help the people of Boston and to elect delegates to the general or Continental Congress when it met in Philadelphia in September. Jefferson's constituents of Albemarle County elected him to represent them at the Virginia convention. He drew up a "draft of instructions" in July which he planned to lay before the members, hoping it might serve to guide the delegates at Philadelphia. The result was the Summary View of the Rights of British America. *While the Virginia convention eventually rejected the* View *as too radical, the effort established Jefferson's reputation as a revolutionary pamphleteer.*

Source: Ford, I, pp. 429-447.

Resolved that it be an instruction to the said deputies when assembled in General Congress with the deputies from the other states of British America to propose to the said Congress that a humble and dutiful address be presented to His Majesty begging leave to lay before him as chief magistrate of the British empire the united complaints of His Majesty's subjects in America; complaints which are excited by many unwarrantable encroachments and usurpations, attempted to be made by the legislature of one part of the empire, upon those rights which God and the laws have given equally and independently to all. To represent to His Majesty that these his states have often individually made humble application to his imperial throne, to obtain through its intervention some redress of their injured rights; to none of which was ever even an answer condescended. Humbly to hope that this their joint address, penned in the language of truth, and divested of those expressions of servility which would persuade His Majesty that we are asking favors and not rights, shall obtain from His Majesty a more respectful acceptance. And this His Majesty will think we have reason to expect when he reflects that he is no more than the chief officer of the people, appointed by the laws, and circumscribed with definite powers, to assist in working the great machine of government erected for their use, and consequently subject to their superintendence. And in order that these our rights, as well as the invasions of them, may be laid more fully before His Majesty, to take a view of them from the origin and first settlement of these countries.

To remind him that our ancestors, before

their emigration to America, were the free inhabitants of the British dominions in Europe, and possessed a right, which nature has given to all men, of departing from the country in which chance, not choice has placed them; of going in quest of new habitations, and of there establishing new societies, under such laws and regulations as to them shall seem most likely to promote public happiness. That their Saxon ancestors had under this universal law, in like manner, left their native wilds and woods in the north of Europe, had possessed themselves of the island of Britain then less charged with inhabitants, and had established there that system of laws which has so long been the glory and protection of that country. Nor was ever any claim of superiority or dependence asserted over them by that mother country from which they had migrated: and were such a claim made it is believed that His Majesty's subjects in Great Britain have too firm a feeling of the rights derived to them from their ancestors to bow down the sovereignty of their state before such visionary pretensions. And it is thought that no circumstance has occurred to distinguish materially the British from the Saxon emigration.

America was conquered, and her settlements made and firmly established, at the expense of individuals, and not of the British public. Their own blood was spilled in acquiring lands for their settlements, their own fortunes expended in making that settlement effectual. For themselves they fought, for themselves they conquered, and for themselves alone they have right to hold. No shilling was ever issued from the public treasures of His Majesty or his ancestors for their assistance, till of very late times, after the colonies had become established on a firm and permanent footing. That then indeed, having become valuable to Great Britain for her commercial purposes, his Parliament was pleased to lend them assistance against an enemy who would fain have drawn to herself the bene-

fits of their commerce to the great aggrandisement of herself and danger of Great Britain. . . . We do not however mean to underrate those aids which to us were doubtless valuable, on whatever principles granted: but we would show that they cannot give a title to that authority which the British Parliament would arrogate over us; and that they may amply be repaid, by our giving to the inhabitants of Great Britain such exclusive privileges in trade as may be advantageous to them, and at the same time not too restrictive to ourselves. That settlements having been thus effected in the wilds of America, the emigrants thought proper to adopt that system of laws under which they had hitherto lived in the mother country, and to continue their union with her by submitting themselves to the same common sovereign, who was thereby made the central link connecting the several parts of the empire thus newly multiplied.

But that not long were they permitted, however far they thought themselves removed from the hand of oppression, to hold undisturbed the rights thus acquired at the hazard of their lives and loss of their fortunes. . . . That country which had been acquired by the lives, the labors, and the fortunes of individual adventurers was by these princes at several times parted out and distributed among favorites and followers of their fortunes; and by an assumed right to the Crown alone were erected into distinct and independent governments; a measure which it is believed His Majesty's prudence and understanding would prevent him from imitating at this day. . . .

That the exercise of a free trade with all parts of the world possessed by the American colonists as of natural right, and which no law of their own had taken away or abridged, was next the object of unjust encroachment. . . . This arbitrary act, however, they soon recalled, and by solemn treaty entered into on March 12, 1651, between the said Commonwealth by their commissioners and the colony of Virginia by their

House of Burgesses, it was expressly stipulated by the 8th Article of the said treaty that they should have "free trade as the people of England do enjoy to all places and with all nations according to the laws of that Commonwealth." But that, upon the restoration of His Majesty King Charles II, their rights of free commerce fell once more a victim to arbitrary power: and by several acts of his reign as well as of some of his successors the trade of the colonies was laid under such restrictions as show what hopes they might form from the justice of a British Parliament were its uncontrolled power admitted over these states.

History has informed us that bodies of men as well as individuals are susceptible of the spirit of tyranny. A view of these acts of Parliament for regulation, as it has been affectedly called, of the American trade, if all other evidence were removed out of the case, would undeniably evince the truth of this observation. Besides the duties they impose on our markets of export and import, they prohibit our going to any markets northward of Cape Finesterre in the kingdom of Spain for the sale of commodities which Great Britain will not take from us, and for the purchase of others with which she cannot supply us. . . . That these acts prohibit us from carrying in quest of other purchasers the surplus of our tobaccos remaining after the consumption of Great Britain is supplied: so that we must leave them with the British merchant for whatever he will please to allow us, to be by him reshipped to foreign markets, where he will reap the benefits of making sale of them for full value.

That to heighten still the idea of parliamentary justice, and to show with what moderation they are like to exercise power, where themselves are to feel no part of its weight, we take leave to mention to His Majesty certain other acts of British Parliament, by which they would prohibit us from manufacturing for our own use the articles we raise on our own lands with our own labor. . . . We do not point out to His Majesty the injustice of these acts with intent to rest on that principle the cause of their nullity, but to show that experience confirms the propriety of those political principles which exempt us from the jurisdiction of the British Parliament. The true ground on which we declare these acts void is that the British Parliament has no right to exercise its authority over us.

That these exercises of usurped power have not been confined to instances alone in which themselves were interested; but they have also intermeddled with the regulation of the internal affairs of the colonies. The act of the ninth year of Anne for establishing a post office in America seems to have had little connection with British convenience, except that of accommodating His Majesty's ministers and favorites with the sale of a lucrative and easy office.

That thus have we hastened through the reigns which preceded His Majesty's, during which the violations of our rights were less alarming, because repeated at more distant intervals, than that rapid and bold succession of injuries which is likely to distinguish the present from all other periods of American story. Scarcely have our minds been able to emerge from the astonishment into which one stroke of parliamentary thunder has involved us, before another more heavy and more alarming is fallen on us. Single acts of tyranny may be ascribed to the accidental opinion of a day; but a series of oppressions, begun at a distinguished period, and pursued unalterably through every change of ministers, too plainly prove a deliberate, systematical plan of reducing us to slavery. . . .

But that one other act passed in the seventh year of his reign, having been a peculiar attempt, must ever require peculiar mention. It is entitled "An Act for Suspending the Legislature of New York." One free and independent legislature hereby takes upon itself to suspend the powers of another, free and independent as itself, thus exhibiting a phenomenon unknown in nature, the creator and creature of his own power. Not only the principles of common sense, but the common feelings of human nature must be surrendered up, before His Majesty's subjects here can be persuaded to believe that they hold their political existence at the will of a British Parliament.

Shall these governments be dissolved, their property annihilated, and their people reduced to a state of nature, at the imperious breath of a body of men whom they never saw, in whom they never confided, and over whom they have no powers of punishment or removal, let their crimes against the American public be ever so great? Can any one reason be assigned why 160,000 electors in the island of Great Britain should give law to 4,000,000 in the states of America, every individual of whom is equal to every individual of them in virtue, in understanding, and in bodily strength? . . .

An act of Parliament had been passed imposing duties on teas to be paid in America, against which act the Americans had protested as inauthoritative. The East India Company, who till that time had never sent a pound of tea to America on their own account, stepped forth on that occasion as the asserters of parliamentary right, and sent hither many ship loads of that obnoxious commodity. The masters of their several vessels, however, on their arrival in America, wisely attended to admonition, and returned with their cargoes.

In the province of New England alone the remonstrances of the people were disregarded, and a compliance, after being many days waited for, was flatly refused. Whether in this the master of the vessel was governed by his obstinacy or his instructions, let those who know, say. There are extraordinary situations which require extraordinary interposition. An exasperated people, who feel that they possess power, are not easily restrained within limits strictly regular. A number of them assembled in the town of Boston, threw the tea into the ocean, and dispersed without doing any other act of violence.

If in this they did wrong, they were known, and were amenable to the laws of the land, against which it could not be objected that they had ever in any instance been obstructed or diverted from their regular course in favor of popular offenders. They should therefore not have been distrusted on this occasion. But that ill-fated colony had formerly been bold in their enmities against the House of Stuart, and were now devoted to ruin by that unseen hand which governs the momentous affairs of this great Empire.

On the partial representations of a few worthless ministerial dependents, whose constant office it has been to keep that government embroiled, and who by their treacheries hope to obtain the dignity of the British knighthood, without calling for the party accused, without asking a proof, without attempting a distinction between the guilty and the innocent, the whole of that ancient and wealthy town is in a moment reduced from opulence to beggary. Men who had spent their lives in extending the British commerce, who had invested in that place the wealth their honest endeavors had merited, found themselves and their families thrown at once on the world for subsistence by its charities. Not the hundredth part of the inhabitants of that town had been concerned in the act complained of; many of them were in Great Britain and in other parts beyond sea; yet all were involved in one indiscriminate ruin, by a new executive power unheard of till then, that of a British Parliament. A property of the value of many millions of money was sacrificed to revenge, not repay, the loss of a few thousands. . . .

By the act for the suppression of riots and tumults in the town of Boston, passed also in the last session of Parliament, a murder committed there is, if the governor pleases, to be tried in a Court of King's Bench in the island of Great Britain, by a jury of Middlesex. The witnesses too, on receipt of such a sum as the governor shall think it reasonable for them to expend, are to enter into recognizance to appear at the trial. This is, in other words, taxing them to the amount of their recognizance; and that amount may be whatever a governor pleases. For who does His Majesty think can be prevailed on to cross the Atlantic for the sole purpose of bearing evidence to a fact? His expenses are to be borne indeed as they shall be estimated by a governor; but who are to feed the wife and children whom he leaves behind, and who have had no other subsistence but his daily labor? . . .

And the wretched criminal, if he happen to have offended on the American side, stripped of his privilege of trial by peers, of his vicinage, removed from the place where alone full evidence could be obtained, without money, without counsel, without friends, without exculpatory proof, is tried before judges predetermined to condemn. The cowards who would suffer a countryman to be torn from the bowels of their society in order to be thus offered a sacrifice to parliamentary tyranny, would merit that everlasting infamy now fixed on the authors of the act! . . .

That these are the acts of power assumed by a body of men foreign to our constitutions, and unacknowledged by our laws; against which we do, on behalf of the inhabitants of British America, enter this our solemn and determined protest. And we do earnestly entreat His Majesty, as yet the only mediatory power between the several states of the British empire, to recommend to his Parliament of Great Britain the total revocation of these acts, which however nugatory they be, may yet prove the cause of further discontents and jealousies among us.

That we next proceed to consider the conduct of His Majesty, as holding the executive powers of the laws of these states, and mark out his deviations from the line of duty. By the constitution of Great Britain as well as of the several American states, His Majesty possesses the power of refusing to pass into a law any bill which has already passed the other two branches of legislature. . . . The addition of new states to the British empire has produced an addition of new, and sometimes opposite interests. It is now therefore the great office of His Majesty to resume the exercise of his negative power, and to prevent the passage of laws by any one legislature of the empire which might bear injuriously on the rights and interests of another.

Yet this will not excuse the wanton exercise of this power which we have seen His Majesty practise on the laws of the American legislatures. For the most trifling reasons, and sometimes for no conceivable reason at all, His Majesty has rejected laws of the most salutary tendency. The abolition of domestic slavery is the great object of desire in those colonies where it was unhappily introduced in their infant state. But previous to the enfranchisement of the slaves we have, it is necessary to exclude all further importations from Africa. Yet our repeated attempts to effect this by prohibitions, and by imposing duties which might amount to a prohibition, have been hitherto defeated by His Majesty's negative, thus preferring the immediate advantages of a few British corsairs to the lasting interests of the American states, and to the rights of human nature deeply wounded by this infamous practice. . . .

With equal inattention to the necessities of his people here has His Majesty permitted our laws to lie neglected in England for years, neither confirming them by his assent, nor annulling them by his negative. . . .

And to render this grievance still more oppressive, His Majesty by his instructions has laid his governors under such restrictions that they can pass no law of any moment unless it has such suspending clause; so that, however immediate may be the call for legislative interposition, the law cannot be executed till it has twice crossed the Atlantic, by which time the evil may have spent its whole force.

But in what terms reconcilable to majesty, and at the same time to truth, shall we speak of a late instruction to His Majesty's governor of the colony of Virginia, by which he is forbidden to assent to any law for the division of a county, unless the new county will consent to have no representative in assembly? That colony has as yet affixed no boundary to the westward. Their western counties therefore are of indefinite extent. Some of them are actually seated many hundred miles from their eastward limits. Is it possible then that His Majesty can have bestowed a single thought on the situation of those people who, in order to obtain justice for injuries however great or small, must, by the laws of that colony, attend their county court at such a distance, with all their witnesses, monthly, till their litigation be determined? Or does His Majesty seriously wish, and publish it to the world, that his subjects should give up the glorious right of representation, with all the benefits derived from that, and submit themselves the absolute slaves of his sovereign will? Or is it rather meant to confine the legislative body to their present numbers, that they may be the cheaper bargain whenever they shall become worth a purchase? . . .

To declare as their duty required, the known rights of their country, to oppose the usurpations of every foreign judicature, to disregard the imperious mandates of a minister or governor, have been the avowed causes of dissolving houses of representatives in America. But if such powers be really vested in His Majesty, can he suppose they are there placed to awe the members from such purposes as these? When the representative body have lost the confidence of their constituents, when they have notoriously made sale of their most valuable rights, when they have assumed to themselves powers which the people never put into their hands, then indeed their continuing in office becomes dangerous to the state, and calls for an exercise of the power of dissolution. Such being the causes for which the representative body should and should not be dissolved, will it not appear strange to an unbiased observer that that of Great Britain was not dissolved, while those of the colonies have repeatedly incurred that sentence?

But Your Majesty or your governors have carried this power beyond every limit known or provided for by the laws. After dissolving one house of representatives, they have refused to call another, so that for a great length of time the legislature provided by the laws has been out of existence. From the nature of things, every society must at all times possess within itself the sovereign powers of legislation. The feelings of human nature revolt against the supposition of a state so situated as that it may not in any emergency provide against dangers which perhaps threaten immediate ruin. While those bodies are in existence to whom the people have delegated the powers of legislation, they alone possess and may exercise those powers. But when they are dissolved by the lopping off one or more of their branches, the power reverts to the people, who may exercise it to unlimited extent, either assembling together in person, sending deputies, or in any other way they may think proper. We forbear to trace consequences further; the dangers are conspicuous with which this practice is replete.

That we shall at this time also take notice of an error in the nature of our landholdings, which crept in at a very early period of our settlement. . . . Our ancestors who emigrated hither were farmers, not lawyers. The fictitious principle that all lands belong originally to the king, they were early persuaded to believe real, and accordingly took grants of their own lands from the Crown. And while the Crown continued to grant for small sums and on reasonable rents, there was no inducement to arrest the error and lay it open to the public view. But His Majesty has lately taken on him to advance the terms of purchase and of holding to the double of what they were, by which means the acquisition of lands being rendered difficult, the population of our country is likely to be checked. It is time therefore for us to lay this matter before His Majesty, and to declare that he has no right to grant lands of himself. From the nature and purpose of civil institutions, all the lands within the limits which any particular society has circumscribed around itself are assumed by that society, and subject to their allotment only. This may be done by themselves assembled collectively, or by their legislature to whom they may have delegated sovereign authority: and, if they are allotted in neither of these ways, each individual of the society may appropriate to himself such lands as he finds vacant, and occupancy will give him title.

That in order to enforce the arbitrary measures before complained of, His Majesty has from time to time sent among us large bodies of armed forces, not made up of the people here, nor raised by the authority of our laws. Did His Majesty possess such a right as this, it might swallow up all our other rights whenever he should think proper. But His Majesty has no right to land a single armed man on our shores; and those whom he sends here are liable to our laws for the suppression and punishment of riots, and unlawful assemblies, or are hostile bodies invading us in defiance of the law. When in the course of the late war it became expedient that a body of Hanoverian troops should be brought over for the defense of Great Britain, His Majesty's grandfather, our late sovereign, did not pretend

to introduce them under any authority he possessed. Such a measure would have given just alarm to his subjects in Great Britain, whose liberties would not be safe if armed men of another country, and of another spirit, might be brought into the Realm at any time without the consent of their legislature.

He therefore applied to Parliament who passed an act for that purpose, limiting the number to be brought in and the time they were to continue. In like manner is His Majesty restrained in every part of the empire. He possesses indeed the executive power of the laws in every state; but they are the laws of the particular state which he is to administer within that state, and not those of any one within the limits of another. Every state must judge for itself the number of armed men which they may safely trust among them, of whom they are to consist, and under what restrictions they shall be laid.

To render these proceedings still more criminal against our laws, instead of subjecting the military to the civil powers, His Majesty has expressly made the civil subordinate to the military. But can His Majesty thus put down all law under his feet? Can he erect a power superior to that which erected himself? He has done it indeed by force; but let him remember that force cannot give right.

That these are our grievances which we have thus laid before His Majesty with that freedom of language and sentiment which becomes a free people, claiming their rights as derived from the laws of nature, and not as the gift of their chief magistrate. Let those flatter, who fear: it is not an American art. . .

You are surrounded by British counselors, but remember that they are parties. You have no minister for American affairs, because you have none taken from among us, nor amenable to the laws on which they are to give you advice. It behooves you therefore to think and to act for yourself and your people. The great principles of right and wrong are legible to every reader: to pursue them requires not the aid of many counselors. The whole art of government consists in the art of being honest. . . .

Let no act be passed by any one legislature which may infringe on the rights and liberties of another. This is the important post in which fortune has placed you, holding the balance of a great, if a well-poised empire. This, sire, is the advice of your great American council, on the observance of which may perhaps depend your felicity and future fame, and the preservation of that harmony which alone can continue both in Great Britain and America and reciprocal advantages of their connection. It is neither our wish nor our interest to separate from her. We are willing on our part to sacrifice everything which reason can ask to the restoration of that tranquillity for which all must wish. . . . The God who gave us life, gave us liberty at the same time: the hand of force may destroy, but cannot disjoin them.

This, sire, is our last, our determined resolution: and that you will be pleased to interpose with that efficacy which your earnest endeavors may insure to procure redress of these our great grievances, to quiet the minds of your subjects in British America against any apprehensions of future encroachment to establish fraternal love and harmony through the whole empire, and that these may continue to the latest ages of time, is the fervent prayer of all British America.

JOSEPH GALLOWAY: A Plan for the Union of Great Britain and the Colonies

To solve the difficulties with Great Britain, Joseph Galloway of Pennsylvania proposed a Plan of Union in the Continental Congress that had convened in Philadelphia in September 1774. Though favorably received by many delegates, the plan was defeated by a six to five vote of colonies. It was the sudden arrival of news concerning the resolutions passed in Suffolk County (Boston), Massachusetts, that turned sentiment away from this effort at compromise. Six years later Galloway reminisced on the fate of this plan, which is reprinted here. "While the two parties in Congress [Loyalist and Republican] remained thus during three weeks on an equal balance," he wrote in 1780, "the republicans were calling to their assistance the aid of their factions without. Continual expresses were employed between Philadelphia and Boston. These were under the management of Samuel Adams — a man, who though by no means remarkable for brilliant abilities, yet is equal to most men in popular intrigue and the management of a faction. . . . It was this man, who by his superior application managed at once the faction in Congress at Philadelphia and the factions in New England. Whatever these patriots in Congress wished to have done by their colleagues without, to induce General Gage, then at the head of his Majesty's army at Boston, to give them a pretext for violent opposition or to promote their measures in Congress, Mr. Adams advised and directed to be done; and when done, it was dispatched by express to Congress. By one of these expresses came the inflammatory resolves of the county of Suffolk, which contained a complete declaration of war against Great Britain."

Source: *Archives*, I, pp. 905-906.

Resolved, that this Congress will apply to His Majesty for a redress of grievances under which his faithful subjects in America labor; and assure him that the colonies hold in abhorrence the idea of being considered independent communities on the British government, and most ardently desire the establishment of a political union, not only among themselves but with the mother state, upon those principles of safety and freedom which are essential in the constitution of all free governments, and particularly that of the British legislature. And as the colonies from their local circumstances cannot be represented in the Parliament of Great Britain, they will humbly propose to His Majesty and his two houses of Parliament the following plan, under which the strength of the whole empire may be drawn together on any emergency, the interest of both countries advanced, and the rights and liberties of America secured: *A Plan for a Proposed Union between Great Britain and the Colonies of New Hampshire, the Massachusetts Bay, Rhode Island, Connecticut, New York, New Jersey, Pennsylvania, Maryland, the Three Lower Counties on the Delaware, Virginia, North Carolina, South Carolina, and Georgia.*

That a British and American legislature, for regulating the administration of the general affairs of America, be proposed and established in America, including all the said colonies; within and under which government each colony shall retain its present constitution and powers of regulating and governing its own internal police, in all cases whatever.

That the said government be administered by a president general, to be appointed by the King, and a Grand Council, to be chosen by the representatives of the people of the several colonies, in their respective assemblies, once in every three years.

That the several assemblies shall choose members for the Grand Council in the following proportions, viz.:

New Hampshire ——, Massachusetts Bay ——, Rhode Island ——, Connecticut ——, New York ——, New Jersey ——, Pennsylvania ——, Delaware Counties ——, Maryland ——, Virginia ——, North Carolina ——, South Carolina ——, Georgia ——, who shall meet at the city of ——— for the first time, being called by the president general as soon as conveniently may be after his appointment.

That there shall be a new election of members for the Grand Council every three years; and on the death, removal, or resignation of any member, his place shall be supplied by a new choice at the next sitting of assembly of the colony he represented.

That the Grand Council shall meet once in every year if they shall think it necessary, and oftener if occasions shall require, at such time and place as they shall adjourn to at the last preceding meeting, or as they shall be called to meet at by the president general on any emergency.

That the Grand Council shall have power to choose their speaker, and shall hold and exercise all the like rights, liberties, and privileges as are held and exercised by and in the House of Commons of Great Britain.

That the president general shall hold his office during the pleasure of the King and his assent shall be requisite to all acts of the Grand Council, and it shall be his office and duty to cause them to be carried into execution.

That the president general, by and with the advice and consent of the Grand Council, hold and exercise all the legislative rights, powers, and authorities necessary for regulating and administering all the general police and affairs of the colonies in which Great Britain and the colonies, or any of them, the colonies in general, or more than one colony, are in any manner concerned, as well civil and criminal as commercial.

That the said president general and the Grand Council be an inferior and distinct branch of the British legislature, united and incorporated with it for the aforesaid general purposes; and that any of the said general regulations may originate and be formed and digested, either in the Parliament of Great Britain or in the said Grand Council, and being prepared, transmitted to the other for their approbation or dissent; and that the assent of both shall be requisite to the validity of all such general acts and stat-utes.

That in time of war, all bills for granting aid to the Crown, prepared by the Grand Council and approved by the president general, shall be valid and passed into a law, without the assent of the British Parliament.

Declaration and Resolves of the Continental Congress

After the rejection of the Galloway Plan of Union the Continental Congress, on October 14, 1774, adopted the following declaration of colonial rights. Major John Sullivan, delegate from New Hampshire, drafted the resolutions. The Congress voted to reconvene the following year unless the grievances set forth in the declaration were settled.

Source: *Journals*, I: "Friday, October 14, 1774."

Whereas, since the close of the last war, the British Parliament, claiming a power of right to bind the people of America by statutes in all cases whatsoever, has in some acts expressly imposed taxes on them, and in others, under various pretenses but in fact for the purpose of raising a revenue, has imposed rates and duties payable in these colonies; established a Board of Commissioners with unconstitutional powers; and extended the jurisdiction of Courts of Admiralty, not only for collecting the said duties but for the trial of causes merely arising within the body of a county.

And whereas, in consequence of other statutes, judges, who before held only estates at will in their offices, have been made dependent on the Crown alone for their salaries, and standing armies kept in times of peace. *And whereas* it has lately been resolved in Parliament that, by force of a statute made in the thirty-fifth year of the reign of King Henry the Eighth, colonists may be transported to England and tried there upon accusations for treasons, and misprisions, or concealments of treasons committed in the colonies; and by a late statute, such trials have been directed in cases therein mentioned.

And whereas, in the last session of Parliament, three statutes were made; one, entitled "An act to discontinue, in such manner and for such time as are therein mentioned, the landing and discharging, lading, or shipping of goods, wares, and merchandise at the town, and within the harbor of Boston, in the province of Massachusetts Bay, in North America"; another, entitled "An act for the better regulating the government of the province of Massachusetts Bay in New England"; and another, entitled "An act for the impartial administration of justice in the cases of persons questioned for any act done by them in the execution of the law, or for the suppression of riots and tumults in the province of the Massachusetts Bay in New England"; and another statute was then made, "for making more effectual provision for the government of the province of Quebec, etc."; all which statutes are impolitic, unjust, and cruel, as well as unconstitutional, and most dangerous and destructive of American rights.

And whereas, assemblies have been frequently dissolved, contrary to the rights of the people, when they attempted to deliberate on grievances; and their dutiful, humble, loyal, and reasonable petitions to the Crown for redress have been repeatedly treated with contempt by His Majesty's ministers of state:

The good people of the several colonies of New Hampshire; Massachusetts Bay; Rhode Island and Providence Plantations; Connecticut; New York; New Jersey; Pennsylvania; Newcastle, Kent, and Sussex on Delaware; Maryland; Virginia; North Carolina; and South Carolina, justly alarmed at these arbitrary proceedings of Parliament and administration, have severally elected, constituted, and appointed deputies to meet and sit in General Congress in the city of Philadelphia in order to obtain such establishment as that their religion, laws, and liberties may not be subverted:

Whereupon the deputies so appointed being now assembled, in a full and free representation of these colonies, taking into their most serious consideration the best means of attaining the ends aforesaid, do, in the first place, as Englishmen, their ancestors in like cases have usually done, for affecting and vindicating their rights and liberties, declare,

That the inhabitants of the English colonies in North America, by the immutable laws of nature, the principles of the English constitution, and the several charters or compacts, have the following rights:

Resolved:

1. That they are entitled to life, liberty, and property, and they have never ceded to any sovereign power whatever a right to dispose of either without their consent.

2. That our ancestors, who first settled these colonies, were at the time of their emigration from the mother country entitled to all the rights, liberties, and immunities of free and natural-born subjects, within the Realm of England.

3. That by such emigration they by no means forfeited, surrendered, or lost any of those rights, but that they were, and their descendants now are, entitled to the exercise and enjoyment of all such of them as their local and other circumstances enable them to exercise and enjoy.

4. That the foundation of English liberty, and of all free government, is a right in the people to participate in their legislative council; and as the English colonists are not represented, and from their local and other circumstances cannot properly be represented in the British Parliament, they are entitled to a free and exclusive power of legislation in their several provincial legislatures, where their right of representation can alone be preserved, in all cases of taxation and internal polity, subject only to the negative of their sovereign, in such manner as has been heretofore used and accustomed. But, from the necessity of the case and a regard to the mutual interest of both countries, we cheerfully consent to the operation of such acts of the British Parliament as are bona fide, restrained to the regulation of our external commerce, for the purpose of securing the commercial advantages of the whole empire to the mother country, and the commercial benefits of its respective members; excluding every idea of taxation, internal or external, for raising a revenue on the subjects in America without their consent.

5. That the respective colonies are entitled to the common law of England, and more especially to the great and inestimable privilege of being tried by their peers of the vicinage according to the course of that law.

6. That they are entitled to the benefit of such of the English statutes as existed at the time of their colonization; and which they have, by experience, respectively found to be applicable to their several local and other circumstances.

7. That these, His Majesty's colonies, are likewise entitled to all the immunities and privileges granted and confirmed to them by royal charters, or secured by their several codes of provincial laws.

Peyton Randolph (1721-1775), president of the 1st Continental Congress; portrait by Wollaston

8. That they have a right peaceably to assemble, consider of their grievances, and petition the King; and that all prosecutions, prohibitory proclamations, and commitments for the same are illegal.

9. That the keeping of a standing army in these colonies, in times of peace, without the consent of the legislature of that colony in which such army is kept is against law.

10. It is indispensably necessary to good government, and rendered essential by the English constitution, that the constituent branches of the legislature be independent of each other; that, therefore, the exercise of legislative power in several colonies, by a council appointed during pleasure by the Crown, is unconstitutional, dangerous, and destructive to the freedom of American legislation.

All and each of which the aforesaid deputies, in behalf of themselves and their constituents, do claim, demand, and insist on as their indubitable rights and liberties; which cannot be legally taken from them, altered or abridged by any power whatever, without their own consent, by their representatives in their several provincial legislatures.

In the course of our inquiry, we find many infringements and violations of the foregoing rights, which, from an ardent desire that harmony and mutual intercourse of affection and interest may be restored, we pass over for the present, and proceed to state such acts and measures as have been adopted since the last war, which demonstrate a system formed to enslave America.

Resolved, that the following acts of Parliament are infringements and violations of the rights of the colonists; and that the repeal of them is essentially necessary in order to restore harmony between Great Britain and the American colonies, viz.:

The several acts . . . which impose duties for the purpose of raising a revenue in America, extend the powers of the Admiralty Courts beyond their ancient limits, deprive the American subject of trial by jury, authorize the judge's certificate to indemnify the prosecutor from damages that he might otherwise be liable to, requiring oppressive security from a claimant of ships and goods seized, before he shall be allowed to defend his property, and are subversive of American rights.

Also [the act] entitled "An act for the better securing His Majesty's dockyards, magazines, ships, ammunition, and stores," which declares a new offense in America, and deprives the American subject of a constitutional trial by jury of the vicinage, by authorizing the trial of any person, charged with the committing any offense described in the said act, out of the Realm, to be indicted and tried for the same in any shire or county within the Realm.

Also the three acts passed in the last session of Parliament for stopping the port and blocking up the harbor of Boston, for altering the charter and government of Massachusetts Bay, and that which is entitled "An act for the better administration of justice, etc."

Also the act passed the same session for establishing the Roman Catholic religion in the province of Quebec, abolishing the equitable system of English laws, and erecting a tyranny there to the great danger, from so total a dissimilarity of religion, law, and government of the neighboring British colonies, by the assistance of whose blood and treasure the said country was conquered from France.

Also the act passed the same session for the better providing suitable quarters for officers and soldiers in His Majesty's service in North America.

Also, that the keeping a standing army in several of these colonies, in time of peace, without the consent of the legislature of that colony in which the army is kept, is against law.

To these grievous acts and measures Americans cannot submit, but in hopes that their fellow subjects in Great Britain will, on a revision of them, restore us to that state in which both countries found happiness and prosperity, we have for the present only resolved to pursue the following peaceable measures:

1. To enter into a nonimportation, nonconsumption, and nonexportation agreement or association.

2. To prepare an address to the people of Great Britain and a memorial to the inhabitants of British America.

3. To prepare a loyal address to His Majesty, agreeable to resolutions already entered into.

JOHN JAY: Address to the People of Great Britain

John Jay, of New York, favored effective central government in the interests of the merchants and property owners. He supported the colonial cause, although he deplored violence in the quarrel between Great Britain and America, hoping, until the eve of independence, for a reconciliation with the mother country. As a member of the First Continental Congress, Jay was appointed in October 1774 to draft the following address, stating the rights of the colonists in a spirit of moderation and conciliation.

Source: Johnston, I, pp. 17-31.

WHEN A NATION, led to greatness by the hand of liberty, and possessed of all the glory that heroism, munificence, and humanity can bestow, descends to the ungrateful task of forging chains for her friends and children, and instead of giving support to freedom, turns advocate for slavery and oppression, there is reason to suspect she has either ceased to be virtuous, or been extremely negligent in the appointment of her rulers.

In almost every age, in repeated conflicts, in long and bloody wars, as well civil as foreign, against many and powerful nations, against the open assaults of enemies and the more dangerous treachery of friends, have the inhabitants of your island, your great and glorious ancestors, maintained their independence, and transmitted the rights of men and the blessings of liberty to you, their posterity.

Be not surprised, therefore, that we, who

are descended from the same common ancestors, that we, whose forefathers participated in all the rights, the liberties, and the constitution you so justly boast of, and who have carefully conveyed the same fair inheritance to us, guaranteed by the plighted faith of government and the most solemn compacts with British sovereigns, should refuse to surrender them to men who found their claims on no principles of reason, and who prosecute them with a design that, by having *our* lives and property in their power, they may with the greater facility enslave *you*.

The cause of America is now the object of universal attention; it has at length become very serious. This unhappy country has not only been oppressed but abused and misrepresented; and the duty we owe to ourselves and posterity, to your interest, and the general welfare of the British empire, leads us to address you on this very important subject.

Know then, that we consider ourselves, and do insist that we are and ought to be, as free as our fellow subjects in Britain, and that no power on earth has a right to take our property from us without our consent.

That we claim all the benefits secured to the subject by the English constitution, and particularly that inestimable one of trial by jury.

That we hold it essential to English liberty that no man be condemned unheard, or punished for supposed offenses without having an opportunity of making his defense.

That we think the legislature of Great Britain is not authorized by the constitution to establish a religion fraught with sanguinary and impious tenets, or to erect an arbitrary form of government in any quarter of the globe. These rights we, as well as you, deem sacred. And yet, sacred as they are, they have, with many others, been repeatedly and flagrantly violated.

Are not the proprietors of the soil of Great Britain lords of their own property? Can it be taken from them without their consent? Will they yield it to the arbitrary disposal of any man or number of men whatever? You know they will not.

Why then are the proprietors of the soil of America less lords of their property than you are of yours? Or why should they submit it to the disposal of your Parliament, or any other parliament or council in the world not of their election? Can the intervention of the sea that divides us cause disparity in rights? Or can any reason be given why English subjects who live 3,000 miles from the royal palace should enjoy less liberty than those who are 300 miles distant from it?

Reason looks with indignation on such distinctions, and freemen can never perceive their propriety. And yet, however chimerical and unjust such discriminations are, the Parliament assert that they have a right to bind us in all cases without exception, whether we consent or not; that they may take and use our property when and in what manner they please; that we are pensioners on their bounty for all that we possess, and can hold it no longer than they vouchsafe to permit. Such declarations we consider as heresies in English politics, and which can no more operate to deprive us of our property, than the interdicts of the pope can divest kings of scepters which the laws of the land and the voice of the people have placed in their hands.

At the conclusion of the late war — a war rendered glorious by the abilities and integrity of a minister to whose efforts the British empire owes its safety and its fame — at the conclusion of this war, which was succeeded by an inglorious peace, formed under the auspices of a minister of principles and of a family unfriendly to the Protestant cause and inimical to liberty; we say, at this period, and under the influence of that man, a plan for enslaving your fellow subjects in America was concerted, and has ever since been pertinaciously carrying into execution.

Prior to this era, you were content with

drawing from us the wealth produced by our commerce. You restrained our trade in every way that could conduce to your emolument. You exercised unbounded sovereignty over the sea. You named the ports and nations to which alone our merchandise should be carried, and with whom alone we should trade; and though some of these restrictions were grievous, we nevertheless did not complain. We looked up to you as to our parent state, to which we were bound by the strongest ties; and were happy in being instrumental to your prosperity and grandeur.

We call upon you yourselves to witness our loyalty and attachment to the common interest of the whole empire. Did we not, in the last war, add all the strength of this vast continent to the force which repelled our common enemy? Did we not leave our native shores, and meet disease and death, to promote the success of British arms in foreign climates? Did you not thank us for our zeal, and even reimburse us large sums of money which, you confessed, we had advanced beyond our proportion; and far beyond our abilities? You did.

To what causes, then, are we to attribute the sudden changes of treatment, and that system of slavery which was prepared for us at the restoration of peace?

Before we had recovered from the distresses which ever attend war, an attempt was made to drain this country of all its money by the oppressive Stamp Act. Paint, glass, and other commodities which you would not permit us to purchase of other nations were taxed; nay, although no wine is made in any country subject to the British state, you prohibited our procuring it of foreigners without paying a tax imposed by your Parliament on all we imported. These and many other impositions were laid upon us most unjustly and unconstitutionally for the express purpose of raising a revenue. In order to silence complaint, it was indeed provided that this revenue should be expended in America for its protection and

defense. These exactions, however, can receive no justification from a pretended necessity of protecting and defending us. They are lavishly squandered on court favorites and ministerial dependents, generally avowed enemies to America, and employing themselves by partial representations to traduce and embroil the colonies.

For the necessary support of government here, we ever were and ever shall be ready to provide. And whenever the exigencies of the state may require it, we shall, as we have heretofore done, cheerfully contribute our full proportion of men and money. To enforce this unconstitutional and unjust scheme of taxation, every fence that the wisdom of our British ancestors had carefully erected against arbitrary power has been violently thrown down in America, and the inestimable right of trial by jury taken away in cases that touch life and property. It was ordained that whenever offenses should be committed in the colonies against particular acts imposing various duties and restrictions upon trade, the prosecutor might bring his action for the penalties in the Courts of Admiralty; by which means the subject lost the advantage of being tried by an honest, uninfluenced jury of the vicinage, and was subjected to the sad necessity of being judged by a single man, a creature of the Crown, and according to the course of a law which exempts the prosecutor from the trouble of proving his accusation, and obliges the defendant either to evince his innocence or to suffer. To give this new judicatory the greater importance, and as if with design to protect false accusers, it is further provided that the judge's certificate of there having been probable causes of seizure and prosecution shall protect the prosecutor from actions at common law for recovery of damages.

By the course of our law, offenses committed in such of the British dominions in which courts are established and justice duly and regularly administered shall be there tried by a jury of the vicinage. There the offenders and witnesses are known, and the degree of credibility to be given to their testimony can be ascertained.

In all these colonies, justice is regularly and impartially administered; and yet, by the construction of some, and the direction of other acts of Parliament, offenders are to be taken by force, together with all such persons as may be pointed out as witnesses, and carried to England, there to be tried in a distant land, by a jury of strangers, and subject to all the disadvantages that result from want of friends, want of witnesses, and want of money.

When the design of raising a revenue from the duties imposed on the importation of tea into America had in a great measure been rendered abortive by our ceasing to import that commodity, a scheme was concerted by the Ministry with the East India Company, and an act passed enabling and encouraging them to transport and vend it in the colonies. Aware of the danger of giving success to this insidious maneuver, and of permitting a precedent of taxation thus to be established among us, various methods were adopted to elude the stroke. The people of Boston, then ruled by a governor whom, as well as his predecessor Sir Francis Bernard, all America considers as her enemy, were exceedingly embarrassed. The ships which had arrived with the tea were by his management prevented from returning. The duties would have been paid, the cargoes landed and exposed to sale; a governor's influence would have procured and protected many purchasers.

While the town was suspended by deliberations on this important subject, the tea was destroyed. Even supposing a trespass was thereby committed, and the proprietors of the tea entitled to damages, the courts of law were open, and judges appointed by the Crown presided in them. The East India Company, however, did not think proper to commence any suits, nor did they even demand satisfaction either from individuals or from the community in general. The Minis-

try, it seems, officiously made the case their own, and the great council of the nation descended to intermeddle with a dispute about private property.

Diverse papers, letters, and other unauthenticated *ex parte* evidence were laid before them; neither the persons who destroyed the tea nor the people of Boston were called upon to answer the complaint. The Ministry, incensed by being disappointed in a favorite scheme, were determined to recur from the little arts of finesse to open force and unmanly violence. The port of Boston was blocked up by a fleet, and an army placed in the town. Their trade was to be suspended, and thousands reduced to the necessity of gaining subsistence from charity till they should submit to pass under the yoke, and consent to become slaves by confessing the omnipotence of Parliament and acquiescing in whatever disposition they might think proper to make of their lives and property.

Let justice and humanity cease to be the boast of your nation! Consult your history, examine your records of former transactions, nay, turn to the annals of the many arbitrary states and kingdoms that surround you, and show us a single instance of men being condemned to suffer for imputed crimes, unheard, unquestioned, and without even the specious formality of a trial; and that, too, by laws made expressly for the purpose, and which had no existence at the time of the fact committed. If it be difficult to reconcile these proceedings to the genius and temper of your laws and constitution, the task will become more arduous when we call upon our ministerial enemies to justify not only condemning men untried and by hearsay but involving the innocent in one common punishment with the guilty, and for the act of 30 or 40, to bring poverty, distress, and calamity on 30,000 souls, and those not your enemies but your friends, brethren, and fellow subjects.

It would be some consolation to us if the catalogue of American oppressions ended here. It gives us pain to be reduced to the necessity of reminding you that under the confidence reposed in the faith of government, pledged in a royal charter from a British sovereign, the forefathers of the present inhabitants of the Massachusetts Bay left their former habitations and established that great, flourishing, and loyal colony. Without incurring or being charged with a forfeiture of their rights, without being heard, without being tried, without law, and without justice, by an act of Parliament their charter is destroyed, their liberties violated, their constitution and form of government changed. And all this upon no better pretense than because in one of their towns a trespass was committed on some merchandise said to belong to one of the companies, and because the Ministry were of opinion that such high political regulations were necessary to compel due subordination and obedience to their mandates.

Nor are these the only capital grievances under which we labor. We might tell of dissolute, weak, and wicked governors having been set over us; of legislatures being suspended for asserting the rights of British subjects; of needy and ignorant dependents on great men advanced to the seats of justice and to other places of trust and importance; of hard restrictions on commerce, and a great variety of lesser evils, the recollection of which is almost lost under the weight and pressure of greater and more poignant calamities.

Now mark the progression of the ministerial plan for enslaving us. Well aware that such hardy attempts to take our property from us, to deprive us of the valuable right of trial by jury, to seize our persons and carry us for trial to Great Britain, to blockade our ports, to destroy our charters, and change our forms of government would occasion, and had already occasioned, great discontent in the colonies, which might produce opposition to these measures; an act was passed to protect, indemnify, and screen from punishment such as might be

guilty even of murder, in endeavoring to carry their oppressive edicts into execution; and by another act the Dominion of Canada is to be so extended, modeled, and governed, as that by being disunited from us, detached from our interests by civil as well as religious prejudices, that by their numbers daily swelling with Catholic emigrants from Europe, and by their devotion to an administration so friendly to their religion, they might become formidable to us, and, on occasion, be fit instruments in the hands of power to reduce the ancient, free, Protestant colonies to the same state of slavery with themselves.

This was evidently the object of the act; and in this view, being extremely dangerous to our liberty and quiet, we cannot forbear complaining of it as hostile to British America. Superadded to these considerations, we cannot help deploring the unhappy condition to which it has reduced the many English settlers who, encouraged by the royal proclamation promising the enjoyment of all their rights, have purchased estates in that country. They are now the subjects of an arbitrary government, deprived of trial by jury, and when imprisoned, cannot claim the benefit of the Habeas Corpus Act, that great bulwark and palladium of English liberty. Nor can we suppress our astonishment that a British Parliament should ever consent to establish in that country a religion that has deluged your island in blood, and dispersed impiety, bigotry, persecution, murder, and rebellion through every part of the world.

This being a state of facts, let us beseech you to consider to what end they lead. Admit that the Ministry, by the powers of Britain and the aid of our Roman Catholic neighbors, should be able to carry the point of taxation, and reduce us to a state of perfect humiliation and slavery. Such an enterprise would doubtless make some addition to your national debt which already presses down your liberties and fills you with pensioners and placemen. We presume, also, that your commerce will somewhat be diminished. However, suppose you should prove victorious, in what condition will you then be? What advantages or what laurels will you reap from such a conquest? May not a Ministry with the same armies enslave you? It may be said you will cease to pay them; but remember, the taxes from America, the wealth, and we may add the men, and particularly the Roman Catholics of this vast continent, will then be in the power of your enemies; nor will you have any reason to expect that after making slaves of us, many among us should refuse to assist in reducing you to the same abject state.

Do not treat this as chimerical. Know that in less than half a century the quitrents reserved to the Crown from the numberless grants of this vast continent will pour large streams of wealth into the royal coffers. And if to this be added the power of taxing America at pleasure, the Crown will be rendered independent of you for supplies, and will possess more treasure than may be necessary to purchase the remains of liberty in your island. In a word, take care that you do not fall into the pit that is preparing for us.

We believe there is yet much virtue, much justice, and much public spirit in the English nation. To that justice we now appeal. You have been told that we are seditious, impatient of government, and desirous of independence. Be assured that these are not facts, but calumnies. Permit us to be as free as yourselves, and we shall ever esteem a union with you to be our greatest glory, and our greatest happiness; we shall ever be ready to contribute all in our power to the welfare of the empire; we shall consider your enemies as our enemies, and your interest as our own.

But if you are determined that your ministers shall wantonly sport with the rights of mankind; if neither the voice of justice, the dictates of the law, the principles of the constitution, or the suggestions of humanity can restrain your hands from shedding human blood in such an impious cause, we must then tell you that we will never submit to be hewers of wood or drawers of water for any ministry or nation in the world.

Place us in the same situation that we were at the close of the last war, and our former harmony will be restored.

But lest the same supineness and the same inattention to our common interest which you have for several years shown should continue, we think it prudent to anticipate the consequences.

By the destruction of the trade of Boston the Ministry have endeavored to induce submission to their measures. The like fate may befall us all. We will endeavor, therefore, to live without trade, and recur for subsistence to the fertility and bounty of our native soil, which affords us all the necessaries and some of the conveniences of life. We have suspended our importation from Great Britain and Ireland; and in less than a year's time, unless our grievances should be redressed, shall discontinue our exports to those kingdoms and the West Indies.

It is with the utmost regret, however, that we find ourselves compelled by the overruling principles of self-preservation to adopt measures detrimental in their consequences to numbers of our fellow subjects in Great Britain and Ireland. But we hope that the magnanimity and justice of the British nation will furnish a Parliament of such wisdom, independence, and public spirit as may save the violated rights of the whole empire from the devices of wicked ministers and evil counselors, whether in or out of office, and thereby restore that harmony, friendship, and fraternal affection between all the inhabitants of His Majesty's kingdoms and territories so ardently wished for by every true and honest American.

John Trumbull: "An Elegy on the Times"

John Trumbull's first poem about national affairs, An Elegy on the Times, *written in 1774, was a "glittering, bombastic piece" that bore a patriotic message. In the role of a liberal, Trumbull attacked British economic policies but was still, at this time, hopeful of avoiding open conflict.*

Source: **Poetical Works**, Hartford, Conn., 1820, Vol. II, p. 205-217.

🙿 AN ELEGY ON THE TIMES

Oh Boston! late with every beauty crowned,
    Where Commerce triumphed on the favoring gales;
And each pleased eye, that roved in prospect round,
    Hailed thy bright spires and blessed thy opening sails!

Thy splendid mart with rich profusion smiled,
    The gay throng crowded in thy spacious streets,
From either Ind, thy cheerful stores were filled,
    Thy haven joyous with unnumbered fleets.

For here, more fair than in their native vales,
    Tall groves of masts arose in beauteous pride;
Glad ocean shone beneath the swelling sails,
    And wafted plenty on the bordering tide.

Alas how changed! the swelling sails no more
    Catch the soft airs and wanton in the sky:
But hostile beaks affright the guarded shore,
    And pointed thunders all access deny.

Where the bold cape its warning forehead rears,
    Where tyrant vengeance waved her fatal wand,
Far from the sight each friendly vessel veers,
    And flies averse the interdicted strand.

Along thy fields, which late in beauty shone,
  With lowing herds and grassy vesture fair,
The insulting tents of barbarous troops are strown,
  And bloody standards stain the peaceful air.

Are these thy deeds, oh Britain? this the praise,
  That gilds the fading luster of thy name,
These the bold trophies of thy later days,
  That close the period of thine early fame?

Shall thy strong fleets, with awful sails unfurled,
  On freedom's shrine the unhallowed vengeance bend,
And leave forlorn the desolated world,
  Crushed every foe and ruined every friend?

And quenched, alas, the soul-inspiring ray,
  Where virtue kindled and where genius soared;
Or damped by darkness and the dismal sway
  Of senates venal and liveried lord?

There pride sits blazoned on the unmeaning brow,
  And over the scene thy factious nobles wait,
Prompt the mixed tumult of the noisy show,
  Guide the blind vote and rule the mock debate.

To these how vain, in weary woes forlorn,
  With abject fear the fond complaint to raise,
Lift fruitless offerings to the ear of scorn
  Of servile vows and well-dissembled praise!

Will the grim savage of the nightly fold
  Learn from their cries the blameless flock to spare?
Will the deaf gods, that frown in molten gold,
  Heed the duped votary and the prostrate prayer?

With what pleased hope before the throne of pride,
  We reared our suppliant hands with filial awe,
While loud Disdain with ruffian voice replied,
  And falsehood triumphed in the garb of law?

While Peers enraptured hail the unmanly wrong,
  See Ribaldry, vile prostitute of shame,
Stretch the bribed hand and dart the envenomed tongue,
  To blast the laurels of a Franklin's fame!

But will the Sage, whose philosophic soul
  Controlled the lightning in its fierce career,
Over heaven's dread vault bade harmless thunders roll,
  And taught the bolts ethereal where to steer;

Will he, while echoing to his just renown,
  The voice of kingdoms swells the loud applause,
Heed the weak malice of a courtier's frown,
  Or dread the insolence of wrested laws?

Yet nought avail the virtues of the heart,
  The vengeful bolt no muse's laurels ward;
From Britain's rage, like death's relentless dart,
  No worth can save us and no fame can guard.

Over hallowed bounds see dire oppression roll,
  Fair Freedom buried in the whelming flood;
Nor chartered rights her tyrant course control,
  Tho' sealed by kings and witnessed in our blood.

In vain we hope from ministerial pride
  A hand to save us or a heart to bless:
'Tis strength, our own, must stem the rushing tide,
  'Tis our own virtue must command success.

But oh my friends, the arm of blood restrain,
  (No rage intemperate aids the public weal;)
Nor basely blend, too daring but in vain,
  The assassin's madness with the patriot's zeal.

Ours be the manly firmness of the sage,
  From shameless foes ungrateful wrongs to bear;
Alike removed from baseness and from rage,
  The flames of faction and the chills of fear.

Repel the torrent of commercial gain,
  That buys our ruin at a price so rare,
And while we scorn Britannia's servile chain,
  Disdain the livery of her marts to wear.

For shall the lust of fashion and of show,
  The curst idolatry of silks and lace,
Bid our gay robes insult our country's woe,
  And welcome slavery in the glare of dress?

No — the rich produce of our fertile soil
  Shall clothe in neat array the cheerful train,
While heaven-born virtues bless the sacred toil,
  And gild the humble vestures of the plain.

No foreign labor in the Asian field
  Shall weave her silks to deck the wanton age:
But as in Rome, the furrowed vale shall yield
  The conquering hero and paternal sage.

And ye, whose heaven in golden pomp to shine,
  And warmly press the dissipated round,
Grace the ripe banquet with the charms of wine,
  And roll the thundering chariot over the ground;

For this, while guised in sycophantic smile,
  With heart regardless of your country's pain,
Your flattering falsehoods feed the ears of guile,
  And barter freedom for the dreams of gain!

Are these the joys on vassal-realms that wait;
  In downs of ease and dalliance to repose,
Quaff streams nectareous in the domes of state,
  And blaze in grandeur of imperial shows?

No — the hard hand, the tortured brow of care,
  The thatch-roofed hamlet and defenseless shed,
The tattered garb, that meets the inclement air,
  The famished table and the matted bed —

These are their fate. In vain the arm of toil
  With gifts autumnal crowns the bearded plain,
In vain glad summer warms the genial soil,
  And spring dissolves in softening showers in vain;

There savage power extends a dreary shade,
  And chill oppression, with her frost severe,
Sheds a dire blast, that nips the rising blade,
  And robs the expecting labors of the year.

So must we sink? and at the stern command,
  That bears the terror of a tyrant's word,
Bend the weak knee and raise the suppliant hand;
  The scorned, dependent vassals of a lord?

The wintry ravage of the storm to meet,
  Brave the scorched vapor of the autumnal air,
Then pour the hard-earned harvest at his feet,
  And beg some pittance from our pains to share.

But not for this, by heaven and virtue led,
  From the mad rule of hierarchal pride,
Over pathless seas our injured fathers fled,
  And followed freedom on the adventurous tide;

Dared the wild horrors of the clime unknown,
  The insidious savage, and the crimson plain,
To us bequeathed the prize their woes had won,
  Nor deemed they suffered, or they bled in vain.

And thinks't thou, *North*,[1] the sons of such a race,
  Whose beams of glory blessed their purpled morn,
Will shrink unnerved before a despot's face,
  Nor meet thy louring insolence with scorn?

Look through the circuit of the extended shore,
  That checks the surges of the Atlantic deep;
What weak eye trembles at the frown of power,
  What torpid soul invites the bands of sleep?

What kindness warms each heaven-illumined heart!
  What generous gifts the woes of want assuage,
And sympathetic tears of pity start,
  To aid the destined victims of thy rage!

No faction, clamorous with unhallowed zeal,
  To wayward madness wakes the impassioned throng;
No thoughtless furies sheath our breasts in steel,
  Or call the sword to avenge the oppressive wrong.

Fraternal bands with vows accordant join,
  One guardian genius, one pervading soul
Nerves the bold arm, inspires the just design,
  Combines, enlivens, and illumes the whole.

Now meet the Fathers of the western clime,
  Nor names more noble graced the rolls of fame,
When Spartan firmness braved the wrecks of time,
  Or Latian virtue fanned the heroic flame.

1. Lord North, prime minister of Great Britain.

Not deeper thought the immortal sage inspired,
  On Solon's lips when Grecian senates hung;
Nor manlier eloquence the bosom fired,
  When genius thundered from the Athenian tongue.

And hopes thy pride to match the patriot strain,
  By the bribed slave in pensioned lists enrolled;
Or awe their councils by the voice profane,
  That wakes to utterance at the call of gold?

Can frowns of terror daunt the warrior's deeds,
  Where guilt is stranger to the ingenuous heart,
Or craft illude, where godlike science sheds
  The beams of knowledge and the gifts of art?

Go, raise thy hand, and with its magic power
  Pencil with night the sun's ascending ray,
Bid the broad veil eclipse the noon-tide hour,
  And damps of Stygian darkness shroud the day;

Bid heaven's dread thunder at thy voice expire,
  Or chain the angry vengeance of the waves;
Then hope thy breath can quench the immortal fire,
  And free souls pinion with the bonds of slaves.

Thou canst not hope! Attend the flight of days,
  View the bold deeds, that wait the dawning age,
Where Time's strong arm, that rules the mighty maze,
  Shifts the proud actors on this earthly stage.

Then tell us, *North:* for thou art sure to know,
  For have not kings and fortune made thee great;
Or lurks not wisdom in the ennobled brow,
  And dwells no prescience in the robes of state?

Tell how the powers of luxury and pride
  Taint thy pure zephyrs with their baleful breath,
How deep corruption spreads the envenomed tide,
  And whelms thy land in darkness and in death.

And tell how rapt by freedom's sacred flame,
  And fostering influence of propitious skies,
This western world, the last recess of fame,
  Sees in her wilds a newborn empire rise —

A newborn empire, whose ascendant hour
    Defies its foes, assembled to destroy,
And like Alcides, with its infant power
    Shall crush those serpents, who its rest annoy.

Then look through time, and with extended eye,
    Pierce the dim veil of fate's obscure domain:
The morning dawns, the effulgent star is nigh,
    And crimson glories deck our rising reign.

Behold, emerging from the cloud of days,
    Where rest the wonders of ascending fame,
What heroes rise, immortal heirs of praise!
    What fields of death with conquering standards flame!

See our thronged cities' warlike gates unfold;
    What towering armies stretch their banners wide,
Where cold Ontario's icy waves are rolled,
    Or far Altama's silver waters glide!

Lo, from the groves, the aspiring cliffs that shade,
    Descending pines the surging ocean brave,
Rise in tall masts, the floating canvas spread,
    And rule the dread dominions of the wave!

Where the clear rivers pour their mazy tide,
    The smiling lawns in full luxuriance bloom;
The harvest wantons in its golden pride,
    The flowery garden breathes a glad perfume.

Behold that coast, which seats of wealth surround,
    That haven, rich with many a flowing sail,
Where friendly ships, from earth's remotest bound,
    Float on the cheerly pinions of the gale;

There Boston smiles, no more the sport of scorn,
    And meanly prisoned by thy fleets no more,
And far as ocean's billowy tides are borne,
    Lifts her dread ensigns of imperial power.

So smile the shores, where lordly Hudson strays,
    Whose floods fair York and deep Albania lave,
Or Philadelphia's happier clime surveys
    Her splendid seats in Delaware's lucid wave:

Or southward far extend thy wondering eyes,
  Where fertile streams the gardened vales divide,
And mid the peopled fields, distinguished rise
  Virginian towers and Charleston's spiry pride.

Genius of arts, of manners and of arms,
  See dressed in glory and the bloom of grace,
This virgin clime unfolds her brightest charms,
  And gives her beauties to thy fond embrace.

Hark, from the glades and every listening spray,
  What heaven-born muses wake the raptured song.
The vocal groves attune the warbling lay,
  And echoing vales the rising strains prolong.

Through the vast series of descending years,
  That lose their currents in the eternal wave,
Till heaven's last trump shall rend the affrighted spheres,
  And ope each empire's everlasting grave;

Propitious skies the joyous field shall crown,
  And robe our valleys in perpetual prime,
And ages blest of undisturbed renown
  Arise in radiance over the imperial clime.

And where is Britain? In the skirt of day,
  Where stormy Neptune rolls his utmost tide,
Where suns oblique diffuse a feeble ray,
  And lonely streams the fated coasts divide,

Seest thou yon Isle, whose desert landscape yields
  The mournful traces of the fame she bore,
Where matted thorns oppress the uncultured fields,
  And piles of ruin load the dreary shore?

From those loved seats, the Virtues sad withdrew
  From fell Corruption's bold and venal hand;
Reluctant Freedom waved her last adieu,
  And devastation swept the vassalled land.

On her white cliffs, the pillars once of fame,
  Her melancholy Genius sits to wail,
Drops the fond tear, and over her latest shame,
  Bids dark Oblivion draw the eternal veil.

John Adams: The Rule of Law and the Rule of Men

As a result of the resolutions of protest against the Stamp Act that he had written for the town of Braintree, Massachusetts, Adams was already identified by 1774 with the patriotic cause. He was therefore selected as a delegate to the First Continental Congress at Philadelphia in that year. Upon his return, he read the "Letters" by "Massachusettensis" [Daniel Leonard] in the Massachusetts Gazette, *arguing the Loyalist point of view. Though he did not then know who the author of the "Letters" was, Adams prepared letters of his own in reply, of which the following appeared in the same paper on February 6, 1775, under the pen name of "Novanglus." He had not yet come to believe in complete independence, as the letter shows. The remarks that he quotes in order to refute them are all those of "Massachusettensis."*

Source: C. F. Adams, IV: "Novanglus, No. VII."

AMERICA HAS ALL ALONG CONSENTED, still consents, and ever will consent that Parliament, being the most powerful legislature in the dominions, should regulate the trade of the dominions. This is founding the authority of Parliament to regulate our trade upon *compact* and *consent* of the colonies, not upon any principle of common or statute law; not upon any original principle of the English constitution; not upon the principle that Parliament is the supreme and sovereign legislature over them in all cases whatsoever. The question is not, therefore, whether the authority of Parliament extends to the colonies in any case, for it is admitted by the Whigs that it does in that of commerce, but whether it extends in all cases. . . .

If the English Parliament were to govern us, where did they get the right, without our consent, to take the Scottish Parliament into a participation of the government over us? When this was done, was the American share of the democracy of the constitution consulted? If not, were not the Americans deprived of the benefit of the democratical part of the constitution? And is not the democracy as essential to the English constitution as the monarchy or aristocracy? Should we have been more effectually deprived of the benefit of the British or English constitution if one or both houses of Parliament, or if our House and Council, had made this union with the two houses of Parliament in Scotland, without the King?

If a new constitution was to be formed for the whole British dominions, and a supreme legislature coextensive with it, upon the general principles of the English constitution, an equal mixture of monarchy, aristocracy, and democracy, let us see what would be necessary. England has 6,000,000 people, we will say; America had 3,000,000. England has 500 members in the House of Commons, we will say; America must have 250. Is it possible she should maintain them there, or could they at such a distance know the state, the sense, or exigencies of their constituents? Ireland, too, must be incorporated and send another hundred or two of members. . . .

Yet, without such a union, a legislature which shall be sovereign and supreme in all cases whatsoever and coextensive with the empire can never be established upon the general principles of the English constitution which Massachusettensis lays down, namely, an equal mixture of monarchy, aristocracy, and democracy. Nay, further, in order to comply with this principle, this new government, this mighty colossus, which is to bestride the narrow world, must have a House of Lords, consisting of Irish, East and West Indian, African, American, as well as English and Scottish noblemen; for the nobility ought to be scattered about all the dominions, as well as the representatives of the Commons.

If, in twenty years more, America should have 6,000,000 inhabitants, as there is a boundless territory to fill up, she must have 500 representatives. Upon these principles, if in forty years she should have 12,000,000 — 1,000; and if the inhabitants of the three kingdoms remain as they are, being already full of inhabitants, what will become of your supreme legislative? It will be translated, Crown and all, to America. This is a sublime system for America. It will flatter those ideas of independency which the Tories impute to them, if they have any such, more than any other plan of independency that I have ever heard projected. . . .

I agree that "two supreme and independent authorities cannot exist in the same state," any more than two supreme beings in one universe; and, therefore, I contend that our provincial legislatures are the only supreme authorities in our colonies. Parliament, notwithstanding this, may be allowed an authority supreme and sovereign over the ocean, which may be limited by the banks of the ocean or the bounds of our charters; our charters give us no authority over the high seas. Parliament has our consent to assume a jurisdiction over them. And here is a line fairly drawn between the rights of Britain and the rights of the colonies, namely, the banks of the ocean, or low watermark; the line of division between common law and civil or maritime law. If this is not sufficient — if Parliament are at

a loss for any principle of natural, civil, maritime, moral, or common law on which to ground any authority over the high seas, the Atlantic especially, let the colonies be treated like reasonable creatures, and they will discover great ingenuity and modesty. The acts of trade and navigation might be confirmed by provincial laws and carried into execution by our own courts and juries, and, in this case, illicit trade would be cut up by the roots forever.

I knew the smuggling Tories in New York and Boston would cry out against this, because it would not only destroy their profitable game of smuggling but their whole place and pension system. But the Whigs, that is, a vast majority of the whole continent, would not regard the smuggling Tories. In one word, if public principles and motives and arguments were alone to determine this dispute between the two countries, it might be settled forever in a few hours; but the everlasting clamors of prejudice, passion, and private interest drown every consideration of that sort and are precipitating us into a civil war.

"If, then, we are a part of the British empire, we must be subject to the supreme power of the state, which is vested in the estates in Parliament."

Here, again, we are to be conjured out of our senses by the magic in the words "British empire," and "supreme power of the state." But, however it may sound, I say we are not a part of the British empire; because the British government is not an empire. The governments of France, Spain, etc., are not empires but monarchies, supposed to be governed by fixed fundamental laws, though not really. The British government is still less entitled to the style of *an empire*. It is a limited monarchy.

If Aristotle, Livy, and Harrington knew what a republic was, the British constitution is much more like a republic than an empire. They define a republic to be a *government of laws*, and *not of men*. If this definition be just, the British constitution is noth-

ing more nor less than a republic, in which
the king is first magistrate. This office being
hereditary, and being possessed of such ample and splendid prerogatives, is no objection to the government's being a republic,
as long as it is bound by fixed laws, which
the people have a voice in making, and a
right to defend. An empire is a despotism,
and an emperor a despot, bound by no law
or limitation but his own will; it is a stretch
of tyranny beyond absolute monarchy. For,
although the will of an absolute monarch is
law, yet his edicts must be registered by
parliaments. Even this formality is not necessary in an empire. . . .

To say that we "must be" subject seems
to betray a consciousness that we are not
by any law or upon any principles but
those of mere power; and an opinion that
we ought to be, or that it is necessary that
we should be. But if this should be admitted for argument's sake only, what is the
consequence? The consequences that may
fairly be drawn are these: that Britain has
been imprudent enough to let colonies be
planted until they are become numerous
and important without ever having wisdom
enough to concert a plan for their government consistent with her own welfare; that
now it is necessary to make them submit to
the authority of Parliament; and, because
there is no principle of law or justice or reason by which she can effect it, therefore,
she will resort to war and conquest — to
the maxim, *delenda est Carthago*.

These are the consequences, according to
this writer's idea. We think the consequences are, that she has, after 150 years,
discovered a defect in her government,
which ought to be supplied by some just
and reasonable means, that is, by the consent of the colonies; for metaphysicians and
politicians may dispute forever, but they
will never find any other moral principle or
foundation of rule or obedience than the
consent of governors and governed. She has
found out that the great machine will not

go any longer without a new wheel. She
will make this herself. We think she is making it of such materials and workmanship as
will tear the whole machine to pieces. We
are willing, if she can convince us of the
necessity of such a wheel, to assist with artists and materials in making it, so that it
may answer the end. But she says we shall
have no share in it; and, if we will not let
her patch it up as she pleases, her Massachusettensis, and other advocates tell us, she
will tear it to pieces herself by cutting our
throats. To this kind of reasoning, we can
only answer that we will not stand still to
be butchered. We will defend our lives as
long as Providence shall enable us. . . .

That the authority of Parliament "has
been exercised almost ever since the first
settlement of the country" is a mistake; for
there is no instance, until the first Navigation Act, which was in 1660, more than
forty years after the first settlement. This
act was never executed nor regarded until
seventeen years afterwards, and then it was
not executed as an act of Parliament but as
a law of the colony, to which the King
agreed.

This "has been expressly acknowledged
by our provincial legislatures." There is too
much truth in this. It has been twice acknowledged by our House of Representatives, that Parliament was the supreme legislative; but this was directly repugnant to a
multitude of other votes, by which it was
denied. This was in conformity to the distinction between taxation and legislation,
which has since been found to be a distinction without a difference.

When a great question is first started,
there are very few, even of the greatest
minds, which suddenly and intuitively com-
prehend it, in all its consequences.

It is both "our interest and our duty to
continue subject to the authority of Parliament," as far as the regulation of our trade,
if it will be content with that, but no
longer.

"If the colonies are not subject to the authority of Parliament, Great Britain and the colonies must be distinct states, as completely so as England and Scotland were before the union, or as Great Britain and Hanover are now." There is no need of being startled at this consequence. It is very harmless. There is no absurdity at all in it. Distinct states may be united under one king. And those states may be further cemented and united together by a treaty of commerce. This is the case. We have, by our own express consent, contracted to observe the Navigation Act and, by our implied consent, by long usage and uninterrupted acquiescence, have submitted to the other acts of trade however grievous some of them may be. This may be compared to a treaty of commerce, by which those distinct states are cemented together, in perpetual league and amity. And if any further ratifications of this pact or treaty are necessary, the colonies would readily enter into them, provided their other liberties were inviolate. . . .

The only proposition in all this writer's long string of pretended absurdities, which he says follows from the position that we are distinct states, is this: That "as the king must govern each state by its parliament, those several parliaments would pursue the particular interest of its own state; and however well-disposed the king might be to pursue a line of interest that was common to all, the checks and control that he would meet with would render it impossible." Every argument ought to be allowed its full weight; and therefore candor obliges me to acknowledge that here lies all the difficulty that there is in this whole controversy. There has been, from first to last, on both sides of the Atlantic, an idea, an apprehension that it was necessary there should be some superintending power to draw together all the wills and unite all the strength of the subjects in all the dominions, in case of war and in the case of trade.

The necessity of this, in case of trade, has been so apparent that, as has often been said, we have consented that Parliament should exercise such a power. In case of war, it has by some been thought necessary. But, in fact and experience, it has not been found so. What though the proprietary colonies, on account of disputes with the proprietors, did not come in so early to the assistance of the general cause in the last war as they ought, and perhaps one of them not at all? The inconveniences of this were small in comparison of the absolute ruin to the liberties of all which must follow the submission to Parliament, in all cases, which would be giving up all the popular limitations upon the government.

These inconveniences fell chiefly upon New England. She was necessitated to greater exertions; but she had rather suffer these again and again than others infinitely greater. However, this subject has been so long in contemplation that it is fully understood now in all the colonies; so that there is no danger, in case of another war, of any colony's failing of its duty.

But, admitting the proposition in its full force, that it is absolutely necessary there should be a supreme power, coextensive with all the dominions, will it follow that Parliament, as now constituted, has a right to assume this supreme jurisdiction? By no means.

A union of the colonies might be projected, and an American legislature; for, if America has 3,000,000 people, and the whole dominions, 12,000,000, she ought to send a quarter part of all the members to the House of Commons; and, instead of holding parliaments always at Westminster, the haughty members for Great Britain must humble themselves, one session in four, to cross the Atlantic, and hold the Parliament in America.

There is no avoiding all inconveniences in human affairs. The greatest possible, or conceivable, would arise from ceding to Parliament power over us without a representation in it. The next greatest would accrue from any plan that can be devised for a representation there. The least of all would arise from going on as we began and fared well for 150 years, by letting Parliament regulate trade, and our own assemblies all other matters. . . .

That a representation in Parliament is impracticable, we all agree; but the consequence is that we must have a representation in our supreme legislatures here. This was the consequence that was drawn by kings, ministers, our ancestors, and the whole nation more than a century ago, when the colonies were first settled, and continued to be the general sense until the last peace; and it must be the general sense again soon, or Great Britain will lose her colonies.

Patrick Henry: Give Me Liberty or Give Me Death

Like Samuel Adams, his counterpart in Massachusetts, Patrick Henry dominated the assembly of his province for ten years before independence was declared. Repeatedly, he overcame the doubts of more cautious leaders — the Randolphs, Pendletons, Harrisons, Carys, and Braxtons — with an eloquence that made him a legend. Unhappily, some of his best speeches were never taken down but survive only as they were remembered. This is the case with what was perhaps the greatest of them, his address on March 23, 1775, to the convention that gathered at Richmond after Lord Dunmore suspended the Virginia Assembly. The speech is best known in the reconstruction, reprinted here, by Henry's early biographer, William Wirt, originally published in 1817. Its last paragraph is among the two or three most famous perorations in American history.

Source: William Wirt, *The Life and Character of Patrick Henry*, Philadelphia, n.d., pp. 137-142.

Mr. Henry was fitted to raise the whirlwind, as well as to ride in and direct it. His was that comprehensive view, that unerring prescience, that perfect command over the actions of men, which qualified him not merely to guide but almost to create the destinies of nations.

He rose at this time with a majesty unusual to him in an exordium, and with all that self-possession by which he was so invariably distinguished. No man, he said, thought more highly than he did of the patriotism, as well as abilities, of the very worthy gentlemen who had just addressed the House. But different men often saw the same subject in different lights; and, therefore, he hoped it would not be thought disrespectful to those gentlemen if, entertaining as he did opinions of a character very opposite to theirs, he should speak forth *his* sentiments freely and without reserve. This, he said, was no time for ceremony. The question before this House was one of awful moment to the country. For his own part, he considered it as nothing less than a question of freedom or slavery. And, in proportion to the magnitude of the subject, ought to be the freedom of the debate. It was only in this way that they could hope to arrive at truth, and fulfill the great responsibility which they held to God and their country. Should he keep back his opinions at such a time through fear of giving offense, he should consider himself as guilty of treason toward his country and of an act of disloyalty toward the Majesty of Heaven, which he revered above all earthly kings.

"Mr. President," said he, "it is natural to man to indulge in the illusions of hope. We are apt to shut our eyes against a painful truth and listen to the song of that siren, till she transforms us into beasts. Is this," he asked, "the part of wise men, engaged in a great and arduous struggle for liberty?" Were we disposed to be of the number of those, who having eyes, see not, and having ears, hear not, the things which so nearly concern their temporal salvation? For his part, whatever anguish of spirit it might cost, *he* was willing to know the whole truth; to know the worst, and to provide for it.

He had, he said, but one lamp by which his feet were guided; and that was the lamp of experience. He knew of no way of judging of the future but by the past. And judging by the past, he wished to know what there had been in the conduct of the British Ministry for the last ten years to justify those hopes with which gentlemen had been pleased to solace themselves and the House?

Is it that insidious smile with which our petition has been lately received? Trust it not, sir; it will prove a snare to your feet. Suffer not yourselves to be betrayed with a kiss. Ask yourselves how this gracious reception of our petition comports with those warlike preparations which cover our waters and darken our land. Are fleets and armies necessary to a work of love and reconciliation? Have we shown ourselves so unwilling to be reconciled that force must be called in to win back our love? Let us not deceive ourselves, sir. These are the implements of war and subjugation — the last arguments to which kings resort. I ask gentlemen, sir, what means this martial array, if its purpose be not to force us to submission? Can gentlemen assign any other possible motive for it? Has Great Britain any enemy in this quarter of the world to call for all this accumulation of navies and armies? No, sir, she has none. They are meant for us; they can be meant for no other. They are sent over to bind and rivet upon us those chains which the British Ministry have been so long forging.

And what have we oppose to them? Shall we try argument? Sir, we have been trying that for the last ten years. Have we anything new to offer upon the subject? Nothing. We have held the subject up in every light of which it is capable; but it has been all in vain. Shall we resort to entreaty and humble supplication? What terms shall we find which have not been already exhausted? Let us not, I beseech you, sir, deceive ourselves longer. Sir, we have done everything that could be done to avert the storm which is now coming on. We have petitioned; we have remonstrated; we have supplicated; we have prostrated ourselves before the throne and have implored its interposition to arrest the tyrannical hands of the Ministry and Parliament. Our petitions have been slighted; our remonstrances have produced additional violence and insult; our supplications have been disregarded; and we have been spurned, with contempt, from the foot of the throne. In vain, after these things, may we indulge the fond hope of peace and reconciliation.

There is no longer any room for hope. If we wish to be free; if we mean to preserve inviolate those inestimable privileges for which we have been so long contending; if we mean not basely to abandon the noble struggle in which we have been so long engaged, and which we have pledged ourselves never to abandon, until the glorious object of our contest shall be obtained; we must fight! I repeat it, sir, we must fight!! An appeal to arms and to the God of hosts is all that is left us!

They tell us, sir . . . that we are weak, unable to cope with so formidable an adversary. But when shall we be stronger. Will it be the next week or the next year? Will it be when we are totally disarmed, and when a British guard shall be stationed in every house? Shall we gather strength by irresolution and inaction? Shall we acquire the means of effectual resistance by lying supinely on our backs and hugging the delusive phantom of hope, until our enemies shall have bound us hand and foot? Sir, we are not weak if we make a proper use of those means which the God of nature has placed in our power. Three millions of people armed in the holy cause of liberty and in such a country as that which we possess are invincible by any force which our enemy can send against us.

Besides, sir, we shall not fight our battles alone. There is a just God who presides over the destinies of nations, and who will raise up friends to fight our battles for us. The battle, sir, is not to the strong alone; it is to the vigilant, the active, the brave. Besides, sir, we have no election. If we were base enough to desire it, it is now too late to retire from the contest. There is no retreat but in submission and slavery! Our chains are forged. Their clanking may be heard on the plains of Boston! The war is inevitable — and let it come!! I repeat it, sir, let it come!!!

It is vain, sir, to extenuate the matter. Gentlemen may cry, peace, peace; but there is no peace. The war is actually begun! The next gale that sweeps from the north will bring to our ears the clash of resounding arms! Our brethren are already in the field! Why stand we here idle? What is it that gentlemen wish? What would they have? Is life so dear or peace so sweet as to be purchased at the price of chains and slavery?

"Forbid it, Almighty God — I know not what course others may take; but as for me," cried he, with both his arms extended aloft, his brows knit, every feature marked with the resolute purpose of his soul, and his voice swelled to its boldest note of exclamation — "give me liberty, or give me death!"

He took his seat. No murmur of applause was heard. The effect was too deep. After the trance of a moment, several members started from their seats. The cry, "To arms!" seemed to quiver on every lip and gleam from every eye.

Preamble to the Massachusetts Articles of War

In February of 1775, a second Massachusetts provincial congress met to prepare for war. It directed the appointed generals to oppose the British by force, if necessary. Directions were also given to gather such military stores as could be procured. On April 5, the congress adopted fifty-three articles of war, to which the following preamble was affixed.

Source: *The Journals of Each Provincial Congress of Massachusetts in 1774 and 1775, etc., etc.,* Boston, 1838, pp. 120-121.

Whereas the lust of power, which of old oppressed, persecuted, and exiled our pious and virtuous ancestors from their fair possessions in Britain, now pursues with tenfold severity us, their guiltless children, who are unjustly and wickedly charged with licentiousness, sedition, treason, and rebellion, and being deeply impressed with a sense of the almost incredible fatigues and hardships our venerable progenitors encountered, who fled from oppression for the sake of civil and religious liberty for themselves and their offspring, and began a settlement here on bare creation, at their own expense; and having seriously considered the duty we owe to God, to the memory of such invincible worthies, to the King, to Great Britain, our country, ourselves, and posterity, do think it our indispensable duty, by all lawful ways and means in our power, to recover, maintain, defend, and preserve the free exercise of all those civil and religious rights and liberties for which many of our forefathers fought, bled, and died, and to hand them down entire for the free enjoyment of the latest posterity;

And whereas the keeping a standing army in any of these colonies in times of peace, without the consent of the legislature of that colony in which such army is kept is against law; *and whereas* such an army with a large naval force is now placed in the town and harbor of Boston for the purpose of subjecting us to the power of the British Parliament; *and whereas* we are frequently told by the tools of administration, dupes to ministerial usurpation, that Great Britain will not, in any degree, relax in her measures until we acknowledge her "right of making laws binding upon us in all cases whatever"; and that if we refuse by our denial of her claim, the dispute must be decided by arms, in which, it is said by our enemies, "we shall have no chance, being undisciplined, cowards, disobedient, impatient of command, and possessed of that spirit of leveling which admits of no order, subordination, rule, or government"; *and whereas,* from the ministerial army and fleet now at Boston, the large reenforcement of troops expected, the late circular letters to the governors upon the continent, the general tenor of intelligence from Great Britain, and the hostile preparations making here, as also from the threats and repeated insults of our

enemies in the capital town, we have reason to apprehend that the sudden destruction of this province is in contemplation, if not determined upon;

And whereas the great law of self-preservation may suddenly require our raising and keeping an army of observation and defense in order to prevent or repel any further attempts to enforce the late cruel and oppressive acts of the British Parliament, which are evidently designed to subject us and the whole continent to the most ignominious slavery; *and whereas* in case of raising and keeping such an army it will be necessary that the officers and soldiers in the same be fully acquainted with their duty, and that the articles, rules, and regulations thereof be made as plain as possible; and having great confidence in the honor and public virtue of the inhabitants of this colony that they will readily obey the officers chosen by themselves, and will cheerfully do their duty when known, without any such severe articles and rules (except in capital cases), and cruel punishments as are usually practised in standing armies; and will submit to all such rules and regulations as are founded in reason, honor, and virtue — :

It is therefore resolved, that the following articles, rules, and regulations for the army that may be raised for the defense and security of our lives, liberties, and estates be, and hereby are, earnestly recommended to be strictly adhered to by all officers, soldiers, and others concerned, as they regard their own honor and the public good.

———◆———

Stand your ground. Don't fire unless fired upon, but if they mean to have a war let it begin here.

Captain John Parker, to his Minute Men on Lexington Green, April 19, 1775

Joseph Warren: The Battles of Lexington and Concord

At the battles of Lexington and Concord, "the shot heard 'round the world" began the bloody clash that would bring on independence. Certainly the political effect of these battles was more significant than the military outcome. American public opinion everywhere was aroused in support of the revolutionary cause. British and American accounts varied greatly in their descriptions of what happened. This account, written on April 26, 1775, by Joseph Warren, president of the Massachusetts Provincial Congress, presents the American version of the event.

Source: Niles: "Address of Provincial Congress of Massachusetts, to the Inhabitants of Great Britain."

Friends and Fellow Subjects:

Hostilities are at length commenced in this colony by the troops under the command of General Gage, and it being of the greatest importance, that an early, true, and authentic account of this inhuman proceeding should be known to you, the Congress of this colony have transmitted the same, and from want of a session of the honorable Continental Congress, think it proper to address you on the alarming occasion.

By the clearest depositions relative to this transaction, it will appear that on the night preceding the 19th of April instant, a body of the King's troops, under the command of Colonel Smith, were secretly landed at Cambridge, with an apparent design to take or destroy the military and other stores provided for the defense of this colony, and deposited at Concord; that some inhabitants of the colony, on the night aforesaid, whilst traveling peaceably on the road between Boston and Concord were seized and greatly abused by armed men, who appeared to be officers of General Gage's army; that the town of Lexington, by these means, was alarmed, and a company of the inhabitants mustered on the occasion; that the regular troops on their way to Concord marched into the said town of Lexington, and the said company, on their approach, began to disperse; that, notwithstanding this, the regulars rushed on with great violence and first began hostilities by firing on said Lexington company, whereby they killed eight, and wounded several others; that the regulars continued their fire, until those of said company, who were neither killed nor wounded, had made their escape; and that Colonel Smith, with the detachment, then marched to Concord, where a number of provincials were again fired on by the troops, two of them killed and several wounded before the provincials fired on them, and that these hostile measures of the troops, produced an engagement that lasted through the day, in which many of the provincials and more of the regular troops were killed and wounded.

To give a particular account of the ravages of the troops as they retreated from Concord to Charlestown would be very difficult, if not impracticable. Let it suffice to say that a great number of the houses on the road were plundered and rendered unfit for use, several were burned, women in childbed were driven by the soldiery naked into the streets, old men peaceably in their houses were shot dead, and such scenes exhibited as would disgrace the annals of the most uncivilized nation.

These, brethren, are marks of ministerial vengeance against this colony for refusing, with her sister colonies, a submission to slavery; but they have not yet detached us from our royal sovereign. We profess to be his loyal and dutiful subjects, and, so hardly dealt with as we have been, are still ready, without lives and fortunes, to defend his person, family, Crown, and dignity. Nevertheless, to the persecution and tyranny of his cruel Ministry we will not tamely submit — appealing to Heaven for the justice of our cause, we determine to die or be free.

We cannot think that the honor, wisdom, and valor of Britons will suffer them to be longer inactive spectators of measures in which they themselves are so deeply interested — measures pursued in opposition to the solemn protests of many noble lords and expressed sense of conspicuous commoners whose knowledge and virtue have long characterized them as some of the greatest men in the nation; measures executed contrary to the interest, petitions, and resolves of many large, respectable, and opulent counties, cities, and boroughs in Great Britain; measures highly incompatible with justice, but still pursued with a specious pretense of easing the nation of its burdens; measures which, if successful, must end in the ruin and slavery of Britain, as well as the persecuted American colonies.

We sincerely hope that the Great Sovereign of the universe, who has so often appeared for the English nation, will support you in every rational and manly exertion with these colonies for saving it from ruin, and that, in a constitutional connection with the mother country, we shall soon be altogether a free and happy people.

Two views of the battles of Lexington and Concord: (left) the first encounter between rebels and British regulars on the Lexington Green; (below) the battle at Concord Bridge. Engravings by Amos Doolittle from sketches by Ralph Earl

The Necessity for Taking Up Arms

A Declaration . . . Setting Forth the Causes and Necessity of Their Taking Up Arms
held out a hope of reconciliation with Britain, but at the same time approved the use
of armed resistance to obtain recognition of the rights of the colonists. The final
draft of the Declaration *was the work of Thomas Jefferson and John Dickinson.*
Approved by the Second Continental Congress on July 6, 1775, the Declaration
disavowed all thoughts of independence. The colonists claimed to be fighting a
"ministerial army" and not the King, who they felt had been misled by evil counselors.
The Americans promised to lay down their arms when the liberties they claimed as
a birthright had been secured.

Source: *Journals,* I: "Thursday, July 6, 1775."

IF IT WAS POSSIBLE for men who exercise their reason to believe that the Divine Author of our existence intended a part of the human race to hold an absolute property in and an unbounded power over others, marked out by His infinite goodness and wisdom, as the objects of a legal domination never rightfully resistible, however severe and oppressive, the inhabitants of these colonies might at least require from the Parliament of Great Britain some evidence that this dreadful authority over them has been granted to that body. But a reverence for our great Creator, principles of humanity, and the dictates of common sense must convince all those who reflect upon the subject that government was instituted to promote the welfare of mankind and ought to be administered for the attainment of that end.

The legislature of Great Britain, however, stimulated by an inordinate passion for a power not only unjustifiable but which they know to be peculiarly reprobated by the very constitution of that kingdom, and desperate of success in any mode of contest where regard should be had to truth, law, or right, have at length, deserting those, attempted to effect their cruel and impolitic purpose of enslaving these colonies by violence, and have thereby rendered it necessary for us to close with their last appeal from reason to arms. Yet, however blinded that assembly may be by their intemperate rage for unlimited domination so to slight justice and the opinion of mankind, we esteem ourselves bound, by obligations of respect to the rest of the world, to make known the justice of our cause.

Our forefathers, inhabitants of the island of Great Britain, left their native land to seek on these shores a residence for civil and religious freedom. At the expense of their blood, at the hazard of their fortunes, without the least charge to the country from which they removed, by unceasing labor and an unconquerable spirit, they effected settlements in the distant and inhospitable wilds of America, then filled with numerous and warlike nations of barbarians. Societies or governments, vested with perfect legislatures, were formed under charters from the Crown, and a harmonious intercourse was established between the colonies and the kingdom from which they derived their origin. The mutual benefits of this union became in a short time so extraordinary as to excite astonishment. It is universally confessed that the amazing increase of the wealth, strength, and navigation of the Realm arose from this source; and the minister, who so wisely and successfully directed the measures of Great Britain in the late war, publicly declared that these colonies enabled her to triumph over her enemies.

Toward the conclusion of that war, it pleased our sovereign to make a change in his counsels. From that fatal moment, the affairs of the British empire began to fall into confusion, and gradually sliding from the summit of glorious prosperity to which they had been advanced by the virtues and abilities of one man, are at length distracted by the convulsions that now shake it to its deepest foundations. The new Ministry finding the brave foes of Britain though frequently defeated yet still contending, took up the unfortunate idea of granting them a hasty peace, and of then subduing her faithful friends.

These devoted colonies were judged to be in such a state as to present victories without bloodshed and all the easy emoluments of statuteable plunder. The uninterrupted tenor of their peaceable and respectful behavior from the beginning of colonization; their dutiful, zealous, and useful services during the war, though so recently and amply acknowledged in the most honorable manner by His Majesty, by the late King, and by Parliament, could not save them from the meditated innovations. Parliament was influenced to adopt the pernicious project, and, assuming a new power over them, have, in the course of eleven years, given

such decisive specimens of the spirit and consequences attending this power as to leave no doubt concerning the effects of acquiescence under it. They have undertaken to give and grant our money without our consent, though we have ever exercised an exclusive right to dispose of our own property; statutes have been passed for extending the jurisdiction of Courts of Admiralty and Vice-Admiralty beyond their ancient limits; for depriving us of the accustomed and inestimable privilege of trial by jury, in cases affecting both life and property; for suspending the legislature of one of the colonies; for interdicting all commerce to the capital of another; and for altering fundamentally the form of government established by charter, and secured by acts of its own legislature solemnly confirmed by the Crown; for exempting the "murderers" of colonists from legal trial and, in effect, from punishment; for erecting in a neighboring province, acquired by the joint arms of Great Britain and America, a despotism dangerous to our very existence; and for quartering soldiers upon the colonists in time of profound peace. It has also been resolved in Parliament that colonists charged with committing certain offenses shall be transported to England to be tried.

But why should we enumerate our injuries in detail? By one statute it is declared that Parliament can "of right make laws to bind us in all cases whatsoever." What is to defend us against so enormous, so unlimited a power? Not a single man of those who assume it is chosen by us, or is subject to our control or influence; but, on the contrary, they are all of them exempt from the operation of such laws; and an American revenue, if not diverted from the ostensible purposes for which it is raised, would actually lighten their own burdens in proportion as they increase ours. We saw the misery to which such despotism would reduce us. We for ten years incessantly and ineffectually besieged the throne as supplicants; we reasoned, we remonstrated with Parliament, in the most mild and decent language.

Administration, sensible that we should regard these oppressive measures as freemen ought to do, sent over fleets and armies to enforce them. The indignation of the Americans was roused, it is true; but it was the indignation of a virtuous, loyal, and affectionate people. A congress of delegates from the United Colonies was assembled at Philadelphia, on the 5th day of last September. We resolved again to offer a humble and dutiful petition to the King, and also addressed our fellow subjects of Great Britain. We have pursued every temperate, every respectful measure; we have even proceeded to break off our commercial intercourse with our fellow subjects, as the last peaceable admonition, that our attachment to no nation upon earth should supplant our attachment to liberty. This, we flattered ourselves, was the ultimate step of the controversy; but subsequent events have shown how vain was this hope of finding moderation in our enemies.

Several threatening expressions against the colonies were inserted in His Majesty's speech; our petition, though we were told it was a decent one, and that His Majesty had been pleased to receive it graciously, and to promise laying it before his Parliament, was huddled into both houses among a bundle of American papers and there neglected. The Lords and Commons in their address, in the month of February, said, that "a rebellion at that time actually existed within the province of Massachusetts Bay; and that those concerned in it had been countenanced and encouraged by unlawful combinations and engagements, entered into by His Majesty's subjects in several of the other colonies; and therefore they besought His Majesty that he would take the most effectual measures to enforce due obedience to the laws and authority of the supreme legislature." Soon after, the commercial intercourse of whole colonies with foreign countries, and with each other, was cut off by an act of Parliament; by another, several of them were entirely prohibited from the fisheries in the seas near their coasts, on which they always depended for their sustenance; and large reinforcements of ships and troops were immediately sent over to General Gage.

Fruitless were all the entreaties, arguments, and eloquence of an illustrious band of the most distinguished peers and commoners, who nobly and strenuously asserted the justice of our cause to stay, or even to mitigate, the heedless fury with which these accumulated and unexampled outrages were hurried on. Equally fruitless was the interference of the City of London, of Bristol, and many other respectable towns in our favor. Parliament adopted an insidious maneuver calculated to divide us, to establish a perpetual auction of taxations where colony should bid against colony, all of them uninformed what ransom would redeem their lives; and thus to extort from us, at the point of the bayonet, the unknown sums that should be sufficient to gratify, if possible to gratify, ministerial rapacity, with the miserable indulgence left to us of raising, in our own mode, the prescribed tribute. What terms more rigid and humiliating could have been dictated by remorseless victors to conquered enemies? In our circumstances to accept them would be to deserve them.

Soon after intelligence of these proceedings arrived on this continent, General Gage, who in the course of the last year had taken possession of the town of Boston in the province of Massachusetts Bay, and still occupied it as a garrison, on the 19th day of April, sent out from that place a large detachment of his army, who made an unprovoked assault on the inhabitants of the said province, at the town of Lexington, as appears by the affidavits of a great number of persons, some of whom were officers and soldiers of that detachment, murdered eight of the inhabitants, and wounded many others. From thence the troops proceeded in warlike array to the town of Concord, where they set upon another party of the inhabitants of the same province, killing several and wounding more, until compelled to retreat by the country people suddenly assembled to repel this cruel aggression. Hostilities, thus commenced by the British troops, have been since prosecuted by them without regard to faith or reputation.

The inhabitants of Boston being confined within that town by the general their governor, and having, in order to procure their dismission, entered into a treaty with him, it was stipulated that the said inhabitants having deposited their arms with their own magistrates, should have liberty to depart, taking with them their other effects. They accordingly delivered up their arms; but in open violation of honor, in defiance of the obligation of treaties, which even savage nations esteemed sacred, the governor ordered the arms deposited as aforesaid, that they might be preserved for their owners, to be seized by a body of soldiers; detained the greatest part of the inhabitants in the town, and compelled the few who were permitted to retire to leave their most valuable effects behind. By this perfidy, wives are separated from their husbands, children from their parents, the aged and the sick from their relations and friends who wish to attend and comfort them; and those who have been used to live in plenty and even elegance are reduced to deplorable distress.

The general, further emulating his ministerial masters by a proclamation bearing date on the 12th day of June, after venting the grossest falsehoods and calumnies against the good people of these colonies, proceeds to "declare them all, either by name or description, to be rebels and traitors, to supersede the course of the common law, and instead thereof to publish and order the use and exercise of the law martial." His troops have butchered our countrymen, have wantonly burned Charlestown, besides a considerable number of houses in other places; our ships and vessels are seized; the necessary supplies of provisions are intercepted; and he is exerting his utmost power to spread destruction and devastation around him.

We have received certain intelligence that General Carleton, the governor of Canada, is instigating the people of that province and the Indians to fall upon us; and we have but too much reason to apprehend that schemes have been formed to excite domestic enemies against us. In brief, a part of these colonies now feel, and all of them are sure of feeling, as far as the vengeance of administration can inflict them, the complicated calamities of fire, sword, and famine. We are reduced to the alternative of choosing an unconditional submission to the tyranny of irritated ministers, or resistance by force.

The latter is our choice. We have counted the cost of this contest and find nothing so dreadful as voluntary slavery. Honor, justice, and humanity forbid us tamely to surrender that freedom which we received from our gallant ancestors, and which our innocent posterity have a right to receive from us. We cannot endure the infamy and guilt of resigning succeeding generations to that wretchedness which inevitably awaits them, if we basely entail hereditary bondage upon them.

Our cause is just. Our union is perfect. Our internal resources are great; and, if necessary, foreign assistance is undoubtedly attainable. We gratefully acknowledge, as signal instances of the divine favor toward us, that His providence would not permit us to be called into this severe controversy until we were grown up to our present strength, had been previously exercised in warlike operation, and possessed of the means of defending ourselves. With hearts fortified with these animating reflections, we most solemnly, before God and the world, *declare* that, exerting the utmost energy of those powers which our beneficent Creator has graciously bestowed upon us, the arms we have been compelled by our enemies to assume, we will, in defiance of every hazard, with unabating firmness and perseverance, employ for the preservation of our liberties; being with one mind resolved to die free men rather than live slaves.

Lest this declaration should disquiet the minds of our friends and fellow subjects in any part of the empire, we assure them that we mean not to dissolve that union which has so long and so happily subsisted between us and which we sincerely wish to see restored. Necessity has not yet driven us into that desperate measure, or induced us to excite any other nation to war against them. We have not raised armies with ambitious designs of separating from Great Britain and establishing independent states. We fight not for glory or for conquest. We exhibit to mankind the remarkable spectacle of a people attacked by unprovoked enemies, without any imputation or even suspicion of offense. They boast of their privileges and civilization, and yet proffer no milder conditions than servitude or death.

In our own native land, in defense of the freedom that is our birthright and which we ever enjoyed till the late violation of it, for the protection of our property acquired solely by the honest industry of our forefathers and ourselves, against violence actually offered, we have taken up arms. We shall lay them down when hostilities shall cease on the part of the aggressors and all danger of their being renewed shall be removed, and not before.

With a humble confidence in the mercies of the supreme and impartial Judge and Ruler of the universe, we most devoutly implore His divine goodness to protect us happily through this great conflict, to dispose our adversaries to reconciliation on reasonable terms, and thereby to relieve the empire from the calamities of civil war.

On a motion made, *Resolved*, that a letter be prepared to the lord mayor, aldermen, and livery of the City of London expressing the thanks of this Congress for their virtuous and spirited opposition to the oppressive and ruinous system of colony administration adopted by the British Ministry.

Ordered, that the committee appointed to draft an address to the people of Great Britain do prepare this.

As to pay, sir, I beg to assure the Congress, that, as no pecuniary consideration could have tempted me to accept this arduous employment, at the expense of my domestic ease and happiness, I do not wish to make any profit from it. I will keep an exact account of my expenses. Those, I doubt not, they will discharge; and that is all I desire.

GEORGE WASHINGTON, answer to Congress on his appointment as commander in chief, June 16, 1775

Horatio Gates: On Recruiting an American Army

As the theater of war expanded in America, the need became evident for an intercolonial military establishment. The Second Continental Congress established the Continental Army in 1775, composing it of the scattered colonial forces outside Boston and appointing George Washington commander in chief. As military organization was developed and funds were raised, fresh units were authorized to supplement the forces already in the field. Horatio Gates, adjutant general of the army, issued instructions to the recruiters on July 10, 1775.

Source: Niles: "Instruction of Adjutant General Horatio Gates for Recruiting Troops, Massachusetts Bay, July 10, 1775."

You ARE NOT TO ENLIST any deserter from the ministerial army, nor any stroller, Negro, or vagabond, or person suspected of being an enemy to the liberty of America, nor any under eighteen years of age.

As the cause is the best that can engage men of courage and principle to take up arms, so it is expected that none but such will be accepted by the recruiting officer; the pay, provision, etc., being so ample, it is not doubted but the officers set upon this service will without delay complete their respective corps, and march the men forthwith to the camp.

You are not to enlist any person who is not an American born, unless such person has a wife and family, and is a settled resident in this country.

The person you enlist must be provided with good and complete arms.

Given at the headquarters at Cambridge, this 10th day of July, 1775.

XXII. *Charge your Bayonet.*

Reconciliation Rejected

Lord North, the prime minister of Great Britain during the Revolutionary War, made an offer for reconciliation to the colonies in May of 1775. Evidence indicates that the purpose of this gesture was to divide parliamentary opposition to ministerial policy and to win support in England for further coercive measures. The Continental Congress was divided between those who favored compromise and those who favored war. On July 31, Congress finally rejected Lord North's motion upon the advice of a committee consisting of Benjamin Franklin, Thomas Jefferson, Richard Henry Lee, and John Adams. In the following document, Congress repeated the colonial claim to the right of self-government and denounced the hypocrisy involved in offering reconciliation while at the same time passing the Restraining Acts.

Source: *Journals*, I: "Monday, July 31, 1775."

THE SEVERAL ASSEMBLIES of New Jersey, Pennsylvania, and Virginia, having referred to the Congress a resolution of the House of Commons of Great Britain, which resolution is in these words:

The House in a committee on the American papers. Motion made, and question proposed:

That it is the opinion of this committee that when the General Council and Assembly, or General Court of any of His Majesty's provinces or colonies in America shall propose to make provision, according to the condition, circumstance, or situation of such province or colony, for contributing their proportion to the common defense (such proportion to be raised under the authority of the General Court or General Assembly of such province or colony and disposable by Parliament) and shall engage to make provision also for the support of the civil government, and the administration of justice in such province or colony, it will be proper, if such proposal shall be approved by His Majesty, and the two houses of Parliament, and for so long as such provision shall be made accordingly, to forbear in respect to such province or colony to lay any duty, tax, or assessment, or to impose any further duty, tax, or assessment, except only such duties as it may be expedient to continue to levy or impose for the regulation of commerce; the net produce or the duties last mentioned to be carried to the account of such province or colony respectively.

The Congress took the said resolution into consideration, and are thereupon of opinion:

That the colonies of America are entitled to the sole and exclusive privilege of giving and granting their own money; that this involves a right of deliberating whether they will make any gift, for what purposes it shall be made, and what shall be its amount; and that it is a high breach of this privilege for any body of men, extraneous to their constitutions, to prescribe the purposes for which money shall be levied on them, to take to themselves the authority of judging of their conditions, circumstances, and situations, and of determining the amount of the contribution to be levied.

That as the colonies possess a right of appropriating their gifts, so are they entitled at all times to inquire into their application, to see that they be not wasted among the venal and corrupt for the purpose of undermining the civil rights of the givers, nor yet be diverted to the support of standing armies, inconsistent with their freedom and subversive of their quiet. To propose, therefore, as this resolution does, that the monies given by the colonies shall be subject to the disposal of Parliament alone, is to propose that they shall relinquish this right of inquiry and put it in the power of others to render their gifts ruinous, in proportion as they are liberal.

That this privilege of giving or of withholding our monies is an important barrier against the undue exertion of prerogative, which, if left altogether without control, may be exercised to our great oppression; and all history shows how efficacious is its intercession for redress of grievances and re-establishment of rights, and how improvident it would be to part with so powerful a mediator.

We are of opinion that the proposition contained in this resolution is unreasonable and insidious: unreasonable, because if we declare we accede to it, we declare without reservation we will purchase the favor of Parliament, not knowing at the same time at what price they will please to estimate their favor. It is insidious because individual colonies, having bid and bidden again till they find the avidity of the seller too great for all their powers to satisfy, are then to return into opposition, divided from their sister colonies whom the minister will have previously detached by a grant of easier terms, or by an artful procrastination of a definitive answer.

That the suspension of the exercise of their pretended power of taxation being ex-

pressly made commensurate with the continuance of our gifts, these must be perpetual to make that so. Whereas no experience has shown that a gift of perpetual revenue secures a perpetual return of duty or of kind disposition. On the contrary, the Parliament itself, wisely attentive to this observation, are in the established practice of granting their supplies from year to year only.

Desirous and determined as we are to consider, in the most dispassionate view, every seeming advance toward a reconciliation made by the British Parliament, let our brethren of Britain reflect what would have been the sacrifice to men of free spirits had even fair terms been proffered, as these insidious proposals were, with circumstances of insult and defiance. A proposition to give our money, accompanied with large fleets and armies, seems addressed to our fears rather than to our freedom. With what patience would Britons have received articles of treaty from any power on earth when borne on the point of the bayonet by military plenipotentiaries?

We think the attempt unnecessary to raise upon us, by force or by threats, our proportional contributions to the common defense, when all know, and themselves acknowledge, we have fully contributed whenever called upon to do so in the character of freemen.

We are of opinion it is not just that the colonies should be required to oblige themselves to other contributions while Great Britain possesses a monopoly of their trade. This of itself lays them under heavy contribution. To demand, therefore, additional aids in the form of a tax is to demand the double of their equal proportion. If we are to contribute equally with the other parts of the empire, let us equally with them enjoy free commerce with the whole world. But while the restrictions on our trade shut to us the resources of wealth, is it just we should bear all other burdens equally with those to whom every resource is open?

We conceive that the British Parliament has no right to intermeddle with our provisions for the support of civil government or administration of justice. The provisions we have made are such as please ourselves, and are agreeable to our own circumstances. They answer the substantial purposes of government and of justice, and other purposes than these should not be answered. We do not mean that our people shall be burdened with oppressive taxes to provide sinecures for the idle or the wicked, under color of providing for a civil list. While Parliament pursue their plan of civil government within their own jurisdiction, we also hope to pursue ours without molestation.

We are of opinion the proposition is altogether unsatisfactory because it imports only a suspension of the mode, not a renunciation of the pretended right to tax us: because, too, it does not propose to repeal the several acts of Parliament passed for the purposes of restraining the trade and altering the form of government of one of our colonies; extending the boundaries and changing the government of Quebec; enlarging the jurisdiction of the Courts of Admiralty and Vice-Admiralty; taking from us the rights of trial by a jury of the vicinage in cases affecting both life and property; transporting us into other countries to be tried for criminal offenses; exempting by mock trial the murderers of colonists from punishment; and quartering soldiers on us in times of profound peace. Nor do they renounce the power of suspending our own legislatures, and for legislating for us themselves in all cases whatsoever. On the contrary, to show they mean no discontinuance of injury, they pass acts, at the very time of holding out this proposition, for restraining the commerce and fisheries of the provinces of New England, and for interdicting the trade of other colonies with all foreign nations, and with each other. This proves unequivocally they mean not to relinquish the exercise of indiscriminate legislation over us.

Upon the whole, this proposition seems to have been held up to the world to deceive it into a belief that there was nothing in dispute between us but the *mode* of levying taxes, and that the Parliament having now been so good as to give up this, the colonies are unreasonable if not perfectly satisfied. Whereas, in truth our adversaries still claim a right of demanding *ad libitum*, and of taxing us themselves to the full amount of their demand if we do not comply with it. This leaves us without anything we can call property. But what is of more importance, and what in this proposal they keep out of sight, as if no such point was now in contest between us, they claim a right to alter our charters and established laws and leave us without any security for our lives or liberties.

The proposition seems also to have been calculated more particularly to lull into fatal security our well-affected fellow subjects on the other side the water till time should be given for the operation of those arms which a British minister pronounced would instantaneously reduce the "cowardly" sons of America to unreserved submission. But when the world reflects how inadequate to justice are these vaunted terms; when it attends to the rapid and bold succession of injuries which during the course of eleven years have been aimed at these colonies; when it reviews the pacific and respectful expostulations which during that whole time were the sole arms we opposed to them; when it observes that our complaints were either not heard at all or were answered with new and accumulated injuries; when it recollects that the minister himself on an early occasion declared "that he would never treat with America, till he had brought her to his feet," and that an avowed partisan of ministry has more lately denounced against us the dreadful sentence, *Delenda est Carthago"* [Let Carthage be destroyed]; that was done in the presence of a British senate, and being unreproved by them must be taken to be their own sentiment (especially as the purpose has already in part been carried into execution by their treatment of Boston and burning of Charlestown); when it considers the great armaments with which they have invaded us and the circumstances of cruelty with which these have commenced and prosecuted hostilities; when these things, we say, are laid together and attentively considered, can the world be deceived into an opinion that we are unreasonable, or can it hesitate to believe with us that nothing but our own exertions may defeat the ministerial sentence of death or abject submission?

The Authority of the People

The Revolution was the occasion for attempts in many of the colonies to make their governments more democratic. That they were insufficiently so was felt with particular passion in North Carolina, where a group of seaboard gentry, allied with the royal governor and his handpicked council, had for all practical purposes ruled the colony. This small minority controlled four-fifths of the representation in the provincial government, since the coastal counties had five members for every two that the inland counties could send to the legislature. The same group taxed the inland region unfairly, was corrupt in its administration of the laws (in 1770 there was at least one defaulting sheriff in every county in the province), and held hard by the established religion. Although the bulk of the population consisted of dissenters, as late as 1769 no marriage was legal unless celebrated by an Anglican clergyman, of whom there were but six to serve a colony of 230,000 persons. The royal governor and the gentry managed to put down the Regulator revolt, but with the coming of the war, the back country was no longer to be denied. On May 31, 1775, only seven weeks after Lexington and Concord, the Scotch-Irish of Mecklenburg County drafted militant resolves declaring that British government was suspended in America. Three months later, on September 1, the same county prepared the following instructions for its delegates to the provincial congress that would consider, among other things, a new constitution for the province. When such a constitution was adopted on December 18, 1776, the province had become a state, and the Mecklenburg demands, at least in principle, were law.

Source: *The Colonial Records of North Carolina, etc., etc.,* William L. Saunders, ed.,
    Vol. X, Raleigh, 1890: "Instructions for the Delegates of Mecklenburg
    County Proposed to the Consideration of the County."

1. You are instructed to vote that the late province of North Carolina is, and of right ought to be, a free and independent state invested with all the power of legislation capable of making laws to regulate all its internal policy, subject only in its external connections and foreign commerce to a negative of a continental senate.

2. You are instructed to vote for the execution of a civil government under the authority of the people for the future security of all the rights, privileges, and prerogatives

of the state and the private, natural, and un-alienable rights of the constituting members thereof, either as men or Christians. If this should not be confirmed in Congress or Convention, protest.

3. You are instructed to vote that an equal representation be established, and that the qualifications required to enable any person or persons to have a voice in legislation may not be secured too high but that every freeman who shall be called upon to support government, either in person or property, may be admitted thereto. If this should not be confirmed, protest and remonstrate.

4. You are instructed to vote that legislation be not a divided right, and that no man or body of men be invested with a negative on the voice of the people duly collected, and that no honors or dignities be conferred for life or made hereditary on any person or persons either legislative or executive. If this should not be confirmed, protest and remonstrate.

5. You are instructed to vote that all and every person or persons seized or possessed of any estate, real or personal, agreeable to the last establishment, be confirmed in their seizures and possession to all intents and purposes in law who have not forfeited their right to the protection of the state by their criminal practice toward the same. If this should not be confirmed, protest.

6. You are instructed to vote that deputies to represent this state in a Continental Congress be appointed in and by the supreme legislative body of the state; the form of nomination to be submitted to if free and also that all officers the influence of whose office is equally to extend to every part of the state be appointed in the same manner and form; likewise give your consent to the establishing the old political divisions if it should be voted in Convention or to new ones if similar. On such establishments taking place, you are instructed to vote in the general that all officers who are

to exercise their authority in any of the said districts be recommended to the trust only by the freemen of the said division — to be subject, however, to the general laws and regulations of the state. If this should not be substantially confirmed, protest.

7. You are instructed to move and insist that the people you immediately represent be acknowledged to be a distinct county of this state, as formerly of the late province, with the additional privilege of annually electing their own officers, both civil and military, together with the elections of clerks and sheriffs by the freemen of the same. The choice to be confirmed by the sovereign authority of the state, and the officers so invested to be under the jurisdiction of the state and liable to its cognizance and inflictions in case of malpractice. If this should not be confirmed, protest and remonstrate.

8. You are instructed to vote that no chief justice, no secretary of state, no auditor general, no surveyor general, no practicing lawyer, no clerk of any court of record, no sheriff, and no person holding a military office in this state shall be a representative of the people in Congress or Convention. If this should not be confirmed, contend for it.

9. You are instructed to vote that all claims against the public, except such as accrue upon attendance upon Congress or Convention, be first submitted to the inspection of a committee of nine or more men, inhabitants of the county where said claimant is a resident, and without the approbation of said committee, it shall not be accepted by the public; for which purpose you are to move and insist that a law be enacted to empower the freemen of each county to choose a committee of not less than nine men, of whom none are to be military officers. If this should not be confirmed, protest and remonstrate.

10. You are instructed to refuse to enter into any combinations of secrecy as members of Congress or Convention and also to

refuse to subscribe any ensnaring tests binding you to an unlimited subjection to the determination of Congress or Convention.

11. You are instructed to move and insist that the public accounts fairly stated shall be regularly kept in proper books open to the inspection of all persons whom it may concern. If this should not be confirmed, contend for it.

12. You are instructed to move and insist that the power of county courts be much more extensive than under the former constitution, both with respect to matters of property and breaches of the peace. If not confirmed, contend for it.

13. You are instructed to assert and consent to the establishment of the Christian religion as contained in the Scriptures of the Old and New Testaments and more briefly comprised in the Thirty-Nine Articles of the Church of England, excluding the 37th Article, together with all the articles excepted, and not to be imposed on dissenters, by the Act of Toleration and clearly held forth in the confession of faith compiled by the Assembly of Divines at Westminster, to be the religion of the state, to the utter exclusion forever of all and every other (falsely so-called) religion, whether pagan or papal; and that the full, free, and peaceable enjoyment thereof be secured to all and every constituent member of the state as their unalienable right as freemen without the imposition of rites and ceremonies, whether claiming civil or ecclesiastic power for their source; and that a confession and profession of the religion so established shall be necessary in qualifying any person for public trust in the state. If this should not be confirmed, protest and remonstrate.

14. You are instructed to oppose to the utmost any particular church or set of clergymen being invested with power to decree rites and ceremonies and to decide in controversies of faith to be submitted to under the influence of penal laws. You are also to oppose the establishment of any mode of worship to be supported to the opposition of the rights of conscience together with the destruction of private property. You are to understand that under modes of worship are comprehended the different forms of swearing by law required. You are, moreover, to oppose the establishing an ecclesiastic supremacy in the sovereign authority of the state. You are to oppose the toleration of the popish idolatrous worship. If this should not be confirmed, protest and remonstrate.

15. You are instructed to move and insist that not less than four-fifths of the body of which you are members shall in voting be deemed a majority. If this should not be confirmed, contend for it.

16. You are instructed to give your voices to and for every motion and bill made or brought into the Congress or Convention where they appear to be for public utility and in no ways repugnant to the above instruction.

17. Gentlemen, the foregoing instructions you are not only to look on as instructions but as charges to which you are desired to take special heed as the general rule of your conduct as our representatives, and we expect you will exert yourselves to the utmost of your ability to obtain the purposes given you in charge. And wherein you fail either in obtaining or opposing, you are hereby ordered to enter your protest against the vote of the Congress or Convention as is pointed out to you in the above instructions.

Thomas Gage: The Rebellion in America

Thomas Gage was relieved of his post as commander in chief of the British forces in America in 1775. On board ship, returning to England, he addressed the following letter of October 15 to Lord Dartmouth, describing the rebellion in America. Gage wanted to convince his superiors that the colonial rebellion could not be disposed of quickly and that a general war would be necessary to insure British domination in North America.

Source: *Archives,* III, pp. 1069-1070.

It will give me pleasure, as I think it my duty, to send Your Lordship every hint or intelligence that can be of use at this important crisis. Nor am I disposed to do it in a secret manner, as it behooves every man in such times as these to declare his sentiments openly.

People agree now that there has been a scheme for a revolt from the mother country long conceived between those who have most influence in the American councils, which has been preparing the people's minds by degrees, for events that at first view they regarded with horror and detestation. If the Boston Port Bill had not furnished a pretext for rebellion, something else would have brought it forward. Unfortunately, few could believe it possible for them to prevail with the people to rise, and to the last the friends of government assured them it was only threats and menaces meant to intimidate.

Misfortune has arisen from this incredulity, for the rebels have been prepared to exercise their plan, while the government, not apprehensive of so general a revolt, has been unprepared to oppose it. The conduct of the leaders on the 19th of April evinced their intention to begin hostilities, and had they not commenced then, they would only have been deferred. Your Lordship has a perfect idea of the transactions of that day, which were so far unlucky as it put an immediate stop to supplies of every kind; otherwise, our magazines would have been better filled.

I am convinced that the promoters of the rebellion have no real desire of peace, unless they have a *carte blanche.* Their whole conduct has been one scene of fallacy, duplicity, and dissimulation, by which they have duped many well-inclined people. Your Lordship will judge if the last petition of the Congress to the King is to be relied upon. And yet we are told that this petition was obtained by the most moderate of the members with great difficulty, and after very long debate.

There has been much heat and division in the Congress and a jealousy of the New England members, and I am told it was owing to jealousy that Washington was appointed to the command of the rebel army, in which there is much discontent. Lee is neither respected nor esteemed among them, though it is said that he is supported by the Boston rulers in opposition to Washington, and that he is for making an attack without delay upon the troops, but that the rest think it too desperate an undertaking. The rebel forces are well fed, but in general ill clothed and badly paid, though paper money has been issued to them lately. The credit of the paper is now kept up by force, and I have not heard that any plan has been fixed upon to redeem it.

They give out that they expect peace on their own terms through the inability of Britain to contend with them; and it is no wonder that such reports gain credit with the people, when letters from England and English newspapers give so much encouragement to rebellion.

Many people are of the opinion that the rebels will not hold together another year; but though the country will be very greatly distressed, and the people tired of the work, I will take the liberty to say, that from their presumption, arrogance, and encouragement from England, we can rely on nothing but our own force to procure even decent terms of peace; and that if it was ever necessary to obtain peace through the means of war, it is highly so in the present juncture.

I transmit to Your Lordship a packet of letters that were picked out from a number of papers scattered about Cushing's house. They contain no intelligence of present transactions but show the nature of the correspondence that the two Lees, Dr. Franklin, and others kept up with the leaders of this rebellion.

Instructions to Vote Against Independence

Well into 1776, there was still some reluctance to declare openly for independence. Apart from their determined opposition to British policy, other factors were operative in the thinking of the colonial leadership. First was an anti-democratic bias: the fear of a popular upheaval in the transition to new forms of government. Second was a fear that strife between the colonies would lead to civil war at a time when Britain was the common enemy. Among the moves which delayed a declaration of independence for some months were the instructions issued November 9, 1775, to the Pennsylvania delegates to the Second Continental Congress.

Source: *Archives*, III, p. 1408.

THE TRUST REPOSED IN YOU is of such a nature and the modes of executing it may be so diversified in the course of your deliberations, that it is scarcely possible to give you particular instructions respecting it.

We, therefore, in general, direct that you, or any four of you, meet in Congress the delegates of the several colonies now assembled in this city and any such delegates as may meet in Congress next year; that you consult together on the present critical and alarming state of public affairs; that you exert your utmost endeavors to agree upon and recommend such measures as you shall judge to afford the best prospect of obtaining redress of American grievances, and restoring that union and harmony between Great Britain and the colonies so essential to the welfare and happiness of both countries.

Though the oppressive measures of the British Parliament and administration have compelled us to resist their violence by force of arms, yet we strictly enjoin you that you, in behalf of this colony, dissent from and utterly reject any propositions, should such be made, that may cause or lead to a separation from our mother country or a change of the form of this government.

You are directed to make report of your proceedings to this House.

ABIGAIL ADAMS: Doubts About Independence

Although Abigail Adams had little formal education, she was intelligent and broadminded and became a terse and vigorous letter writer. That she was concerned with the growth of the new nation can be seen in her numerous letters to her husband John Adams. In the following letter, written November 27, 1775, Mrs. Adams expresses her doubts about the ability of the Americans to form a viable government.

Source: *Letters of Mrs. Adams, the Wife of John Adams*, Charles Francis
Adams, ed., 4th edition, Boston, 1848.

COLONEL WARREN RETURNED last week to Plymouth, so that I shall not hear anything from you until he goes back again, which will not be till the last of this month. He damped my spirits greatly by telling me that the court had prolonged your stay another month. I was pleasing myself with the thought that you would soon be upon your return. It is in vain to repine. I hope the public will reap what I sacrifice.

I wish I knew what mighty things were fabricating. If a form of government is to be established here, what one will be assumed? Will it be left to our assemblies to choose one? And will not many men have many minds? And shall we not run into dissensions among ourselves?

I am more and more convinced that man is a dangerous creature; and that power, whether vested in many or a few, is ever grasping, and, like the grave, cries "Give," give." The great fish swallow up the small; and he who is most strenuous for the rights of the people when vested with power, is as eager after the prerogatives of government. You tell me of degrees of perfection to which human nature is capable of arriving, and I believe it, but, at the same time, lament that our admiration should arise from the scarcity of the instances.

The building up a great empire, which was only hinted at by my correspondent, may now, I suppose, be realized even by the unbelievers. Yet, will not ten thousand difficulties arise in the formation of it? The reins of government have been so long slackened that I fear the people will not quietly submit to those restraints which are necessary for the peace and security of the community. If we separate from Britain, what code of laws will be established? How shall we be governed so as to retain our liberties? Can any government be free which is not administered by general stated laws? Who shall frame these laws? Who will give them force and energy? It is true your resolutions, as a body, have hitherto had the force of laws; but will they continue to have?

When I consider these things, and the prejudices of people in favor of ancient customs and regulations, I feel anxious for the fate of our monarchy or democracy, or whatever is to take place. I soon get lost in a labyrinth of perplexities; but, whatever occurs, may justice and righteousness be the stability of our times, and order arise out of confusion. Great difficulties may be surmounted by patience and perseverance.

I believe I have tired you with politics. As to news, we have not any at all. I shudder at the approach of winter, when I think I am to remain desolate.

I must bid you good night; 'tis late for me, who am much of an invalid. I was disappointed last week in receiving a packet by the post, and, upon unsealing it, finding only four newspapers. I think you are more cautious than you need be. All letters, I believe, have come safe to hand. I have sixteen from you, and wish I had as many more.

"Yankee Doodle"

France, Spain, the Netherlands, Germany, and Hungary have all claimed "Yankee Doodle," but the melody seems to have come first from England, where it was a children's game song called "Lucy Locket." Brought to America by the English soldiers who fought in the French and Indian War, the song became popular among the colonists, each settlement having its own set of lyrics. During the Revolutionary War, the British soldiers used a derisive set of lyrics to mock the shabby colonial soldiers, and the colonists in turn had another set of words that eventually became their battle cry. "Yankee" was a contemptuous nickname the British used for the New Englanders, and "doodle" meant "dope, half-wit, fool."

YANKEE DOODLE

Father and I went down to camp
Along with Captain Gooding,
And there we saw the men and boys
As thick as hasty pudding.

Yankee Doodle keep it up,
Yankee Doodle Dandy,
Mind the music and the step,
And with the girls be handy.

There was Captain Washington
Upon a slapping stallion
A-giving orders to his men —
There must have been a million.

Then I saw a swamping gun
As large as logs of maple
Upon a very little cart,
A load for Father's cattle.

Every time they shot it off
It took a horn of powder
And made a noise like father's gun
Only a nation louder.

There I saw a wooden keg
With heads made out of leather;
They knocked upon it with some sticks
To call the folks together.

Then they'd fife away like fun
And play on cornstalk fiddles,
And some had ribbons red as blood
All bound around their middles.

I can't tell you all I saw —
They kept up such a smother.
I took my hat off, made a bow,
And scampered home to mother.

Massachusetts Suspends the Royal Authority

Early in 1776, most features of royal authority had vanished in the colonies, although reconciliation with Britain still seemed possible. On January 23, the General Court of Massachusetts, at the urging of the Continental Congress, issued a proclamation ousting the royal governor. The management of the colony's affairs reverted to the assembly until such time as the King would appoint a new governor compatible with the spirit of the old charter.

Source: Niles: "Proclamation by the Great and General Court of the
Colony of Massachusetts Bay, January 23, 1776."

As THE HAPPINESS of the people is the sole end of government, so the consent of the people is the only foundation of it, in reason, morality, and the natural fitness of things. And, therefore, every act of government, every exercise of sovereignty against or without the consent of the people is injustice, usurpation, and tyranny.

It is a maxim that in every government there must exist, somewhere, a supreme, sovereign, absolute, and uncontrollable power; but this power resides always in the body of the people; and it never was, or can be delegated to one man, or a few; the great Creator has never given to men a right to vest others with authority over them, unlimited, either in duration or degree.

When kings, ministers, governors, or legislators, therefore, instead of exercising the powers entrusted with them, according to the principles, forms and proportions stated by the constitution, and established by the original compact, prostitute those powers to the purposes of oppression — to subvert, instead of supporting a free constitution; to

destroy, instead of preserving the lives, liberties and properties of the people — they are no longer to be deemed magistrates vested with a sacred character, but become public enemies, and ought to be resisted.

The administration of Great Britain, despising equally the justice, humanity, and magnanimity of their ancestors, and the rights, liberties, and courage of *Americans,* have, for a course of years, labored to establish a sovereignty in America, not founded in the consent of the people but in the mere will of persons, a thousand leagues from us, whom we know not, and have endeavored to establish this sovereignty over us, against our consent, in all cases whatsoever.

The colonies, during this period, have recurred to every peaceable resource in a free constitution, by petitions and remonstrances, to obtain justice; which has been not only denied to them but they have been treated with unexampled indignity and contempt; and, at length, open war of the most atrocious, cruel, and sanguinary kind has been commenced against them. To this an open, manly, and successful resistance has hitherto been made; thirteen colonies are now firmly united in the conduct of this most just and necessary war, under the wise councils of their Congress.

It is the will of Providence for wise, righteous, and gracious ends that this colony should have been singled out, by the enemies of America, as the first object, both of their envy and their revenge; and, after having been made the subject of several merciless and vindictive statutes, one of which was intended to subvert our constitution by charter, is made the seat of war.

No effectual resistance to the system of tyranny prepared for us could be made without either instant recourse to arms or a temporary suspension of the ordinary powers of government and tribunals of justice. To the last of which evils, in hope of a speedy reconciliation with Great Britain, upon equitable terms, the Congress advised us to submit: — And mankind has seen a phenomenon, without example in the political world, a large and populous colony, subsisting in great decency and order, for more than a year, under such a suspension of government.

But as our enemies have proceeded to such barbarous extremities, commencing hostilities upon the good people of this colony, and with unprecedented malice exerting their power to spread the calamities of fire, sword, and famine through the land, and no reasonable prospect remains of a speedy reconciliation with Great Britain, the Congress have resolved:

That no obedience being due to the act of Parliament for altering the charter of the colony of Massachusetts Bay, nor to a governor or lieutenant governor, who will not observe the directions of, but endeavor to subvert that charter, the governor and lieutenant governor of that colony are to be considered as absent, and their offices vacant. And as there is no council there, and inconveniences arising from the suspension of the powers of

government are intolerable, especially at a time when General Gage has actually levied war, and is carrying on hostilities against His Majesty's peaceable and loyal subjects of that colony: that, in order to conform as near as may be to the spirit and substance of the charter, it be recommended to the provincial convention to write letters to the inhabitants of the several places which are entitled to representation in assembly, requesting them to choose such representatives; and that the assembly, when chosen, elect counselors; and that such assembly and council exercise the powers of government, until a governor of His Majesty's appointment will consent to govern the colony according to its charter.

In pursuance of which advice, the good people of this colony have chosen a full and free representation of themselves, who, being convened in assembly, have elected a Council; who, as the executive branch of government, have constituted necessary officers through the colony. The present generation, therefore, may be congratulated on the acquisition of a form of government more immediately, in all its branches, under the influence and control of the people; and therefore more free and happy than was enjoyed by their ancestors. But as a government so popular can be supported only by universal knowledge and virtue in the body of the people, it is the duty of all ranks to promote the means of education, for the rising generation, as well as true religion, purity of manners, and integrity of life among all orders and degrees.

As an army has become necessary for our defense, and in all free states the civil must provide for and control the military power, the major part of the Council have appointed magistrates and courts of justice in every county whose happiness is so connected with that of the people that it is difficult to suppose they can abuse their trust. The business of it is to see those laws enforced which are necessary for the preservation of peace, virtue, and good order. And the

Great and General Court expects and requires that all necessary support and assistance be given, and all proper obedience yielded to them; and will deem every person who shall fail of his duty in this respect toward them a disturber of the peace of this colony, and deserving of exemplary punishment.

That piety and virtue, which alone can secure the freedom of any people, may be encouraged, and vice and immorality suppressed, the Great and General Court have thought fit to issue this proclamation, commanding and enjoining it upon the good people of this colony, that they lead sober, religious, and peaceable lives, avoiding all blasphemies, contempt of the Holy Scriptures, and of the Lord's Day, and all other crimes and misdemeanors, all debauchery, profaneness, corruption, venality, all riotous and tumultuous proceedings, and all immoralities whatsoever; and that they decently and reverently attend the public worship of God, at all times acknowledging with gratitude His merciful interposition in their behalf, devoutly confiding in Him, as the God of armies, by whose favor and protection alone they may hope for success in their present conflict.

TOM PAINE: Plain Arguments for Independence

As the Revolutionary War progressed, the attitude of the British authorities made it apparent that no concessions could be expected. The idea of complete independence, which was beginning to win more and more support, was the subject of discussion in a pamphlet written by a newly arrived English immigrant Tom Paine. Published in January 1776, Common Sense *pressed the argument for independence in logically compelling terms. Paine's reasoning convinced George Washington who wrote to Joseph Reed of Pennsylvania on January 31, 1776: "A few more of such flaming arguments, as were exhibited at Falmouth and Norfolk, added to the sound doctrine and unanswerable reasoning contained in the pamphlet* Common Sense, *will not leave numbers at a loss to decide upon the propriety of a separation."*

Source: *Common Sense*, Boston, 1856, pp. 33-47.

IN THE FOLLOWING PAGES I offer nothing more than simple facts, plain arguments, and common sense; and have no other preliminaries to settle with the reader than that he will divest himself of prejudice and prepossession, and suffer his reason and his feelings to determine for themselves; that he will put *on*, or rather that he will not put *off*, the true character of a man, and generously enlarge his views beyond the present day.

Volumes have been written on the subject of the struggle between England and America. Men of all ranks have embarked in the controversy, from different motives and with various designs; but all have been ineffectual, and the period of debate is closed. Arms, as the last resource, must decide the contest; the appeal was the choice of the king, and the continent has accepted the challenge.

It has been reported of the late Mr. Pelham (who, though an able minister, was not without his faults) that on his being attacked in the House of Commons, on the score that his measures were only of a temporary kind, replied, "They will last my time." Should a thought so fatal and unmanly possess the colonies in the present contest, the name of ancestors will be remembered by future generations with detestation.

The sun never shone on a cause of greater worth. 'Tis not the affair of a city, a county, a province, or a kingdom but of a continent — of at least one-eighth part of the habitable globe. 'Tis not the concern of a day, a year, or an age; posterity are virtually involved in the contest and will be more or less affected even to the end of time by the proceedings now. Now is the seedtime of continental union, faith, and honor. The least fracture now will be like a name engraved with the point of a pin on the tender rind of a young oak; the wound will enlarge with the tree, and posterity read it in full-grown characters.

By referring the matter from argument to arms, a new area for politics is struck; a new method of thinking has arisen. All plans, proposals, etc., prior to the 19th of April, i.e., to the commencement of hostilities, are like the almanacs of last year; which, though proper then, are superseded and useless now. Whatever was advanced by the advocates on either side of the question then terminated in one and the same point, viz., a union with Great Britain. The only difference between the parties was the method of effecting it, the one proposing force, the other friendship; but it has so far happened that the first has failed, and the second has withdrawn her influence.

As much has been said of the advantages of reconciliation, which, like an agreeable dream, have passed away and left us as we were, it is but right that we should examine the contrary side of the argument, and inquire into some of the many material injuries which these colonies sustain, and always will sustain, by being connected with and dependent on Great Britain. To examine that connection and dependence, on the principles of nature and common sense, to see what we have to trust to if separated, and what we are to expect if dependent.

I have heard it asserted by some that as America has flourished under her former connection with Great Britain, the same connection is necessary toward her future happiness, and will always have the same effect. Nothing can be more fallacious than this kind of argument. We may as well assert that because a child has thrived upon milk . . . it is never to have meat, or that the first twenty years of our lives is to become a precedent for the next twenty. But even this is admitting more than is true, for I answer roundly that America would have flourished as much, and probably much more, had no European power had anything to do with her. The articles of commerce, by which she has enriched herself, are the necessaries of life, and will always have a market while eating is the custom of Europe.

But she has protected us, say some. That she has engrossed us is true, and defended the continent at our expense as well as her own is admitted, and she would have defended Turkey from the same motives, viz., for the sake of trade and dominion.

Alas! we have been long led away by ancient prejudices, and made large sacrifices to superstition. We have boasted the protection of Great Britain without considering that her motive was *interest* not *attachment;* and that she did not protect us from *our enemies* on *our account* but from *her enemies* on *her own account,* from those who had no quarrel with us on any *other account,* and who will always be our enemies on the *same account.* Let Britain waive her pretensions to the continent, or the continent throw off the dependence, and we should be at peace with France and Spain, were they at war with Britain. The miseries of Hanover last war ought to warn us against connections.

It has lately been asserted in Parliament that the colonies have no relation to each other but through the parent country, i.e., that Pennsylvania and the Jerseys, and so on for the rest, are sister colonies by the way of England. This is certainly a very roundabout way of proving relationship, but it is the nearest and only true way of proving enemyship, if I may so call it. France and Spain never were, nor perhaps ever will be, our enemies as *Americans* but as our being the *subjects of Great Britain*.

But Britain is the parent country, say some. Then the more shame upon her conduct. Even brutes do not devour their young, nor savages make war upon their families; wherefore, the assertion, if true, turns to her reproach. But it happens not to be true, or only partly so, and the phrase "parent" or "mother country" has been jesuitically adopted by the king and his parasites, with a low papistical design of gaining an unfair bias on the credulous weakness of our minds. Europe, and not England, is the parent country of America. This New World has been the asylum for the persecuted lovers of civil and religious liberty from *every part* of Europe. Hither have they fled, not from the tender embraces of the mother but from the cruelty of the monster; and it is so far true of England that the same tyranny which drove the first emigrants from home pursues their descendants still.

In this extensive quarter of the globe, we forget the narrow limits of 360 miles (the extent of England) and carry our friendship on a larger scale; we claim brotherhood with every European Christian, and triumph in the generosity of the sentiment.

It is pleasant to observe by what regular gradations we surmount local prejudices as we enlarge our acquaintance with the world. A man born in any town in England divided into parishes will naturally associate most with his fellow parishioners (because their interests in many cases will be common) and distinguish him by the name of "neighbor"; if he meet him but a few miles from home, he drops the narrow idea of a street and salutes him by the name of "townsman"; if he travel out of the county and meet him in any other, he forgets the minor divisions of street and town and calls him "countryman," *i.e.*, "countyman." But if in their foreign excursions they should associate in France or any other part of Europe, their local remembrance would be enlarged into that of "Englishmen." And by a just parity of reasoning, all Europeans meeting in America, or any other quarter of the globe, are "countrymen"; for England, Holland, Germany, or Sweden, when compared with the whole, stand in the same places on the larger scale, which the divisions of street, town, and county do on the smaller one — distinctions too limited for continental minds. Not one-third of the inhabitants, even of this province, are of English descent. Wherefore, I reprobate the phrase of "parent" or "mother country" applied to England only as being false, selfish, narrow, and ungenerous.

But, admitting that we were all of English descent, what does it amount to? Nothing. Britain, being now an open enemy, extinguishes every other name and title; and to say that reconciliation is our duty is truly farcical. The first king of England, of the present line (William the Conqueror), was a Frenchman, and half the peers of England are descendants from the same country; wherefore, by the same method of reasoning, England ought to be governed by France.

Much has been said of the united strength of Britain and the colonies — that in conjunction they might bid defiance to the world. But this is mere presumption. The fate of war is uncertain, neither do the expressions mean anything; for this continent would never suffer itself to be drained of inhabitants to support the British arms in either Asia, Africa, or Europe.

Besides, what have we to do with setting the world at defiance? Our plan is commerce, and that, well attended to, will secure us the peace and friendship of all Europe; because it is the interest of all Europe to have America a *free port*. Her trade will always be a protection, and her barrenness of gold and silver secure her from invaders.

I challenge the warmest advocate for reconciliation to show a single advantage that this continent can reap by being connected with Great Britain. I repeat the challenge; not a single advantage is derived. Our corn will fetch its price in any market in Europe, and our imported goods must be paid for, buy them where we will.

But the injuries and disadvantages which we sustain by that connection are without number; and our duty to mankind at large, as well as to ourselves, instructs us to renounce the alliance, because any submission to or dependence on Great Britain tends directly to involve this continent in European wars and quarrels, and sets us at variance with nations who would otherwise seek our friendship, and against whom we have neither anger nor complaint. As Europe is our market for trade, we ought to form no partial connection with any part of it. It is the true interest of America to steer clear of European contentions which she never can do, while, by her dependence on Britain, she is made the makeweight in the scale of British politics.

Europe is too thickly planted with kingdoms to be long at peace; and whenever a war breaks out between England and any foreign power, the trade of America goes to ruin *because of her connection with Britain*. The next war may not turn out like the last, and should it not, the advocates for reconciliation now will be wishing for separation then, because neutrality in that case would be a safer convoy than a man-of-war. Everything that is right or natural pleads for separation. The blood of the slain, the weeping voice of nature cries, "'tis time to part." Even the distance at which the Almighty has placed England and America is a strong and natural proof that the authority of the one over the other was never the design of Heaven. The time, likewise, at which the continent was discovered adds weight to the argument, and the manner in which it was peopled increases the force of it. The Reformation was preceded by the discovery of America, as if the Almighty graciously meant to open a sanctuary to the persecuted in future years, when home should afford neither friendship nor safety.

The authority of Great Britain over this continent is a form of government which sooner or later must have an end; and a serious mind can draw no true pleasure by looking forward, under the painful and positive conviction that what he calls "the present constitution" is merely temporary. As parents, we can have no joy knowing that *this government* is not sufficiently lasting to ensure anything which we may bequeath to posterity; and by a plain method of argument, as we are running the next generation into debt, we ought to do the work of it, otherwise we use them meanly and pitifully. In order to discover the line of our duty rightly, we should take our children in our hand and fix our station a few years further into life; that eminence will present a prospect which a few present fears and prejudices conceal from our sight.

Though I would carefully avoid giving unnecessary offense, yet I am inclined to believe that all those who espouse the doctrine of reconciliation may be included within the following descriptions: Interested men who are not to be trusted; weak men who *cannot* see; prejudiced men who *will not* see; and a certain set of moderate men who think better of the European world than it deserves; and this last class, by an ill-judged deliberation, will be the cause of more calamities to this continent than all the other three.

It is the good fortune of many to live distant from the scene of sorrow; the evil is not sufficiently brought to *their* doors to make *them* feel the precariousness with which all American property is possessed. But let our imaginations transport us a few moments to Boston; that seat of wretchedness will teach us wisdom and instruct us forever to renounce a power in whom we can have no trust. The inhabitants of that unfortunate city, who but a few months ago were in ease and affluence, have now no other alternative than to stay and starve, or turn out to beg. Endangered by the fire of their friends if they continue within the city, and plundered by the soldiery if they leave it, in their present situation they are prisoners without the hope of redemption, and in a general attack for their relief, they would be exposed to the fury of both armies.

Men of passive tempers look somewhat lightly over the offenses of Britain, and, still hoping for the best, are apt to call out, "Come, come, we shall be friends again for all this." But examine the passions and feelings of mankind, bring the doctrine of reconciliation to the touchstone of nature, and then tell me whether you can hereafter love, honor, and faithfully serve the power that has carried fire and sword into your land. If you cannot do all these then are you only deceiving yourselves, and by your delay bringing ruin upon your posterity. Your future connection with Britain, whom you can neither love nor honor, will be forced and unnatural, and being formed only on the plan of present convenience, will in a little time fall into a relapse more wretched than the first. But if you say you can still pass the violations over, then I ask, has your house been burned? Has your property been destroyed before your face? Are your wife and children destitute of a bed to lie on or bread to live on? Have you lost a parent or child by their hands, and yourself the ruined and wretched survivor? If you have not, then are you not a judge of those who have? But if you have, and can still shake hands with the murderers, then are you unworthy the name of husband, father, friend, or lover, and whatever may be your rank or title in life, you have the heart of a coward and the spirit of a sycophant.

This is not inflaming or exaggerating matters but trying them by those feelings and affections which nature justifies, and without which we should be incapable of discharging the social duties of life or enjoying the felicities of it. I mean not to exhibit horror for the purpose of provoking revenge but to awaken us from fatal and unmanly slumbers, that we may pursue determinately some fixed object. It is not in the power of Britain or of Europe to conquer America, if she does not conquer herself by *delay* and *timidity*. The present winter is worth an age if rightly employed, but if lost or neglected, the whole continent will partake of the misfortune; and there is no punishment which that man will not deserve, be he who or what or where he will, that may be the means of sacrificing a season so precious and useful.

It is repugnant to reason and the universal order of things [and] to all examples from former ages to suppose that this continent can longer remain subject to any external power. The most sanguine in Britain do not think so. The utmost stretch of human wisdom cannot, at this time, compass a plan short of separation which can promise the continent even a year's security. Reconciliation is *now* a fallacious dream. Nature has deserted the connection, and art cannot supply her place. For, as Milton wisely expresses, "never can true reconcilement grow, where wounds of deadly hate have pierced so deep."

Every quiet method for peace has been ineffectual. Our prayers have been rejected with disdain, and only tended to convince us that nothing flatters vanity or confirms obstinancy in kings more than repeated petitioning; nothing has contributed more than this very measure to make the kings of Europe absolute — witness Denmark and Sweden. Wherefore, since nothing but blows will do, for God's sake let us come to a final separation and not leave the next generation to be cutting throats under the violated unmeaning names of parent and child.

To say they will never attempt it again is

idle and visionary. We thought so at the repeal of the Stamp Act, yet a year or two undeceived us, as well may we suppose that nations which have been once defeated will never renew the quarrel.

As to government matters, it is not in the power of Britain to do this continent justice. The business of it will soon be too weighty and intricate to be managed with any tolerable degree of convenience by a power so distant from us, and so very ignorant of us; for if they cannot conquer us, they cannot govern us. To be always running 3,000 or 4,000 miles with a tale or a petition, waiting four or five months for an answer, which, when obtained, requires five or six more to explain it in, will in a few years be looked upon as folly and childishness — there was a time when it was proper, and there is a proper time for it to cease.

Small islands not capable of protecting themselves are the proper objects for kingdoms to take under their care; but there is something absurd in supposing a continent to be perpetually governed by an island. In no instance has nature made the satellite larger than its primary planet; and as England and America, with respect to each other, reverses the common order of nature, it is evident that they belong to different systems: England to Europe, America to itself.

I am not induced by motives of pride, party, or resentment to espouse the doctrine of separation and independence; I am clearly, positively, and conscientously persuaded that it is the true interest of this continent to be so; that everything short of *that* is mere patchwork; that it can afford no lasting felicity; that it is leaving the sword to our children and shrinking back at a time when going a little further would have rendered this continent the glory of the earth.

As Britain has not manifested the least inclination toward a compromise, we may be assured that no terms can be obtained worthy the acceptance of the continent, or anyway equal to the expense of blood and treasure we have been already put to.

The object contended for ought always to bear some just proportion to the expense. The removal of North, or the whole detestable junto, is a matter unworthy the millions we have expended. A temporary stoppage of trade was an inconvenience which would have sufficiently balanced the repeal of all the acts complained of had such repeals been obtained; but if the whole continent must take up arms, if every man must be a soldier, it is scarcely worth our while to fight against a contemptible Ministry only. Dearly, dearly do we pay for the repeal of the acts, if that is all we fight for; for, in a just estimation, it is as great a folly to pay a Bunker-Hill price for law as for land. I have always considered the independency of this continent as an event which sooner or later must take place, and, from the late rapid progress of the continent to maturity, the event cannot be far off. Wherefore, on the breaking out of hostilities, it was not worth the while to have disputed a matter which time would have finally redressed, unless we meant to be in earnest; otherwise, it is like wasting an estate on a suit at law to regulate the trespasses of a tenant whose lease is just expiring. No man was a warmer wisher for a reconciliation than myself before the fatal 19th of April, 1775; but the moment the event of that day was made known, I rejected the hardened, sullen-tempered Pharaoh of England forever; and disdain the wretch, that with the pretended title of "Father of his people" can unfeelingly hear of their slaughter, and composedly sleep with their blood upon his soul.

But admitting that matters were now made up, what would be the event? I answer, the ruin of the continent. And that for several reasons.

First, the powers of governing still remaining in the hands of the king, he will have a negative over the whole legislation of this continent. And as he has shown himself such an inveterate enemy to liberty, and discovered such a thirst for arbitrary power, is he, or is he not, a proper person to say to these colonies, "You shall make no laws but what I please!" And is there any inhabitant of America so ignorant as not to know that according to what is called the *present constitution,* this continent can make no laws but what the king gives leave to? And is there any man so unwise as not to see that (considering what has happened) he will suffer no law to be made here but such as suits *his* purpose? We may be as effectually enslaved by the want of laws in America as by submitting to laws made for us in England. After matters are made up (as it is called), can there be any doubt but the whole power of the Crown will be exerted to keep this continent as low and humble as possible? Instead of going forward we shall go backward, or be perpetually quarreling, or ridiculously petitioning. We are already greater than the king wishes us to be, and will he not hereafter endeavor to make us less? To bring the matter to one point: Is the power who is jealous of our prosperity a proper power to govern us? Whoever says "No" to this question is an *independent,* for independency means no more than this — whether we shall make our own laws, or, whether the king, the greatest enemy which this continent has or can have, shall tell us "There shall be no laws but such as I like."

But the king, you will say, has a negative in England; the people there can make no laws without his consent. In point of right and good order, it is something very ridiculous that a youth of twenty-one (which has often happened) shall say to several millions of people, older and wiser than himself, I forbid this or that act of yours to be law. But in this place I decline this sort of reply, though I will never cease to expose the absurdity of it; and only answer that England being the king's residence, and America not,

makes quite another case. The king's negative *here* is ten times more dangerous and fatal than it can be in England; for *there* he will scarcely refuse his consent to a bill for putting England into as strong a state of defense as possible, and in America he would never suffer such a bill to be passed.

America is only a secondary object in the system of British politics; England consults the good of *this* country no further than it answers her *own* purpose. Wherefore, her own interest leads her to suppress the growth of *ours* in every case which does not promote her advantage, or in the least interferes with it. A pretty state we should soon be in under such a secondhand government, considering what has happened! Men do not change from enemies to friends by the alteration of a name; and in order to show that reconciliation *now* is a dangerous doctrine, I affirm *that it would be policy in the king at this time to repeal the acts, for the sake of reinstating himself in the government of the provinces, in order that he may accomplish by craft and subtlety, in the long run, what he cannot do by force in the short one.* Reconciliation and ruin are nearly related.

Second, that as even the best terms which we can expect to obtain can amount to no more than a temporary expedient, or a kind of government by guardianship which can last no longer than till the colonies come of age, so the general face and state of things, in the interim, will be unsettled and unpromising. Emigrants of property will not choose to come to a country whose form of government hangs but by a thread, and which is every day tottering on the brink of commotion and disturbance; and numbers of the present inhabitants would lay hold of the interval to dispose of their effects and quit the continent.

But the most powerful of all arguments is that nothing but independence, *i.e.,* a continental form of government, can keep the peace of the continent and preserve it inviolate from civil wars. I dread the event of a reconciliation with Britain now, as it is more than probable that it will be followed by a revolt somewhere or other, the consequences of which may be far more fatal than all the malice of Britain.

Thousands are already ruined by British barbarity. (Thousands more will probably suffer the same fate.) Those men have other feelings than us who have nothing suffered. All they *now* possess is liberty; what they before enjoyed is sacrificed to its service; and having nothing more to lose, they disdain submission. Besides, the general temper of the colonies toward a British government will be like that of a youth who is nearly out of his time; they will care very little about her. And a government which cannot preserve the peace is no government at all, and in that case we pay our money for nothing. And pray what is it that Britain can do, whose power will be wholly on paper, should a civil tumult break out the very day after reconciliation?

I have heard some men say, many of whom I believe spoke without thinking, that they dreaded an independence, fearing that it would produce civil wars. It is but seldom that our first thoughts are truly correct, and that is the case here; for there is ten times more to dread from a patched up connection than from independence. I make the sufferer's case my own, and I protest that were I driven from house and home, my property destroyed, and my circumstances ruined, that as a man sensible of injuries, I could never relish the doctrine of reconciliation, or consider myself bound thereby.

The colonies have manifested such a spirit of good order and obedience to continental government as is sufficient to make every reasonable person easy and happy on that head. No man can assign the least pretense for his fears on any other grounds than such as are truly childish and ridiculous, viz., that one colony will be striving for superiority over another.

Where there are no distinctions there can be no superiority; perfect equality affords no temptation. The republics of Europe are all (and we may say always) in peace. Holland and Switzerland are without wars, foreign or domestic; monarchical governments, it is true, are never long at rest; the crown itself is a temptation to enterprising ruffians at home; and that degree of pride and insolence ever attendant on regal authority swells into a rupture with foreign powers in instances where a republican government, by being formed on more natural principles, would negotiate the mistake.

If there is any true cause of fear respecting independence, it is because no plan is yet laid down. Men do not see their way out; wherefore, as an opening into that business, I offer the following hints, at the same time modestly affirming that I have no other opinion of them myself than that they may be the means of giving rise to something better. Could the straggling thoughts of individuals be collected, they would frequently form materials for wise and able men to improve into useful matter.

Let the assemblies be annual, with a president only; the representation more equal; their business wholly domestic and subject to the authority of a continental congress.

Let each colony be divided into six, eight, or ten convenient districts, each district to send a proper number of delegates to Congress, so that each colony send at least 30. The whole number in Congress will be at least 390. Each Congress to sit ——— and to choose a president by the following method. When the delegates are met, let a colony be taken from the whole thirteen colonies by lot, after which, let the Congress choose (by ballot) a president from out of the delegates of that province. In the next Congress, let a colony be taken by lot from twelve only, omitting that colony from which the president was taken in the former Congress, and so proceeding on till the whole thirteen shall have had their proper rotation. And in order that nothing may pass into a law but what is satisfactorily just, not less than three-fifths of the Congress to be called a majority. He that will promote discord, under a government so equally formed as this, would have joined Lucifer in his revolt.

But as there is a peculiar delicacy from whom, or in what manner, this business must first arise, and as it seems most agreeable and consistent that it should come from some intermediate body between the governed and the governors, that is, between the Congress and the people, let a continental conference be held, in the following manner, and for the following purpose:

A committee of twenty-six members of Congress, viz., two for each colony; two members from each house of assembly, or provincial convention; and five representatives of the people at large, to be chosen in the capital city or town of each province, for and in behalf of the whole province, by as many qualified voters as shall think proper to attend from all parts of the province for that purpose; or, if more convenient, the representatives may be chosen in two or three of the most populous parts thereof. In this conference, thus assembled, will be united the two grand principles of business, *knowledge* and *power*. The members of Congress, assemblies, or conventions, by having had experience in national concerns, will be able and useful counselors; and the whole, being empowered by the people, will have a truly legal authority.

The conferring members being met, let their business be to frame a continental charter, or charter of the united colonies (answering to what is called the Magna Charta of England), fixing the number and manner of choosing members of congress and members of assembly, with their date of sitting, and drawing the line of business and jurisdiction between them (always remembering that our strength is continental, not provincial), securing freedom and property to all men, and, above all things, the free exercise of religion, according to the dictates of conscience, with such other matter as it is necessary for a charter to contain. Immediately after which, the said conference to dissolve, and the bodies which shall be chosen conformable to the said charter to be the legislators and governors of this continent for the time being, whose peace and happiness may God preserve. Amen.

Should any body of men be hereafter delegated for this or some similar purpose, I offer them the following extracts from that wise observer on governments, Dragonetti.

The science of the politician consists in fixing the true point of happiness and freedom. Those men would deserve the gratitude of ages who should discover a mode of government that contained the greatest sum of individual happiness, with the least national expense.

But where, say some, is the king of America? I'll tell you, friend, He reigns above, and does not make havoc of mankind like the royal brute of Britain. Yet, that we may not appear to be defective even in earthly honors, let a day be solemnly set apart for proclaiming the charter; let it be brought forth placed on the divine law, the word of God; let a crown be placed thereon, by which the world may know that so far as we approve of monarchy, that in America *the law is king*. For as in absolute governments the king is law, so in free countries the law ought to be king; and there ought to be no other. But lest any ill use should afterward arise, let the crown at the conclusion of the ceremony be demolished and scattered among the people whose right it is.

A government of our own is our natural right; and when a man seriously reflects on the precariousness of human affairs, he will become convinced that it is infinitely wiser and safer, to form a constitution of our own in a cool deliberate manner, while we have it in our power, than to trust such an interesting event to time and chance. If we omit it now, some Massanello [Thomas Anello] may hereafter arise, who, laying hold of popular disquietudes, may collect together the desperate and the discontented, and by assuming to themselves the powers of government, finally sweep away the liberties of the continent like a deluge. Should the government of America return again into the hands of Britain, the tottering situation of things will be a temptation for some desperate adventurer to try his fortune; and in such a case, what relief can Britain give? 'Ere she could hear the news, the fatal business might be done; and ourselves suffering like the wretched Britons under the oppression of the Conqueror. Ye that oppose independence now, ye know not what ye do; ye are opening a door to eternal tyranny by keeping vacant the seat of government. There are thousands and tens of thousands who would think it glorious to expel from the continent that barbarous and hellish power which has stirred up the Indians and Negroes to destroy us; the cruelty has a double guilt — it is dealing brutally by us and treacherously by them.

To talk of friendship with those in whom our reason forbids us to have faith, and our affections, wounded through a thousand pores, instruct us to detest, is madness and folly. Every day wears out the little remains of kindred between us and them; and can there be any reason to hope that as the relationship expires, the affection will increase, or that we shall agree better when we have ten times more and greater concerns to quarrel over than ever?

Ye that tell us of harmony and reconciliation, can ye restore to us the time that is past? Can ye give to prostitution its former innocence? Neither can ye reconcile Britain and America. The last cord now is broken; the people of England are presenting addresses against us. There are injuries which nature cannot forgive; she would cease to be nature if she did. As well can the lover forgive the ravisher of his mistress as the continent forgive the murders of Britain. The Almighty has implanted in us these unextinguishable feelings, for good and wise purposes. They are the guardians of His image in our hearts, and distinguish us from the herd of common animals. The social compact would dissolve and justice be extirpated from the earth, or have only a casual existence, were we callous to the touches of affection. The robber and the murderer would often escape unpunished did not the injuries which our tempers sustain provoke us into justice.

O! ye that love mankind! Ye that dare oppose, not only the tyranny but the tyrant, stand forth! Every spot of the Old World is overrun with oppression. Freedom has been haunted round the globe. Asia and Africa have long expelled her. Europe regards her like a stranger, and England has given her warning to depart. O! receive the fugitive, and prepare in time an asylum for mankind.

———————◆———————

E Pluribus Unum.
>ANON., used on title page of *Gentleman's Journal,* January 1692. Motto for seal of U.S. proposed originally on Aug. 10, 1776, by a committee composed of Franklin, Adams and Jefferson; adopted June 20, 1782; the motto added to certain coins, 1796. The actual selection of the motto for the seal is sometimes credited to Pierre Eugène du Simitière, who submitted a design for the seal that was not accepted, but that is said to have contained the words.

JOHN ADAMS: The Foundation of Government

The prospect of independence meant more than fighting a war with Britain. It also entailed the formation of new governments in America. In January of 1776, George Wythe, of Virginia, asked John Adams to draw up a plan that would enable the colonies to make this transition. Adams responded with the following letter.

Source: C. F. Adams, IV, pp. 193-200.

IF I WAS EQUAL TO THE TASK of forming a plan for the government of a colony, I should be flattered with your request, and very happy to comply with it; because, as the divine science of politics is the science of social happiness, and the blessings of society depend entirely on the constitutions of government, which are generally institutions that last for many generations, there can be no employment more agreeable to a benevolent mind than a research after the best. . . .

We ought to consider what is the end of government before we determine which is the best form. Upon this point all speculative politicians will agree, that the happiness of society is the end of government, as all divines and moral philosophers will agree that the happiness of the individual is the end of man. From this principle it will follow that the form of government which communicates ease, comfort, security, or, in one word, happiness to the greatest number of persons, and in the greatest degree, is the best.

All sober inquirers after truth, ancient and modern, pagan and Christian, have declared that the happiness of man, as well as his dignity, consists in virtue. . . . If there is a form of government, then, whose principle and foundation is virtue, will not every sober man acknowledge it better calculated to promote the general happiness than any other form?

Fear is the foundation of most governments; but it is so sordid and brutal a passion, and renders men in whose breasts it predominates so stupid and miserable, that Americans will not be likely to approve of any political institution which is founded on it.

Honor is truly sacred, but holds a lower rank in the scale of moral excellence than virtue. Indeed, the former is but a part of the latter and, consequently, has not equal pretensions to support a frame of government productive of human happiness.

The foundation of every government is some principle or passion in the minds of the people. The noblest principles and most generous affections in our nature, then, have the fairest chance to support the noblest and most generous models of government. . . . That, as a republic is the best of governments, so that particular arrangement of the powers of society, or, in other words, that form of government which is best contrived to secure an impartial and exact execution of the laws, is the best of republics.

Of republics there is an inexhaustible variety, because the possible combinations of the powers of society are capable of innumerable variations.

As good government is an empire of laws, how shall your laws be made? In a large society inhabiting an extensive country, it is impossible that the whole should assemble to make laws. The first necessary step, then, is to depute power from the many to a few of the most wise and good. But by what rules shall you choose your representatives? Agree upon the number and qualifications of persons who shall have the benefit of choosing, or annex this privilege to the inhabitants of a certain extent of ground.

The principal difficulty lies, and the greatest care should be employed, in constituting this representative assembly. It should be in miniature an exact portrait of the people at large. It should think, feel, reason, and act like them. That it may be the interest of this assembly to do strict justice at all times, it should be an equal representation, or, in other words, equal interests among the people should have equal interests in it. Great care should be taken to effect this, and to prevent unfair, partial, and corrupt elections. Such regulations, however, may be better made in times of greater tranquillity than the present; and they will spring up themselves naturally when all the powers of government come to be in the hands of the people's friends. At present, it will be safest to proceed in all established modes to which the people have been familiarized by habit.

A representation of the people in one assembly being obtained, a question arises, whether all the powers of government, legislative, executive, and judicial, shall be left in this body? I think a people cannot be long free, nor ever happy, whose government is in one assembly. My reasons for this opinion are as follow:

1. A single assembly is liable to all the vices, follies, and frailties of an individual; subject to fits of humor, starts of passion, flights of enthusiasm, partialities, or prejudice, and consequently productive of hasty results and absurd judgments. And all these errors ought to be corrected and defects supplied by some controlling power.

2. A single assembly is apt to be avaricious, and in time will not scruple to exempt itself from burdens which it will lay, without compunction, on its constituents.

3. A single assembly is apt to grow ambitious, and after a time will not hesitate to vote itself perpetual. . . .

To avoid these dangers, let a distinct assembly be constituted as a mediator between the two extreme branches of the legislature, that which represents the people, and that which is vested with the executive power. . . .

The dignity and stability of government in all its branches, the morals of the people, and every blessing of society depend so much upon an upright and skilful administration of justice that the judicial power ought to be distinct from both the legislative and executive, and independent upon both, that so it may be a check upon both, as both should be checks upon that. . . .

A militia law requiring all men, or with very few exceptions besides cases of conscience, to be provided with arms and ammunition, to be trained at certain seasons; and requiring counties, towns, or other small districts to be provided with public stocks of ammunition and entrenching utensils, and with some settled plans for transporting provisions after the militia, when marched to defend their country against sudden invasions; and requiring certain districts to be provided with fieldpieces, companies of matrosses [gunner's mates], and perhaps some regiments of light-horse [men], is always a wise institution, and, in the present circumstances of our country, indispensable.

Laws for the liberal education of youth, especially of the lower class of people, are so extremely wise and useful that, to a humane and generous mind, no expense for this purpose would be thought extravagant. . . .

A constitution founded on these principles introduces knowledge among the people and inspires them with a conscious dignity becoming freemen; a general emulation takes place which causes good humor, sociability, good manners, and good morals to be general. That elevation of sentiment inspired by such a government makes the common people brave and enterprising. That ambition which is inspired by it makes them sober, industrious, and frugal. You will find among them some elegance, perhaps, but more solidity; a little pleasure, but a great deal of business; some politeness, but more civility. If you compare such a country with the regions of domination, whether monarchical or aristocratical, you will fancy yourself in Arcadia or Elysium.

If the colonies should assume governments separately, they should be left entirely to their own choice of the forms; and if a continental constitution should be formed, it should be a congress containing a fair and adequate representation of the colonies, and its authority should sacredly be confined to these cases; namely, war, trade, disputes between colony and colony, the post office, and the unappropriated lands of the Crown, as they used to be called.

These colonies under such forms of government, and in such a union, would be unconquerable by all the monarchies of Europe.

You and I, my dear friend, have been sent into life at a time when the greatest lawgivers of antiquity would have wished to live. How few of the human race have ever enjoyed an opportunity of making an election of government, more than of air, soil, or climate, for themselves or their children! When, before the present epoch, had 3,000,000 people full power and a fair opportunity to form and establish the wisest and happiest government that human wisdom can contrive? I hope you will avail yourself and your country of that extensive learning and indefatigable industry which you possess to assist her in the formation of the happiest governments and the best character of a great people.

In the new code of laws which I suppose it will be necessary for you to make I desire you would remember the ladies and be more generous and favorable to them than your ancestors.

ABIGAIL ADAMS, letter to John Adams, March 31, 1776

James Wilson: The Legal Right to Form a Government

James Wilson was a delegate from Pennsylvania to the Second Continental Congress.
On February 13, 1776, he prepared an address to the inhabitants of all the colonies that
was meant to prepare public opinion for eventual independence. However, as public
sentiment had already anticipated his position, the address was not published at the time.

Source: *Selected Political Essays of James Wilson*, Randolph G. Adams, ed., New York, 1930:
"An Address to the Inhabitants of the Colonies of New Hampshire, etc., etc."

Friends and Countrymen:

History, we believe, cannot furnish an example of a trust higher and more important than that which we have received from your hands. It comprehends in it everything that can rouse the attention and interest the passions of a people, who will not reflect disgrace upon their ancestors, nor degrade themselves, nor transmit infamy to their descendants. It is committed to us at a time when everything dear and valuable to such a people is in imminent danger. This danger arises from those whom we have been accustomed to consider as our friends; who really were so while they continued friendly to themselves; and who will again be so when they shall return to a just sense of their own interests. The calamities which threaten us would be attended with a total loss of those constitutions, formed upon the venerable model of British liberty, which have been long our pride and felicity. To avert those calamities we are under the disagreeable necessity of making temporary deviations from those constitutions.

Such is the trust reposed in us. Much does it import you and us that it be executed with skill and with fidelity. That we have discharged it with fidelity, we enjoy the testimony of a good conscience. How far we have discharged it with skill must be determined by you, who are our principals and judges, to whom we esteem it our duty to render an account of our conduct. To enable you to judge of it, as we would wish you to do, it is necessary that you should be made acquainted with the situation in which your affairs have been placed; the principles on which we have acted; and the ends, which we have kept and still keep in view.

That all power was originally in the people — that all the powers of government are derived from them — that all power, which they have not disposed of, still continues theirs — are maxims of the English constitution, which, we presume, will not be disputed. The share of power which the king derives from the people, or, in other words, the prerogative of the Crown, is well known and precisely ascertained. It is the same in Great Britain and in the colonies. The share of power which the House of Commons derives from the people is likewise well known — the manner in which it is conveyed is by election.

But the House of Commons is not elected by the colonists; and, therefore, from them that body can derive no authority.

Besides, the powers which the House of Commons receives from its constituents are entrusted by the colonies to their assemblies in the several provinces. Those assemblies have authority to propose and assent to laws for the government of their electors, in the same manner as the House of Commons has authority to propose and assent to laws for the government of the inhabitants of Great Britain. Now the same collective body cannot delegate the same powers to distinct representative bodies. The undeniable result is that the House of Commons neither has nor can have any power derived from the inhabitants of these colonies.

In the instance of imposing taxes, this doctrine is clear and familiar; it is true and just in every other instance. If it would be incongruous and absurd that the same property should be liable to be taxed by two bodies independent of each other, would less incongruity and absurdity ensue if the same offense were to be subjected to different and perhaps inconsistent punishments? Suppose the punishment directed by the laws of one body to be death, and that directed by those of the other body be banishment for life; how could both punishments be inflicted?

Though the Crown possesses the same prerogative over the colonies which it possesses over the inhabitants of Great Britain; though the colonists delegate to their assemblies the same powers which our fellow subjects in Britain delegate to the House of Commons; yet by some inexplicable mystery in politics, which is the foundation of the odious system that we have so much reason to deplore, additional powers over you are ascribed to the Crown, as a branch of the British legislature. And the House of Commons — a body which acts solely by derivative authority — is supposed entitled to exert over you an authority which you cannot give and which it cannot receive.

The sentence of universal slavery gone forth against you is: *that the British Parliament have power to make laws, without your consent, building you in all cases whatever.* Your fortunes, your liberties, your reputations, your lives, everything that can render you and your posterity happy, all are the objects of the laws; all must be enjoyed, impaired, or destroyed as the laws direct. And are you the wretches who have nothing that you can or ought to call your own? Were all the rich blessings of nature, all the bounties of indulgent Providence poured upon you, not for your own use but for the use of those upon whom neither nature nor Providence has bestowed qualities or advantages superior to yours?

From this root of bitterness numerous are the branches of oppression that have sprung. Your most undoubted and highest-prized rights have been invaded; heavy and unnecessary burdens have been imposed on you; your interests have been neglected and sometimes wantonly sacrificed to the interests and even to the caprice of others. When you felt, for your enemies have not yet made any laws to divest you of feeling, uneasiness under your grievances, and expressed it in the natural tone of complaint, your murmurs were considered and treated as the language of faction, and your uneasiness was ascribed to a restive disposition, impatient of control.

In proportion, however, as your oppressions were multiplied and increased, your opposition to them became firm and vigorous. Remonstrances succeeded petitions; a resolution carried into effect not to import goods from Great Britain succeeded both. The acts of Parliament then complained of were in part repealed. Your good humor and unsuspicious fondness returned. Short — alas! too short — was the season allowed for indulging them. The former system of rigor was renewed.

The colonies, wearied with presenting

fruitless supplications and petitions separately; or prevented by arbitrary and abrupt dissolutions of their assemblies from using even those fruitless expedients for redress, determined to join their counsels and their efforts. Many of the injuries flowing from the unconstitutional and ill-advised acts of the British legislature affected all the provinces equally; and even in those cases in which the injuries were confined, by the acts to one or to a few, the principles on which they were made extended to all. If common rights, common interests, common dangers and common sufferings are principles of union, what could be more natural than the union of the colonies?

Delegates authorized by the several provinces from Nova Scotia to Georgia to represent them and act in their behalf met in General Congress.

It has been objected that this measure was unknown to the constitution; that the Congress was, of consequence, an illegal body; and that its proceedings could not, in any manner, be recognized by the government of Britain. To those who offer this objection and have attempted to vindicate, by its supposed validity, the neglect and contempt with which the petition of that Congress to His Majesty was treated by the Ministry, we beg leave, in our turn, to propose that they would explain the principles of the constitution, which warranted the Assembly of the Barons at Runnymede, when Magna Charta was signed, the Convention-Parliament that recalled Charles II, and the Convention of Lords and Commons that placed King William on the throne. When they shall have done this, we shall perhaps be able to apply their principles to prove the necessity and propriety of a congress.

But the objections of those who have done so much and aimed so much against the liberties of America are not confined to the meeting and the authority of the Congress; they are urged with equal warmth against the views and inclinations of those who composed it. We are told, in the name of majesty itself, "that the authors and promoters of this desperate conspiracy," as those who have framed His Majesty's speech are pleased to term our laudable resistance, "have, in the conduct of it, derived great advantage from the difference of His Majesty's intentions and theirs. That they meant only to amuse by vague expressions of attachment to the parent state, and the strongest protestations of loyalty to the King, whilst they were preparing for a general revolt. That on the part of His Majesty and the Parliament, the wish was rather to reclaim than to subdue." It affords us some pleasure to find that the protestations of loyalty to His Majesty which have been made are allowed to be strong; and that attachment to the parent state is owned to be expressed. Those protestations of loyalty and expressions of attachment ought, by every rule of candor, to be presumed to be sincere, unless proofs evincing their insincerity can be drawn from the conduct of those who used them.

In examining the conduct of those who directed the affairs of the colonies at the time when, it is said, they were preparing for a general revolt, we find it an easy undertaking to show that they merited no reproach from the British Ministry by making any preparations for that purpose. We wish it were as easy to show that they merited no reproach from their constituents by neglecting the necessary provisions for their security. Has a single preparation been made which has not been found requisite for our defense? Have we not been attacked in places where fatal experience taught us we were not sufficiently prepared for a successful opposition? On which side of this unnatural controversy was the ominous intimation first given that it must be decided by force? Were arms and ammunition imported into America, before the importation of them was prohibited? What reason can

Miniature portrait of James Wilson by an unidentified artist

be assigned for this prohibition, unless it be this, that those who made it had determined upon such a system of oppression as they knew would force the colonies into resistance? And yet, they "wished only to reclaim!"

The sentiments of the colonies, expressed in the proceedings of their delegates assembled in 1774, were far from being disloyal or disrespectful. Was it disloyal to offer a petition to your sovereign? Did your still-anxious impatience for an answer, which your hopes, founded only on your wishes, as you too soon experienced, flattered you would be a gracious one — did this impatience indicate a disposition only to amuse? Did the keen anguish with which the fate of the petition filled your breasts betray an inclination to avail yourselves of the indignity with which you were treated for forwarding favorite designs of revolt?

Was the agreement not to import merchandise from Great Britain or Ireland, nor after the 10th day of September last to ex-

port our produce to those kingdoms and the West Indies — was this a disrespectful or a hostile measure? Surely we have a right to withdraw or to continue our own commerce. Though the British Parliament have exercised a power of directing and restraining our trade; yet, among all their extraordinary pretensions, we recollect no instance of their attempting to force it contrary to our inclinations. It was well known, before this measure was adopted, that it would be detrimental to our own interest, as well as to that of our fellow subjects. We deplored it on both accounts. We deplored the necessity that produced it. But we were willing to sacrifice our interest to any probable method of regaining the enjoyment of those rights which, by violence and injustice, had been infringed.

Yet even this peaceful expedient, which faction surely never suggested, has been represented, and by high authority too, as a seditious and unwarrantable combination. We are, we presume, the first rebels and conspirators who commenced their conspiracy and rebellion with a system of conduct immediately and directly frustrating every aim which ambition or rapaciousness could propose. Those whose fortunes are desperate may upon slight evidence be charged with desperate designs; but how improbable is it that the colonists, who have been happy, and have known their happiness in the quiet possession of their liberties; who see no situation more to be desired than that in which, till lately, they have been placed; and whose warmest wish is to be reinstalled in the enjoyment of that freedom which they claim and are entitled to as men and as British subjects — how improbable is it that such would, without any motives that could tempt even the most profligate minds to crimes, plunge themselves headlong into all the guilt and danger and distress with which those that endeavor to overturn the constitution of their country are always surrounded and frequently overwhelmed?

The humble, unaspiring colonists asked only for "peace, liberty and safety." This, we think, was a reasonable request. Reasonable as it was, it has been refused. Our ministerial foes, dreading the effects which our commercial opposition might have upon their favorite plan of reducing the colonies to slavery, were determined not to hazard it upon that issue. They employed military force to carry it into execution. Opposition of force by force or unlimited subjection was now our only alternative. Which of them did it become freemen, determined never to surrender that character, to choose? The choice was worthily made. We wish for peace — we wish for safety; but we will not, to obtain either or both of them, part with our liberty. The sacred gift descended to us from our ancestors; we cannot dispose of it; we are bound by the strongest ties to transmit it, as we have received it, pure and inviolate to our posterity.

We have taken up arms in the best of causes. We have adhered to the virtuous principles of our ancestors, who expressly stipulated in their favor, and in ours, a right to resist every attempt upon their liberties. We have complied with our engagements to our sovereign. He should be the ruler of a free people; we will not, as far as his character depends upon us, permit him to be degraded into a tyrant over slaves.

Our troops are animated with the love of freedom. They have fought and bled and conquered in the discharge of their duty as good citizens as well as brave soldiers. Regardless of the inclemency of the seasons, and of the length and fatigue of the march, they go with cheerfulness wherever the cause of liberty and their country requires their service. We confess that they have not the advantages arising from experience and discipline. But facts have shown that native courage warmed with patriotism is sufficient to counterbalance these advantages. The experience and discipline of our troops will

daily increase; their patriotism will receive no diminution; the longer those who have forced us into this war oblige us to continue it, the more formidable we shall become.

The strength and resources of America are not confined to operations by land. She can exert herself likewise by sea. Her sailors are hardy and brave; she has all the materials for shipbuilding; her artificers can work them into form. We pretend not to vie with the Royal Navy of England though that navy had its beginnings; but still we may be able in a great measure to defend our own coasts, and may intercept, as we have been hitherto successful in doing, transports and vessels laden with stores and provisions.

Possessed of so many advantages; favored with the prospect of so many more; threatened with the destruction of our constitutional rights; cruelly and illiberally attacked because we will not subscribe to our own slavery — ought we to be animated with vigor or to sink into despondency? When the forms of our governments are, by those entrusted with the direction of them, perverted from their original design, ought we to submit to this perversion? Ought we to sacrifice the forms when the sacrifice becomes necessary for preserving the spirit of our constitution? Or ought we to neglect and, neglecting, to lose the spirit by a superstitious veneration for the forms? We regard those forms and wish to preserve them as long as we can consistently with higher objects. But much more do we regard essential liberty, which, at all events, we are determined not to lose but with our lives. In contending for this liberty, we are willing to go through good report and through evil report.

In our present situation, in which we are called to oppose an attack upon your liberties, made under bold pretensions of authority from that power, to which the executive part of government is, in the ordinary course of affairs, committed — in the situation, every mode of resistance, though directed by necessity and by prudence, and authorized by the spirit of the constitution, will be exposed to plausible objections drawn from its forms. Concerning such objections, and the weight that may be allowed to them, we are little solicitous. It will not discourage us to find ourselves represented as "laboring to inflame the minds of the people of America, and openly avowing revolt, hostility, and rebellion." We deem it an honor to "have raised troops, and collected a naval force"; and, clothed with the sacred authority of the people, from whom all legitimate authority proceeds, "to have exercised legislative, executive and judicial powers." For what purposes were those powers instituted? For your safety and happiness. You and the world will judge whether those purposes have been best promoted by us; or by those who claim the powers which they charge us with assuming.

But while we feel no mortification at being misrepresented with regard to the measures employed by us for accomplishing the great ends which you have appointed us to pursue, we cannot sit easy under an accusation which charges us with laying aside those ends and endeavoring to accomplish such as are very different. We are accused of carrying on the war "for the purpose of establishing an independent empire."

We disavow the intention. We declare that what we aim at, and what we are entrusted by you to pursue, is the defense and the reestablishment of the constitutional rights of the colonies. Whoever gives impartial attention to the facts we have already stated, and to the observations we have already made, must be fully convinced that all the steps which have been taken by us in this unfortunate struggle can be accounted for as rationally and as satisfactorily by supposing that the defense and reestablishment of their rights were the objects which the colonists and their representatives had in view, as by supposing that an independent empire was their aim. Nay, we may safely go farther and affirm, without the most distant apprehension of being refuted, that many of those steps can be accounted for rationally and satisfactorily only upon the former supposition, and cannot be accounted for in that manner upon the latter. The numerous expedients that were tried, though fruitlessly, for avoiding hostilities; the visible and unfeigned reluctance and horror with which we entered into them; the caution and reserve with which we have carried them on; the attempts we have made by petitioning the Throne and by every other method which might probably, or could possibly, be of any avail for procuring an accommodation — these are not surely the usual characteristics of ambition.

In what instance have we been the aggressors? Did our troops take the field before the ministerial forces began their hostile march to Lexington and Concord? Did we take possession or did we form any plan for taking possession of Canada before we knew that it was a part of the ministerial system to pour the Canadians upon our frontiers? Did we approach the Canadians, or have we treated them as enemies? Did we take the management of the Indian tribes into our hands before we were well assured that the emissaries of administration were busy in persuading them to strike us? When we treated with them, did we imitate the barbarous example? Were not our views and persuasions confined to keeping them in a state of neutrality? Did we seize any vessel of our enemies before our enemies had seized some of ours? Had we yet seized any, except such as were employed in the service of administration, and in supplying those that were in actual hostilities against us? Cannot our whole conduct be reconciled to principles and views of self-defense? Whence then the uncandid imputation of aiming at an independent empire?

Is no regard to be had to the professions

and protestations made by us, on so many different occasions, of attachment to Great Britain, of allegiance to His Majesty; and of submission to his government upon the terms on which the constitution points it out as a duty, and on which alone a British sovereign has the right to demand it?

When the hostilities commenced by the ministerial forces in Massachusetts Bay and the imminent dangers threatening the other colonies rendered it absolutely necessary that they should be put into a state of defense — even on that occasion, we did not forget our duty to His Majesty and our regard for our fellow subjects in Britain. Our words are these:

But as we most ardently wish for a restoration of the harmony formerly subsisting between our mother country and these colonies, the interruption of which must at all events be exceedingly injurious to both countries: resolved, that with a sincere design of contributing, by all means in our power not incompatible with a just regard for the undoubted rights and true interests of these colonies, to the promotion of this most desirable reconciliation, a humble and dutiful address be presented to His Majesty.

If the purposes of establishing an independent empire had lurked in our breasts, no fitter occasion could have been found for giving intimations of them than in our declaration setting forth the causes and necessity of our taking up arms. Yet even there no pretense can be found for fixing such an imputation on us.

Lest this declaration should disquiet the minds of our friends and fellow subjects in any part of the empire, we assure them that we mean not to dissolve that union which has so long and so happily subsisted between us, and which we sincerely wish to see restored. Necessity has not yet driven us into that desperate measure, or induced us to excite any other nation to war against them. We have not raised armies with the ambitious designs of separating from Great

Britain and establishing independent states.

Our petition to the King has the following asseveration:

By such arrangements as Your Majesty's wisdom can form for collecting the united sense of your American people, we are convinced Your Majesty would receive such satisfactory proofs of the disposition of the colonists toward their Sovereign and the parent state, that the wished for opportunity would be soon restored to them, of evincing the sincerity of their professions by every testimony of devotion becoming the most dutiful subjects and the most affectionate colonists.

In our address to the inhabitants of Great Britain, we say:

We are accused of aiming at independence. But how is this accusation supported? By the allegations of your ministers, not by our actions. Give us leave most solemnly to assure you that we have not yet lost sight of the object we have ever had in view, a reconciliation with you on constitutional principles, and a restoration of that friendly intercourse which to the advantage of both we till lately maintained.

If we wished to detach you from your allegiance to His Majesty and to wean your affections from a connection with your fellow subjects in Great Britain, is it likely that we would have taken so much pains, upon every proper occasion, to place those objects before you in the most agreeable points of view?

If any equitable terms of accommodation had been offered us, and we had rejected them, there would have been some foundation for the charge that we endeavored to establish an independent empire. But no means have been used either by Parliament or by administration for the purpose of bringing this contest to a conclusion besides penalties directed by statutes or devastations occasioned by war. Alas! how long will

Britons forget that kindred blood flows in your veins? How long will they strive with hostile fury to sluice it out from bosoms that have already bled in their cause; and, in their cause, would still be willing to pour out what remains, to the last precious drop?

We are far from being insensible of the advantages which have resulted to the colonies as well as to Britain from the connection which has hitherto subsisted between them; we are far from denying them, or wishing to lessen the ideas of their importance. But the nature of this connection, and the principles on which it was originally formed and on which alone it can be maintained, seem unhappily to have been misunderstood or disregarded by those who laid or conducted the late destructive plan of colony administration. It is a connection founded upon mutual benefits; upon religion, laws, manners, customs and habits common to both countries. Arbitrary exertions of power on the part of Britain, and servile submission on the part of the colonies, if the colonies should ever become degenerate enough to accept it, would immediately rend every generous bond asunder. An intimate connection between freemen and slaves cannot be continued without danger and, at last, destruction to the former. Should your enemies be able to reduce you to slavery, the baneful contagion would spread over the whole empire. We verily believe that the freedom, happiness, and glory of Great Britain, and the prosperity of His Majesty and his family, depend upon the success of your resistance. You are now expending your blood and your treasure in promoting the welfare and the true interests of your sovereign and your fellow subjects in Britain in opposition to the most dangerous attacks that have been ever made against them.

The ideas of deriving emolument to the mother country by taxing you and depriving you of your constitutions and liberties were not introduced till lately. The experiments to which those ideas have given birth have proved disastrous; the voice of wisdom calls loudly that they should be laid aside. Let them not, however, be removed from view. They may serve as beacons to prevent future shipwrecks.

Britain and these colonies have been blessings to each other. Sure we are that they might continue to be so. Some salutary system might certainly be devised which would remove from both sides jealousies that are ill-founded and causes of jealousies that are well-founded; which would restore to both countries those important benefits that nature seems to have intended them reciprocally to confer and to receive; and which would secure the continuance and the increase of those benefits to numerous succeeding generations. That such a system may be formed is our ardent wish.

But as such a system must affect the interest of the colonies as much as that of the mother country, why should the colonies be excluded from a voice in it? Should not, to say the least upon this subject, their consent be asked and obtained as to the general ends which it ought to be calculated to answer? Why should not its validity depend upon us as well as upon the inhabitants of Great Britain? No disadvantage will result to them; an important advantage will result to us. We shall be affected by no laws, the authority of which, as far as they regard us, is not founded on our own consent. This consent may be expressed as well by a solemn compact, as if the colonists, by their representatives, had an immediate voice in passing the laws. In a compact we would concede liberally to Parliament, for the bounds of our concessions would be known.

We are too much attached to the English laws and constitution, and know too well their happy tendency to diffuse freedom, prosperity, and peace wherever they prevail, to desire an independent empire. If one part of the constitution be pulled down, it is impossible to foretell whether the other parts of it may not be shaken, and, perhaps, overthrown. It is a part of our constitution to be under allegiance to the Crown, limited and ascertained as the prerogative is, the position — that a king can do no wrong — may be founded in fact as well as in law, if you are not wanting to yourselves.

We trace your calamities to the House of Commons. They have undertaken to give and grant your money. From a supposed virtual representation in their House it is argued that you ought to be bound by the acts of the British Parliament in all cases whatever. This is no part of the constitution. This is the doctrine to which we will never subscribe our assent; this is the claim to which we adjure you, as you tender your own freedom and happiness and the freedom and happiness of your posterity, never to submit. The same principles which directed your ancestors to oppose the exorbitant and dangerous pretensions of the Crown should direct you to oppose the no less exorbitant and dangerous claims of the House of Commons. Let all communication of despotic power through that channel be cut off, and your liberties will be safe.

Let neither our enemies nor our friends make improper inferences from the solicitude which we have discovered to remove the imputation of aiming to establish an independent empire. Though an independent empire is not our wish, it may — let your oppressors attend — it may be the fate of our countrymen and ourselves. It is in the power of your enemies to render independency or slavery your and our alternative. Should we — will you, in such an event — hesitate a moment about the choice? Let those who drive us to it answer to their King and to their country for the consequences. We are desirous to continue subjects; but we are determined to continue freemen. We shall deem ourselves bound to renounce, and we hope you will follow our example in renouncing, the former character whenever it shall become incompatible with the latter.

While we shall be continued by you in the very important trust which you have committed to us, we shall keep our eyes constantly and steadily fixed upon the grand object of the union of the colonies — the reestablishment and security of their constitutional rights. Every measure that we employ shall be directed to the attainment of this great end; no measure necessary, in our opinion, for attaining it shall be declined. If any such measure should, against our principal intention, draw the colonies into engagements that may suspend or dissolve their union with their fellow subjects in Great Britain, we shall lament the effect, but shall hold ourselves justified in adopting the measure. That the colonies may continue connected, as they have been, with Britain is our second wish. Our first is — *That America may be free.*

Instructions for a Declaration of Independence

Pressure for a complete break with Britain gained momentum in the early months of 1776. Rhode Island took matters into its own hands by declaring its independence early in May. Several of the other colonies sent instructions to their delegates in the Continental Congress to call for a declaration of independence. On May 9, the Massachusetts House of Representatives, in an effort to ascertain the sentiments of the colony with respect to independence, requested each town to instruct its representatives. The instructions from the town of Malden, on May 27, were typical of many voted in Massachusetts.

Source: Niles: "Instructions of the Inhabitants of Malden, Mass. to Their Representative in Congress, May 27, 1776."

Sir:

A resolution of the honorable House of Representatives, calling upon the several towns in this colony to express their minds with respect to the important question of American independence, is the occasion of our now instructing you. The time was, sir, when we loved the King and the people of Great Britain with an affection truly filial; we felt ourselves interested in their glory; we shared in their joys and sorrows; we cheerfully poured the fruit of all our labors into the lap of our mother country, and without reluctance expended our blood and our treasure in their cause.

These were our sentiments toward Great Britain while she continued to act the part of a parent state; we felt ourselves happy in our connection with her, nor wished it to be dissolved; but our sentiments are altered. It is now the ardent wish of our souls that America may become a free and independent state.

A sense of unprovoked injuries will arouse the resentment of the most peaceful.

Such injuries these colonies have received from Britain. Unjustifiable claims have been made by the King and his minions to tax us without our consent; these claims have been prosecuted in a manner cruel and unjust to the highest degree. The frantic policy of administration has induced them to send fleets and armies to America; that, by depriving us of our trade, and cutting the throats of our brethren, they might awe us into submission and erect a system of despotism in America which should so far enlarge the influence of the Crown as to enable it to rivet their shackles upon the people of Great Britain.

This plan was brought to a crisis upon the ever memorable 19th of April. We remember the fatal day! The expiring groans of our countrymen yet vibrate on our ears! And we now behold the flames of their peaceful dwellings ascending to Heaven! We hear their blood crying to us from the ground for vengeance! And charging us, as we value the peace of their [names], to have no further connection with [him], who can

unfeelingly hear of the slaughter of [them], and composedly sleep with their blood upon his soul. The manner in which the war has been prosecuted has confirmed us in these sentiments; piracy and murder, robbery and breach of faith, have been conspicuous in the conduct of the King's troops. Defenseless towns have been attacked and destroyed, the ruins of Charlestown, which are daily in our view, daily remind of this. The cries of the widow and the orphan demand our attention; they demand that the hand of pity should wipe the tear from their eye, and that the sword of their country should avenge their wrongs. We long entertained hopes that the spirit of the British nation would once more induce them to assert their own and our rights, and bring to condign punishment the elevated villains who have trampled upon the sacred rights of men and affronted the majesty of the people. We hoped in vain; they have lost their love to freedom, they have lost their spirit of just resentment; we therefore renounce with disdain our connection with a kingdom of slaves; we bid a final adieu to Britain.

Could an accommodation now be effected, we have reason to think that it would be fatal to the liberties of America; we should soon catch the contagion of venality and dissipation, which has subjected Britons to lawless domination. Were we placed in the situation we were in 1763, were the powers of appointing to offices and commanding the militia in the hands of governors, our arts, trade and manufactures would be cramped; nay, more than this, the life of every man who has been active in the cause of his country would be endangered.

For these reasons, as well as many others which might be produced, we are confirmed in the opinion that the present age would be deficient in their duty to God, their posterity, and themselves if they do not establish an American republic. This is the only form of government which we wish to see established; for we can never be willingly subject to any other king than He who, being possessed of infinite wisdom, goodness and rectitude, is alone fit to possess unlimited power.

We have freely spoken our sentiments upon this important subject, but we mean not to dictate; we have unbounded confidence in the wisdom and uprightness of the Continental Congress: with pleasure we recollect that this affair is under their direction; and we now instruct you, sir, to give them the strongest assurance that, if they should declare America to be a free and independent republic, your constituents will support and defend the measure to the last drop of their blood and the last farthing of their treasure.

Don't give up the ship! You will beat them off!

JAMES MUGFORD, last words, as he lay dying in his schooner, the *Franklin*, during a British attack in Boston Harbor, May 19, 1776

Virginia Declaration of Rights

Virginia's Declaration of Rights was in many ways a central document of its era. Drawn upon by Jefferson for the opening paragraphs of the Declaration of Independence, it was widely copied by the other colonies, became the basis of the Bill of Rights in the Constitution, and had considerable influence in France at the time of the French Revolution. It was written by George Mason and adopted by the Virginia Constitutional Convention on June 12, 1776, as the theoretical foundation of all government.

Source: Thorpe, VII, pp. 3812-3814.

A DECLARATION OF RIGHTS made by the representatives of the good people of Virginia, assembled in full and free convention: which rights do pertain to them and their posterity, as the basis and foundation of government.

Section 1. That all men are by nature equally free and independent and have certain inherent rights, of which, when they enter into a state of society, they cannot, by any compact, deprive or divest their posterity; namely, the enjoyment of life and liberty, with the means of acquiring and possessing property, and pursuing and obtaining happiness and safety.

Section 2. That all power is vested in, and consequently derived from, the people; that magistrates are their trustees and servants and at all times amenable to them.

Section 3. That government is, or ought to be, instituted for the common benefit, protection, and security of the people, nation, or community; of all the various modes and forms of government, that is best which is capable of producing the greatest degree of happiness and safety and is most effectually secured against the danger of maladministration. And that, when any government shall be found inadequate or contrary to these purposes, a majority of the community has an indubitable, inalienable, and indefeasible right to reform, alter, or abolish it, in such manner as shall be judged most conducive to the public weal.

Section 4. That no man, or set of men, is entitled to exclusive or separate emoluments or privileges from the community, but in consideration of public services; which, not being descendible, neither ought the offices of magistrate, legislator, or judge to be hereditary.

Section 5. That the legislative and executive powers of the state should be separate and distinct from the judiciary; and that the members of the two first may be restrained from oppression, by feeling and participating the burdens of the people, they should, at fixed periods, be reduced to a private station, return into that body from which they were originally taken, and the vacancies be supplied by frequent, certain, and regular elections, in which all, or any part, of the former members, to be again eligible, or ineligible, as the laws shall direct.

Section 6. That elections of members to serve as representatives of the people, in assembly, ought to be free; and that all men, having sufficient evidence of permanent common interest with, and attachment to, the community, have the right of suffrage and cannot be taxed or deprived of their property for public uses without their own consent, or that of their representatives so elected, nor bound by any law to which they have not, in like manner, assembled for the public good.

Section 7. That all power of suspending laws, or the execution of laws, by any authority, without consent of the representatives of the people, is injurious to their rights and ought not to be exercised.

Section 8. That in all capital or criminal prosecutions a man has a right to demand the cause and nature of his accusation, to be confronted with the accusers and witnesses, to call for evidence in his favor, and to a speedy trial by an impartial jury of twelve men of his vicinage, without whose unanimous consent he cannot be found guilty; nor can he be compelled to give evidence against himself; that no man be deprived of his liberty except by the law of the land or the judgment of his peers.

Section 9. That excessive bail ought not to be required, nor excessive fines imposed, nor cruel and unusual punishments inflicted.

Section 10. That general warrants, whereby an officer or messenger may be commanded to search suspected places without evidence of a fact committed, or to seize any person or persons not named, or whose offense is not particularly described and supported by evidence, are grievous and oppressive and ought not to be granted.

Section 11. That in controversies respecting property, and in suits between man and man, the ancient trial by jury is preferable to any other and ought to be held sacred.

Section 12. That the freedom of the press is one of the great bulwarks of liberty and can never be restrained but by despotic governments.

Section 13. That a well-regulated militia, composed of the body of the people, trained to arms, is the proper, natural, and safe defense of a free state; that standing armies, in time of peace, should be avoided as dangerous to liberty; and that in all cases the military should be under strict subordination to, and governed by, the civil power.

Section 14. That the people have a right to uniform government; and, therefore, that no government separate from or independent of the government of Virginia ought to be erected or established within the limits thereof.

Section 15. That no free government, or the blessings of liberty, can be preserved to any people but by a firm adherence to justice, moderation, temperance, frugality, and virtue, and by frequent recurrence to fundamental principles.

Section 16. That religion, or the duty which we owe to our Creator, and the manner of discharging it, can be directed only by reason and conviction, not by force or violence; and therefore all men are equally entitled to the free exercise of religion, according to the dictates of conscience; and that it is the mutual duty of all to practise Christian forbearance, love, and charity toward each other.

———◆———

This day the Continental Congress declared the United Colonies free and independent states.

ANON., notice, quoted in its entirety, on the last page of the Pennsylvania *Evening Post*, July 2, 1776

John Dickinson: Speech Against Independence

On June 7, 1776, following the instructions of the Virginia Convention, Richard Henry Lee submitted to the Second Continental Congress three resolutions calling for American independence. There was an initial two-day debate, but a vote on the issue was successfully delayed for three weeks by a few delegations that still opposed independence. When debate resumed on July 1, John Dickinson of Pennsylvania made his last protest against a declaration. The speech was probably not published at the time it was given. The text that follows is a reconstruction, printed — with his comments — by Hezekiah Niles in his Principles and Acts of the Revolution in America.

Source: Niles: "Speech of John Dickinson of Pennsylvania, Favoring a Condition of Union with England, Delivered July 1, 1776."

JOHN DICKINSON, one of the deputies of the province to the General Congress, a man of prompt genius, of extensive influence, and one of the most zealous partisans of American liberty, restricted, however, to the condition of union with England, harangued, it is said, in the following manner against independence:

It too often happens, fellow citizens, that men, heated by the spirit of party, give more importance in their discourses, to the surface and appearance of objects, than either to reason or justice; thus evincing that their aim is not to appease tumults but to excite them; not to repress the passions but to inflame them; not to compose ferocious discords but to exasperate and embitter them more and more. They aspire but to please the powerful, to gratify their own ambition, to flatter the caprices of the multitude in order to captivate their favor. Accordingly, in popular commotions, the party of wisdom and of equity is commonly found in the minority; and, perhaps, it would be safer, in difficult circumstances, to consult the smaller instead of the greater number. Upon this principle I invite the attention of those who hear me, since my opinion may differ from that of the majority; but I dare believe it will be shared by all impartial and moderate citizens who condemn this tumultuous proceeding, this attempt to coerce our opinions, and to drag us, with so much precipitation, to the most serious and important of decisions.

But, coming to the subject in controversy, I affirm that prudent men do not abandon objects which are certain to go in pursuit of those which offer only uncertainty. Now, it is an established fact that America can be well and happily governed by the English laws, under the same king and the same Parliament. Two hundred years of happiness furnish the proof of it; and we find it also in the present prosperity, which is the result of these venerable laws and of this ancient union. It is not as independent, but as subjects; not as republic, but as monarchy, that we have arrived at this degree of power and of greatness. What then is the object of these chimeras, hatched in the days of discord and war? Shall the transports of fury have more power over us than the experience of ages? Shall we destroy, in a moment of anger, the work cemented and tested by time?

I know the name of liberty is dear to each one of us; but have we not enjoyed liberty even under the English monarchy? Shall we this day renounce that to go and seek it in I know not what form of republic, which will soon change into a licentious anarchy and popular tyranny? In the human body the head only sustains and governs all the members, directing them, with admirable harmony, to the same object, which is self-preservation and happiness; so the head of the body politic, that is the king, in concert with the Parliament, can alone maintain the union of the members of this Empire, lately so flourishing, and prevent civil war by obviating all the evils produced by variety of opinions and diversity of interests. And so firm is my persuasion of this that I fully believe the most cruel war which Great Britain could make upon us would be that of not making any; and that the surest means of bringing us back to her obedience would be that of employing none. For the dread of the English arms, once removed, provinces would rise up against provinces and cities against cities; and we shall be seen to turn against ourselves the arms we have taken up to combat the common enemy.

Insurmountable necessity would then compel us to resort to the tutelary authority which we should have rashly abjured, and, if it consented to receive us again under its aegis, it would be no longer as free citizens but as slaves. Still inexperienced and in our infancy, what proof have we given of our ability to walk without a guide? None, and, if we judge the future by the past, we must conclude that our concord will continue as long as the danger, and no longer.

Even when the powerful hand of England supported us, for the paltry motives of territorial limits and distant jurisdictions, have we not abandoned ourselves to discords, and sometimes even to violence? And what must we not expect, now that minds are heated, ambitions roused, and arms in the hands of all?

If, therefore, our union with England offers us so many advantages for the mainte-

nance of internal peace, it is no less necessary to procure us, with foreign powers, that condescension and respect which is so essential to the prosperity of our commerce,

Historical Society of Pennsylvania

John Dickinson, portrait by Charles Willson Peale

to the enjoyment of any consideration, and to the accomplishment of any enterprise. Hitherto in our intercourse with the different nations of the world, England has lent us the support of her name and of her arms. We have presented ourselves in all the ports and in all the cities of the globe, not as Americans, a people scarcely heard of, but as English. Under shadow of this respected name, every port was open to us, every way was smooth, every demand was heard with favor. From the moment when our separation shall take place, everything will assume a contrary direction. The nations will accustom themselves to look upon us with disdain; even the pirates of Africa and Europe will fall upon our vessels, will massacre our seamen, or lead them into a cruel and perpetual slavery.

There is in the human species, often so inexplicable in their affections, a manifest propensity to oppress the feeble as well as to flatter the powerful. Fear always carries it against reason, pride against moderation, and cruelty against clemency.

Independence, I am aware, has attractions for all mankind; but I maintain that, in the present quarrel, the friends of independence are the promoters of slavery, and that those who desire to separate us would but render us more dependent, if independence means the right of commanding and not the necessity of obeying, and if being dependent is to obey and not command. If, in rendering ourselves independent of England, supposing, however, that we should be able to effect it, we might be so, at the same time, of all other nations, I should applaud the project; but to change the condition of English subjects for that of slaves to the whole world is a step that could only be counseled by insanity. If you would reduce yourselves to the necessity of obeying, in all things, the mandates of supercilious France, who is now kindling fire under our feet, declare yourselves independent. If, to British liberty, you prefer the liberty of Holland, of Venice, of Genoa, or of Ragusa, declare yourselves independent. But, if we would not change the signification of words, let us preserve and carefully maintain this dependence which has been, down to this very hour, the principle and source of our prosperity, of our liberty, of our real independence.

But here I am interrupted and told that no one questions the advantages which America derived at first from her conjunction with England; but that the new pretensions of the ministers have changed all, have subverted all. If I should deny that, for the last twelve years, the English government has given the most fatal direction to the affairs of the colonies, and that its measures toward us savor of tyranny, I should deny not only what is the manifest truth but even what I have so often advanced and supported. But is there any doubt that it already feels a secret repentance? These

arms, these soldiers it prepares against us are not designed to establish tyranny upon our shores but to vanquish our obstinacy, and to compel us to subscribe to conditions of accommodation.

In vain is it asserted that the Ministry will employ all means to make themselves quite sure of us in order to exercise upon us, with impunity, all the rigor of their power; for to pretend to reduce us to an absolute impossibility of resistance, in cases of oppression, would be, on their part, a chimerical project. The distance of the seat of government, the vast extent of intervening seas, the continual increase of our population, our warlike spirit, our experience in arms, the lakes, the rivers, the forests, the defiles which abound in our territory, are our pledges that England will always prefer to found her power upon moderation and liberty rather than upon rigor and oppression. An uninterrupted succession of victories and of triumphs could alone constrain England to acknowledge American independence; which, whether we can expect, whoever knows the instability of fortune can easily judge.

If we have combated successfully at Lexington and at Boston, Quebec and all Canada have witnessed our reverses. Everyone sees the necessity of opposing the extraordinary pretensions of the ministers; but does everybody see also that of fighting for independence?

It is to be feared that, by changing the object of the war, the present harmony will be interrupted, that the ardor of the people will be chilled by apprehensions for their new situation. By substituting a total dismemberment to the revocation of the laws we complain of, we should fully justify the ministers; we should merit the infamous name of rebels, and all the British nation would arm, with an unanimous impulse, against those who, from oppressed and complaining subjects, should have become all at once irreconcilable enemies. The English cherish the liberty we defend; they respect the dignity of our cause; but they will blame, they will detest our recourse to independence, and will unite with one consent to combat us.

The propagators of the new doctrine are pleased to assure us that, out of jealousy toward England, foreign sovereigns will lavish their succors upon us, as if these sovereigns could sincerely applaud rebellion; as if they had not colonies, even here in America, in which it is important for them to maintain obedience and tranquility. Let us suppose, however, that jealousy, ambition, or vengeance should triumph over the fear of insurrection; do you think these princes will not make you pay dear for the assistance with which they flatter you? Who has not learned, to his cost, the perfidy and the cupidity of Europeans? They will disguise their avarice under pompous words; under the most benevolent pretexts they will despoil us of our territories, they will invade our fisheries and obstruct our navigation, they will attempt our liberty and our privileges. We shall learn too late what it costs to trust to those European flatteries, and to place that confidence in inveterate enemies which has been withdrawn from long tried friends.

There are many persons who, to gain their ends, extol the advantages of a republic over monarchy. I will not here undertake to examine which of these two forms of government merits the preference. I know, however, that the English nation, after having tried them both, has never found repose except in monarchy. I know, also, that in popular republics themselves, so necessary is monarchy to cement human society, it has been requisite to institute monarchical powers, more or less extensive, under the names of *archons*, of *consuls*, of *doges*, of *gonfaloniers*, and finally of *kings*. Nor should I here omit an observation, the truth of which ap-

pears to me incontestible — the English constitution seems to be the fruit of the experience of all anterior time, in which monarchy is so tempered that the monarch finds himself checked in his efforts to seize absolute power; and the authority of the people is so regulated that anarchy is not to be feared. But for us it is to be apprehended that, when the counterpoise of monarchy shall no longer exist, the democratic power may carry all before it and involve the whole state in confusion and ruin. Then an ambitious citizen may arise, seize the reins of power, and annihilate liberty forever; for such is the ordinary career of ill-balanced democracies, they fall into anarchy, and thence under despotism.

Such are the opinions which might have been offered you with more eloquence, but assuredly not with more zeal or sincerity. May heaven grant that such sinister forebodings be not one day accomplished! May it not permit that, in this solemn concourse of the friends of country, the impassioned language of presumptuous and ardent men should have more influence than the pacific exhortations of good and sober citizens; prudence and moderation found and preserve empires; temerity and presumption occasion their downfall.

The discourse of Dickinson was heard with attention; but the current flowed irresistibly strong in a contrary direction, and, fear acting upon many more powerfully even than their opinion, the majority pronounced in favor of independence. The deputies of Pennsylvania were accordingly authorized to return to Congress, and to consent that the Confederate Colonies should declare themselves free and independent states.

THOMAS JEFFERSON: Debate on Independence

During the debate on R. H. Lee's resolution for independence in June 1776, many of the old arguments for and against independence were restated. Thomas Jefferson recorded the views of both sides in notes that he made during the proceedings of the Continental Congress. These notes were later included in Jefferson's Autobiography.

Source: H. A. Washington, VIII, pp. 12-26.

Friday, June 7, 1776. The delegates from Virginia moved, in obedience to instructions from their constituents, that the Congress should declare that these United Colonies are and of right ought to be free and independent states; that they are absolved from all allegiance to the British Crown, and that all political connection between them and the state of Great Britain is and ought to be totally dissolved; that measures should be immediately taken for procuring the assistance of foreign powers, and a confederation be formed to bind the colonies more closely together.

The House being obliged to attend at that time to some other business, the proposition was referred to the next day, when the members were ordered to attend punctually at 10 o'clock.

Saturday, June 8. They proceeded to take it into consideration and referred it to a committee of the whole, into which they immediately resolved themselves, and passed that day and Monday, the 10th, in debating on the subject.

It was argued by Wilson, Robert R. Livingston, E. Rutledge, Dickinson, and others:

That, though they were friends to the measures themselves and saw the impossibility that we should ever again be united with Great Britain, yet they were against adopting them at this time;

That the conduct we had formerly observed was wise and proper now, of deferring to take any capital step till the voice of the people drove us into it;

That they were our power, and without them our declarations could not be carried into effect;

That the people of the middle colonies (Maryland, Delaware, Pennsylvania, the Jerseys, and New York) were not yet ripe for bidding adieu to British connection, but that they were fast ripening and in a short time would join in the general voice of America;

That the resolution entered into by this House on the 15th of May for suppressing the exercise of all powers derived from the Crown had shown, by the ferment into which it had thrown these middle colonies, that they had not yet accommodated their minds to a separation from the mother country;

That some of them had expressly forbidden their delegates to consent to such a declaration, and others had given no instructions and, consequently, no powers to give such consent;

That if the delegates of any particular colony had no power to declare such colony independent, certain they were the others could not declare it for them, the colonies being as yet perfectly independent of each other;

That the Assembly of Pennsylvania was now sitting abovestairs, their convention would sit within a few days, the convention of New York was now sitting, and those of the Jerseys and Delaware counties would meet on the Monday following; and it was probable these bodies would take up the question of independence and would declare to their delegates the voice of their state;

That if such a declaration should now be agreed to, these delegates must retire, and possibly their colonies might secede from the Union;

That such a secession would weaken us more than could be compensated by any foreign alliance;

That in the event of such a division, foreign powers would either refuse to join themselves to our fortunes, or, having us so much in their power as that desperate declaration would place us, they would insist on terms proportionably more hard and prejudicial;

That we had little reason to expect an alliance with those to whom alone, as yet, we had cast our eyes;

That France and Spain had reason to be jealous of that rising power which would one day certainly strip them of all their American possessions;

That it was more likely they should form a connection with the British court, who, if they should find themselves unable otherwise to extricate themselves from their difficulties, would agree to a partition of our territories, restoring Canada to France and the Floridas to Spain, to accomplish for themselves a recovery of these colonies;

That it would not be long before we should receive certain information of the disposition of the French court from the agent whom we had sent to Paris for that purpose;

That if this disposition should be favorable, by waiting the event of the present campaign, which we all hoped would be successful, we should have reason to expect an alliance on better terms;

That this would in fact work no delay of any effectual aid from such ally, as, from the advance of the season and distance of

Independence National Historical Park

Charles Thomson, secretary of the Continental Congress

our situation, it was impossible we could receive any assistance during this campaign;

That it was prudent to fix among ourselves the terms on which we should form alliance before we declared we would form one at all events;

And that if these were agreed on and our Declaration of Independence ready by the time our ambassador should be prepared to sail, it would be as well as to go into that Declaration at this day.

On the other side it was urged by J. Adams, Lee, Wythe, and others:

That no gentleman had argued against the policy or the right of separation from Britain, nor had supposed it possible we should ever renew our connection; that they had only opposed its being now declared;

That the question was not whether, by a Declaration of Independence, we should make ourselves what we are not, but whether we should declare a fact which already exists;

That, as to the people or Parliament of England, we had always been independent of them, their restraints on our trade deriving efficacy from our acquiescence only and not from any rights they possessed of imposing them, and that so far our connection had been federal only and was now dissolved by the commencement of hostilities;

That, as to the King, we had been bound to him by allegiance, but that this bond was now dissolved by his assent to the last act of Parliament, by which he declares us out of his protection, and by his levying war on us, a fact which had long ago proved us out of his protection, it being a certain position in law that allegiance and protection are reciprocal, the one ceasing when the other is withdrawn;

That James II never declared the people of England out of his protection, yet his actions proved it and the Parliament declared it;

No delegates then can be denied, or ever want, a power of declaring an existing truth;

That the delegates from the Delaware counties having declared their constituents ready to join, there are only two colonies, Pennsylvania and Maryland, whose delegates are absolutely tied up, and that these had, by their instructions, only reserved a right of confirming or rejecting the measure;

That the instructions from Pennsylvania might be accounted for from the times in which they were drawn, near a twelvemonth ago, since which the face of affairs has totally changed;

That within that time it had become apparent that Britain was determined to accept nothing less than a *carte blanche*, and that the King's answer to the lord mayor, aldermen, and Common Council of London, which had come to hand four days ago, must have satisfied everyone of this point;

That the people wait for us to lead the way;

That *they* are in favor of the measure, though the instructions given by some of their *representatives* are not;

That the voice of the representatives is not always consonant with the voice of the people, and that this is remarkably the case in these middle colonies;

That the effect of the resolution of the 15th of May has proved this, which, raising the murmurs of some in the colonies of Pennsylvania and Maryland, called forth the opposing voice of the freer part of the people and proved them to be the majority, even in these colonies;

That the backwardness of these two colonies might be ascribed partly to the influence of proprietary power and connections, and partly to their having not yet been attacked by the enemy;

That these causes were not likely to be soon removed, as there seemed no probability that the enemy would make either of these the seat of this summer's war;

That it would be vain to wait either weeks or months for perfect unanimity, since it was impossible that all men should ever become of one sentiment on any question;

That the conduct of some colonies, from the beginning of this contest, had given reason to suspect it was their settled policy to keep in the rear of the Confederacy, that their particular prospect might be better even in the worst event;

That, therefore, it was necessary for those colonies who had thrown themselves forward and hazarded all from the beginning to come forward now also, and put all again to their own hazard;

That the history of the Dutch revolution, of whom three states only confederated at first, proved that a secession of some colonies would not be so dangerous as some apprehended;

That a Declaration of Independence alone could render it consistent with European delicacy for European powers to treat with us, or even to receive an ambassador from us;

That till this they would not receive our vessels into their ports, nor acknowledge the adjudications of our Courts of Admiralty to be legitimate in cases of capture of British vessels;

That, though France and Spain may be jealous of our rising power, they must think it will be much more formidable with the addition of Great Britain, and will therefore see it their interest to prevent a coalition; but should they refuse, we shall be but where we are; whereas, without trying, we shall never know whether they will aid us or not;

That the present campaign may be unsuccessful, and therefore we had better propose an alliance while our affairs wear a hopeful aspect;

That to wait the event of this campaign will certainly work delay, because, during this summer, France may assist us effectually by cutting off those supplies of provisions from England and Ireland on which the enemy's armies here are to depend; or by setting in motion the great power they have collected in the West Indies, and calling our enemy to the defense of the possessions they have there;

That it would be idle to lose time in settling the terms of alliance till we had first determined we would enter into alliance;

That it is necessary to lose no time in opening a trade for our people, who will want clothes and will want money, too, for the payment of taxes;

And that the only misfortune is that we did not enter into alliance with France six months sooner, as, besides opening her ports for the vent [sale] of our last year's produce, she might have marched an army into Germany and prevented the petty princes there from selling their unhappy subjects to subdue us.

It appearing in the course of these debates that the colonies of New York, New Jersey, Pennsylvania, Delaware, Maryland, and South Carolina were not yet matured for falling from the parent stem, but that they were fast advancing to that state, it was thought most prudent to wait a while for them, and to postpone the final decision to July 1; but, that this might occasion as little delay as possible, a committee was appointed to prepare a Declaration of Independence. The committee were John Adams, Dr. Franklin, Roger Sherman, Robert R. Livingston, and myself. Committees were also appointed at the same time to prepare a plan of confederation for the colonies, and to state the terms proper to be proposed for foreign alliance. The committee for drawing the Declaration of Independence desired me to do it. It was accordingly done, and, being approved by them, I reported it to the House on Friday, the 28th of June, when it was read and ordered to lie on the table.

On Monday, the 1st of July, the House resolved itself into a committee of the whole and resumed the consideration of the original motion made by the delegates of Virginia, which, being again debated through the day, was carried in the affirmative by the votes of New Hampshire, Connecticut, Massachusetts, Rhode Island, New Jersey, Maryland, Virginia, North Carolina, and Georgia. South Carolina and Pennsylvania voted against it. Delaware had but two members present, and they were divided. The delegates from New York declared they were for it themselves, and were assured their constituents were for it, but that their instructions having been drawn near a twelvemonth before, when reconciliation was still the general object, they were enjoined by them to do nothing which should impede that object. They therefore thought themselves not justifiable in voting on either side and asked leave to withdraw from the question, which was given them. The committee rose and reported their resolution to the House.

Mr. Edward Rutledge of South Carolina then requested the determination might be put off to the next day, as he believed his colleagues, though they disapproved of the resolution, would then join in it for the sake of unanimity. The ultimate question, whether the House would agree to the resolution of the committee, was accordingly postponed to the next day, when it was again moved and South Carolina concurred in voting for it. In the meantime, a third member had come post from the Delaware counties and turned the vote of that colony in favor of the resolution. Members of a different sentiment attending that morning from Pennsylvania also, her vote was changed, so that the whole twelve colonies who were authorized to vote at all gave their voices for it; and within a few days the convention of New York approved of it and thus supplied the void occasioned by the withdrawing of her delegates from the vote.

Congress proceeded the same day to consider the Declaration of Independence, which had been reported and lain on the table the Friday preceding, and on Monday referred to a committee of the whole. The pusillanimous idea that we had friends in England worth keeping terms with still haunted the minds of many. For this reason, those passages which conveyed censures on the people of England were struck out, lest they should give them offense. The clause, too, reprobating the enslaving the inhabitants of Africa was struck out in complaisance to South Carolina and Georgia, who had never attempted to restrain the importation of slaves, and who, on the contrary, still wished to continue it. Our Northern brethren, also, I believe, felt a little tender under those censures; for though their people had very few slaves themselves, yet they had been pretty considerable carriers of them to others.

The debates, having taken up the greater parts of the 2nd, 3rd, and 4th days of July, were, on the evening of the last, closed. The Declaration was reported by the committee, agreed to by the House, and signed by every member present, except Mr. Dickinson.

The Declaration of Independence

The Declaration of Independence was formally adopted by the delegates to the Second Continental Congress, meeting in Philadelphia, on July 4, 1776. Two days earlier, a resolution had been passed which said "that these United Colonies are, and of right ought to be, free and independent States, that they are absolved from all allegiance to the British Crown, and that all political connection between them and the state of Great Britain is and ought to be totally dissolved." The introduction on June 7 of this resolution, by Richard Henry Lee of Virginia, had been followed by the appointment of a committee to draft a statement declaring the reasons for the impending separation. Of the members of this committee, which included Thomas Jefferson, John Adams, Benjamin Franklin, Roger Sherman, and Robert Livingston, it was Jefferson who prepared the draft, submitting it to the others for consideration. Minor changes in Jefferson's draft were suggested by Adams and Franklin. Some further alterations were made after it was presented to the Congress on June 28. The final words, however, were still largely those of Jefferson. At its passage it was signed only by John Hancock, the presiding officer. Four days later the Declaration of Independence was read aloud in the city of Philadelphia at what later became Independence Square. Copies were made, sent to the legislatures of the colonies, and published throughout the country. The Declaration was not signed by the other members of the Congress until August 2, when a copy engrossed on parchment was witnessed with their names.

Source: *Journals*, I: "Thursday, July 4, 1776."

WHEN, IN THE COURSE OF HUMAN EVENTS, it becomes necessary for one people to dissolve the political bands which have connected them with another, and to assume, among the powers of the earth, the separate and equal station to which the laws of nature and of nature's God entitle them, a decent respect to the opinions of mankind requires that they should declare the causes which impel them to the separation.

We hold these truths to be self-evident, that all men are created equal, that they are endowed by their Creator with certain unalienable rights, that among these are life, liberty, and the pursuit of happiness. That, to secure these rights, governments are instituted among men, deriving their just powers from the consent of the governed. That, whenever any form of government becomes destructive of these ends, it is the right of the people to alter or to abolish it, and to institute new government, laying its foundation on such principles, and organizing its powers in such form, as to them shall seem most likely to effect their safety and happiness.

Prudence, indeed, will dictate that governments long established should not be changed for light and transient causes; and, accordingly, all experience has shown, that mankind are more disposed to suffer, while evils are sufferable, than to right themselves by abolishing the forms to which they are accustomed.

But, when a long train of abuses and usurpations, pursuing invariably the same object, evinces a design to reduce them under absolute despotism, it is their right, it is their duty, to throw off such government, and to provide new guards for their future security. Such has been the patient sufferance of these colonies; and such is now the necessity which constrains them to alter their former systems of government. The history of the present King of Great Britain is a history of repeated injuries and usurpations, all having in direct object the establishment of an absolute tyranny over these states. To prove this, let facts be submitted to a candid world.

He has refused his assent to laws the most wholesome and necessary for the public good.

He has forbidden his governors to pass laws of immediate and pressing importance, unless suspended in their operation till his assent should be obtained; and when so suspended, he has utterly neglected to attend to them.

He has refused to pass other laws for the accommodation of large districts of people, unless those people would relinquish the right of representation in the legislature; a right inestimable to them and formidable to tyrants only.

He has called together legislative bodies at places unusual, uncomfortable, and distant from the depository of their public records, for the sole purpose of fatiguing them into compliance with his measures.

He has dissolved representative houses repeatedly, for opposing, with manly firmness, his invasions on the rights of the people.

He has refused for a long time, after such dissolutions, to cause others to be elected; whereby the legislative powers, incapable of annihilation, have returned to the people at large for their exercise; the state remaining in the meantime exposed to all the dangers of invasion from without, and convulsions within.

He has endeavored to prevent the population of these states; for that purpose obstructing the laws for naturalization of foreigners; refusing to pass others to encourage their migrations hither, and raising the conditions of new appropriations of lands.

He has obstructed the administration of justice, by refusing his assent to laws for establishing judiciary powers.

He has made judges dependent on his will alone, for the tenure of their offices, and the amount and payment of their salaries.

He has erected a multitude of new offices, and sent hither swarms of officers to harass our people, and eat out their substance.

He has kept among us, in times of peace, standing armies, without the consent of our legislatures.

He has affected to render the military independent of and superior to the civil power.

He has combined with others to subject us to a jurisdiction foreign to our constitution, and unacknowledged by our laws; giving his assent to their acts of pretended legislation:

For quartering large bodies of armed troops among us;

For protecting them, by a mock trial, from punishment for any murders which they should commit on the inhabitants of these states;

For cutting off our trade with all parts of the world;

For imposing taxes on us without our consent;

For depriving us, in many cases, of the benefits of trial by jury;

For transporting us beyond seas to be tried for pretended offenses;

For abolishing the free system of English laws in a neighboring province, establishing therein an arbitrary government, and enlarging its boundaries, so as to render it at once an example and fit instrument for introducing the same absolute rule into these colonies;

For taking away our charters, abolishing our most valuable laws, and altering fundamentally the forms of our governments;

For suspending our own legislatures, and declaring themselves invested with power to legislate for us in all cases whatsoever.

He has abdicated government here, by declaring us out of his protection, and waging war against us.

He has plundered our seas, ravaged our coasts, burnt our towns, and destroyed the lives of our people.

He is at this time transporting large armies of foreign mercenaries to complete the works of death, desolation, and tyranny, already begun with circumstances of cruelty and perfidy scarcely paralleled in the most barbarous ages, and totally unworthy the head of a civilized nation.

He has constrained our fellow citizens, taken captive on the high seas, to bear arms against their country, to become the executioners of their friends and brethren, or to fall themselves by their hands.

He has excited domestic insurrections amongst us, and has endeavored to bring on the inhabitants of our frontiers, the merciless Indian savages, whose known rule of warfare is an undistinguished destruction of all ages, sexes, and conditions.

In every stage of these oppressions, we have petitioned for redress, in the most humble terms. Our repeated petitions have been answered only by repeated injury. A prince, whose character is thus marked by every act which may define a tyrant, is unfit to be the ruler of a free people.

Nor have we been wanting in attentions to our British brethren. We have warned them from time to time of attempts by their legislature to extend an unwarrantable jurisdiction over us. We have reminded them of the circumstances of our emigration and settlement here. We have appealed to their native justice and magnanimity, and we have conjured them by the ties of our common kindred, to disavow these usurpations, which would inevitably interrupt our connections and correspondence. They too have been deaf to the voice of justice and of consanguinity. We must, therefore, acquiesce in the necessity, which denounces our separation, and hold them, as we hold the rest of mankind, enemies in war, in peace friends.

We, therefore, the representatives of the United States of America, in General Congress assembled, appealing to the Supreme Judge of the world for the rectitude of our intentions, do, in the name, and by authority of the good people of these colonies, solemnly publish and declare, that these

United Colonies are, and of right ought to be free and independent states; that they are absolved from all allegiance to the British Crown, and that all political connection between them and the state of Great Britain is and ought to be totally dissolved; and that, as free and independent states, they have full power to levy war, conclude peace, contract alliances, establish commerce, and to do all other acts and things which independent states may of right do. And for the support of this declaration, with a firm reliance on the protection of Divine Providence, we mutually pledge to each other our lives, our fortunes, and our sacred honor.

Concord's Call for a State Constitutional Convention

In creating new state governments, the mechanics of constitution making was probably the heart of the problem. The great question was: Who possessed the rightful authority to make a constitution? The Concord town meeting felt that the authority rested only with the people of the state. In their proposals of October 22, 1776, they urged the suggestion of a state-wide constitutional convention which has since become the traditional American practice. In Massachusetts, the suggestions of the Concord meeting were not heeded until 1779.

Source: *Bulletins for the Constitutional Convention 1917-1918*, Boston, 1919, Vol. II, Bulletin No. 35: "The Proceedings of the Town of Concord, Massachusetts, October 22, 1776."

A MEETING OF THE INHABITANTS (free men and twenty-one years of age and older) of the town of Concord met by adjournment on October 21, 1776, to take into consideration a resolve of the honorable House of Representatives of this state made on September 17. The town resolved as follows:

Resolve 1. This state being presently destitute of a properly established form of government, it is absolutely necessary that a government should be immediately formed and established.

Resolve 2. The supreme legislative, either in its proper capacity or in a joint committee, is by no means a body proper to form and establish a constitution or form a government, for the following reasons:

First, because we conceive that a constitution in its proper idea intends a system of principles established to secure the subject in the possession and enjoyment of their rights and privileges against any encroachments of the governing part.

Second, because the same body that forms a constitution has a power to alter it.

Third, because a constitution alterable by the supreme legislature is no security at all to the subject against any encroachment of the governing part on any or on all of their rights and privileges.

Resolve 3. It appears highly necessary and expedient to this town that a convention or congress be immediately chosen to form and establish a constitution by the inhabitants of the respective towns in this state, who are free and twenty-one years of age and older, in proportion as the representatives of this state formerly were chosen. The convention or congress is not to consist of a greater number than the House of Assembly of this state might consist of, except that each town and district shall have liberty to send one representative, or otherwise as shall appear meet to the inhabitants of this state in general.

Resolve 4. When the convention or congress has formed a constitution, they are to adjourn for a short time and publish their proposed constitution for the inspection of the inhabitants of this state.

Resolve 5. The honorable House of As-sembly of this state desires to recommend to the inhabitants of the state to proceed to choose a convention or congress for the purpose abovesaid as soon as possible.

Tom Paine: The American Crisis

Tom Paine was the author of a series of patriotic tracts called The Crisis *papers, which appeared in print from 1776 to 1783. The first of these so stirred General Washington that he ordered it read to his troops late in December 1776 at a time when the American cause seemed to be faltering. This paper, combined with the subsequent victory of his army at Trenton, New Jersey, later in the month, had the probable effect of inspiring many soldiers, whose term of service would expire January 1, to reenlist. The first* Crisis *paper appeared in the* Pennsylvania Journal, *December 19, 1776, and within a week was reissued as a pamphlet.*

Source: *The Political Writings of Thomas Paine,* New York, 1830, Vol. I, pp. 75-82.

THESE ARE THE TIMES that try men's souls. The summer soldier and the sunshine patriot will, in this crisis, shrink from the service of his country; but he that stands it now deserves the love and thanks of man and woman. Tyranny, like hell, is not easily conquered; yet we have this consolation with us — that the harder the conflict, the more glorious the triumph. What we obtain too cheap, we esteem too lightly: It is dearness only that gives everything its value. Heaven knows how to put a proper price upon its goods; and it would be strange indeed if so celestial an article as freedom should not be highly rated. Britain, with an army to enforce her tyranny, has declared that she has a right not only to tax but "to bind us in all cases whatsoever," and if being bound in that manner is not slavery, then is there not such a thing as slavery upon earth. Even the expression is impious, for so unlimited a power can belong only to God.

Whether the independence of the conti-nent was declared too soon or delayed too long, I will not now enter into as an argu-ment; my own simple opinion is, that had it been eight months earlier, it would have been much better. We did not make a proper use of last winter; neither could we, while we were in a dependent state. How-ever, the fault, if it were one, was all our own; we have none to blame but ourselves. But no great deal is lost yet; all that Howe has been doing for this month past is rather a ravage than a conquest, which the spirit of the Jerseys a year ago would have quick-ly repulsed, and which time and a little res-olution will soon recover.

I have as little superstition in me as any man living, but my secret opinion has ever been, and still is, that God Almighty will not give up a people to military destruction, or leave them unsupportedly to perish, who have so earnestly and so repeatedly sought to avoid the calamities of war by every de-cent method which wisdom could invent. Neither have I so much of the infidel in me as to suppose that He has relinquished the government of the world and given us up to the care of devils; and as I do not, I cannot see on what grounds the king of Britain can look up to Heaven for help against us — a common murderer, a highwayman, or a housebreaker has as good a pretense as he.

It is surprising to see how rapidly a panic will sometimes run through a country. All nations and ages have been subject to them: Britain has trembled like an ague at the report of a French fleet of flat-bottomed boats; and in the 14th century the whole English Army, after ravaging the kingdom of France, was driven back like men petrified with fear; and this brave exploit was performed by a few broken forces collected and headed by a woman, Joan of Arc. Would that Heaven might inspire some Jersey maid to spirit up her countrymen and save her fair fellow sufferers from ravage and ravishment! Yet panics, in some cases, have their uses; they produce as much good as hurt. Their duration is always short; the mind soon grows through them and acquires a firmer habit than before. But their peculiar advantage is that they are the touchstones of sincerity and hypocrisy, and bring things and men to light which might otherwise have lain forever undiscovered. In fact, they have the same effect on secret traitors which an imaginary apparition would have upon a private murderer. They sift out the hidden thoughts of man and hold them up in public to the world. Many a disguised Tory has lately shown his head, that shall penitentially solemnize with curses the day on which Howe arrived upon the Delaware.

As I was with the troops at Fort Lee, and marched with them to the edge of Pennsylvania, I am well acquainted with many circumstances which those who live at a distance know but little or nothing of. Our situation there was exceedingly cramped, the place being a narrow neck of land between the North River and the Hackensack. Our force was inconsiderable, being not one-fourth so great as Howe could bring against us. We had no army at hand to have relieved the garrison, had we shut ourselves up and stood on our defense. Our ammunition, light artillery, and the best part of our stores had been removed on the apprehension that Howe would endeavor to penetrate the Jerseys, in which case Fort Lee could be of no use to us; for it must occur to every thinking man, whether in the army or not, that these kind of field forts are only for temporary purposes, and last in use no longer than the enemy directs his force against the particular object, which such forts are raised to defend.

Such was our situation and condition at Fort Lee on the morning of the 20th of November, when an officer arrived with information that the enemy with 200 boats had landed about seven miles above. Major General Green, who commanded the garrison, immediately ordered them under arms, and sent express to General Washington at the town of Hackensack, distant, by the way of the ferry, six miles. Our first object was to secure the bridge over the Hackensack, which laid up the river between the enemy and us, about six miles from us, three from them. General Washington arrived in about three-quarters of an hour, and marched at the head of the troops toward the bridge, which place I expected we should have a brush for; however, they did not choose to dispute it with us, and the greatest part of our troops went over the bridge, the rest over the ferry, except some which passed at a mill on a small creek, between the bridge and the ferry, and made their way through some marshy grounds up to the town of Hackensack, and there passed the river. We brought off as much baggage as the wagons could contain; the rest was lost. The simple object was to bring off the garrison and march them on till they could be strengthened by the Jersey or Pennsylvania militia, so as to be enabled to make a stand.

We stayed four days at Newark, collected our outposts with some of the Jersey militia, and marched out twice to meet the enemy, on being informed that they were advancing, though our numbers were greatly inferior to theirs. Howe, in my little opinion, committed a great error in generalship in not throwing a body of forces off from Staten Island through Amboy, by which means he might have seized all our stores at Brunswick and intercepted our march into Pennsylvania. But if we believe the power of hell to be limited, we must likewise believe that their agents are under some providential control.

I shall not now attempt to give all the particulars of our retreat to the Delaware; suffice it for the present to say that both officers and men, though greatly harassed and fatigued, frequently without rest, covering, or provision — the inevitable consequences of a long retreat — bore it with a manly and martial spirit. All their wishes centered in one, which was, that the country would turn out and help them to drive the enemy back. Voltaire has remarked that King William never appeared to full advantage but in difficulties and in action; the same remark may be made on General Washington, for the character fits him. There is a natural firmness in some minds which cannot be unlocked by trifles, but which, when unlocked, discovers a cabinet of fortitude; and I reckon it among those kind of public blessings which we do not immediately see, that God has blessed him with uninterrupted health, and given him a mind that can even flourish upon care.

I shall conclude this paper with some miscellaneous remarks on the state of our affairs; and shall begin with asking the following question: Why is it that the enemy have left the New England provinces and made these middle ones the seat of war? The answer is easy: New England is not infested with Tories, and we are. I have been tender in raising the cry against these men, and used numberless arguments to show them their danger, but it will not do to sacrifice a world either to their folly or their baseness. The period is now arrived in which either they or we must change our sentiments, or one or both must fall. And what is a Tory? Good God! What is he? I should not be afraid to go with a hundred Whigs against a thousand Tories, were they to attempt to get into arms. Every Tory is a coward, for servile, slavish, self-interested fear is the foundation of Toryism; and a man under such influence, though he may be cruel, never can be brave.

But, before the line of irrecoverable separation be drawn between us, let us reason the matter together. Your conduct is an invitation to the enemy, yet not one in a thousand of you has heart enough to join him. Howe is as much deceived by you as the American cause is injured by you. He expects you will all take up arms and flock to his standard, with muskets on your shoulders. Your opinions are of no use to him, unless you support him personally, for it is soldiers, and not Tories, that he wants.

I once felt all that kind of anger which a man ought to feel against the mean principles that are held by the Tories. A noted one, who kept a tavern at Amboy, was standing at his door with as pretty a child in his hand, about eight or nine years old, as I ever saw, and after speaking his mind as freely as he thought was prudent, finished with this unfatherly expression. "Well! give me peace in my day." Not a man lives on the continent but fully believes that a separation must some time or other finally take place; and a generous parent should have said, "If there must be trouble, let it be in my day, that my child may have peace." And this single reflection, well applied, is sufficient to awaken every man to duty.

Not a place upon earth might be so happy as America. Her situation is remote from all the wrangling world, and she has nothing to do but to trade with them. A man can distinguish himself between temper and principle, and I am as confident, as I am that God governs the world, that America will never be happy till she gets clear of foreign dominion. Wars, without ceasing, will break out till that period arrives, and the continent must in the end be conqueror; for though the flame of liberty may sometimes cease to shine, the coal can never expire.

America did not, nor does not want force; but she wanted a proper application of that force. Wisdom is not the purchase of a day, and it is no wonder that we should err at the first setting off. From an excess of tenderness, we were unwilling to raise an army, and trusted our cause to the temporary defense of a well-meaning militia. A summer's experience has now taught us better; yet with those troops, while they were collected, we were able to set bounds to the progress of the enemy, and, thank God! they are again assembling. I always considered militia as the best troops in the world for a sudden exertion, but they will not do for a long campaign.

Howe, it is probable, will make an attempt on this city. Should he fail on this side the Delaware, he is ruined; if he succeeds, our cause is not ruined. He stakes all on his side against a part on ours; admitting he succeeds, the consequences will be that armies from both ends of the continent will march to assist their suffering friends in the middle states; for he cannot go everywhere, it is impossible. I consider Howe as the greatest enemy the Tories have; he is bringing war into their country, which, had it not been for him and partly for themselves, they had been clear of. Should he now be expelled, I wish, with all the devotion of a Christian, that the names of Whig and Tory may never more be mentioned; but should the Tories give him encouragement to come, or assistance if he come, I as sincerely wish that our next year's arms may expel them from the continent, and the Congress appropriate their possessions to the relief of those who have suffered in well-doing. A single successful battle next year will settle the whole.

America could carry on a two years' war by the confiscation of the property of disaffected persons, and be made happy by their expulsion. Say not that this is revenge, call it rather the soft resentment of a suffering people, who, having no object in view but the good of all, have staked their own all upon a seemingly doubtful event. Yet it is folly to argue against determined hardness; eloquence may strike the ear, and the language of sorrow draw forth the tear of compassion, but nothing can reach the heart that is steeled with prejudice.

Quitting this class of men, I turn with the warm ardor of a friend to those who have nobly stood and are yet determined to stand the matter out. I call not upon a few, but upon all; not in this state or that state, but on every state. Up and help us; lay your shoulders to the wheel; better have too much force than too little, when so great an object is at stake. Let it be told to the future world that in the depth of winter, when nothing but hope and virtue could survive, that the city and country, alarmed at one common danger, came forth to meet and to repulse it. Say not that thousands are gone, turn out your tens of thousands; throw not the burden of the day upon Providence, but "show your faith by your works," that God may bless you. It matters not where you live, or what rank of life you hold, the evil or the blessing will reach you all. The far and the near, the home counties and the back, the rich and the poor will suffer or rejoice alike. The heart that feels not now is dead; the blood of his children will curse his cowardice who shrinks back at a time when a little might have saved the whole, and made *them* happy. I love the man that can smile in trouble, that can gather strength from distress, and grow brave by reflection. It is the business of little minds to shrink; but he whose heart is firm, and whose conscience approves his conduct, will pursue his principles unto death.

My own line of reasoning is to myself as straight and clear as a ray of light. Not all the treasures of the world, so far as I believe, could have induced me to support an offensive war, for I think it murder; but if a thief breaks into my house, burns and destroys my property, and kills or threatens to kill me, or those that are in it, and to "bind me in all cases whatsoever" to his absolute will, am I to suffer it? What signifies it to me whether he who does it is a king or a common man; my countryman or not my countryman; whether it be done by an individual villain or an army of them? If we reason to the root of things we shall find no difference; neither can any just cause be assigned why we should punish in the one case and pardon in the other. Let them call me rebel and welcome, I feel no concern from it; but I should suffer the misery of devils were I to make a whore of my soul by swearing allegiance to one whose character is that of a sottish, stupid, stubborn, worthless, brutish man. I conceive likewise a horrid idea in receiving mercy from a being who at the last day shall be shrieking to the rocks and mountains to cover him, and fleeing with terror from the orphan, the widow, and the slain of America.

There are cases which cannot be overdone by language, and this is one. There are persons, too, who see not the full extent of the evil which threatens them; they solace themselves with hopes that the enemy, if he succeed, will be merciful. It is the madness of folly to expect mercy from those who have refused to do justice; and even mercy, where conquest is the object, is only a trick of war. The cunning of the fox is as murderous as the violence of the wolf, and we ought to guard equally against both. Howe's first object is, partly by threats and partly by promises, to terrify or seduce the people to deliver up their arms

and receive mercy. The Ministry recommended the same plan to Gage, and this is what the Tories call making their peace, "a peace which passeth all understanding," indeed! — a peace which would be the immediate forerunner of a worse ruin than any we have yet thought of.

Ye men of Pennsylvania, do reason upon these things! Were the back counties to give up their arms, they would fall an easy prey to the Indians, who are all armed; this perhaps is what some Tories would not be sorry for. Were the home counties to deliver up their arms, they would be exposed to the resentment of the back counties, who would then have it in their power to chastise their defection at pleasure. And were any one state to give up its arms, that state must be garrisoned by all Howe's army of Britons and Hessians to preserve it from the anger of the rest. Mutual fear is the principal link in the chain of mutual love, and woe be to that state that breaks the compact. Howe is mercifully inviting you to barbarous destruction, and men must be either rogues or fools that will not see it. I dwell not upon the vapors of imagination; I bring reason to your ears, and, in language as plain as A, B, C, hold up truth to your eyes.

I thank God that I fear not. I see no real cause for fear. I know our situation well, and can see the way out of it. While our army was collected, Howe dared not risk a battle; and it is no credit to him that he decamped from the White Plains and waited a mean opportunity to ravage the defenseless Jerseys. But it is great credit to us that, with a handful of men, we sustained an orderly retreat for near a hundred miles, brought off our ammunition, all our field-pieces, the greatest part of our stores, and had four rivers to pass. None can say that our retreat was precipitate, for we were near three weeks in performing it, that the country might have time to come in. Twice we marched back to meet the enemy, and remained out till dark. The sign of fear was not seen in our camp, and had not some of the cowardly and disaffected inhabitants spread false alarms through the country, the Jerseys had never been ravaged. Once more we are again collected and collecting, our new army at both ends of the continent is recruiting fast, and we shall be able to open the next campaign with sixty thousand men, well armed and clothed.

This is our situation, and who will may know it. By perseverance and fortitude we have the prospect of a glorious issue; by cowardice and submission, the sad choice of a variety of evils — a ravaged country — a depopulated city — habitations without safety and slavery without hope — our homes turned into barracks and bawdy houses for Hessians, and a future race to provide for, whose fathers we shall doubt of. Look on this picture and weep over it! And if there yet remains one thoughtless wretch who believes it not, let him suffer it unlamented.

"Johnny Has Gone for a Soldier"

In one form or another the feelings expressed by the following song must have been shared by thousands of young girls in every war in history. "Johnny Has Gone for a Soldier," a lament of one girl a soldier left behind, is said to date from the American Revolution.

✺ JOHNNY HAS GONE FOR A SOLDIER

Here I sit on Buttermilk Hill,
Who could blame me cry me fill?
And every tear would turn a mill;
Johnny has gone for a soldier.

 Shool, shool, shool a-roo,
 Shool a-sac-a-rac-ca bib-ba-lib-ba-boo.
 If I should die for Sally Bobolink
 Come bib-ba-lib-ba-boo so rare-o.

I'd sell my clock, I'd sell my reel,
Likewise I'd sell my spinning wheel
To buy my love a sword of steel;
Johnny has gone for a soldier.

 Shool, shool, shool a-roo,
 Shool a-sac-a-rac-ca bib-ba-lib-ba-boo.
 If I should die for Sally Bobolink
 Come bib-ba-lib-ba-boo so rare-o.

THE HORSE AMERICA, *throwing his Master.*

Pub.d as the Act directs Aug.st 1.st 1779 by W.m White, Angel Court, Westminster.

THE REVOLUTIONARY WAR

The struggle for the control of North America, which had seemed decisively ended by Britain's victory over France in 1763, was renewed when the rebellion of the American colonies became in 1776 a war for independence. In this conflict the British had many material advantages, including a large population and a regular army. But they overestimated the support that Loyalists in America would give, for Loyalists were not well organized and their enthusiasm seldom matched that of the revolutionaries. Indeed, unlike the earlier wars, in which the colonies had supplied many British needs, practically everything the Red-coats required had to be shipped 3,000 miles across the Atlantic. The American Army, on the other hand, was seldom better provisioned than the British since Congress had little power to requisition supplies, and much of the fighting was by state militias, whose numbers depended on the nearness of the enemy. Most important in raising American strength was the aid of the French, especially the French Navy, whose king wished to see Britain's empire weakened and her armies defeated. Thus the longest American war became an international war whose outcome, so familiar today, remained long in doubt.

Officers and Men

Congress chose George Washington as commander in chief of the Army. His character and ability as a leader of men made up for any lack of training or experience. Against Washington the British first placed William Howe, an experienced officer of high reputation. Richard Howe, the general's brother, was admiral of the fleet. They were authorized to seek peace as well as to wage war and this confusion of purpose may account for what seemed to be a lack of aggressiveness on their part.

New York Public Library

"English recruits for America," engraving dated 1780

Sir William Howe, 1778

Library of Congress

George Washington, by C. W. Peale, 1772

Washington and Lee University

National Gallery of Art

Richard, Earl Howe, by Joseph Wright

Letter to British troops en route to America

Library of Congress

Address to the Soldiers.

GENTLEMEN,

YOU are about to embark .... your Fellow Subjects there to .... to POPERY and SLAVERY.

It is the Glory of the British Soldier, that he is the *Defender*, not the *Destroyer*, of the Civil and Religious Rights of the People. The *English* Soldiery are immortalized in History, for their Attachment to the Religion and Liberties of their Country.

When King JAMES the Second endeavoured to introduce the Roman-catholic Religion and arbitrary Power into ..... *Britain*, he had an Army encamped on *Hounslow* ....., to terrify the People. Seven Bishops were seized upon, and sent to the Tower. But they appealed to the Laws of their Country, and were set at Liberty. When this News reached the Camp, the Shouts of Joy were so great, that they re-echoed in the Royal Palace. This, however, did not quite convince the King, of the Aversion of the Soldiers to be the Instruments of Oppression against their Fellow Subjects. He therefore made another Trial. He ordered the Guards to be drawn up, and the Word was given, that those who did not chuse to support the King's Measures, should ground their Arms. When, behold, to his utter Confusion, and their eternal Honour—the whole Body grounded their Arms.

You, Gentlemen, will soon have an Opportunity of shewing equal Virtue. You will be called upon to imbrue your Hands in the Blood of your Fellow Subjects in *America*, because they will not admit to be Slaves, and are alarmed at the Establishment of Popery and Arbitrary Power in one Half of their Country.

Whether you will draw those Swords which have defended them against their Enemies, to butcher them into a Resignation of their Rights, which they hold as the Sons of *Englishmen*, is in your Breasts. That you will not stain the Laurels you have gained from *France*, by dipping them in Civil Blood, is every good Man's Hope.

Arts will no doubt be used to persuade you, that it is your Duty to obey Orders, and that you are sent upon the just and righteous Errand of crushing Rebellion. But your own Hearts will tell you, that the People may be so ill treated, as to make Resistance necessary. You know, that Violence and Injury offered from one Man to ......her, has always some Pretence of Right or Reason ...... it. So it is between the People and their Ru.....

......, whatever hard Names and heavy Accusa..... be bestowed upon your Fellow Subjects, in ....ared they have not deserved them; but ...... the most cruel Treatment, into Despair. In this Despair they are compelled to defend their Liberties, after having tried, in Vain, every peaceable Means of obtaining Redress of their manifold Grievances.

Before God and Man they are right.

Your Honour then, Gentlemen, as Soldiers, and your Humanity as Men, forbid you to be the Instruments of forcing Chains upon your injured and oppressed Fellow Subjects. Remember that your first Obedience is due to God, and that whoever bids you shed innocent Blood, bids you act contrary to his Commandments.

I am, GENTLEMEN,

your sincere Well-wisher,

AN OLD SOLDIER.

Isaac Royall, portrait by Copley

Loyalists

Loyalists, or "Tories," were of many kinds: conservative people of all classes tended to be Loyalists, as did Anglican clergymen and crown officials. Some were Tories after analysis of the issues, some simply because personal enemies were rebels. There was no freedom of speech for Loyalists in the colonies, many of whom had their property confiscated or burned. During and after the war, many Loyalists fled north to Canada, where they made an important contribution to that country's growth.

Rivington James, Tory who later aided the patriots

The TORY'S Day of JUDGMENT.

Two engravings showing the American treatment of Loyalists from "M'Fingal" by John Trumbull

The PROCESSION.

1776

With the Declaration of Independence fresh in their minds, the colonists were confident of victory. In July the Howe brothers landed at Staten Island, bringing a pardon from the British crown as an effort to halt hostilities. When this was rejected, there ensued the Battle of Long Island in which Washington and his unskilled militia were badly beaten by the British regulars. The Americans retreated to New Jersey and with winter approaching, Howe did not pursue. This gave Washington a chance to regroup his forces, enabling them to muster strength to attack and capture Trenton in December, restoring the colonists' confidence in their military leader.

Library of Congress

Hessian troops captured at Trenton by Washington

Historical Society of Pennsylvania

Americans defeat British forces at Princeton

Library of Congress

Burning of New York City

British and Hessian forces attack the Americans at Fort Washington

Stokes Collection, New York Public Library

Negotiations with the French

Although the French had fought the Americans in the colonial wars before 1763, they were eager to give aid against their real enemy, Great Britain. The French secretly supplied cannons and gunpowder from almost the beginning of the Revolution. Much of this aid was arranged by Pierre de Beaumarchais. Meanwhile, American agents in France were attempting to secure open and increased aid from Louis XVI. But since the colonies had won no major battles, the French hesitated as long as there was the possibility that the Americans would accept peace without independence.

Bibliotheque Nationale
King Louis XVI of France

Conn. Historical Society
Silas Deane, portrait by Peale

Virginia Historical Society
Arthur Lee, portrait by Peale

City Art Museum of St. Louis
Benjamin Franklin, America's chief negotiator with France

Beaumarchais
New York Public Library

Franklin's home in Passy, France, sketched by Hugo
New York Public Library

Dissent in Parliament

Lord North's ministry was anxious to bring the war to a conclusion in 1777. After a long and costly conflict with France, the British could ill afford the expense of the war in America. In addition, the possibility of an alliance between France and America demanded that the war be ended quickly. Meanwhile, a few members of Parliament, including such eloquent and controversial figures as John Wilkes, Isaac Barre, and Charles Fox, were openly critical of the war and urged conciliation. For these reasons, Burgoyne's advance south from Canada was planned as the decisive blow to bring the colonists to their knees.

National Portrait Gallery, London

Frederick, Lord North; portrait by N. Dance

Historical Society of Pennsylvania

George III; portrait by Benjamin West

National Portrait Gallery, London

Charles Fox, portrait by Hickel

The Brooklyn Museum

Isaac Barre

Library of Congress

Cartoon reflecting English view that Fox belonged in America

Howe Takes Philadelphia

General Howe's main effort for 1777 was the capture in September of the American capital city, Philadelphia. A few days later he repelled a poorly executed American attack at Germantown, a Philadelphia suburb. But in taking the capital, Howe had gained little more than some real estate, for the Congress escaped with their records to York, and Washington's Army remained intact.

COURT-HOUSE, YORK, PA.

The Building in which the American Congress sat during the gloomiest period of the Revolution.

The American Congress retreated to York after the British captured Philadelphia

Henry Laurens, president of Congress

Battle of Germantown in which British troops withstood the American attack

Saratoga

The British plan was to divide and conquer: Burgoyne was instructed to lead an army down the Champlain-Hudson River route to New York and split the colonies in two. But as he moved south, Burgoyne's supply lines became dangerously extended, casualties and desertions depleted his ranks, and most of his Indians disappeared. Meanwhile, the American forces daily grew larger as reinforcements arrived. On September 19 and again on October 7, 1777, British efforts to move south from encampment at Saratoga were halted in fierce battles. The American forces, by now three times those of Burgoyne, held an impregnable position at Bemis Heights, which had been fortified on the advice of Tadeusz Kosciuszko. Attempting to retreat from Saratoga, Burgoyne was surrounded and surrendered his entire army to General Gates on October 17.

Saratoga was a significant turning point in the war. Not only were British hopes for an early victory smashed and American morale boosted, but more importantly, France was convinced that the Americans were worthy of open support. Negotiations to that end were soon underway in Paris.

Library of Congress

The Frick Collection

(Above left) French engraving showing the surrender of Burgoyne; (above right) portrait of Burgoyne by Joshua Reynolds; (below) Burgoyne's army encamped on the left bank of the Hudson

Library of Congress

Tadeusz Kosciuszko

Gen. Horatio Gates

Daniel Morgan

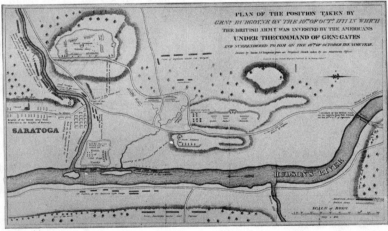

Plan showing positions of the two armies during the battle at Saratoga

Prison camp for Burgoyne's army at Charlotte, Va.

Dr. Franklin erhält, als Gesandter des Americanischen Frey Staats, seine fte Audienz in Frankreich, zu Ver- failles. am 20ten März 1778.

(Left) Franklin's first audience with Louis XVI; (above) English cartoon shows Lord North's peace commission scorned by three members of Congress in Tartar dress

The French Alliance

Armed with news of the victory at Saratoga, Benjamin Franklin, America's commissioner to France, feigned interest in conciliation with the British. French foreign minister Vergennes wanted the war to continue and persuaded the king to offer the Americans an alliance. Lord North tardily dispatched a peace commission to America to keep Congress from ratifying the French treaty. But the English did not offer the colonies independence, and Congress would not receive them. The alliance was ratified on May 4, 1778, and the French Navy was soon on its way.

Drawing at left pities America for her "Popish Leagues"; (below) "The Curious Zebra" is examined by English and French statesmen

Freedom, Peace, Plenty, all in vain advance,
Spurnd by Brittannia's Children, dupaste France:
Aspiring Chiefs in congrefs scourge the land;
All Laws subverting to usurp command.

Tyrants they prove, while Patriots they appear,
And Popish Leagues mark their absurd career:
May Heav'n in timely mercy make them wise,
Ere French and Spanish Chains their crimes chastize.

L'Escadre française sortant de la Mediterranée le 16. Mai 1778.

A Le Mont Gibraltar. | C Corvette Angloise mettant en panne dans la baye | D Batiments hollandois
B Le Mont aux Singes. | de Gibraltar en essuyant son canon à Terre. | sortant de la Mediterranée.

(Above) D'Estaing's fleet sails out of the Mediterranean Sea, bound for America

(Right) The Angel of France depicted as driving the English from Philadelphia while Americans rejoice in the background

Cow representing English commerce is milked and de-horned by France, Spain, Holland, and America while the British lion sleeps

[French handwritten caption beneath the engraving:]

...re françoise entrant dans Newport sous le feu des Batteries en forçant le passage le 8 Aoust 1778. Jour que les Améri... passèrent sur l'Isle de Rode Island par le chemin d'howland's Ferry.

... de Newport .
... sur Rode Island faisant feu ... Vaisseaux .
... sur Goat Island faisant feu sur ... aisseaux .
Nᵗᵃ Les Anglois brulerent ou coulerent a Rode Island, les Frégates L'Orphée, la Junon, le Lark en la flore de 32 Canons le Cerbere en le Faucon de 28. Sans par... grand nombre de Batiments Marchands.

D Isle de Conanicut .
E Vaisseaux françois forçant le passage .
F Vaisseaux François tournant ou qui on tourné l'Isle de Conanicut .
G Batiments Anglois en feu .

H Batterie qui fut abandonnée aprés avoir tiré sur le premier Vaisseau françois qui tourn... Conanicut .
I Frégate françoise restant mouillée en dehors avec une prise tandis que les deux autre Fr... sont dans le Canal de l'En ou elles assurent le passage d'howland's ferry aprés fait brulés les deux Batiments Gardes cotes Anglois qui deffendoient ce Canal.

(Above) The French fleet sails into Newport; (below) Comte d'Estaing, commander of the fleet

The French Arrive

Seventeen French warships arrived in America in July 1778, and promptly disappointed the patriots. Comte d'Estaing, an army officer for most of his career, proved cautious as a naval commander, and the Americans thought he was too reluctant to fight. Later, under Admiral de Grasse, the French fleet was important in forcing Cornwallis' surrender at Yorktown.

Siege of Rhode Island at Newport, August 1778

Foreign Officers

Many European officers volunteered to serve in the American forces, but since Americans would rarely agree to serve under foreign officers, most of the volunteers served as special advisors in artillery, military engineering, and battlefield tactics where their professional training was most useful. Some of those not pictured elsewhere, who made significant contributions to the American cause, are shown here.

Massachusetts Historical Society

Marquis de Lafayette, outstanding soldier and invaluable liason between the French and American governments; portrait by Joseph Boze

Giraudon

Comte Rochambeau, leader of the French forces in America, who donated several thousand dollars to the Continental Army

Baron von Steuben, who supervised the military drilling of the troops at Valley Forge; portrait by C. W. Peale

Independence National Historical Park

Johann, baron de Kalb, who came to America with Lafayette, was killed at the battle of Camden, 1780; portrait by C. W. Peale

Independence National Historical Park

Southern Campaigns

The defeat at Saratoga and continued failure to draw Washington into battle caused the British to turn south, where they expected wide Loyalist support. The British won major victories in Georgia and in South Carolina. However, these initial successes were followed by the brilliant victory of the colonials under General Daniel Morgan at Cowpens, near the Carolinas' border, and by guerilla action that destroyed the outposts left behind by the main British advance. Loyalist support had been overestimated, and by 1781 only Savannah and Charleston in the South were held by British forces.

Benjamin Lincoln (below left) was forced to surrender Charleston (above) to the British, May 1780. General Gates (below right) was relieved of his command after surrendering at Camden, S.C., in August 1780

(Above) The victory at Cowpens, led by Daniel Morgan (bottom); Thomas Sumter (below left) excelled in guerilla warfare; Nathanael Greene (below right) directed operations in the South

NGTON

Yorktown

Cornwallis, the British commander in the South, was trying to concentrate his strength in Virginia in October 1781, when he found himself surrounded at Yorktown by the armies of Washington and Rochambeau. Meanwhile, De Grasse's fleet had arrived off the Yorktown peninsula to prevent Cornwallis from escaping by sea. After a long siege the British surrendered. Although few on the battlefield realized its significance, Yorktown was the last major battle of the war. When news of the defeat reached London, the government resolved to end the protracted and costly war.

(Above) George Washington, painted in 1784 by C. W. Peale; Charles Cornwallis, first marquis of Cornwallis, by Gainsborough, 1783; plan of the siege of Yorktown, with the British surrounded on three sides and backed up against the river

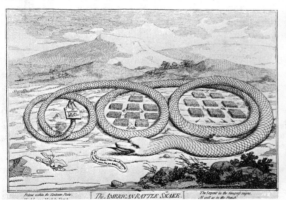

(Top) Painting of the allied armies at the siege, by a French eyewitness; (above left) the snake has "Burgoyn'd" two armies and has "room for more"; (above right and below) fanciful versions of the landing of British forces at Yorktown and of the surrender of Cornwallis

Peace

In accordance with the terms of the alliance with France, Congress instructed the peace commissioners not to negotiate without French cooperation. But Franklin and his colleagues found that American and French interests were not parallel. France supported independence, but sought terms that would keep America dependent on France. But, in order to end the war and weaken Franco-American ties, Great Britain offered the Americans very generous peace terms. In light of this, the commissioners ignored French objections and their instructions from Congress by signing a separate treaty with Great Britain; it was quickly approved by Congress.

(Above) Spain and France try to keep America and Britain apart, while the Dutch await a victor; West's painting, showing Jay, Adams, Franklin, Laurens and William Franklin, is unfinished because the British commissioners refused to sit with their American counterparts

Winterthur Museum

LIBERTY.

Ende der Feindseeligkeiten. Die Engländer räumen den Americanern Neu-Yorck ein. ——— 1783.

(Above left) an engraving celebrating independence; (right) New Yorkers watch the Redcoats leave; (below) inaccuracies in this map used by the commissioners led to later boundary disputes

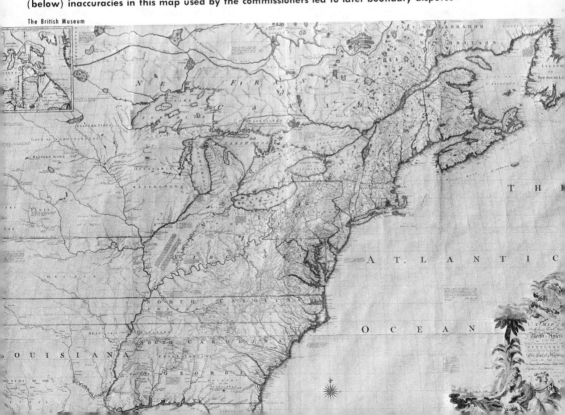

BENJAMIN RUSH: On the Progress of the War

*Dr. Benjamin Rush was a member of the Second Continental Congress and a signer of the
Declaration of Independence. He made the following cautious appraisal of the war's
progress in a letter to Richard Henry Lee, who was serving in Congress at the time.
The letter was written on December 30, 1776, while Rush was stationed with the
American Army in New Jersey.*

Source: Richard H. Lee, *Memoir of the Life of Richard Henry Lee, etc., etc.,*
Philadelphia, 1825, Vol. II, pp. 161-163.

THERE IS NO SOIL so dear to a soldier as that which is marked with the footsteps of a flying enemy — everything looks well. Our army increases daily, and our troops are impatient to avenge the injuries done to the state of New Jersey; the Tories fly with the precipitation of guilty fear to General Howe. A detachment from our body yesterday took four of them, and killed one; two of the former were officers of Howe's new militia establishment.

We suffer much for the want of intelligence, which can only be procured by money that will pass in both camps. Howe owes the superiority and regularity of his intelligence above ours, not so much to the voluntary information of the Tories as to the influence of his gold. Pray send £ 2,000 or £ 3,000 in hard money immediately to General Washington; it will do you more service than twenty new regiments. Let not this matter be debated and postponed in the usual way for two or three weeks; the salvation of America, under God, depends upon its being done in an *instant*.

I beg leave for a moment to call off your attention from the affairs of the public to inform you that I have heard from good authority that my much honored father-in-law, who is now a prisoner with General Howe, suffers many indignities and hardships from the enemy, from which not only his rank but his being a man ought to exempt him. I wish you would propose to Congress to pass a resolution in his favor similar to that they have passed in favor of General Lee; they owe it to their own honor as well as to a member of their body. I did not want this intelligence to rouse my resentment against the enemy, but it has increased it. Every particle of my blood is electrified with revenge, and if justice cannot be done to him in any other way, I declare I will, in defiance of the authority of the Congress and the power of the army, drive the first rascally Tory I meet with a hundred miles barefooted through the first deep snow that falls in our country.

Two small brigades of New England troops have consented to serve a month after the time of their enlistments expire. There is reason to believe all the New England troops in their predicament will follow their example. We have just learned that the enemy are preparing to retreat from Princeton. Adieu. General Washington must be invested with dictatorial power for a few months, or we are undone. The *vis inertiae* of the Congress has almost ruined this country.

Negro Voices Raised for Freedom

Negroes in America took the words of the Declaration of Independence seriously. It seemed to many of them to verge on hypocrisy that 700,000 people should be held in bondage while the nation fought a war under the banner of liberty and equality. The following petition against slavery was presented to the Massachusetts House of Representatives on January 13, 1777.

Source: MHSC, 5th series, III.

THE PETITION OF A GREAT NUMBER of blacks detained in a state of slavery in the bowels of a free and Christian country humbly shows that your petitioners apprehend that they have in common with all other men a natural and unalienable right to that freedom which the Great Parent of the universe has bestowed equally on all mankind and which they have never forfeited by any compact or agreement whatever. But they were unjustly dragged by the hand of cruel power from their dearest friends and some of them even torn from the embraces of their tender parents, from a populous, pleasant, and plentiful country and in violation of laws of nature and of nations and in defiance of all the tender feelings of humanity, brought here either to be sold like beasts of burden and, like them, condemned to slavery for life — among a people professing the mild religion of Jesus; a people not insensible of the secrets of rational being, nor without spirit to resent the unjust endeavors of others to reduce them to a state of bondage and subjection. Your Honor need not be informed that a life of slavery like that of your petitioners, deprived of every social privilege of everything requisite to render life tolerable, is far worse then nonexistence.

In imitation of the laudable example of the good people of these states, your petitioners have long and patiently awaited the event of petition after petition presented by them to the legislative body of this state, and cannot but with grief reflect that their success has been but too similar. They cannot but express their astonishment that it has never been considered that every principle from which America has acted in the course of their unhappy difficulties with Great Britain pleads stronger than a thousand arguments in favor of your petitioners.

They therefore humbly beseech Your Honors to give this petition its due weight and consideration, and cause an act of legislation to be passed whereby they may be restored to the enjoyments of that which is the natural right of all men, and that their children, who were born in this land of liberty, may not be held as slaves after they arrive at the age of twenty-one years. So may the inhabitants of this state, no longer chargeable with the inconsistency of acting themselves the part which they condemn and oppose in others, be prospered in their present glorious struggle for liberty and have those blessings for themselves.

NICHOLAS CRESSWELL: On General Washington

Nicholas Cresswell came to America from England in 1774 at the age of twenty-four. It is likely that he hoped to stay in the colonies and establish a new life for himself, but the growing enmity with the mother country made it difficult for him to remain. He felt he was regarded as a Tory and a spy by the rebelling Americans and so returned home three years later. During these years he kept a diary from which the following entry of July 13, 1777, is taken.

Source: *The Journal of Nicholas Cresswell*, New York, 1924.

Sunday, July 13th, 1777. News that our army has surprised Washington and taken him prisoner. Afraid it is too good to be authentic. His great caution will always prevent him being made a prisoner to our inactive general. Washington is certainly a most surprising man, one of nature's geniuses, a heaven-born general, if there is any of that sort. That a Negro-driver should, with a ragged banditti of undisciplined people, the scum and refuse of all nations on earth, so long keep a British general at bay, nay, even oblige him, with as fine an army of veteran soldiers as ever England had on the American continent, to retreat — it is astonishing. It is too much. By Heavens, there must be double-dealing somewhere. General Howe, a man brought up to war from his youth, to be puzzled and plagued for two years together, with a Virginia tobacco planter. O! Britain, how thy laurels tarnish in the hands of such a lubber! The life of General Washington will be a most copious subject for some able biographer to exercise his pen upon. Nature did not make me one of the biographic order. However, I will make some remarks concerning this great and wonderful man.

George Washington, the American hero, was second son of a creditable Virginia tobacco planter (which I suppose may, in point of rank, be equal to the better sort of yeomanry in England). I believe his mother is still living and two of his brothers. One of them lives in Berkley County in Virginia, the other in Faquire County in Virginia. Both able planters and men of good character. In the early part of his life he was surveyor of Fairfax County in Virginia. It was then a frontier county and his office was attended with much trouble but not any considerable profit. This business accustomed him to the woods and gained him the character of the best woodsman in the colony. His older brother, Mr. Augustine Washington, was a captain in the American troops raised for the expedition against Cartagena, but afterward incorporated with the regulars. He died in the service, and our hero George came to the patrimonial estate.

In the year 1755 he was chosen by the Assembly of Virginia to go to the French forts on the Ohio to know the reason why they made encroachments on the back parts of Virginia, which office he performed to the entire satisfaction of his employers. On his return he published his journal which did him great credit and first made him popular amongst his countrymen.

In the year 1754 the governor of Virginia gave him the command of about 1,000 troops (all Virginians), with orders to drive the French from their encroachments in the back settlements. In this expedition he proved unsuccessful. On the 3rd of July, 1754, he suffered himself to be surrounded by the French and Indians at the Big Meadows in the Allegheny Mountain and was obliged to capitulate, but upon what terms I do not recollect. He by some means or other got from the French very soon and had the command of a regiment of Virginians, and was with the unfortunate General Braddock when he was defeated by the French and Indians on the banks of the Monongahela River, July 9, 1755, prior to which he, with a part of his regiment, fell in with a scouting party of his own in the woods, an engagement began, and a number of men were killed before the mistake was discovered. He continued in the Army most of the war, but never performed any action to render himself conspicuous.

Before the expiration of the war he married a Mrs. Custis, a widow lady, with whom he had a very good fortune. By her entreaties he left the Army, in which he never gained any great esteem by his own country officers or men. By all accounts it was his frugality that lost him the goodwill of his officers, and the strict discipline he always observed, the love of his men. Indeed, any kind of order or subordination ill agrees with his countrymen in general. After he quitted the Army, he was made a member of the Virginia House of Burgesses, in which he was much respected for his good private character, but always looked upon as too bashful and timid for an orator. He lived as a country gentleman, much noted for his hospitality, great knowledge in agriculture, and industry in carrying his various manufactories of linen and woolen to greater perfection than any man in the colony.

On the breaking out of these troubles he was chosen, in company with Messrs. Peyton Randolph, Richard Henry Lee, Patrick Henry, Richard Bland, Benjamin Harrison, and Edmund Pendleton, Esqs., to act as deputies or delegates for the colony of Virginia in the first Congress or Sanhedrin held at Philadelphia, September 5, 1774, and appointed general and commander in chief of all the rebel forces (by Congress) June 17, 1775. I believe he accepted this post with reluctance, but the great and almost unexpected success he has had may now soothe and become agreeable to his natural ambitious temper. He undoubtedly pants for military fame, and, considering the little military knowledge and experience he had before he was made a general, he has performed wonders. He was generally unfortunate (indeed I may with propriety say always) in every action where he was immediately concerned until the affair at Trenton in the Jerseys. Since that unlucky period (for us) he has only been too successful.

His education is not very great nor his parts shining, his disposition is rather heavy than volatile, much given to silence. In short, he is but a poor speaker and but shines in the epistolary way. His person is tall and genteel, age between forty and fifty, his behavior and deportment is easy, genteel, and obliging, with a certain something about him which pleases everyone who has anything to do with him. There cannot be a greater proof of his particular address and good conduct than his keeping such a number of refractory, headstrong people together in any tolerable degree of decorum.

His house is at a place called Mount Vernon, about twelve miles below Alexandria on the banks of the Potomac River in Virginia, where he has a very fine plantation and farm, but, by the best accounts I could get, his estate, altogether, before these troubles did not amount to more than £ 300 a year in Virginia currency. But estates in this country are seldom valued by the year; it is some difficulty to know exactly what they are worth where they keep great numbers of Negroes and make large crops of tobacco. His friends and acquaintances reckon him a just man, exceedingly honest, but not very generous. Perhaps they may give him this character because he manages his estate with industry and economy, and very seldom enters into those foolish, giddy, and expensive frolics natural to a Virginian.

He keeps an excellent table, and a stranger, let him be of what country or nation, he will always meet with a most hospitable reception at it. His entertainments were always conducted with the most regularity and in the genteelest manner of any I ever was at on the continent (and I have been at several of them, that is, before he was made a general). Temperance he always observed, was always cool-headed and exceedingly cautious himself, but took great pleasure in seeing his friends entertained in the way most agreeable to themselves. His lady is of a hospitable disposition, always good-humored and cheerful, and seems to be actuated by the same motives with himself, but she is rather of a more lively disposition. They are to all appearances a happy pair.

He has no children by his wife, but she had two by her first husband, a son and daughter. The daughter died unmarried; the son, Mr. John Custis, a very worthy young gentleman, is lately married and lives with his mother at Mount Vernon. He lives entirely as a country gentleman; has no post, civil or military.

The general seems by nature calculated for the post he is in; he has a manner and behavior peculiar to himself and particularly adapted to his present station and rank in life. It is said (and I believe with great truth) that he never had an intimate, particular bosom friend, or an open professed enemy in his life. By this method of behavior he in a great measure prevents all parties and factions, and raises a spirit of emulation among his officers and men. As there is no favorite to pay their court to and pave their way to preferment, and the general, I believe, is proof against bribery, they have no way to advance themselves but by merit alone. His private character is amiable; he is much beloved and respected by all his acquaintances.

From my personal acquaintance with him, and from everything that I have been able to learn of him, I believe him to be a worthy, honest man, guilty of no bad vice, except we reckon ambition among the number, and here we ought to judge charitably. The temptation was very great to a mind naturally ambitious. Nature made him too weak to resist it.

As an officer, he is quite popular, almost idolized by the southern provinces, but I think he is not so great a favorite with the northern ones. The ignorant and deluded part of the people look up to him as the savior and protector of their country, and have implicit confidence in everything he does. The artful and designing part of the people, that is, the Congress and those at the head of affairs, look upon him as a necessary tool to compass their diabolical purposes.

He certainly deserves some merit as a general, that he, with his banditti, can keep General Howe dancing from one town to another for two years together, with such an army as he has. Confound the great chucklehead, he will not unmuzzle the mastiffs, or they would eat him and his ragged crew in a little time were they properly conducted with a man of resolution and spirit. Washington, my enemy as he is, I should be sorry if he should be brought to an ignominious death.

GEORGE WASHINGTON: On the Organization of the Army

After the Battle of Bunker Hill, General George Washington was put in command of the Continental Army in Massachusetts. His task was to transform a disorganized mob of patriotic recruits into a disciplined army, all the while fighting a war. By early 1778, several deficiencies in the military establishment had become apparent. Discipline, officer status, and short-term enlistments were among the problems that caused Washington to appeal to Congress for a reorganization of the army. The following communication was addressed to a committee of Congress on January 28, 1778, while the army was in camp at Valley Forge. It was issued under Washington's name, but it was written by Alexander Hamilton, who was Washington's confidential aide from 1777 to 1781.

Source: J. C. Hamilton, II, pp. 139-152: "Reorganization of the Army."

THE NUMEROUS DEFECTS in our present military establishment, rendering many reformations and many new arrangements absolutely necessary, and Congress having been pleased to appoint you a committee, in concert with me, to make and recommend such as shall appear eligible, in pursuance of the various objects expressed in the resolution, for that purpose; I have, in the following sheets, briefly delivered my sentiments upon such of them as appeared to me most essential, so far as observation has suggested and leisure permitted. These are submitted to consideration, and I shall be happy, if they are found conducive to remedying the evils and inconveniences we are now subject to, and putting the army upon a more respectable footing. Something must be done; important alterations must be made; necessity requires that our resources should be enlarged and our system improved, for without it, if the dissolution of the army should not be the consequence, at least its operations must be feeble, languid, and ineffectual.

As I consider a proper and satisfactory provision for officers as the basis of every other arrangement and regulation necessary to be made (since without officers no army can exist) and unless some measures be devised to place those officers in a more desirable condition, few of them would be able, if willing, to continue in it. . . .

A HALF-PAY AND PENSIONARY ESTABLISHMENT

A SMALL KNOWLEDGE of human nature will convince us that, with far the greatest part of mankind, interest is the governing principle, and that almost every man is more or less under its influence. Motives of public virtue may, for a time, or in particular instances, actuate men to the observance of a conduct purely disinterested, but they are not sufficient of themselves to produce a persevering conformity to the refined dictates of social duty. Few men are capable of making a continual sacrifice of all views of private interest or advantage, to the common good. It is in vain to exclaim against the depravity of human nature on this account; the fact is so, the experience of every age and nation has proved it, and we must in a great measure change the constitution of man before we can make it otherwise. No institution not built on the presumptive truth of these maxims can succeed.

We find them exemplified in the American officers as well as in all other men. At the commencement of the dispute, in the first effusions of their zeal, and looking upon the service to be only temporary, they entered into it without paying any regard to pecuniary or selfish considerations. But, finding its duration to be much longer than they at first expected, and that instead of deriving any advantage from the hardships and dangers to which they were exposed, they, on the contrary, were losers by their patriotism, and fell far short even of a competency to supply their wants; they have gradually abated in their ardor, and, with many, an entire disinclination to the service, under its present circumstances, has taken place. To this, in an eminent degree, must be ascribed the frequent resignations daily happening, and the more frequent importunities for permission to resign, and from some officers of the greatest merit. To this also may we ascribe the apathy, inattention, and neglect of duty which pervade all ranks, and which will necessarily continue and increase while an officer, instead of gaining, is impoverished by his commission, and conceives he is conferring, not receiving, a favor in holding it. There can be no tie upon men possessing such sentiments, nor can we adopt any method to oblige those to a punctual discharge of their duty who are indifferent about their continuance in the service, and are often seeking a pretext to disengage themselves from it. Punishment, in this case, will be unavailing; but when an officer's commission is made valuable to him, and he fears to lose it, then may you exact obedience from him.

It is not indeed consistent with reason or justice to expect that one set of men should make a sacrifice of property, domestic ease and happiness, encounter the rigors of the field, the perils and vicissitudes of war to obtain those blessings which every citizen will enjoy in common with them, without some adequate compensation.

It must also be a comfortless reflection to any man that, after he may have contributed to the securing the rights of his country at the risk of his life and the ruin of his fortune, there would be no provision to prevent himself and family from sinking into indigence and wretchedness. I urge these sentiments with the greater freedom because I cannot, and shall not, receive the smallest benefit from the establishment, and have no other inducement for proposing it, than a full conviction of its utility and propriety. . . .

OF COMPLETING THE REGIMENTS AND ALTERING THEIR ESTABLISHMENT

THE NECESSITY OF THE FIRST, in the most expeditious manner possible, is too self-evident to need illustrations or proof; and I shall, therefore, only beg leave to offer some reflections on the mode. Voluntary enlistments seem to be totally out of the question; all the allurements of the most exorbitant bounties, and every other inducement that could be thought of, have been tried in vain, and seem to have had little other effect than to increase rapacity and raise the demands of those to whom they were held out. We may fairly infer that the country has been already pretty well drained of that class of men whose tempers, attachments, and circumstances disposed them to enter permanently, or for a length of time, into the army; and that the residue of such men who, from different motives, have kept out of the army, if collected, would not augment our general strength in any proportion to what they require. If experience has demonstrated that little more can be done by voluntary enlistments, some other mode must be concerted, and no other presents itself than that of filling the regiments by drafts from the militia. This is a disagreeable alternative but it is an unavoidable one.

As drafting for the war, or for a term of years, would probably be disgusting and dangerous, perhaps impracticable, I would propose an annual draft of men, without officers, to serve till the 1st day of January in each year. That on or before the 1st day of October preceding, these drafted men should be called upon to reenlist for the succeeding year; and as an incitement to doing it, those being much better and less expensive than raw recruits, a bounty of $25 should be offered. That upon ascertaining at this period the number of men willing to reengage, exact returns should be made to Congress of the deficiency in each regiment and transmitted by them to the respective states, in order that they may have their several quotas immediately furnished and sent on to camp, for the service of the ensuing year, so as to arrive by or before the 1st day of January.

This method, though not so good as that of obtaining men for the war, is perhaps the best our circumstances will allow; and, as we shall always have an established corps of experienced officers, may answer tolerably well. It is the only mode I can think of for completing our battalions in time that promises the least prospect of success; the accomplishment of which is an object of the last importance; and it has this advantage, that the minds of the people being once reconciled to the experiment, it would prove a source of continual supplies hereafter.

Men drafted in this manner should not, in the first instance, receive any bounty from the public; which being solemnly enjoined upon each state, and a stop put to the militia substitution laws, would probably be attended with very happy consequences.

A number of idle mercenary fellows would be thrown out of employment, precluded from their excessive wages as substitutes for a few weeks or months, and constrained to enlist in the Continental Army. In speaking of abolishing the militia substitution laws, it is not meant to hinder a person who might be drafted in the annual allotments from procuring a substitute in his stead, himself in consequence being excused. This indulgence would be admissible, and, considering all things, necessary, as there are many individuals whose dispositions and private affairs would make them irreconcilably averse from giving their personal services for so long a duration, and with whom it would be impolitic to use compulsion. The allowance of substitution upon a smaller scale, in the occasional coming out of the militia for a few weeks, a month or two, is the thing meant to be reprobated. It is highly productive of the double disadvantage of preventing the growth of the army and depreciating our currency. . . .

OF THE ARRANGEMENT OF THE ARMY

VIRGINIA, I UNDERSTAND, though not from any direct authority, has resolved to draft toward the completion of her battalions; and as this mode seems to be the only one calculated to answer the end, it is to be hoped she will be able to furnish her full complement of fifteen, including the state regiment. What plan Maryland has fallen upon, or may adopt, to fill her battalions I know not, but as the powers of government are with her in full vigor, and the abilities of the state entirely adequate, I think her original quota ought to be depended upon. Delaware must, undoubtedly, contribute one battalion; no change having happened

since that portion was assigned her sufficient to afford a plea for reducing it. In behalf of Pennsylvania, much may be said; the
exhausted state of her regiments; loss of her
capital, and intestine divisions, ever destructive to the energy of government, may perhaps incapacitate her from completing her
thirteen regiments now on foot. I suppose
the number should be, for the present, diminished to eight, and the state should exert herself to fill them in the first place.
When this shall be accomplished, if her resources appear equal to any further efforts,
she may proceed to raising the remaining
five. Jersey, New York, Connecticut, Rhode
Island, Massachusetts, and New Hampshire
are fully competent to the quotas respectively required of them, and no abatement
seems necessary with respect to either. We
have reason to hope their exertions will
keep pace with their abilities, and that they
will take decisive measures to send their
several proportions into the field.

I am at a loss what to propose concerning the German battalion, Hazen's regiment, and the sixteen additionals. Apper-
taining to no particular state or states, they
will have no chance of being filled by
drafts, and as little by any other means.
They must either remain weak and imperfect corps, be adopted by the states, or incorporated into each other, and then, if possible, be recruited. The first, upon every
principle, ought not to be the case, and as
the second would not be altogether eligible,
from the difficulty of apportioning them
without dividing and subdividing the regiments, the third seems to be the expedient
to which we must have recourse. Let Maryland take the German battalion, wholly, as
one of her eight, for she already claims a
part of it; and then let the sixteen additionals, none of which are strong, some extremely weak, and others only partly organized, be thrown into nine. There is this
number of them, which, comparatively
speaking, are tolerably respectable, and have

undergone a good deal of hard service in
the course of the campaign. These, after
having received the men out of the reduced
corps, licensed, though a barren experiment,
ought to try what can be done by voluntary
enlistments throughout the continent at
large. Hazen's regiment might be added to
them, and united in the same privilege.

If these propositions are approved, the
whole number of battalions on the establishment will be eighty, and, if complete,
the total amount of them 40,320 rank and
file. Upon this number of battalions, I shall
make my arrangements. Whether full or not
they will require to be thrown into brigades. . . .

PAYMASTER GENERAL

This department is well conducted, so far
as depends upon the gentleman at the head
of it, but the want of money, which too
frequently happens, is extremely injurious to
our affairs. It is unnecessary to observe that
besides feeding and clothing a soldier well,
nothing is of greater importance than paying him punctually; and it is perhaps more
essential in our army than any other, because our men are worse supplied and more
necessitous; and the notions of implicit subordination not being as yet sufficiently ingrafted among them, they are more apt to
reason upon their rights, and rendered read-
ier to manifest their sensibility of anything
that has the appearance of injustice to them,
in which light they consider their being
kept out of their pay after it is due. Nor
does the evil end here. The inhabitants who
through choice, accident, or necessity have
any pecuniary concerns with the army, finding themselves frequently disappointed in
the payments they have a right to expect,
grow dissatisfied and clamorous; the credit
of the army, and, which is nearly the same
thing, the credit of the continent, is impaired, our supplies of course are impeded,

and the price of every article we want raised. This circumstance is not among the least causes of the depreciation of the currency.

A question has arisen whether officers, prisoners with the enemy, who come out on parole, and are not provided for by any actual appointments, are entitled to pay during their imprisonment.

A resolve of Congress of the 19th instant provides that all continental officers, prisoners with the enemy, either while in confinement or on parole, so long as they continue officers of the United States, shall be entitled to their pay and rations, liable to a deduction for what they may have received in confinement; and that all flying camp and militia officers should be entitled to the same while in confinement only. This resolve excludes from pay all officers liberated on parole who have not actual appointments in the Continental Army. Will it not be deemed a hardship and injustice to such officers, especially to those who merely from their absence have been neglected in arrangements posterior to their capture, as has been too much the case?

While they continue prisoners, whether in possession of the enemy or out on parole, they can have little opportunity of prosecuting any business for a livelihood, and must be in a distressful situation, unless they have a private fortune sufficient to maintain them. It has in many instances happened that officers in captivity have been omitted in promotions made in their absence, upon which a question has arisen whether there should not be a restoration of rank with respect to those who are men of merit. It seems but reasonable there should.

Several new regulations will, I imagine, be found useful in the articles of war, which the judge advocate, from his official experience of the deficiency, can more accurately indicate. One thing we have suffered much from is the want of a proper gradation of punishments. The interval between a hundred lashes and death is too great, and requires to be filled up by some intermediate stages. Capital crimes in the army are frequently commuted, particularly in the instance of desertion. Actually to inflict capital punishment or death upon every deserter, or other heinous offender, would incur the imputation of cruelty, and by the too common exhibition of the example, destroy its efficacy. On the other hand, to give only a hundred lashes to such criminals is rather a burlesque on the crime than a serious correction, and affords encouragement to obstinacy and to imitation. The courts are often in a manner compelled, by the enormity of the facts, to pass sentences of death. I am as often obliged to remit, on account of the number in the same circumstances, and let the offenders pass wholly unpunished. This would be avoided if there were other punishments short of the destruction of life in some degree adequate to the crime. These the courts would ordain, and I should have executed. . . .

THE POSITION

THE REGIMENTAL SURGEONS complain that for want of medicines and other necessaries they are disabled from giving that assistance in slight cases, and in the first stages of dangerous complaints, which would serve to check their progress to maturity and save the lives of the soldiery. The hospital surgeons reply that their stores are incapable of bearing the excessive drafts which the profusion and carelessness of the regimental surgeons would make upon them if indulged in their demands.

I shall not attempt to decide the merits of this dispute, nor can I conceive any adequate mode of adjusting the difference. But one would imagine it might not be impossible to fix some general rule of allowance by which the supplies to the regimental surgeons might be regulated, and to make them accountable for the right and economical application of what they received.

At all events, as the accommodation of the sick and the preservation of men's lives are the first and great objects to be consulted, the regimental surgeons ought not to be destitute of a reasonable quantity of medicines and other conveniences of which the sick stand in need. The ill effects resulting from it are many and glaring.

Either men, at every slight indication of disease, must be sent away to distant hospitals, and the army unnecessarily deprived of the services of numbers who, if the means were at hand, might in a day or two be restored; or they must remain without proper assistance till their disorders confirm themselves, and with many get beyond the power of cure.

Other ill consequences that have attended the sending so many men away to a distance from the army are desertions and the waste of arms and clothing, for which rea-

son it ought to be avoided as much as possible. To prevent these evils, as far as can be done, a field officer is stationed at each hospital to see the arms of the soldiers carefully deposited at their admission into it, take care of them in their convalescent state, and send them on to join their regiments under proper officers, as soon as they are fit for duty. . . .

Upon the whole, gentlemen, I doubt not you are fully impressed with the defects of our present military system, and of the absolute necessity of speedy and decisive measures to put it upon a satisfactory footing. The disagreeable picture I have given you of the wants and sufferings of the army and the discontents reigning among the officers is a just representation of evils equally melancholy and important; and unless effectual remedies be applied without loss of time, the most alarming and ruinous consequences are to be apprehended.

George Washington: Against the Appointment of Foreign Officers

Unemployed professional soldiers were plentiful in Europe, and when war broke out in America they were eager to serve in the Continental Army. Securing passage money and letters of recommendation from Benjamin Franklin, the American representative in France, they came to America and offered their services to the army. Congress appointed these mercenaries to ranks as high as major general, leaving it to General Washington to find something for them to do. Most of them were given positions on Washington's staff because some Americans disliked serving under foreigners. With this situation in view, Washington addressed a letter to Gouverneur Morris, from White Plains, New York, on July 24, 1778.

Source: John P. Sanderson, *The Views and Opinions of American Statesmen on Foreign Immigration*, Philadelphia, 1856, pp. 108-109.

THE DESIGN OF THIS is to touch cursorily upon a subject of very great importance to the being of these states; much more so than will appear at first view, I mean the appointment of so many foreigners to offices of high rank and trust in our service.

The lavish manner in which rank has hitherto been bestowed on these gentlemen will certainly be productive of one or the other of these two evils, either to make us despicable in the eyes of Europe, or become a means of pouring them in upon us like a torrent, and adding to our present burden.

But it is neither the expense nor the trouble of them I most dread; there is an evil more extensive in its nature and fatal in its consequence to be apprehended, and that is the driving of all our officers out of the service, and throwing not only our own Army, but our military councils entirely into the hands of foreigners.

The officers, my dear sir, on whom you must depend for the defense of the cause, distinguished by length of service and military merit, will not submit much, if any, longer to the unnatural promotion of men over them who have nothing more than a little plausibility, unbounded pride and ambition, and a perseverance in the application to support their pretensions, not to be resisted but by uncommon firmness; men who, in the first instance, say they wish for nothing more than the honor of serving so glorious a cause as volunteers, the next day solicit rank without pay; the day following want money advanced to them; and in the course of a week, want further promotion. The expediency and policy of the measure remain to be considered, and whether it is consistent with justice or prudence to promote these military fortune hunters at the hazard of our Army.

Baron Steuben, I now find, is also wanting to quit his inspectorship for a command in the line. This will be productive of much discontent. In a word, although I think the Baron an excellent officer, I do most devoutly wish that we had not a single foreigner among us except the Marquis de Lafayette, who acts upon very different principles from those which govern the rest. Adieu.

John Adams: On an Alliance with France

France had been giving aid secretly to the American cause for at least two years. However, she was unwilling to enter into an open alliance until it became certain that there would be no reconciliation between America and Britain. Washington's conduct of the war in the winter of 1777-1778 convinced France of the practicability of a treaty. On February 6, 1778, two agreements were signed with France: a treaty of alliance and a treaty of amity and commerce. On July 28, John Adams, then commissioner to France, discussed the merits of the alliance in a letter to Sam Adams.

Source: *The Revolutionary Diplomatic Correspondence of the United States,*
Francis Wharton, ed., Washington, 1889, Vol. II, pp. 667-668.

THE SOVEREIGN OF BRITAIN and his Council have determined to instruct their commissioners to offer you independence, provided you will disconnect yourselves from France. The question arises, how came the King and Council by authority to offer this? It is certain that they have it not.

In the next place, is the treaty of alliance between us and France now binding upon us? I think there is not room to doubt it; for declarations and manifestos do not make the state of war — they are only publications of the reasons of war. Yet the message of the King of Great Britain to both houses of Parliament, and their answers to that message, were as full a declaration of war as ever was made, and, accordingly, hostilities have been frequent ever since. This proposal, then, is a modest invitation to a gross act of infidelity and breach of faith. It is an observation that I have often heard you make that "France is the natural ally of the United States." This observation is, in my opinion, both just and important. The reasons are plain. As long as Great Britain shall have Canada, Nova Scotia, and the Floridas, or any of them, so long will Great Britain be the enemy of the United States, let her disguise it as much as she will.

It is not much to the honor of human nature, but the fact is certain that neighboring nations are never friends in reality. In the times of the most perfect peace between them their hearts and their passions are hostile, and this will certainly be the case forever between the thirteen United States and the English colonies. France and England, as neighbors and rivals, never have been and never will be friends. The hatred and jealousy between the nations are eternal and irradicable. As we, therefore, on the one hand, have the surest ground to expect the jealousy and hatred of Great Britain, so on the other we have the strongest reasons to depend upon the friendship and alliance of France, and no one reason in the world to expect her enmity or her jealousy, as she has given up every pretension to any spot of ground on the continent.

The United States, therefore, will be for ages the natural bulwark of France against the hostile designs of England against her, and France is the natural defense of the United States against the rapacious spirit of Great Britain against them. France is a nation so vastly eminent, having been for so many centuries what they call the dominant power of Europe, being incomparably the most powerful at land, that united in a close alliance with our states, and enjoying the benefit of our trade, there is not the smallest reason to doubt but both will be a sufficient curb upon the naval power of Great Britain.

This connection, therefore, will forever secure a respect for our states in Spain, Portugal, and Holland too, who will always choose to be upon friendly terms with powers who have numerous cruisers at sea, and indeed, in all the rest of Europe. I presume, therefore, that sound policy as well as good faith will induce us never to renounce our alliance with France, even although it should continue us for some time in war. The French are as sensible of the benefits of this alliance to them as we are, and they are determined as much as we to cultivate it.

In order to continue the war, or at least that we may do any good in the common cause, the credit of our currency must be supported. But how? Taxes, my dear sir, taxes! Pray let our countrymen consider and be wise; every farthing they pay in taxes is a farthing's worth of wealth and good policy. If it were possible to hire money in Europe to discharge the bills, it would be a dreadful drain to the country to pay the interest of it. But I fear it will not be. The house of Austria has sent orders to Amsterdam to hire a very great sum, England is borrowing great sums, and France is borrowing largely. Amidst such demands for money, and by powers who offer better terms, I fear we shall not be able to succeed.

Alexander Hamilton: War Profiteering

As a soldier, Alexander Hamilton shared Washington's disgust with civilians who would turn the opportunity offered by the war to their own economic benefit. One case of such profiteering came to light in the person of Congressman Samuel Chase of Maryland, who took advantage of his position in the government to make extensive grain purchases that he knew would be needed by the French fleet when it arrived. It was this occurrence that set Hamilton to writing the letters signed "Publius" to the New-York Journal *in the fall of 1778. The letter of October 19 is reprinted here.*

Source: J. C. Hamilton, II, pp. 156-157.

WHILE EVERY METHOD IS TAKEN to bring to justice those men whose principles and practices have been hostile to the present revolution, it is to be lamented that the conduct of another class, equally criminal, and if possible more mischievous, has hitherto passed with impunity, and almost without notice. I mean that tribe who, taking advantage of the times, have carried the spirit of monopoly and extortion to an excess, which scarcely admits of a parallel. Emboldened by the success of progressive impositions, it has extended to all the necessaries of life. The exorbitant price of every article, and the depreciation upon our currency, are evils derived essentially from this source. When avarice takes the lead in a state, it is commonly the forerunner of its fall. How shocking is it to discover among ourselves, even at this early period, the strongest symptoms of this fatal disease.

There are men in all countries, the business of whose lives it is to raise themselves above indigence by every little art in their power. When these men are observed to be influenced by the spirit I have mentioned, it is nothing more than might be expected, and can only excite contempt. When others,

who have characters to support, and credit enough in the world to satisfy a moderate appetite for wealth in an honorable way, are found to be actuated by the same spirit, our contempt is mixed with indignation. But when a man, appointed to be the guardian of the state, and the depositary of the happiness and morals of the people, forgetful of the solemn relation in which he stands, descends to the dishonest artifices of a mercantile projector, and sacrifices his conscience and his trust to pecuniary motives, there is no strain of abhorrence of which the human mind is capable, no punishment the vengeance of the people can inflict, which may not be applied to him with justice.

If it should have happened that a member of Congress has been this degenerate character, and has been known to turn the knowledge of secrets, to which his office gave him access, to the purposes of private profit by employing emissaries to engross an article of immediate necessity to the public service, he ought to feel the utmost rigor of public resentment, and be detested as a traitor of the worst and most dangerous kind.

George Washington: On the Lack of a National Spirit

At no time during the Revolution was there unity of public mind or purpose in America.
Even many of those who generally accepted independence were reluctant to give
wholehearted support with taxes or military service. General Washington's unequivocal
devotion to the American cause made him unwilling, perhaps unable, to accept anything
less from the public. He could not help censuring the men whose sense of duty did not
equal his own and whose private interest normally came before the common cause. In
the following letter of December 30, 1778, to Benjamin Harrison, Speaker of the
Virginia House of Delegates, Washington expressed himself in no uncertain terms.

Source: *The Writings of George Washington*, John C. Fitzpatrick, ed., Vol. XIII,
Washington, 1936, pp. 466-468.

I HAVE SEEN NOTHING since I came here to change my opinion . . . but abundant reason to be convinced that our affairs are in a more distressed, ruinous, and deplorable condition than they have been in since the commencement of the war. By a faithful laborer then in the cause; by a man who is daily injuring his private estate without even the smallest earthly advantage not common to all in case of a favorable issue to the dispute; by one who wishes the prosperity of America most devoutly and sees or thinks he sees it on the brink of ruin, you are beseeched, most earnestly, my dear Colonel Harrison, to exert yourself in endeavoring to rescue your country by (let me add) sending your ablest and best men to Congress. These characters must not slumber nor sleep at home in such times of pressing danger; they must not content themselves in the enjoyment of places of honor or profit in their own country while the common interests of America are moldering and sinking into irretrievable (if a remedy is not soon applied) ruin, in which theirs also must ultimately be involved.

If I was to be called upon to draw a picture of the times and of men from what I have seen, heard, and in part know, I should in one word say that idleness, dissipation, and extravagance seems to have laid fast hold of most of them; that speculation, peculation, and an insatiable thirst for riches seems to have got the better of every other consideration and almost of every order of men; that party disputes and personal quarrels are the great business of the day, while the momentous concerns of an empire — a great and accumulated debt, ruined finances, depreciated money, and want of credit (which in their consequences is the want of everything) — are but secondary considerations and postponed from day to day, from week to week, as if our affairs wear the most promising aspect. After drawing this picture, which from my soul I believe to be a true one, I need not repeat to you that I am alarmed and wish to see my countrymen roused.

I have no resentments, nor do I mean to point at any particular characters; this I can declare upon my honor, for I have every attention paid me by Congress than I can possibly expect and have reason to think that I stand well in their estimation. But in the present situation of things I cannot help asking — Where is Mason, Wythe, Jefferson, Nicholas, Pendleton, Nelson, and another I could name? And why, if you are sufficiently impressed with your danger, do you not (as New York has done in the case of Mr. Jay) send an extra member or two for at least a certain limited time till the great business of the nation is put upon a more respectable and happy establishment?

Your money is now sinking 5 percent a day in this city; and I shall not be surprised if in the course of a few months a total stop is put to the currency of it. And yet an assembly, a concert, a dinner or supper (that will cost £ 300 or £ 400) will not only take men off from acting in, but even from thinking of, this business, while a great part of the officers of your Army, from absolute necessity, are quitting the service; and the more virtuous few, rather than do this, are sinking by sure degrees into beggary and want.

I again repeat to you that this is not an exaggerated account. That it is an alarming one I do not deny, and confess to you that I feel more real distress on account of the present appearances of things than I have done at any one time since the commencement of the dispute. But it is time to bid you once more adieu. Providence has heretofore taken us up when all other means and hope seemed to be departing from us.

Two Patriotic Songs

In the minds of patriots, George Washington inevitably became the living embodiment of the American cause and the natural subject for many songs. Several rousing (if not very graceful) songs about Washington were written by his friend Francis Hopkinson, an author and musician and father of the composer of "Hail Columbia!" The "Toast to Washington" reprinted here is a good example of the elder Hopkinson's work. William Billings was a singing master and composer of hymns; after about 1775 his productions took on a decidedly patriotic tenor. "Let Tyrants Shake" (also known as "Chester") was the most popular of his patriotic hymns; it followed the soldiers to camp and became a favorite of the fife and drum corps.

Source: "A Favorite New Patriotic Song in Honor of Washington, To Which Is Added A Toast Written and Composed by F. Hopkinson, Esq.," Philadelphia, 1799.

[William Billings] *The Singing Master's Assistant or Key to Practical Music, etc., etc.*, Boston, 1778.

A TOAST

'Tis Washington's health fill a bumper all round,
    For he is our glory and pride;
Our arms shall in battle with conquest be crowned
    Whilst virtue and he's on our side;
Our arms shall in battle with conquest be crowned
    Whilst virtue and he's on our side
      And he's on our side.

'Tis Washington's health loud cannons should roar,
   And trumpets the truth should proclaim;
There cannot be found, search all the world o'er,
   His equal in virtue and fame;
There cannot be found, search all the world o'er,
   His equal in virtue in fame
     In virtue and fame.

'Tis Washington's health our hero to bless,
   May heaven look graciously down;
Oh! long may he live, our hearts to possess,
   And freedom still call him her own;
Oh! long may he live, our hearts to possess,
   And freedom still call him her own
     Still call him her own.

FRANCIS HOPKINSON

LET TYRANTS SHAKE (CHESTER)

Let tyrants shake their iron rod,
And slavery clank her galling chains,
We fear them not, we trust in God,
New England's God forever reigns.

Howe and Burgoyne and Clinton too,
With Prescott and Cornwallis joined,
Together plot our overthrow
In one infernal league combined.

When God inspired us for the fight,
Their ranks were broke, their lines were forced,
Their ships were shattered in our sight,
Or swiftly driven from our coast.

The foe comes on with haughty stride,
Our troops advance with martial noise,
Their veterans flee before our youth,
And generals yield to beardless boys.

What grateful offering shall we bring,
What shall we render to the Lord?
Loud Hallelujahs let us sing,
And praise His name on every chord.

WILLIAM BILLINGS

While Commerce spreads her canvass o'er the main,
And Agriculture ploughs the grateful plain
Minerva aids Columbia's rising race
With arms to triumph and with arts to grace

Independence
the reward of
Wisdom
Fortitude
and
Perseverance

THE INGREDIENTS
FOR A NEW NATION

By the 1770s an American culture was emerging in the heterogeneous colonies strung out along the coast. The English heritage was adapted to the varying locales, incorporating rather than smothering the customs of other European settlers. As cities grew, they acquired distinctive characters, reflecting new colonial interest in architecture and in enjoying the comforts common-place in England. Having provided for basic needs, the colonists devoted more energy to education, invention, and scientific inquiry. Expanded newspaper circulation kept colonists aware of the political ideas and activities in Europe. Because traveling between the colonies was difficult, the newspapers also served as a major link in communications and as a forum for debate.

Boston

Boston, the second largest town in the colonies, was one of a dozen prosperous seaports in New England. The inhabitants reflected the homogeneity of New England with fewer extremes in wealth and no dominant landed aristocracy. Suffrage was extended to almost all adult white males. The church and the town meeting exposed Bostonians to democratic principles, making the city highly antagonistic to England's hard line tactics.

(Right) View from Beacon Hill in Boston drawn by a British officer during the Battle of Charlestown, 1775; (below) woodcut from a broadside distributed in Boston following the execution of Levi Ames and intended to instruct "thoughtless Youth"

(Below) Plan of Boston, 1769; (right and below right) the opposing sides in the conflict with Britain are represented in Copley's portraits of Nathaniel Hurd, a silversmith and patriot and Joseph Green, a Loyalist merchant

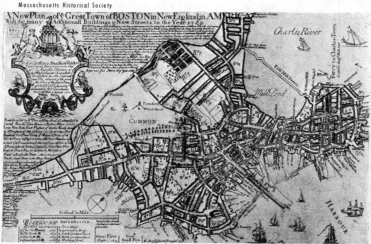

(Above) Freelove Ol-
ney by J. S. Copley;
(above right) Boston
state house

Boston Common with
British troops in drill
formation

New York

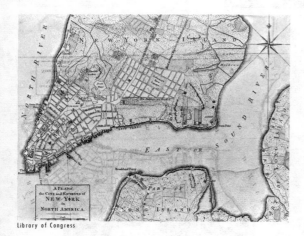

The cosmopolitan nature of New York was already in evidence by the 1770s. Stately homes of the merchants lined the river while nearby were slums occupied by day laborers, dockhands, and free Negroes. Up the river lived the landed gentry. Because the franchise was restricted to property owners, this group controlled the colony's politics.

(Top) New York from Brooklyn Heights, by Archibald Robertson, 1778; (bottom) view to the southeast on Manhattan Island, 1768

(Top) New York along the Battery; (left) Hudson River at Ft. Montgomery, showing chain which the Americans stretched across the river to stop British vessels; (above) Philipse Manor, Yonkers; (bottom) French vessels blocking English ships from New York harbor

L'Escadre française mouillée devant New york, bloquans l'Escadre Angloise et interceptans les Batimens qui vouloient y entrer. Le 12 juillet 1778.

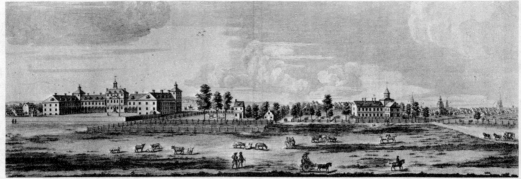

Philadelphia

(Top) The Pennsylvania Hospital, almshouse, and the house of employment, located on the outskirts of the city; (center) the Quaker meetinghouse and the almshouse run by the Friends

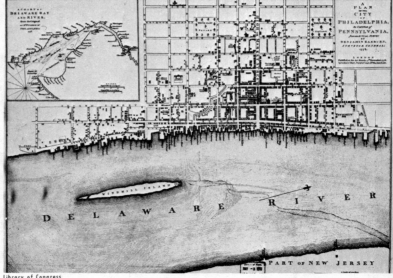

By the 1770s Philadelphia had become a highly cultured and prosperous city, the largest in America. It possessed many fine public buildings, semi-public libraries, a college, and the only hospital and medical school in the colonies. Many of the neatly laid out streets were paved, lined with sidewalks, and lighted and policed at night. The city also possessed the only Catholic church outside Maryland. Its central position in the colonies made it an ideal location for the political gatherings that preceded the war for independence.

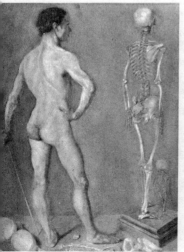

Pennsylvania Hospital

(Top left) Old Swedes' Church (Gloria Dei); (top right) Christ Church; (left) drawing by Dr. Fothergill, one of 18 donated to Pennsylvania Hospital (above) for use in anatomy class at the medical school in the 1760s

David Rittenhouse, by C. W. Peale

Science

Rittenhouse's orrery, built in 1767, traced the relative positions and motions of bodies in the solar system

The Franklin stove, adapted from a German model, provided better ventilation and more heat than a fireplace

The general prosperity of the colonies brought increasing interest in and support for scientific and educational endeavors. In addition to the medical research at the Pennsylvania Hospital and the activities of the American Philosophical Society, David Rittenhouse, an astronomer and mathematician, and the botanist John Bartram gained international reputations.

Map of the Gulf Stream drawn by Benjamin Franklin

John Bartram, the American botanist, produced many improved hybrids by crossing native and imported plants

Samuel Johnson, first president of King's College (right), a nonsectarian school founded in New York City in 1754. It was renamed Columbia College in 1784. Portrait by Smibert

(Left) Samuel Davies, a Presbyterian minister, was president of the College of New Jersey 1759-61; (below) Nassau Hall, built in 1756, was the college's first and largest building

Education

Among the academies and colleges founded before the Revolution were several that later grew to major importance. Education of the clergy was still a primary motive for the colleges, but there was increasing pressure for secular instruction, particularly in law.

(Above) Rhode Island College (Baptist), founded in 1764, and renamed Brown University in 1804; (left) Ezra Stiles, president of Yale University in 1777 and a founder of Brown

Cartoon emphasizing the folly of ruining the country's wealth and trade in war, 1779

Politics

In innumerable meetings and congresses and a flood of pamphlets and broadsides, political opinion in the colonies gradually polarized around the issue of independence. Many who eventually supported independence had earlier advocated less radical means and the war's economic disruptions led even some who were not Loyalists to argue for early settlement. In addition to a basic conflict between Loyalists and radicals, disagreement over the form and structure of the new government was revealed in the Articles of Confederation and its rejection of central authority.

THE NEW *MASSACHUSETTS*
LIBERTY SONG,
[*To the Tune of the* British Grenadier.]

I.

THAT Seat of Science ATHENS, and Earth's great Miſtreſs ROME,
Where now are all their Glories, we ſcarce can find their Tomb:
Then guard your Rights, AMERICANS! nor ſtoop to lawleſs Sway,
Oppoſe, oppoſe, oppoſe, oppoſe,—thy brave AMERICA.

II.

Proud ALBION bow'd to *Cæſar,* and num'rous *Lords* before,
To *Picts,* to *Danes,* to *Normans,* and many Maſters more:
But we can boaſt AMERICANS! we never fell a Prey;
Huzza, huzza, huzza, huzza, for brave AMERICA.

Patriotic "Liberty Song" composed in 1770

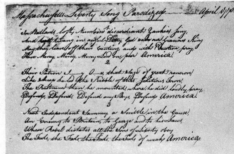

Parody of the "Liberty Song" which satirizes the activities of James Otis and Samuel Adams

Conflicting viewpoints at a town meeting

Dickinson draft of the Articles of Confederation

View of Portsmouth, N.H., from "Atlantic Neptune"

Town and Country

In spite of the growth of several cities in the colonies, the vast majority of the population at the time of the Revolution (perhaps as much as 90 percent) lived in small towns or in the country and earned their living from the land or the sea. Particularly in New England, the numerous villages came to exemplify an ideal of local self-government, where an enterprising man could parlay the fruits of his labors into a position of respect.

"Moses Marcey of Sturbridge," painting by an unknown artist

"Village Common," watercolor by an anonymous artist, 1780

By the Revolution most of the coastal areas and river valleys from New Hampshire to Virginia were dotted with towns, but even with designated local responsibility for maintaining roads, travel was difficult. Tolls for private roads and ferries, where they existed, were an added burden.

The town of Concord in 1776 from "Massachusetts Magazine"

View from Bushongo Tavern near Yorktown on the Baltimore Road from "Columbian Magazine"

Ferry three miles below Bristol, Pa.

Map of Fairfield County, Connecticut, c. 1775

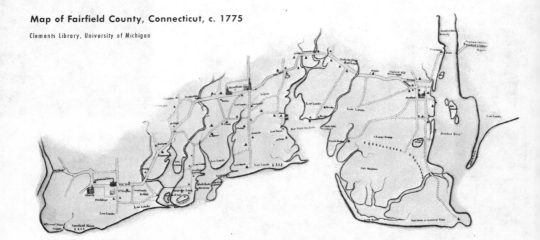

Plan of a granary drawn for "Columbian Magazine," 1779

View of a frontier sawmill and blockhouse

Generally, farming outside the South was a subsistence enterprise, little improved by experiments with new tools or methods. Large landowners, however, profited by demands for such basics as timber. The war increased the need for salt and other products formerly imported.

VENERATE THE PLOUGH

Salt works in Salisbury, Massachusetts, 1776

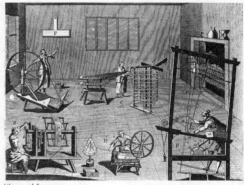

Various steps in the manufacture of woolens

New method of reaping as illustrated in "Columbian Magazine" in 1780

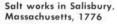

A Bird in the Hand is worth two in the Bush

(Above left) Two woodcuts from "A New Guide to the English Tongue," 1770; (top right) plate from "The Frugal Housewife," 1772; (center) contents page for Dilworth's "New Guide"; (center right) poem dedicated to his patrons by a newsboy; (bottom) covers of two almanacs published in the colonies

Popular Reading

In addition to political tracts and the Bible, colonial presses put forth a variety of material of general interest, from an array of popular almanacs containing weather information and helpful hints to "primers" filled with aphorisms and moral lessons for the younger generation to learn.

Folk Art

In matters of artistic patronage even the cities could barely sustain the few trained portraitists available. A small-town patron bought plain likenesses by itinerant limners or the local sign painter. In the German settlements there was a genuine and vibrant decorative folk art, derived from native styles.

(Above) "The Domino Girl," artist unknown; (right) "Capt. Samuel Chandler" by Winthrop Chandler, most accomplished of the primitives; (below) "Lady Washingdon - Exselence George General Washingdon" by an unknown artist; fraktur of a parrot by Heinrich Otto, 1785

Furniture

The decorative arts flourished in America from early in the 17th century with the arrival of immigrant European craftsmen. Furniture designs reflected familiar Renaissance and Baroque styles, learned before emigration. The two room settings recreate a large hall used for cooking, eating, and sleeping, as in the medieval tradition, and a formal dining room later in the century.

(Top left) 17th-century room from a house at Essex, Mass.; (top right) oak armchair attributed to Thomas Dennis, Ipswich, 1660-75; (left) Queen Anne style dining room with paneling from New Hampshire and chairs from New York; (below, left to right) slat-back armchair, probably New York, about 1700; tip-top table, Philadelphia; easy chair, New England, 1700-25

Glass and Metalwork

(Left) Loving cup by John Coney, 1701; (center) sugar bowl by Jacob Ten Eyck, about 1720; (right) pewter chalice, mid-18th century

(Both) Winterthur Museum

The designs of colonial silversmiths were distinguished for their simplicity and grace. Of these craftsmen, John Coney and Paul Revere of Boston were most famous.

"Baron" Stiegel established an "industrial plantation" on the Delaware River where he produced ironware and glassware of high quality.

(Right) Silver tea service by Paul Revere; (below, left to right) glass sugar bowl and "Valentine" tumbler, both c. 1764-74, and cast iron stove plate, c. 1760, all by Henry William Stiegel

Minneapolis Institute of Arts

Corning Museum of Glass

Corning Museum of Glass

Philadelphia Museum of Art

On the Formation of New States

The original Crown charters by which the colonies were created failed in many cases to set western boundaries to their territories, which in theory thus extended indefinitely toward the Mississippi River, and even beyond it. The potential of these western regions was early apparent to provincial entrepreneurs, so the Proclamation of 1763 that closed the country west of the Appalachians to colonial settlement was greatly resented, and had much to do with creating the movement toward independence. After independence was achieved, or at least announced, the states had to clarify their western claims, which overlapped and were otherwise conflicting. There was general sentiment, particularly among those states without such claims, that they should all be ceded to the central government, which could then decide how to administer the vast expanse of land involved. As a result, and in anticipation of this cession, the Continental Congress on October 10, 1780, passed the following resolution indicating the policy it would follow toward any territory placed in its charge.

Source: *Journals*, III: "Tuesday, October 10, 1780."

Resolved, that the unappropriated lands that may be ceded or relinquished to the United States by any particular states, pursuant to the recommendation of Congress on the 6th day of September last, shall be disposed of for the common benefit of the United States and be settled and formed into distinct republican states which shall become members of the federal Union, and shall have the same rights of sovereignty, freedom, and independence as the other states.

That each state which shall be so formed shall contain a suitable extent of territory, not less than 100 nor more than 150 miles square, or as near thereto as circumstances will admit.

That the necessary and reasonable expenses which any particular state shall have incurred since the commencement of the present war, in subduing any of the British posts or in maintaining forts or garrisons within and for the defense, or in acquiring any part of the territory that may be ceded or relinquished to the United States, shall be reimbursed.

That the said lands shall be granted and settled at such times and under such regulations as shall hereafter be agreed on by the United States in Congress assembled, or any nine or more of them.

THOMAS POWNALL: The New Relation Between the Old and the New World

Thomas Pownall, former governor of Massachusetts and member of Parliament since 1767, had considerable experience in administering colonial affairs. The Revolutionary War led him to survey the policy that he felt the European powers should adopt in their commercial and political relations with the new nation. Pownall wrote a tract in July of 1780, entitled A Memorial Most Humbly Addressed to the Sovereigns of Europe. *Pownall did not permit his name to appear on the title page, but he used so many quotations from his earlier work,* The Administration of the Colonies, *that its authorship was easily recognized. The editor of the* Monthly Review *lauded the work as a scholarly presentation by a competent authority, even though the authorship was not known at the time.*

Source: *A Memorial Most Humbly Addressed to the Sovereigns of Europe on the Present State of Affairs, Between the Old and New World,* 2nd edition, London, 1780, pp. 4-71.

NORTH AMERICA is *de facto* an independent power which has taken its equal station with other powers, and must be so *de jure*. The politicians of the governments of Europe may reason or negotiate upon this idea, as a matter *sub lite* [under consideration]. The powers of those governments may fight about it as a new power coming into establishment; such negotiations and such wars are of no consequence either to the right or the fact. It would be just as wise, and just as effectual, if they were to go to war to decide or set on foot negotiations to settle to whom for the future the sovereignty of the moon should belong. The moon has been long common to them all, and they may all in their turns profit of her reflected light.

The independence of America is fixed as fate; she is mistress of her own fortune, knows that she is so, and will actuate that power which she feels she has so as to establish her own system and to change the system of Europe.

I will not lose time, in a useless waste of words, by attempting to prove the existence of this fact. The rapid progress of events at this crisis will not wait for such trifling. The only thing which can be useful to the world is to examine what the precise change of system is; what will be the general consequence of such change; and with what spirit and by what conduct the advancing state of things should be met.

If the powers of Europe will view the state of things *as they do really exist*, and will treat them *as being what they are*, the lives of thousands may be spared; the happiness of millions may be secured; and the peace of the whole world preserved. If they will not, they will be plunged into a sea of troubles, a sea of blood, fathomless and bound-

less. The war that has begun to rage between Britain, France, and Spain, which is
almost gorged between Britain and America, will extend itself to all the maritime, and
most likely, afterwards, to all the inland
powers of Europe; and like the Thirty
Years' War of the 16th and 17th centuries,
will not end but as that did — by a new
and general resettlement of powers and interests, according to the new spirit of the
new system which has taken place.

Why may not all this be done by a congress of all the powers before as well as after war? If the powers of the present world
fought for dominion by extirpation, then
war is the proper engine; but if they war in
order to treat for settlements of power, as
has been long the system of Europe, then is
war a wanton, clumsy, useless cruelty. . . .

There is nowhere in the European part of
the Old World such a greatness of interwoven and combined interest, communicating
through such largeness of territory, as that
in North America, possessed and actuated
by the English nation. The northern and
southern parts of Europe are possessed by
different nations, actuated by different spirits, and conducted under very different systems. Instead of actuating an intercommu-
nion by an attractive [system], their intercourse is at perpetual variance under a repellent principle; their communion also is
obstructed by the difficulties of intercourse,
both over land and through the seas. They
are, moreover, cut off, as it were, in the
middle by other intervening nations, whose
principles and systems are alike repellent
and obstructive of free communion.

On the contrary, when the site and circumstances of the large extended territories
of North America are examined, one finds
everything united in it which forms greatness of dominions, *amplitude and growth of
state*.

The nature of the coast and of the winds
upon that coast is such as renders marine
navigation, from one end of its extent to
the other, a perpetually moving intercourse
of communion; and the nature of the rivers,
which open (where marine navigation ends)
an inland navigation which, with short in-
terruptions, carries on a circulation throughout the whole, renders such inland navigation but a further process of that communion — all which becomes, as it were, a
one vital principle of life, extended through
a one organized being.

While the country, by the *capability* of
this natural communion, becomes thus united at its root, its largeness of territory, expanded through such a variety of climates,
produces, upon this communion, everything
that nature requires, that luxury loves to
abound in, or that power can use as an instrument of its activity. All those things
which the different nations in Europe (under every difficulty that a defect of natural
communion, under every obstruction that
an artificial and perverted system threw in
their way) barter for in the Old World are
here in the New World possessed, under an
uninterrupted natural communion, by an
unobstructed navigation, under a universal
freedom of commerce, by one nation.

The naval stores, the timber, the hemp,
the fisheries, the salted provisions of the
North; the tobacco, rice, cotton, silk, indigo, finer fruits, and perhaps, in no very distant period, the wines, the resin and tar of
the South, form the reciprocation of wants
and supplies of each respectively. The
bread-corn, the flour, the produce of agriculture in every form of farming, and the
several increasing articles of manufactures
which the middle colonies produce, not
only fill up the communion but complete
its system. They unite those parts which
were before connected, and organize (as I
have said) the several parts into a one
whole. . . .

In this New World we see all the inhabitants not only free but allowing a universal
naturalization to all who wish to be so; and
an uncontrolled liberty of using any mode

of life they choose, or any means of getting a livelihood that their talents lead them to. Free of all restraints which take the property of themselves out of their own hands, their souls are their own, and their reason; they are their own masters, and they act; their labor is employed on their own property, and what they produce is their own. In a country like this, where every man has the full and free exertion of his powers, where every man may acquire any share of the good things thereof, or of interest and power which his spirit can work him up to — there, an unabated application of the powers of individuals and a perpetual struggle of their spirits sharpens their wits and gives constant training to the mind.

The acquirement of information in things and business which becomes necessary to this mode of life gives the mind, thus sharpened and thus exercised, a turn of inquiry and investigation which forms a *character peculiar to these people*, which is not to be met with, nor ever did exist in any other to the same degree, unless in some of the ancient republics, where the people were under the same predicament. This turn of character, which in the ordinary occurrences of life is called "inquisitiveness," and which, when exerted about trifles, goes even to a degree of ridicule in many instances, is yet, in matters of business and commerce, a most useful and efficient talent. Whoever knows these people and has viewed them in this light will consider them as *animated in this New World* (if I may so express myself) *with the spirit of the new philosophy*. Their system of life is a course of experiments; and, standing on that high ground of improvement up to which the most enlightened parts of Europe have advanced, like eaglets they commence the first efforts of their pinions from a towering advantage.

Nothing in the Old World is less regarded than a poor man's wisdom; and yet a rich man's wisdom is generally naught but the impression of what others teach him.

On the other hand, the poor man's wisdom is not learning but knowledge of his own acquiring and picking up, and founded upon fact and nature by simple experience. In America, the wisdom and not the man is attended to; and *America is peculiarly a poor man's country*. Everything in this wilderness of woods being totally different from an Old World, almost worn out; and every person here far removed from the habits, example, and perversion, or obstruction, of those who assume the power of directing them — the settlers reason not from what they hear but from what they see and feel. They move not but as nature calls forth their activity, nor fix a step but where use marks the ground, and take the direction of their courses by that line only, where truth and nature lead hand in hand. They find themselves at liberty to follow what mode they like; they feel that they can venture to try experiments, and that the advantages of their discoveries are their own. They, therefore, try what the soil claims, what the climate permits, and what both will produce and sustain to the greatest advantage. Advancing in this line of labor *by such a spirit of induction*, they have brought forward into culture an abundant produce, more than any other nation of the Old World ever did or could. . . .

When the field of agriculture shall be filled with husbandmen, and the classes of handicrafts fully stocked — as there are here no laws that frame conditions on which a man is to become entitled to exercise this or that trade, or by which he is excluded from exercising the one or the other, in this or that place; as there are here no laws that prescribe the manner in which, and the prices at which, he is to work, or that lock him up in that trade which it has been his misfortune to have attached himself to, although, while he is starving in that, he could, in some other line of business which his circumstances point out and his talents lead him to be useful to the public, and maintain himself; as there are none of those oppressing, obstructing, dead-doing laws here, the moment that the progress of civilization, carried thus on in its natural course, is ripe for it — the branch of manufactures will take its shoot and will grow and increase with an astonishing exuberancy.

Although the civilizing activity of America does not, by artificial and false helps contrary to the natural course of things, inconsistent with, and checking the first applications of, its natural labor, and before the community is ripe for such endeavor, attempt to force the establishment of manufactures; yet following, as use and experience lead, the natural progress of improvement, it is every year producing a surplus profit; which surplus, as it enters again into the circulation of productive employment, creates an accumulating, accelerated, progressive series of surpluses. *With these accumulated surpluses* of the produce of the earth and seas, *and not with manufactures,* the Americans carry on their *commercial* exertions. Their fish, wheat, flour, rice, tobacco, indigo, livestock, barrel pork and beef (some of these articles being peculiar to the country and staple commodities) form the exports of their commerce. This has given them a direct trade to Europe; and, with some additional articles, a circuitous trade to Africa and the West Indies.

The same ingenuity of mechanic handicraft, which arises concomitant with agriculture, does here also rise concomitant with commerce and is exerted in shipbuilding. It is carried on not only to serve all the purposes of their own carriage, and that of the West Indies in part, but to an extent of sale, so as to supply a great part of the shipping of Britain. And, further, if it continues to advance with the same progress, it will supply a great part of the trade of Europe, also, with shipping, at cheaper rates than they can anywhere, or by any means, supply themselves.

Thus, their commerce, although subsisting (while they were subordinate provinces) under various restrictions, by its advancing progress in shipbuilding has been striking deep root, and is now shot forth an *active commerce,* growing into *amplitude of state* and great power.

Stating the ground on which an objection is made to this description of the improving commerce of America will open to view another extraordinary source of *amplitude and growth of state.* It will be said that the fact of the balance of trade being at all times, and in every channel, finally against America, so as to draw all the gold and silver it can collect from it, is but a damning circumstance of its progressive advance in commerce and opulence. . . .

North America has advanced, and is every day advancing, to growth of state, with a steady and continually accelerating motion, of which there has never yet been any example in Europe. . . .

When one looks to the progressive *population* which this fostering happiness does, of course, produce, one cannot but see, in North America, that God's first blessing, "Be fruitful and multiply; replenish the earth and subdue it," has operated in full manifestation of His will. In Europe, on the contrary, where a wretched, selfish, self-obstructing policy has rendered barren not only fruitful countries but even the womb itself; one may say, in melancholy truth, that the first curse, "I will greatly multiply thy sorrow in procreation; in sorrow shalt thou bring forth children," seems to have been executed in judgment. . . . In North America, children are a blessing, are riches and strength to the parents; and *happy is every man that has his quiver full of them.* . . .

Let us here view this world . . . now separated and fallen off from that vital union by which it was once an organized member of the English Empire. Let us view it *as it now is* — AN INDEPENDENT STATE *that has taken its equal station amid the nations of the earth* — as an empire, the spirit of whose government extends from the center to its extreme parts, exactly in proportion as the will of those parts does reciprocally unite in that center. Here we shall find (as has always been found) "That universal participation of council creates reciprocation of universal obedience. The seat of government will be well informed of the state and condition of the remote and extreme parts; and the remote and extreme parts, by participation in the legislature, will from self-consciousness, be informed and satisfied in the reasons and necessity of the measures of government. These parts will consider themselves as acting in every grant that is made and in every tax which is imposed. This consideration alone will give efficacy to government, and will create that *consensus obedientium* on which only the permanent power of the imperium of a state can be founded. This will give extension and stability of empire as far as it can extend its dominions."

This might have been, indeed, the spirit of the British Empire, America being a part of it. *This is the spirit* of the government of the new empire of America, Great Britain being no part of it. It is a vitality liable, indeed, to many disorders, many dangerous diseases; but it is young and strong, and will struggle, by the vigor of internal healing principles of life, against those evils and surmount them. Like the infant Hercules, it will strangle these serpents in its cradle. Its strength will grow with its years, and it will establish its constitution, and perfect adultness in growth of state.

To this greatness of empire it will certainly arise. That it is removed 3,000 miles distant from its enemy; that it lies on another side of the globe where it has no enemy; that it is earthborn and like a giant ready to run its course are not alone the grounds and reasons on which a speculatist may pronounce this. The fostering care with which the rival powers of Europe will nurse it, ensures its establishment beyond all doubt or danger.

Where a state is founded on such amplitude of base as the union of territory in this New World forms, whose communion is actuated by such a spirit of civilization; where all is enterprise and experiment; where agriculture, led by this spirit, has made discoveries in so many new and peculiar articles of culture, and has carried the ordinary produce of bread-corn to a degree that has wrought it to a staple export for the supply of the Old World; whose fisheries are mines producing more solid riches to those who work them than all the silver of Potosi; where experimental application of the understanding as well as labor to the several branches of the mechanics has invented so many new and ingenious improvements; where the arts and sciences, legislation and politics are soaring, with a strong and extended pinion, to such heights of philosophic induction; where, under this blessedness, population has multiplied like the seeds of the harvest; where the strength of these numbers, taking a military form, "shall lift up itself as a young lion"; where trade, of a most extensive orbit circulated in its own shipping, has wrought up this effort of the community to an *active commerce;* where all these powers unite and take the form of establishment of empire — I may suppose that I cannot err, nor give offense to the greatest power in Europe, when, upon a comparison of the state of mankind and of the states of those powers in Europe with that of America, I venture to suggest to their contemplation that America is growing too large for any government in Europe to govern as subordinate; that the government of North America is too firmly fixed in the hands of its own community to be either directed by other hands or taken out of the hands in which it is; and that the power in men and arms (be they contemned or contemptible, as the wisdom of Europe may suppose) is too much to be forced at the distance of 3,000 miles.

Thomas Rodney: First Steps Toward Peace

Between 1781 and 1788 Thomas Rodney was five times elected by the General Assembly of Delaware to membership in the Confederation Congress. On June 14, 1781, Rodney wrote a letter from Philadelphia to his brother Caesar, at that time president of Delaware. In the letter, Thomas Rodney described European attempts to negotiate a peace between America and Britain.

Source: Niles: "Thos. Rodney to C. Rodney."

You will find by the contents of this that it is a confidential letter, conveying you very important and pleasing intelligence.

Congress has received a letter from the king of France, and also otherwise officially informed by his minister here, that the empress of Russia threw out an invitation for the belligerent powers to apply for her mediation, at which the court of London eagerly caught, and mentioned the emperor of Germany as another mediator — and a congress was proposed to be opened at Vienna for the purpose of settling a general peace. The answer of the court of France was that they could send no plenipotentiaries to said congress till they had consulted their allies; but, in [that] the mediators are such respectable powers, and may be so fully relied on for justice, the king presses the United States to submit to the mediation — and that the first preliminary he will insist on, previous to any other negotiation, shall be the independence of the United States in full — and upon obtaining this, request that the states may be as moderate in all other demands as possible, that the mediating powers may thereby receive favorably impressions of our equity and justice.

The same mediating application was made to the court of Spain, and their answer was that they could not do anything but in conjunction with their ally, the king of France — so that the congress of mediation is likely to be delayed till our despatches reach France. However, the king says that if he is so pressed that he cannot decently delay sending a plenipotentiary till that time, he shall insist on the preliminary before mentioned, and then only proceed in the negotiation so as to have it in such forwardness as will not injure America against their plenipotentiaries and instructions arrived.

The king of France thinks that very equitable terms of peace may be obtained through this mediation, but urges us strongly to exert ourselves this campaign — as the wresting of the southern states out of the hands of the British will contribute greatly to lessen their demands and make them more readily incline to equitable terms of peace. . . . Our exertions ought to be quick and vigorous, lest a truce should take place. . . . To ensure the success of this mediation we ought to make the most ample and vigorous preparations for carrying on the war.

Britain made an attempt, through a Mr. Cumberland, to negotiate a separate treaty with Spain; but this has failed, though Mr. Cumberland is still at Madrid. Spain would not treat but in conjunction with France, and France cannot treat but in conjunction with America. Thus are we linked together, so that the independence of America now stands on prosperous ground, and no further doubt need to remain about it. For this much is certain — all the powers of Europe (Britain excepted) wish us to be independent.

Thus far in confidence, with this addition, that Congress have appointed Dr. Franklin, J. Adams, J. Jay, H. Laurens and Governor Jefferson plenipotentiaries for settling the peace. They first agreed to appoint but one, and Adams was appointed before I came up; they then agreed to add two more, then Jay was appointed — then Jefferson had five votes, Franklin four, and Laurens one. The states voted the same way three times.

Then I proposed to the members of Virginia and Pennsylvania that we should appoint them both, which being generally agreed to, this day was appointed for the purpose, and then Laurens was included — so the appointment now consists of five; New Hampshire, Pennsylvania, Delaware and Maryland were for Franklin, South Carolina for Laurens, and Massachusetts, Connecticut, Jersey, Virginia and North Carolina for Jefferson, Rhode Island and New York unrepresented; Georgia absent. Mr. M'Kean wanted to alter in favor of Jefferson and leave Franklin out, which, upon Georgia's coming in, would have carried him; but I would not give up Franklin, and by the manner of proposing to appoint them both, got him appointed — though this was exceedingly against the grain of several members. He will not be put at the head of the commission. His abilities, character, and influence are what will be of most use to us in Europe.

He defeated the Americans with great slaughter.
Inscription on the tomb of Lord Cornwallis, in Westminster Abbey. The surrender of Cornwallis at Yorktown, Oct. 17, 1781, virtually ended the Revolutionary War.

ALEXANDER HAMILTON: Arguments for Increasing the Power of the Federal Government

Hardly had the new government begun to function, under the Articles of Confederation, when voices began calling for a stronger central authority. One such critic was Alexander Hamilton, who published a series of articles under the pseudonym, "The Continentalist." The last of these, which is reprinted here, appeared on July 4, 1782. By this time Hamilton had resigned his position on Washington's staff and was taking steps to implement his proposals in Congress.

Source: J. C. Hamilton, II, pp. 194-201: "The Continentalist, No. VI."

LET US SEE what will be the consequences of not authorizing the federal government to regulate the trade of these states. Besides the want of revenue and of power; besides the immediate risk to our independence, the dangers of all the future evils of a precarious Union; besides the deficiency of a wholesome concert and provident superintendence to advance the general prosperity of trade — the direct consequence will be that the landed interest and the laboring poor will, in the first place, fall a sacrifice to the trading interest, and the whole eventually to a bad system of policy made necessary by the want of such regulating power.

Each state will be afraid to impose duties on its commerce lest the other states, not doing the same, should enjoy greater advantages than itself by being able to afford native commodities cheaper abroad and foreign commodities cheaper at home.

A part of the evils resulting from this would be a loss to the revenue of those moderate duties, which, without being injurious to commerce are allowed to be the most agreeable species of taxes to the people. Articles of foreign luxury, while they would contribute nothing to the income of the state being less dear by an exemption from duties, would have a more extensive consumption.

Many branches of trade, hurtful to the common interest, would be continued for want of proper checks and discouragements. As revenues must be found to satisfy the public exigencies in peace and in war, too great a proportion of taxes will fall directly upon land and upon the necessaries of life — the produce of that land. The influence of these evils will be to render landed property fluctuating and less valuable — to oppress the poor by raising the prices of necessaries; to injure commerce by encouraging the consumption of foreign luxuries; by increasing the value of labor; by lessening the quantity of home productions, enhancing their prices at foreign markets, of course obstructing their sale, and enabling other nations to supplant us.

Particular caution ought at present to be observed in this country not to burden the soil itself and its productions with heavy impositions, because the quantity of unimproved land will invite the husbandmen to abandon old settlements for new, and the disproportion of our population for some time to come will necessarily make labor dear — to reduce which, and not to increase it, ought to be a capital object of our policy.

Easy duties, therefore, on commerce, especially on imports, ought to lighten the burdens which will unavoidably fall upon land. Though it may be said that, on the principle of a reciprocal influence of prices whereon the taxes are laid in the first instance, they will in the end be borne by all classes, yet it is of the greatest importance that no one should sink under the immediate pressure. The great art is to distribute the public burdens well, and not suffer them, either first or last, to fall too heavily on parts of the community; else, distress and disorder must ensue — a shock given to any part of the political machine vibrates through the whole.

As a sufficient revenue could not be raised from trade to answer the public purposes, other articles have been proposed. A moderate land and poll tax being of easy and unexpensive collection, and leaving nothing to discretion, are the simplest and best that could be devised.

It is to be feared the avarice of many of the landholders will be opposed to a perpetual tax upon land, however moderate. They will ignorantly hope to shift the burdens of the national expense from themselves to others — a disposition as iniquitous as it is fruitless — the public necessities must be satisfied; this can only be done by the contributions of the whole society. Particular classes are neither able nor will be willing to pay for the protection and security of the others; and where so selfish a spirit discovers itself in any member, the rest of the community will unite to compel it to do its duty.

Indeed, many theorists in political economy have held that all taxes, wherever they originate, fall upon land, and have therefore been of opinion that it would be best to draw the whole revenue of the state immediately from that source to avoid the expense of a more diversified collection, and the accumulations which will be heaped in their several stages upon the primitive sums advanced in those stages which are imposed on our trade. But though it has been demonstrated that this theory has been carried

to an extreme, impracticable in fact, yet it is evident, in tracing the matter, that a large part of all taxes, however remotely laid, will, by an insensible circulation, come at last to settle upon land — the source of most of the materials employed in commerce.

It appears from calculation made by the ablest master of political arithmetic about sixty years ago that the yearly product of all the lands in England amounted to £42 million sterling, and the whole annual consumption at that period, of foreign as well as domestic commodities, did not exceed £49 million, and the surplus of the exportation above the importation, £2 million, on which sums arise all the revenues in whatever shape which go into the treasury. It is easy to infer from this, how large a part of them must, directly or indirectly, be derived from land.

Nothing can be more mistaken than the collision and rivalship which almost always subsist between the landed and trading interests; for the truth is, they are so inseparably interwoven that one cannot be injured without injury nor benefited without benefit to the other. Oppress trade, lands sink in value; make it flourish, their value rises — incumber husbandry, trade declines; encourage agriculture, commerce revives. The progress of this mutual reaction might be easily delineated, but it is too obvious to every man who turns his thoughts, however superficially, upon the subject to require it. It is only to be regretted that it is too often lost sight of, when the seductions of some immediate advantage or exemption tempt us to sacrifice the future to the present.

But perhaps the class is more numerous of those who, not unwilling to bear their share of public burdens, are yet averse to the idea of perpetuity, as if there ever would arrive a period when the state would cease to want revenues, and taxes become unnecessary. It is of importance to unmask this delusion and open the eyes of the people to the truth. It is paying too great a tribute to the idol of popularity to flatter so injurious and so visionary an expectation. The error is too gross to be tolerated anywhere but in the cottage of the peasant. Should we meet with it in the Senate house, we must lament the ignorance or despise the hypocrisy, on which it is ingrafted.

Expense is, in the present state of things, entailed upon all governments; though, if we continue united, we shall be hereafter less exposed to wars by land than most other countries; yet, while we have powerful neighbors on either extremity, and our frontier is embraced by savages whose alliance they may without difficulty command, we cannot, in prudence, dispense with the usual precautions for our interior security. As a commercial people, maritime power must be a primary object of our attention, and a navy cannot be created or maintained without ample revenues. The nature of our popular institutions requires a numerous magistracy, for whom competent provision must be made; or we may be certain our affairs will always be committed to improper hands, and experience will teach us that no government costs so much as a bad one.

We may preach, till we are tired of the theme, the necessity of disinterestedness in republics without making a single proselyte. The virtuous declaimer will neither persuade himself nor any other person to be content with a double mess of pottage instead of a reasonable stipend for his services. We might as soon reconcile ourselves to the Spartan community of goods and wives, to their iron coin, their long beards, or their black broth. There is a total dissimilarity in the circumstances, as well as the manners of society among us, and it is as ridiculous to seek for models in the small ages of Greece and Rome as it would be to go in quest of them among the Hottentots and Laplanders.

The public, for the different purposes that have been mentioned, must always have large demands upon its constituents, and the only question is, whether these shall be satisfied by annual grants, perpetually renewed by a perpetual grant, once for all, or by a compound of permanent and occasional supplies. The last is the wisest course. The federal government should neither be independent nor too much dependent. It should neither be raised above responsibility or control, nor should it want the means of maintaining its own weight, authority, dignity and credit. To this end, permanent funds are indispensable, but they ought to be of such a nature and so moderate in their amount as never to be inconvenient. Extraordinary supplies can be the objects of extraordinary emergencies, and in that salutary medium will consist our true wisdom.

It would seem as if no mode of taxation could be relished but the worst of all modes, which now prevails by assessment. Every proposal for a specific tax is sure to meet with opposition. It has been objected to a poll tax at a fixed rate that it will be unequal, and the rich will pay no more than the poor. In the form in which it has been offered in these papers, the poor, properly speaking, are not comprehended, though it is true that beyond the exclusion of the indigent the tax has no reference to the proportion of property; but it should be remembered that it is impossible to devise any specific tax that will operate equally on the whole community. It must be the province of the legislature to hold the scales with a judicious hand and balance one by another. The rich must be made to pay for their luxuries, which is the only proper way of taxing their superior wealth.

Do we imagine that our assessments operate equally? Nothing can be more contrary to the fact. Wherever a discretionary power is lodged in any set of men over the property of their neighbors, they will abuse it; their passions, prejudices, partialities, dislikes will have the principal lead in measuring the abilities of those over whom their power extends; and assessors will ever be a set of petty tyrants, too unskillful, if honest, to be possessed of so delicate a trust, and too seldom honest to give them the excuse of want of skill.

The genius of liberty reprobates everything arbitrary or discretionary in taxation. It exacts that every man, by a definite and general rule, should know what proportion of his property the state demands; whatever liberty we may boast in theory, it cannot exist in fact while assessments continue. The admission of them among us is a new proof how often human conduct reconciles the most glaring opposites; in the present case, the most vicious practice of despotic governments with the freest constitutions and the greatest love of liberty.

The establishment of permanent funds would not only answer the public purposes infinitely better than temporary supplies but it would be the most effectual way of easing the people.

With this basis for procuring credit, the amount of present taxes might be greatly diminished. Large sums of money might be borrowed abroad, at a low interest, and introduced into the country to defray the current expenses and pay the public debts; which would not only lessen the demand for immediate supplies but would throw more money into circulation, and furnish the people with greater means of paying the taxes.

Though it be a just rule that we ought not to run in debt to avoid present expense, so far as our faculties extend, yet the propriety of doing it cannot be disputed when it is apparent that these are incompetent to the public necessities. Efforts beyond our abilities can only tend to individual distress and national disappointment. The product of the three foregoing articles will be as little as can be required to enable Congress to pay their debts and restore order into their finances. In addition to them:

The disposal of the unlocated lands will hereafter be a valuable source of revenue, and an immediate one of credit. As it may be liable to the same condition with the duties on trade, that is, the product of the sales within each state to be credited to that state, and as the rights of jurisdiction are not infringed, it seems to be susceptible of no reasonable objection.

Mines in every country constitute a branch of the revenue. In this, where nature has so richly impregnated the bowels of the earth, they may in time become a valuable one; and as they require the care and attention of government to bring them to perfection, this care and a share in the profits of it will very properly devolve upon Congress. All the precious metals should absolutely be the property of the federal government, and with respect to the others, it should have a discretionary power of reserving, in the nature of a tax, such part as it may judge not inconsistent with the encouragement due to so important an object. This is rather a future than a present resource.

The reason of allowing Congress to appoint its own officers of the customs, collectors of the taxes, and military officers of every rank is to create in the interior of each state a mass of influence in favor of the federal government. The great danger has been shown to be that it will not have power enough to defend itself and preserve the Union, not that it will ever become formidable to the general liberty; a mere regard to the interests of the confederacy will never be a principle sufficiently active to crush the ambition and intrigues of different members.

Force cannot effect it. A contest of arms will seldom be between the common sovereign and a single refractory member, but between distinct combinations of the several parts against each other. A sympathy of situations will be apt to produce associates to the disobedient. The application of force is always disagreeable — the issue uncertain. It will be wise to obviate the necessity of it by interesting such a number of individuals in each state, in support of the federal government, as will be counterpoised to the ambition of others, and will make it difficult for them to unite the people in opposition to the first and necessary measures of the Union.

There is something noble and magnificent in the perspective of a great federal republic, closely linked in the pursuit of a common interest — tranquil and prosperous at home, respectable abroad. But there is something proportionably diminutive and contemptible in the prospect of a number of petty states, with the appearance only of union, jarring, jealous, and perverse, without any determined direction, fluctuating and unhappy at home, weak and insignificant by their dissensions in the eyes of other nations.

Happy America, if those to whom thou has entrusted the guardianship of thy infancy know how to provide for thy future repose, but miserable and undone if their negligence or ignorance permits the spirit of discord to erect her banner on the ruins of thy tranquillity!

Michel Guillaume Jean de Crèvecoeur: What Is an American?

Crèvecoeur came to the British-American colonies in 1759, and by 1765 had become a naturalized citizen. From 1769 to 1780 he owned a farm in New York. A Loyalist in the Revolution, Crèvecoeur refused to accept the excesses of those who, in his words, were "perpetually bawling about liberty without knowing what it was." In 1780, he left America for France until the war in America was over. It was during his years as a New York farmer that he wrote his best-known collection of essays, Letters from an American Farmer, *from which the following selection is taken. They were originally published in London, in 1782, under the pen name of "J. Hector St. John."*

Source: *Letters from an American Farmer,* London, 1782, pp. 45-86.

I wish I could be acquainted with the feelings and thoughts which must agitate the heart and present themselves to the mind of an enlightened Englishman when he first lands on this continent. He must greatly rejoice that he lived at a time to see this fair country discovered and settled; he must necessarily feel a share of national pride when he views the chain of settlements which embellishes these extended shores. When he says to himself, this is the work of my countrymen, who, when convulsed by factions, afflicted by a variety of miseries and wants, restless and impatient, took refuge here. They brought along with them their national genius, to which they principally owe what liberty they enjoy and what substance they possess. Here he sees the industry of his native country displayed in a new manner, and traces in their works the embryos of all the arts, sciences, and ingenuity which flourish in Europe. Here he beholds fair cities, substantial villages, extensive fields, an immense country filled with decent houses, good roads, orchards, meadows, and bridges, where a hundred years ago all was wild, woody, and uncultivated!

What a train of pleasing ideas this fair spectacle must suggest! It is a prospect which must inspire a good citizen with the most heartfelt pleasure. The difficulty consists in the manner of viewing so extensive a scene. He is arrived on a new continent; a modern society offers itself to his contemplation, different from what he had hitherto seen. It is not composed, as in Europe, of great lords who possess everything, and of a herd of people who have nothing. Here are no aristocratical families, no courts, no kings, no bishops, no ecclesiastical dominion, no invisible power giving to a few a very visible one, no great manufacturers employing thousands, no great refinements of luxury. The rich and the poor are not so far removed from each other as they are in Europe.

Some few towns excepted, we are all tillers of the earth, from Nova Scotia to West Florida. We are a people of cultivators, scattered over an immense territory, communicating with each other by means of good roads and navigable rivers, united by the silken bands of mild government, all respecting the laws without dreading their power, because they are equitable. We are all animated with the spirit of industry, which is unfettered and unrestrained, because each person works for himself. If he travels through our rural districts, he views not the hostile castle and the haughty mansion, contrasted with the clay-built hut and miserable cabin, where cattle and men help to keep each other warm, and dwell in meanness, smoke, and indigence. A pleasing uniformity of decent competence appears throughout our habitations. The meanest of our log houses is a dry and comfortable habitation.

Lawyer or merchant are the fairest titles our towns afford; that of a farmer is the only appellation of the rural inhabitants of our country. It must take some time before he can reconcile himself to our dictionary, which is but short in words of dignity and names of honor. There, on a Sunday, he sees a congregation of respectable farmers and their wives, all clad in neat homespun, well mounted, or riding in their own humble wagons. There is not among them an esquire, saving the unlettered magistrate. There he sees a parson as simple as his flock, a farmer who does not riot on the labor of others. We have no princes for whom we toil, starve, and bleed; we are the most perfect society now existing in the world. Here man is free as he ought to be; nor is this pleasing equality so transitory as many others are. Many ages will not see the shores of our great lakes replenished with inland nations, nor the unknown bounds of North America entirely peopled. Who can tell how far it extends? Who can tell the millions of men whom it will feed and contain? For no European foot has as yet traveled half the extent of this mighty continent!

The next wish of this traveler will be to know whence came all these people. They are a mixture of English, Scotch, Irish, French, Dutch, Germans, and Swedes. From this promiscuous breed that race now called Americans have arisen. The eastern provinces must indeed be excepted as being the unmixed descendants of Englishmen. I have heard many wish they had been more intermixed also; for my part, I am no wisher; and think it much better as it has happened. They exhibit a most conspicuous figure in this great and variegated picture; they too enter for a great share in the pleasing perspective displayed in these thirteen provinces. I know it is fashionable to reflect on them, but I respect them for what they have done; for the accuracy and wisdom with which they have settled their territory; for the decency of their manners: for their early love of letters; their ancient college, the first in this hemisphere; for their industry, which to me, who am but a farmer, is the criterion of everything. There never was a people, situated as they are, who, with so ungrateful a soil, have done more in so short a time. Do you think that the monarchial ingredients which are more prevalent in other governments have purged them from all foul stains? Their histories assert the contrary.

In this great American asylum, the poor of Europe have by some means met together, and in consequence of various causes; to what purpose should they ask one another, what countrymen they are? Alas, two-thirds of them had no country. Can a wretch who wanders about, who works and starves, whose life is a continual scene of sore affliction or pinching penury — can that man call England or any other kingdom his country? A country that had no bread for him, whose fields procured him no harvest, who met with nothing but the frowns of the rich, the severity of the laws, with jails and punishments, who owned not a single foot of the extensive surface of this planet? No! urged by a variety of motives, here they came. Everything has tended to regenerate them: new laws, a new mode of living, a new social system. Here they are become men; in Europe they were as so many useless plants, wanting vegetative mold and refreshing showers; they withered and were mowed down by want, hunger, and war — But now, by the power of transplantation, like all other plants, they have taken root

and flourished! Formerly they were not numbered in any civil list of their country, except in those of the poor; here they rank as citizens. By what invisible power has this surprising metamorphosis been performed? By that of the laws and that of their industry.

The laws, the indulgent laws, protect them as they arrive, stamping on them the symbol of adoption; they receive ample rewards for their labors; these accumulated rewards procure them lands; those lands confer on them the title of freemen; and to that title every benefit is affixed which men can possibly require. This is the great operation daily performed by our laws. From whence proceed these laws? From our government. Whence that government? It is derived from the original genius and strong desire of the people, ratified and confirmed by the Crown. This is the great chain which links us all; this is the picture which every province exhibits, Nova Scotia excepted. There the Crown has done all; either there were no people who had genius, or it was not much attended to. The consequence is that the province is very thinly inhabited indeed; the power of the Crown, in conjunction with the mosquitos, has prevented men from settling there. Yet some part of it flourished once, and it contained a mild, harmless set of people. But for the fault of a few leaders the whole were banished. The greatest political error the Crown ever committed in America was to cut off men from a country which wanted nothing but men.

What attachment can a poor European emigrant have for a country where he had nothing? The knowledge of the language, the love of a few kindred as poor as himself were the only cords that tied him. His country is now that which gives him land, bread, protection, and consequence. *Ubi panis ibi patria* [where my bread is earned, there is my country] is the motto of all emigrants. What then is the American, this new man? He is either a European or the descendant of a European; hence that strange mixture of blood which you will find in no other country. I could point out to you a man whose grandfather was an Englishman whose wife was Dutch, whose son married a French woman, and whose present four sons have now four wives of different nations. *He* is an American who, leaving behind him all his ancient prejudices and manners, receives new ones from the new mode of life he has embraced, the new government he obeys, and the new rank he holds. He becomes an American by being received in the broad lap of our great alma mater.

Here individuals of all nations are melted into a new race of men, whose labors and posterity will one day cause great change in the world. Americans are the western pilgrims who are carrying along with them that great mass of arts, sciences, vigor, and industry which began long since in the east; they will finish the great circle. The Americans were once scattered all over Europe; here they are incorporated into one of the finest systems of population which has ever appeared, and which will hereafter become distinct by the power of the different climates they inhabit. The American ought, therefore, to love this country much better than that wherein either he or his forefathers were born. Here the rewards of his industry follow with equal steps the progress of his labor; his labor is founded on the basis of nature, self-interest. Can it want a stronger allurement? Wives and children, who before in vain demanded of him a morsel of bread, now, fat and frolicsome, gladly help their father to clear those fields whence exuberant crops are to arise to feed and to clothe them all, without any part being claimed, either by a despotic prince, a rich abbot, or a mighty lord. Here, religion demands but little of him; a small voluntary salary to the minister, and gratitude to God. Can he refuse these?

The American is a new man, who acts upon new principles; he must, therefore, entertain new ideas and form new opinions. From involuntary idleness, servile dependence, penury, and useless labor he has passed to toils of a very different nature, rewarded by ample subsistence. This is an American.

North America is divided into many provinces, forming a large association, scattered along a coast 1,500 miles extent and about 200 wide. This society I would fain examine, at least such as it appears in the middle provinces. If it does not afford that variety of tinges and gradations which may be observed in Europe, we have colors peculiar to ourselves. For instance, it is natural to conceive that those who live near the sea must be very different from those who live in the woods; the intermediate space will afford a separate and distinct class.

Men are like plants; the goodness and flavor of the fruit proceed from the peculiar soil and exposition in which they grow. We are nothing but what we derive from the air we breathe, the climate we inhabit, the government we obey, the system of religion we profess, and the nature of our employment. Here you will find but few crimes; these have acquired as yet no root among us. I wish I were able to trace all my ideas. If my ignorance prevents me from describing them properly, I hope I shall be able to delineate a few of the outlines, which are all I propose.

Those who live near the sea feed more on fish than on flesh, and often encounter that boisterous element. This renders them more bold and enterprising; this leads them to neglect the confined occupations of the land. They see and converse with a variety of people; their intercourse with mankind becomes extensive. The sea inspires them with a love of traffic, a desire of transporting produce from one place to another; leads them to a variety of resources, which supply the place of labor. Those who inhabit the middle settlements, by far the most numerous, must be very different. The simple cultivation of the earth purifies them; but the indulgences of the government, the soft remonstrances of religion, the rank of independent freeholders must necessarily inspire them with sentiments very little known in Europe among people of the same class.

What do I say? Europe has no such class of man. The early knowledge they acquire, the early bargains they make, give them a great degree of sagacity. As freemen, they will be litigious; pride and obstinacy are often the cause of lawsuits; the nature of our laws and governments may be another. As citizens, it is easy to imagine that they will carefully read the newspapers, enter into every political disquisition, freely blame or censure governors and others. As farmers, they will be careful and anxious to get as much as they can, because what they get is their own. As northern men, they will love the cheerful cup. As Christians, religion curbs them not in their opinions. The general indulgence leaves everyone to think for himself in spiritual matters; the laws inspect our actions; our thoughts are left to God. Industry, good living, selfishness, litigiousness, country politics, the pride of freemen, religious indifference are their characteristics. If you recede still farther from the sea, you will come into more modern settlements; they exhibit the same strong lineaments in a ruder appearance. Religion seems to have still less influence, and their manners are less improved.

Now we arrive near the great woods, near the last inhabited districts. There men seem to be placed still farther beyond the reach of government, which in some measure leaves them to themselves. How can it pervade every corner? As they were driven there by misfortunes, necessity of beginnings, desire of acquiring large tracts of land, idleness, frequent want of economy, ancient debts — the reunion of such people

does not afford a very pleasing spectacle. When discord, want of unity and friendship — when either drunkenness or idleness prevail in such remote districts — contention, inactivity, and wretchedness must ensue. There are not the same remedies to these evils as in a long-established community. The few magistrates they have are in general little better than the rest. They are often in a perfect state of war; that of man against man, sometimes decided by blows, sometimes by means of the law; that of man against every wild inhabitant of these venerable woods, of which they are come to dispossess them. There men appear to be no better than carnivorous animals of a superior rank, living on the flesh of wild animals when they can catch them; and when they are not able, they subsist on grain.

He who would wish to see America in its proper light and have a true idea of its feeble beginnings and barbarous rudiments must visit our extended line of frontiers where the last settlers dwell, and where he may see the first labors of settlement, the mode of clearing the earth, in all their different appearances; where men are wholly left dependent on their native tempers and on the spur of uncertain industry, which often fails when not sanctified by the efficacy of a few moral rules. There, remote from the power of example and check of shame, many families exhibit the most hideous parts of our society. They are a kind of forlorn hope, preceding by ten or twelve years the most respectable army of veterans which come after them. In that space, prosperity will polish some; vice and the law will drive off the rest, who, uniting again with others like themselves, will recede still farther, making room for more industrious people, who will finish their improvements, convert the log house into a convenient habitation, and, rejoicing that the first heavy labors are finished, will change in a few years that hitherto barbarous country into a fine, fertile, well-regulated district.

Such is our progress, such is the march of the Europeans toward the interior parts of this continent. In all societies there are offcasts; this unpure part serves as our precursors or pioneers. My father himself was one of that class; but he came upon honest principles and was therefore one of the few who held fast. By good conduct and temperance, he transmitted to me his fair inheritance when not above one in fourteen of his contemporaries had the same good fortune.

Forty years ago this smiling country was thus inhabited; it is now purged, a general decency of manners prevails throughout; and such has been the fate of our best countries.

Exclusive of those general characteristics, each province has its own, founded on the government, climate, mode of husbandry, customs, and peculiarity of circumstances. Europeans submit insensibly to these great powers, and become in the course of a few generations not only Americans in general but either Pennsylvanians, Virginians, or provincials under some other name. Whoever traverses the continent must easily observe those strong differences, which will grow more evident in time. The inhabitants of Canada, Massachusetts, the middle provinces, the southern ones will be as different as their climates; their only points of unity will be those of religion and language. . . .

Europe contains hardly any other distinctions but lords and tenants. This fair country alone is settled by freeholders, the possessors of the soil they cultivate, members of the government they obey, and the framers of their own laws by means of their representatives. This is a thought which you have taught me to cherish; our distance from Europe, far from diminishing, rather adds to our usefulness and consequence as men and subjects. Had our forefathers remained there, they would only have crowded it, and perhaps prolonged those convulsions which had shaken it so long. Every industrious European who transports himself here may be compared to a sprout growing at the foot of a great tree; it enjoys and draws but a little portion of sap. Wrench it from the parent roots, transplant it, and it will become a tree bearing fruit also. Colonists are therefore entitled to the consideration due to the most useful subjects. A hundred families barely existing in some parts of Scotland will here in six years cause an annual exportation of 10,000 bushels of wheat, 100 bushels being but a common quantity for an industrious family to sell if they cultivate good land. It is here, then, that the idle may be employed, the useless become useful, and the poor become rich. But by riches I do not mean gold and silver; we have but little of those metals. I mean a better sort of wealth: cleared lands, cattle, good houses, good clothes, and an increase of people to enjoy them.

There is no wonder that this country has so many charms and presents to Europeans so many temptations to remain in it. A traveler in Europe becomes a stranger as soon as he quits his own kingdom; but it is otherwise here. We know, properly speaking, no strangers; this is every person's country; the variety of our soils, situations, climates, governments, and produce has something which must please everybody. No sooner does a European arrive, no matter of what condition, than his eyes are opened upon the fair prospects. He hears his language spoken; he retraces many of his own country manners; he perpetually hears the names of families and towns with which he is acquainted; he sees happiness and prosperity in all places disseminated; he meets with hospitality, kindness, and plenty everywhere. He beholds hardly any poor; he seldom hears of punishments and executions; and he wonders at the elegance of our towns, those miracles of industry and freedom. He cannot admire enough our rural districts, our convenient roads, good taverns, and our many accommodations; he involuntarily loves a country where everything is so lovely.

When in England, he was a mere Englishman; here he stands on a larger portion of the globe, not less than its fourth part, and may see the productions of the north in iron and naval stores; the provisions of Ireland, the grain of Egypt, the indigo, the rice of China. He does not find, as in Europe, a crowded society, where every place is overstocked; he does not feel that perpetual collision of parties, that difficulty of beginning, that contention which oversets so many.

There is room for everybody in America. Has he any particular talent or industry? He exerts it in order to procure a livelihood, and it succeeds. Is he a merchant? The avenues of trade are infinite. Is he eminent in any respect? He will be employed and respected. Does he love a country life? Pleasant farms present themselves; he may purchase what he wants, and thereby become an American farmer. Is he a laborer, sober and industrious? He need not go many miles nor receive many informations before he will be hired, well-fed at the table of his employer, and paid four or five times more than he can get in Europe. Does he want uncultivated lands? Thousands of acres present themselves, which he may purchase cheap. Whatever be his talents or inclinations, if they are moderate, he may satisfy them.

I do not mean that everyone who comes will grow rich in a little time; no, but he may procure an easy, decent maintenance by his industry. Instead of starving, he will be fed; instead of being idle, he will have employment; and these are riches enough for such men as come over here. The rich stay in Europe; it is only the middling and poor that emigrate. Would you wish to travel in independent idleness, from north to south, you will find easy access and the most cheerful reception at every house; society without ostentation, good cheer without pride, and every decent diversion which the country affords, with little expense. It is no wonder that the European who has lived here a few years is desirous to remain. Europe with all its pomp is not to be compared to this continent for men of middle stations or laborers.

A European, when he first arrives, seems limited in his intentions as well as in his views; but he very suddenly alters his scale; 200 miles formerly appeared a very great distance; it is now but a trifle. He no sooner breathes our air than he forms schemes and embarks in designs he never would have thought of in his own country. There the plenitude of society confines many useful ideas, and often extinguishes the most laudable schemes which here ripen into maturity. Thus Europeans become Americans.

But how is this accomplished in that crowd of low, indigent people who flock here every year from all parts of Europe? I will tell you: they no sooner arrive than they immediately feel the good effects of that plenty of provisions we possess; they fare on our best food and are kindly entertained; their talents, character, and peculiar industry are immediately inquired into; they find countrymen everywhere disseminated, let them come from whatever part of Europe.

Let me select one as an epitome of the rest. He is hired, he goes to work and works moderately. Instead of being employed by a haughty person, he finds himself with his equal, placed at the substantial table of the farmer, or else at an inferior one as good. His wages are high, his bed is not like that bed of sorrow on which he used to lie. If he behaves with propriety and is faithful, he is caressed and becomes, as it were, a member of the family. He begins to feel the effects of a sort of resurrection; hitherto he had not lived but simply vegetated; he now feels himself a man, because he is treated as such. The laws of his own country had overlooked him in his insignificancy; the laws of this cover him with their mantle.

Judge what an alteration there must arise in the mind and thoughts of this man; he begins to forget his former servitude and dependence; his heart involuntarily swells and glows; this first swell inspires him with those new thoughts which constitute an American. What love can he entertain for a country where his existence was a burden to him! if he is a generous, good man, the love of his new adoptive parent will sink deep into his heart. He looks around and sees many a prosperous person who but a few years before was as poor as himself. This encourages him much; he begins to form some little scheme, the first, alas, he ever formed in his life. If he is wise, he thus spends two or three years, in which time he acquires knowledge, the use of tools, the modes of working the lands, felling trees, etc. This prepares the foundation of a good name, the most useful acquisition he can make. He is encouraged; he has gained friends; he is advised and directed; he feels bold; he purchases some land; he gives all the money he has brought over, as well as what he has earned, and trusts to the God of harvests for the discharge of the rest. His good name procures him credit; he is now possessed of the deed conveying to him and his posterity the fee simple and absolute property of 200 acres of land, situated on such a river.

What an epoch in this man's life! He has become a freeholder, from perhaps a German boor — he is now an American, a Pennsylvanian, an English subject. He is naturalized; his name is enrolled with those of the other citizens of the province. Instead of being a vagrant, he has a place of residence; he is called the inhabitant of such a county, or of such a district, and for the first time in his life counts for something; for hitherto he had been a cipher. I only repeat what I have heard many say, and no wonder their hearts should glow and be agitated with a multitude of feelings not easy to describe. From nothing to start into being; from a servant to the rank of master; from being the slave of some despotic prince to become a free man, invested with lands, to which every municipal blessing is

annexed! What a change indeed! It is in consequence of that change that he becomes an American.

This great metamorphosis has a double effect; it extinguishes all his European prejudices; he forgets that mechanism of subordination, that servility of disposition which poverty had taught him, and sometimes he is apt to forget it too much, often passing from one extreme to the other. If he is a good man, he forms schemes of future prosperity; he proposes to educate his children better than he has been educated himself; he thinks of future modes of conduct, feels an ardor to labor he never felt before. Pride steps in and leads him to everything that the laws do not forbid; he respects them; with a heartfelt gratitude he looks toward that government from whose wisdom all his new felicity is derived and under whose wings and protection he now lives. These reflections constitute him the good man and the good subject.

Ye poor Europeans; ye who sweat and work for the great — ye, who are obliged to give so many sheaves to the church, so many to your lords, so many to your government, and have hardly any left for yourselves — ye, who are held in less estimation than favorite hunters or useless lapdogs — ye, who only breathe the air of nature because it cannot be withheld from you; it is here that ye can conceive the possibility of those feelings I have been describing; it is here the laws of naturalization invite everyone to partake of our great labors and felicity, to till unrented, untaxed lands!

Many, corrupted beyond the power of amendment, have brought with them all their vices and, disregarding the advantages held out to them, have gone on in their former career of iniquity until they have been overtaken and punished by our laws. It is not every emigrant who succeeds; no, it is only the sober, the honest, and the industrious. Happy those to whom this transition has served as a powerful spur to labor, to prosperity, and to the good establishment of children, born in the days of their poverty; and who had no other portion to expect but the rags of their parents, had it not been for their happy emigration. Others again have been led astray by this enchanting scene; their new pride, instead of leading them to the fields, has kept them in idleness; the idea of possessing lands is all that satisfies them; though surrounded with fertility, they have moldered away their time in inactivity, misinformed husbandry, and ineffectual endeavors.

How much wiser, in general, the honest Germans than almost all other Europeans. They hire themselves to some of their wealthy landsmen, and in that apprenticeship learn everything that is necessary. They attentively consider the prosperous industry of others, which imprints on their minds a strong desire of possessing the same advantages. This forcible idea never quits them; they launch forth, and by dint of sobriety, rigid parsimony, and the most persevering industry, they commonly succeed. Their astonishment at their first arrival from Germany is very great; it is to them a dream. The contrast must be very powerful indeed. They observe their countrymen flourishing in every place; they travel through whole counties where not a word of English is spoken; and in the names and the language of the people they retrace Germany. They have been a useful acquisition to this continent, and to Pennsylvania in particular — to them it owes some share of its prosperity; to their mechanical knowledge and patience, it owes the finest mills in all America, the best teams of horses, and many other advantages. The recollection of their former poverty and slavery never quits them as long as they live.

The Scotch and the Irish might have lived in their own country perhaps as poor, but enjoying more civil advantages. The effects of their new situation do not strike them so forcibly, nor has it so lasting an effect. From whence the difference arises, I know not; but out of twelve families of emigrants of each country, generally, seven Scotch will succeed; nine German, and four Irish. The Scotch are frugal and laborious; but their wives cannot work so hard as the German women, who, on the contrary, vie with their husbands and often share with them the most severe toils of the field, which they understand better. They have therefore nothing to struggle against but the common casualties of nature. The Irish do not prosper so well; they love to drink and to quarrel, they are litigious, and soon take to the gun, which is the ruin of everything. They seem, besides, to labor under a greater degree of ignorance in husbandry than the others; perhaps it is that their industry had less scope and was less exercised at home. I have heard many relate how the land was parceled out in that kingdom. Their ancient conquest has been a great detriment to them, by oversetting their landed property. The lands, possessed by a few, are leased down *ad infinitum*; and the occupiers often pay five guineas an acre. The poor are worse lodged there than anywhere else in Europe. Their potatoes, which are easily raised, are perhaps an inducement to laziness. Their wages are too low and their whiskey too cheap.

There is no tracing observations of this kind without making at the same time very great allowances, as there are everywhere to be found a great many exceptions. The Irish themselves, from different parts of that kingdom, are very different. It is difficult to account for this surprising locality. One would think on so small an island all Irishmen must be alike, yet it is not so; they are different in their aptitude to and in their love of labor.

The Scotch, on the contrary, are all industrious and saving. They want nothing more than a field to exert themselves in; and they are commonly sure of succeeding.

The only difficulty they labor under is, that technical American knowledge, which requires some time to obtain. It is not easy for those who seldom saw a tree to conceive how it is to be felled, cut up, and split into rails and posts. . . .

After a foreigner from any part of Europe has arrived and become a citizen, let him devoutly listen to the voice of our great parent, which says to him, "Welcome to my shores, distressed European; bless the hour in which thou didst see my verdant fields, my fair navigable rivers, and my green mountains! If thou wilt work, I have bread for thee; if thou wilt be honest, sober, and industrious, I have greater rewards to confer on thee — ease and independence. I will give thee fields to feed and clothe thee; a comfortable fireside to sit by, and tell thy children by what means thou hast prospered; and a decent bed to repose on. I shall endow thee, besides, with the immunities of a freeman. If thou wilt carefully educate thy children, teach them gratitude to God, and reverence to that government, that philanthropic government which has collected here so many men and made them happy, I will also provide for thy progeny. And to every good man this ought to be the most holy, the most powerful, the most earnest wish he can possibly form, as well as the most consolatory prospect when he dies. Go thou, and work and till; thou shalt prosper, provided thou be just, grateful, and industrious."

———————◆———————

I cannot conclude without mentioning how sensibly I feel the dismemberment of America from this empire, and that I should be miserable indeed if I did not feel that no blame on that account can be laid at my door, and did I not also know that knavery seems to be so much the striking feature of its inhabitants that it may not in the end be an evil that they will become aliens to this kingdom.

GEORGE III, letter to Shelburne, Nov. 10, 1782

George Washington: Address to the Officers of the Army

By the end of the Revolutionary War, the financial resources of the Americans were exhausted. Soldiers who had fought for independence had to be sent home without pay. Some members of the army hoped to be able to take by force what they felt entitled to. One officer, Major John Armstrong, in what is known as the "Newburgh Address," urged the army to override civilian authority and disown a government that was unable to fulfill its obligations. General Washington met and defeated this suggestion in his address to the officers of the army on March 15, 1783. Promising that Congress would do them justice, Washington rebuked all those who would use the military to coerce the civilian authority.

Source: John Marshall, *The Life of George Washington, etc., etc.,* 2nd edition, Philadelphia, 1848, Vol. II, pp. 46-52.

Gentlemen:

By an anonymous summons, an attempt has been made to convene you together. How inconsistent with the rules of propriety! How unmilitary! And how subversive of all order and discipline, let the good sense of the Army decide.

In the moment of this summons, another anonymous production was sent into circulation, addressed more to the feelings and passions than to the reason and judgment of the Army. The author of the piece is entitled to much credit for the goodness of his pen, and I could wish he had as much credit for the rectitude of his heart; for, as men see through different optics and are induced by the reflecting faculties of the mind to use different means to attain the same end, the author of the address should have had more charity than to mark for suspicion the man who should recommend moderation and longer forbearance — or, in other words, who should not think as he thinks and acts as he advises. But he had another plan in view, in which candor and liberality of sentiment, regard to justice, and love of country have no part; and he was right to insinuate the darkest suspicion to effect the blackest design.

That the address is drawn with great art and is designed to answer the most insidious purposes; that it is calculated to impress the mind with an idea of premeditated injustice in the sovereign power of the United States, and rouse all those resentments which must unavoidably flow from such a belief; that the secret mover of this scheme (whoever he may be) intended to take advantage of the passions while they were warmed by the recollection of past distresses, without giving time for cool, deliberative thinking, and that composure of mind which is so necessary to give dignity and stability to measures is rendered too obvious, by the mode of conducting the business, to need other proof than a reference to the proceedings.

Thus much, gentlemen, I have thought it incumbent on me to observe to you, to show upon what principles I opposed the irregular and hasty meeting which was proposed to have been held on Tuesday last, and not because I wanted a disposition to give you every opportunity consistent with your own honor and the dignity of the Army to make known your grievances. If my conduct heretofore has not evinced to you that I have been a faithful friend to the Army, my declaration of it at this time would be equally unavailing and improper. But as I was among the first who embarked in the cause of our common country; as I have never left your side one moment but when called from you on public duty; as I have been the constant companion and witness of your distresses, and not among the last to feel and acknowledge your merits; as I have ever considered my own military reputation as inseparably connected with that of the Army; as my heart has ever expanded with joy when I have heard its praises, and my indignation has arisen when the mouth of detraction has been opened against it, it can *scarcely be supposed*, at this late stage of the war, that I am indifferent to its interests. But how are they to be promoted? The way is plain, says the anonymous addresser.

If war continues, remove into the unsettled country; there establish yourselves and leave an ungrateful country to defend itself. But who are they to defend? Our wives, our children, our farms, and other property which we leave behind us, or, in this state of hostile separation, are we to take the two first (the latter cannot be removed) to perish in a wilderness, with hunger, cold, and nakedness?

If peace takes place, never sheath your swords, says he, until you have obtained full and ample justice. This dreadful alternative, of either deserting our country in the extremest hour of her distress or turning our arms against it (which is the apparent object, unless Congress can be compelled into instant compliance), has something so shocking in it that humanity revolts at the idea. My God! What can this writer have in view, by recommending such measures? Can he be a friend to the Army? Can he be a friend to this country? Rather, is he not an insidious foe? Some emissary, perhaps, from New York, plotting the ruin of both by sowing the seeds of discord and separation between the civil and military powers of the continent? And what a compliment does he pay to our understandings when he recommends measures in either alternative, impracticable in their nature?

But here, gentlemen, I will drop the curtain, because it would be as imprudent in me to assign my reasons for this opinion as it would be insulting to your conception to suppose you stood in need of them. A moment's reflection will convince every dispassionate mind of the physical impossibility of carrying either proposal into execution.

There might, gentlemen, be an impropriety in my taking notice, in this address to you, of an anonymous production; but the manner in which that performance has been introduced to the Army, the effect it was intended to have, together with some other circumstances, will amply justify my observations on the tendency of that writing.

With respect to the advice given by the

author, to suspect the man who shall recommend moderate measures and longer forbearance, I spurn it, as every man who regards that liberty and reveres that justice for which we contend undoubtedly must; for if men are to be precluded from offering their sentiments on a matter which may involve the most serious and alarming consequences that can invite the consideration of mankind, reason is of no use to us — the freedom of speech may be taken away and, dumb and silent, we may be led, like sheep, to the slaughter.

I cannot, in justice to my own belief and what I have great reason to conceive is the intention of Congress, conclude this address without giving it as my decided opinion that that honorable body entertains exalted sentiments of the services of the Army; and, from a full conviction of its merits and sufferings, will do it complete justice. That their endeavors to discover and establish funds for this purpose have been unwearied, and will not cease till they have succeeded, I have not a doubt.

But like all other large bodies where there is a variety of different interests to reconcile, their deliberations are slow. Why then should we distrust them, and, in consequence of that distrust, adopt measures which may cast a shade over that glory which has been so justly acquired, and tarnish the reputation of an Army which is celebrated through all Europe for its fortitude and patriotism? And for what is this done? To bring the object we seek nearer? No! Most certainly, in my opinion, it will cast it at a greater distance.

For myself (and I take no merit in giving the assurance, being induced to it from principles of gratitude, veracity, and justice), a grateful sense of the confidence you have ever placed in me, a recollection of the cheerful assistance and prompt obedience I have experienced from you, under every vicissitude of fortune, and the sincere affection I feel for an Army I have so long had

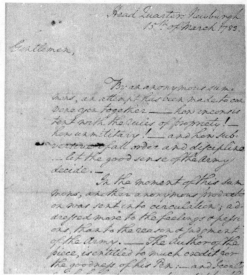

Massachusetts Historical Society

Manuscript of Washington's address to the Army, March 15, 1783

the honor to command, will oblige me to declare in this public and solemn manner that, in the attainment of complete justice for all your toils and dangers, and in the gratification of every wish, so far as may be done consistently with the great duty I owe my country and those powers we are bound to respect, you may freely command my services to the utmost of my abilities.

While I give you these assurances and pledge myself in the most unequivocal manner to exert whatever ability I am possessed of, in your favor, let me entreat you, gentlemen, on your part, not to take any measures which, viewed in the calm light of reason, will lessen the dignity and sully the glory you have hitherto maintained. Let me request you to rely on the plighted faith of your country, and place a full confidence in the purity of the intentions of Congress; that, previous to your dissolution as an Army they will cause all your accounts to be fairly liquidated, as directed in their resolutions, which were published to you two days ago, and that they will adopt the most effectual measures in their power to render ample justice to you for your faithful and meritorious services. And let me conjure you, in the name of our common country, as you value your own sacred honor, as you respect the rights of humanity, and as you regard the military and national character of America, to express your utmost horror and detestation of the man who wishes, under any specious pretenses, to overturn the liberties of our country, and who wickedly attempts to open the floodgates of civil discord and deluge our rising empire in blood.

By thus determining, and thus acting, you will pursue the plain and direct road to the attainment of your wishes. You will defeat the insidious designs of our enemies, who are compelled to resort from open force to secret artifice. You will give one more distinguished proof of unexampled patriotism and patient virtue, rising superior to the pressure of the most complicated sufferings; and you will, by the dignity of your conduct, afford occasion for posterity to say, when speaking of the glorious example you have exhibited to mankind, "had this day been wanting, the world had never seen the last stage of perfection to which human nature is capable of attaining."

George Washington: On Disbanding the Army

After the Revolution was over and while he waited for the British to evacuate New York, George Washington wrote a circular letter to the state governors, expressing his hopes for the future of the United States. Claiming that the basic requirement for future happiness and security was "an indissoluble union," Washington asserted that the honor of the country required that the public debt and the nation's defenders be paid. His letter is a forthright statement of the problems facing the Confederation.

Source: *The Writings of George Washington*, John C. Fitzpatrick, ed., Vol. XXVI, Washington, 1938, pp. 483-496.

THE GREAT OBJECT for which I had the honor to hold an appointment in the service of my country being accomplished, I am now preparing to resign it into the hands of Congress, and to return to that domestic retirement which, it is well known, I left with the greatest reluctance; a retirement for which I have never ceased to sigh, through a long and painful absence, and in which (remote from the noise and trouble of the world) I meditate to pass the remainder of my life in a state of undisturbed repose. But before I carry this resolution into effect, I think it a duty incumbent on me to make this my last official communication; to congratulate you on the glorious events which heaven has been pleased to produce in our favor; to offer my sentiments respecting some important subjects which appear to me to be intimately connected with the tranquility of the United States; to take my leave of Your Excellency as a public character; and to give my final blessing to that country in whose service I have spent the prime of my life, for whose sake I have consumed so many anxious days and watchful nights, and whose happiness, being extremely dear to me, will always constitute no inconsiderable part of my own.

Impressed with the liveliest sensibility on this pleasing occasion, I will claim the indulgence of dilating the more copiously on the subjects of our mutual felicitation. When we consider the magnitude of the prize we contended for, the doubtful nature of the contest, and the favorable manner in which it has terminated, we shall find the greatest possible reason for gratitude and rejoicing. This is a theme that will afford infinite delight to every benevolent and liberal mind, whether the event in contemplation be considered as the source of present enjoyment or the parent of future happiness; and we shall have equal occasion to felicitate ourselves on the lot which Providence has assigned us, whether we view it in a natural, a political, or moral point of light.

The citizens of America, placed in the most enviable condition as the sole lords and proprietors of a vast tract of continent, comprehending all the various soils and climates of the world and abounding with all the necessaries and conveniences of life, are now, by the late satisfactory pacification, acknowledged to be possessed of absolute freedom and independency. They are, from this period, to be considered as the actors on a most conspicuous theater, which seems to be peculiarly designated by Providence for the display of human greatness and felicity. Here they are not only surrounded with everything which can contribute to the completion of private and domestic enjoyment, but Heaven has crowned all its other blessings by giving a fairer opportunity for political happiness than any other nation has ever been favored with. Nothing can illustrate these observations more forcibly than a recollection of the happy conjuncture of times and circumstances under which our republic assumed its rank among the nations.

The foundation of our empire was not laid in the gloomy age of ignorance and superstition but at an epoch when the rights of mankind were better understood and more clearly defined than at any former period. The researches of the human mind, after social happiness, have been carried to a great extent; the treasures of knowledge, acquired by the labors of philosophers, sages, and legislators through a long succession of years, are laid open for our use; and their collected wisdom may be happily applied in the establishment of our forms of government. The free cultivation of letters, the unbounded extension of commerce, the progressive refinement of manners, the growing liberality of sentiment, and, above all, the pure and benign light of revelation have had a meliorating influence on mankind and increased the blessings of society. At this auspicious period, the United States came into existence as a nation; and, if their citizens should not be completely free and happy, the fault will be entirely their own.

Such is our situation, and such are our prospects; but notwithstanding the cup of blessing is thus reached out to us; notwithstanding happiness is ours, if we have a disposition to seize the occasion and make it our own; yet it appears to me there is an option still left to the United States of America, that it is in their choice, and depends upon their conduct, whether they will be respectable and prosperous, or contemptible and miserable, as a nation. This is the time of their political probation; this is the moment when the eyes of the whole world are turned upon them; this is the moment to establish or ruin their national character forever; this is the favorable moment to give such a tone to our federal government as will enable it to answer the ends of its institution; or this may be the ill-fated moment for relaxing the powers of the Union, annihilating the cement of the Confederation, and exposing us to become the sport of European politics, which may play one state against another, to prevent their growing importance and to serve their own interested purposes. For, according to the system of policy the states shall adopt at this moment, they will stand or fall; and by their confirmation or lapse, it is yet to be decided whether the Revolution must ultimately be considered as a blessing or a curse — a blessing or a curse not to the present age alone, for with our fate will the destiny of unborn millions be involved.

With this conviction of the importance of the present crisis, silence in me would be a crime. I will therefore speak to Your Excellency the language of freedom and of sincerity without disguise. I am aware, however, that those who differ from me in political sentiment may perhaps remark I am stepping out of the proper line of my duty, and may possibly ascribe to arrogance or ostentation what I know is alone the result of the purest intention. But the rectitude of my own heart, which disdains such unworthy motives; the part I have hitherto acted in life; the determination I have formed of not taking any share in public business hereafter; the ardent desire I feel, and shall continue to manifest, of quietly enjoying in private life, after all the toils of war, the benefits of a wise and liberal government will, I flatter myself, sooner or later convince my countrymen that I could have no sinister views in delivering, with so little reserve, the opinions contained in this address.

There are four things which, I humbly conceive, are essential to the well-being, I may even venture to say to the existence, of the United States as an independent power.

First, an indissoluble union of the states under one federal head.

Second, a sacred regard to public justice.

Third, the adoption of a proper peace establishment; and,

Fourth, the prevalence of that pacific and friendly disposition among the people of the United States which will induce them to forget their local prejudices and policies; to make those mutual concessions which are requisite to the general prosperity; and, in some instances, to sacrifice their individual advantages to the interest of the community.

These are the pillars on which the glorious fabric of our independency and national character must be supported. Liberty is the basis; and whoever would dare to sap the foundation, or overturn the structure, under whatever specious pretext he may attempt it, will merit the bitterest execration and the severest punishment which can be inflicted by his injured country.

On the three first articles I will make a few observations, leaving the last to the good sense and serious consideration of those immediately concerned.

Under the first head, although it may not be necessary or proper for me, in this place, to enter into a particular disquisition on the principles of the Union, and to take up the great question which has been frequently agitated — whether it be expedient and requisite for the states to delegate a larger proportion of power to Congress or not — yet it will be a part of my duty, and that of every true patriot, to assert without reserve, and to insist upon, the following positions: That, unless the states will suffer Congress to exercise those prerogatives they are undoubtedly invested with by the constitution, everything must very rapidly tend to anarchy and confusion. That it is indispensable to the happiness of the individual states that there should be lodged somewhere a supreme power to regulate and govern the general concerns of the confederated republic, without which the Union cannot be of long duration. That there must be a faithful and pointed compliance, on the part of every state, with the late proposals and demands of Congress, or the most fatal consequences will ensue. That whatever measures have a tendency to dissolve the Union, or contribute to violate or lessen the sovereign authority, ought to be considered as hostile to the liberty and independency of America, and the authors of them treated accordingly. And lastly, that unless we can be enabled, by the concurrence of the states, to participate of the fruits of the Revolution and enjoy the essential benefits of civil society, under a form of government so free and uncorrupted, so happily guarded against the danger of oppression as has been devised and adopted by the Articles of Confederation, it will be a subject of regret that so much blood and treasure have been lavished for no purpose, that so many sufferings have been encountered without a compensation, and that so many sacrifices have been made in vain.

Many other considerations might here be adduced to prove that, without an entire conformity to the spirit of the Union, we cannot exist as an independent power. It will be sufficient for my purpose to mention but one or two which seem to me of the greatest importance.

It is only in our united character, as an empire, that our independence is acknowledged, that our power can be regarded, or our credit supported, among foreign nations. The treaties of the European powers with the United States of America will have no validity on a dissolution of the Union. We shall be left nearly in a state of nature; or we may find, by our own unhappy experience, that there is a natural and necessary progression from the extreme of anarchy to the extreme of tyranny, and that arbitrary power is most easily established on the ruins of liberty abused to licentiousness.

As to the second article, which respects the performance of public justice, Congress have, in their late address to the United States, almost exhausted the subject. They have explained their ideas so fully, and have enforced the obligations the states are under to render complete justice to all the public creditors with so much dignity and energy that, in my opinion, no real friend to the honor or independency of America can hesitate a single moment respecting the propriety of complying with the just and honorable measures proposed. If their arguments do

not produce conviction, I know of nothing that will have greater influence, especially when we recollect that the system referred to, being the result of the collected wisdom of the continent, must be esteemed, if not perfect, certainly the least objectionable of any that could be devised; and that, if it shall not be carried into immediate execution, a national bankruptcy, with all its deplorable consequences, will take place before any different plan can possibly be proposed and adopted. So pressing are the present circumstances, and such is the alternative now offered to the states.

The ability of the country to discharge the debts which have been incurred in its defense is not to be doubted; an inclination, I flatter myself, will not be wanting. The path of our duty is plain before us; honesty will be found, on every experiment, to be the best and only true policy. Let us then, as a nation, be just; let us fulfill the public contracts, which Congress had undoubtedly a right to make for the purpose of carrying on the war, with the same good faith we suppose ourselves bound to perform our private engagements. In the meantime, let an attention to the cheerful performance of their proper business, as individuals and as members of society, be earnestly inculcated on the citizens of America; then will they strengthen the hands of government and be happy under its protection. Everyone will reap the fruit of his labors, everyone will enjoy his own acquisitions, without molestation and without danger.

In this state of absolute freedom and perfect security, who will grudge to yield a very little of his property to support the common interest of society and ensure the protection of government? Who does not remember the frequent declarations, at the commencement of the war, that we should be completely satisfied if, at the expense of one-half, we could defend the remainder of our possessions? Where is the man to be found who wishes to remain indebted for the defense of his own person and property to the exertions, the bravery, and the blood of others without making one generous effort to repay the debt of honor and gratitude? In what part of the continent shall we find any man, or body of men, who would not blush to stand up and propose measures purposely calculated to rob the soldier of his stipend and the public creditor of his due? And were it possible that such a flagrant instance of injustice could ever happen, would it not excite the general indignation, and tend to bring down upon the authors of such measures the aggravated vengeance of heaven?

If, after all, a spirit of disunion, or a temper of obstinacy and perverseness, should manifest itself in any of the states; if such an ungracious disposition should attempt to frustrate all the happy effects that might be expected to flow from the Union; if there should be a refusal to comply with the requisition for funds to discharge the annual interest of the public debts; and if that refusal should revive again all those jealousies and produce all those evils which are now happily removed, Congress, who have, in all their transactions, shown a great degree of magnanimity and justice, will stand justified in the sight of God and man. And the state alone which puts itself in opposition to the aggregate wisdom of the continent, and follows such mistaken and pernicious counsels, will be responsible for all the consequences.

For my own part, conscious of having acted, while a servant of the public, in the manner I conceived best suited to promote the real interests of my country; having, in consequence of my fixed belief, in some measure pledged myself to the Army that their country would finally do them complete and ample justice; and not wishing to conceal any instance of my official conduct from the eyes of the world, I have thought proper to transmit to Your Excellency the enclosed collection of papers, relative to the half pay and commutation granted by Congress to the officers of the Army.

From these communications, my decided sentiments will be clearly comprehended, together with the conclusive reasons which induced me, at an early period, to recommend the adoption of this measure, in the most earnest and serious manner. As the proceedings of Congress, the Army, and myself are open to all, and contain, in my opinion, sufficient information to remove the prejudices and errors which may have been entertained by any, I think it unnecessary to say anything more than just to observe that the resolutions of Congress now alluded to are undoubtedly as absolutely binding upon the United States as the most solemn acts of confederation or legislation.

As to the idea, which, I am informed, has in some instances prevailed, that the half pay and commutation are to be regarded merely in the odious light of a pension, it ought to be exploded forever. That provision should be viewed as it really was — a reasonable compensation offered by Congress at a time when they had nothing else to give to the officers of the Army for services then to be performed. It was the only means to prevent a total dereliction of the service. It was a part of their hire. I may be allowed to say, it was the price of their blood, and of your independency. It is therefore more than a common debt; it is a debt of honor; it can never be considered as a pension or gratuity, nor be canceled until it is fairly discharged.

With regard to a distinction between officers and soldiers, it is sufficient that the uniform experience of every nation of the world, combined with our own, proves the utility and propriety of the discrimination. Rewards, in proportion to the aids the public derives from them, are unquestionably due to all its servants. In some lines, the soldiers have perhaps generally had as ample a compensation for their services by the large bounties which have been paid to them as their officers will receive in the proposed commutation; in others if, besides the donation of lands, the payment of arrearages of clothing and wages (in which articles all the component parts of the Army must be put upon the same footing), we take into the estimate the *douceurs* [presents] many of the soldiers have received, and the gratuity of one year's full pay, which is promised to all, possibly their situation (every circumstance being duly considered) will not be deemed less eligible than that of the officers. Should a further reward, however, be judged equitable, I will venture to assert no one will enjoy greater satisfaction than myself on seeing an exemption from taxes for a limited time (which has been petitioned for in some instances) or any other adequate immunity or compensation granted to the brave defenders of their country's cause; but neither the adoption nor rejection of this proposition will in any manner affect, much less militate against, the act of Congress by which they have offered five years' full pay, in lieu of the half pay for life, which had been before promised to the officers of the Army.

Before I conclude the subject of public justice, I cannot omit to mention the obligations this country is under to that meritorious class of veteran noncommissioned officers and privates who have been discharged for inability, in consequence of the resolution of Congress of April 23, 1782, on an annual pension for life. Their peculiar sufferings, their singular merits, and claims to that provision need only be known to interest all the feelings of humanity in their behalf. Nothing but a punctual payment of their annual allowance can rescue them from the most complicated misery; and nothing could be a more melancholy and distressing sight than to behold those who have shed their blood or lost their limbs in the service of their country without a shelter, without a friend, and without the means of obtaining any of the necessaries or comforts of life, compelled to beg their daily bread from door to door. Suffer me to recommend those of this description belonging to your state to the warmest patronage of Your Excellency and your legislature.

It is necessary to say but a few words on the third topic which was proposed, and which regards particularly the defense of the republic, as there can be little doubt but Congress will recommend a proper peace establishment for the United States, in which a due attention will be paid to the importance of placing the militia of the Union upon a regular and respectable footing. If this should be the case, I would beg leave to urge the great advantage of it in the strongest terms. The militia of this country must be considered as the palladium of our security, and the first effectual resort in case of hostility. It is essential, therefore, that the same system should pervade the whole; that the formation and discipline of the militia of the continent should be absolutely uniform; and that the same species of arms, accouterments, and military apparatus should be introduced in every part of the United States. No one who has not learned it from experience can conceive the difficulty, expense, and confusion which result from a contrary system, or the vague arrangements which have hitherto prevailed.

If, in treating of political points, a greater latitude than usual has been taken in the course of this address, the importance of the crisis and the magnitude of the objects in discussion must be my apology. It is, however, neither my wish nor expectation that the preceding observations should claim any regard, except so far as they shall appear to be dictated by a good intention, consonant to the immutable rules of justice, calculated to produce a liberal system of policy, and founded on whatever experience may have been acquired by a long and close attention to public business.

Here I might speak with the more confidence from my actual observations; and if it would not swell this letter (already too prolix) beyond the bounds I had prescribed to myself, I could demonstrate to every mind open to conviction that in less time, and with much less expense than has been incurred the war might have been brought to the same happy conclusion if the resources of the continent could have been properly drawn forth; that the distresses and disappointments which have very often occurred have, in too many instances, resulted more from a want of energy in the continental government than a deficiency of means in the particular states; that the inefficacy of measures arising from the want of an adequate authority in the supreme power, from a partial compliance with the requisitions of Congress in some of the states, and from a failure of punctuality in others, while it tended to damp the zeal of those which were more willing to exert themselves, served also to accumulate the expenses of the war and to frustrate the best concerted plans; and that the discouragement occasioned by the complicated difficulties and embarrassments in which our affairs were by this means involved would have long ago produced the dissolution of any army less patient, less virtuous, and less persevering than that which I have had the honor to command. But, while I mention these things, which are notorious facts, as the defects of our federal constitution, particularly in the prosecution of a war, I beg it may be understood that, as I have ever taken a pleasure in gratefully acknowledging the assistance and support I have derived from every class of citizens, so shall I always be happy to do justice to the unparalleled exertions of the individual states on many interesting occasions.

I have thus freely disclosed what I wished to make known before I surrendered up my public trust to those who committed it to me. The task is now accomplished. I now bid adieu to Your Excellency as the chief magistrate of your state, at the same time I bid a last farewell to the cares of office and all the employments of public life.

It remains, then, to be my final and only request that Your Excellency will communicate these sentiments to your legislature at their next meeting, and that they may be considered as the legacy of one who has ardently wished, on all occasions, to be useful to his country, and who, even in the shade of retirement, will not fail to implore the divine benediction upon it.

I now make it my earnest prayer that God would have you, and the state over which you preside, in His holy protection; that He would incline the hearts of the citizens to cultivate a spirit of subordination and obedience to government; to entertain a brotherly affection and love for one another, for their fellow citizens of the United States at large, and particularly for their brethren who have served in the field; and finally, that He would most graciously be pleased to dispose us all to do justice, to love mercy, and to demean ourselves with that charity, humility, and pacific temper of mind which were the characteristics of the Divine Author of our blessed religion, and without a humble imitation of whose example in these things we can never hope to be a happy nation.

May we never see another war! For in my opinion there never was a good war or a bad peace.

BENJAMIN FRANKLIN, letter to Josiah Quincy, Sept. 1783

George Washington: Public Lands for Veterans

Washington's army throughout the Revolution had suffered from official neglect and meager pay. Washington repeatedly urged Congress to meet its obligations to the soldiers of the Continental Army. "If, retiring from the field, they [the officers] are to grow old in poverty, wretchedness and contempt," he wrote in 1782; "if they are to wade thro' the vile mire of dependency, and owe the miserable remnant of that life to charity, which has hitherto been spent in honor; then shall I have learned what ingratitude is, then shall I have realized a tale, which will embitter every moment of my future life." On June 17, 1783, Washington requested, in a letter to Congress, that it set aside public lands for the veterans of the war.

Source: William Parker Cutler and Julia Perkins Cutler, *Life, Journals, and Correspondence of Rev. Manasseh Cutler*, Cincinnati, 1888, Vol. I, pp. 172-174.

I have the honor of transmitting to Your Excellency, for the consideration of Congress, a petition from a large number of officers of the army in behalf of themselves and such other officers and soldiers of the Continental Army as are entitled to rewards in lands, and may choose to avail themselves of any privileges and grants which may be obtained in consequence of the present solicitation. I enclose also the copy of a letter from Brigadier General Putnam, in which the sentiments and expectations of the petitioners are more fully explained, and in which the ideas of occupying the posts in the western country will be found to correspond very nearly with those I have some time since communicated to a committee of Congress, in treating of the subject of a peace establishment. I will beg leave to make a few more observations on the general benefits of the location and settlement now proposed, and then submit the justice

and policy of the measure to the wisdom of Congress.

Although I pretend not myself to determine how far the district of unsettled country, which is described in the petition, is free from the claim of every state, or how far this disposal of it may interfere with the views of Congress, yet it appears to me this is the tract which, from local position and peculiar advantages, ought to be first settled in preference to any other whatever; and I am perfectly convinced that it can not be so advantageously settled by any other class of men as by disbanded officers and soldiers of the Army to whom the faith of government has long since been pledged, that lands should be granted at the expiration of the war in certain proportions, agreeably to their respective grades.

I am induced to give my sentiments thus freely on the advantages to be expected from this plan of colonization, because it would connect our governments with the frontiers, extend our settlements progressively, and plant a brave, a hardy, and respectable race of people as our advanced post, who would be always ready and willing (in case of hostility) to combat the savages and check their incursions. A settlement formed by such men would give security to our frontiers; the very name of it would awe the Indians, and more than probably prevent the murder of many innocent families, who frequently, in the usual mode of extending our settlements and encroachments on the hunting grounds of the natives, fall the hapless victims to savage barbarity. Besides the emoluments which might be derived from the peltry trade at our factories, if such should be established, the appearance of so formidable a settlement in the vicinity of their towns (to say nothing of the barrier it would form against our other neighbors) would be the most likely means to enable us to purchase, upon equitable terms, of the aborigines, their right of preoccupancy, and to induce them to relinquish our territories and to remove into the illimitable regions of the West.

Much more might be said of the public utility of such a location, as well as of the private felicity it would afford to the individuals concerned in it. I will venture to say it is the most rational and practicable scheme which can be adopted by a great proportion of the officers and soldiers of our Army, and promises them more happiness than they can expect in any other way. The settlers being in the prime of life, inur-

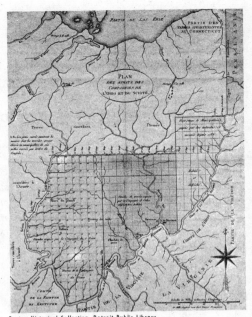

Burton Historical Collection, Detroit Public Library

Tardieu map of Ohio, showing lands designated for veterans in the northern part of the territory

ed to hardship, and taught by experience to accommodate themselves in every situation, going in a considerable body, and under the patronage of government, would enjoy in the first instance advantages in procuring subsistence, and all the necessaries for a comfortable beginning, superior to any common class of emigrants, and quite unknown to those who have heretofore extended themselves beyond the Appalachian Mountains. They may expect, after a little perseverance, competence and independence for themselves, a pleasant retreat in old age, and the fairest prospects for their children.

If to be venerated for benevolence: if to be admired for talents: if to be esteemed for patriotism: if to be beloved for philanthropy, can gratify the human mind, you must have the pleasing consolation that you have not lived in vain.
GEORGE WASHINGTON, letter to Benjamin Franklin, 1789

Noah Webster: The Union of the American States

The problem of copyrighting a speller that he had compiled brought Noah Webster into politics in 1782. At that time the federal government had no authority in copyright matters, and none of the newly established states had enacted a copyright law. Webster began to promote copyright legislation in thirteen state capitals. These efforts led him to become one of the early advocates of a strong federal government. In Sketches of American Policy, *a pamphlet printed in 1785, Webster stated his views on government.*

Source: *Sketches of American Policy,* 1785 [Harry R. Warfel, ed., New York, 1937, pp. 3-48].

No PERSON can be said to enjoy civil liberty who has no share in legislation, and no person is secure in society unless the laws are known and respected.

In despotic governments, where the scepter is swayed by an individual, the ruler, whether denominated an emperor, a king, or a bashaw [pasha], having the sole right of making and executing laws, is the only person who enjoys any liberty. Every individual within his dominions is a slave. In this case, the interest of the individual, of the magistrate, and of the supreme power are all united, and government is of course as active as possible. Hence the vigor and decision of military operations when the power of the general is without limitation.

Despotic power is not always tyrannical; in the hands of a mild prince, it may be favorable to the rights of the subject. But such is the depravity of human nature that it is madness in a people to vest such power in an individual. Denmark furnishes the only instance of absolute power conferred on an individual by the solemn act of the people; and it furnishes perhaps the only instance of absolute power that has not been abused.

A limited monarchy, where the power of the sovereign is restrained by certain laws, is far preferable to despotism. But if a monarch has the power of making *any* laws, the people are so far slaves. However such power may be sanctified by time, custom, or hereditary succession, the exercise of it, in a single instance, is an act of tyranny. The king of Great Britain cannot make a single law binding upon his subjects, but he can defeat every bill that is proposed by Parliament. Is such a nation free? The English boast of their privileges, and with some reason, when they draw a comparison between themselves and the vassals of a Polish nobleman. But when compared with the eternal immutable rights of man, their privileges shrink into insignificance. With what face can a nation boast of their liberties, when an individual of that nation can, with a single expression, "the king will consider of it," defeat any measure that the Parliament may adopt? Neither the title nor the dignities of royalty can make a king more honest or less fallible than another man; and upon the principles of natural right, any member of Parliament might as well negative an act of that body as the king. A nation which is subject to the will of an individual is a nation of slaves, whether that nation receives its laws from the arbitrary will of its sovereign, or whether the people reserve to themselves the right of making their own laws and give their sovereign full power to annihilate them at pleasure. In either case a nation is at the mercy of an individual.

An aristocracy is a form of government of all others the most to be dreaded; I mean where the right of legislation is vested in a hereditary nobility. The idea of being born a legislator is shocking to common sense, and the fact is a reproach to human nature. In such a government, the interest of the people is out of question. The interest of the supreme power, of the magistracy, and of the individual are here blended, and they are distinct and independent of the interest of the people. The consequence is that when these interests coincide in all the members of the legislature, they are combined to oppress their subjects, and when they clash, as often happens, the state is torn with dissensions and civil war.

From the preceding consideration, I deduce this definition of the most perfect practicable system of government; "a government where the right of making laws is vested in the greatest number of individuals, and the power of executing them in the smallest number." In large communities, the individuals are too numerous to assemble for the purpose of legislation; for which reason the people appear by substitutes or agents; persons of their own choice. A representative democracy seems therefore to be the most perfect system of government that is practicable on earth. . . .

The theory of civil government exhibited in the preceding pages [is] designed as introductory to some remarks on the American states.

A tolerable acquaintance with history and a small knowledge of the English settlements on this continent teach us that the situation of these states is, in every point of view, the reverse of what has been the infant situation of all other nations.

In the first place, our constitutions of civil government have been framed in the most enlightened period of the world. All other systems of civil polity have been begun in the rude times of ignorance and savage ferocity; fabricated at the voice of necessity, without science and without experience. America, just beginning to exist in an advanced period of human improvement, has the science and the experience of all nations to direct her in forming plans of government. By this advantage she is enabled to supply the defects and avoid the errors incident to the policy of uncivilized nations, and to lay a broad basis for the perfection of human society. The legislators of the American states are neither swayed by a blind veneration for an independent clergy nor awed by the frowns of a tyrant. Their civil policy is or ought to be the result of the collected wisdom of all nations, and their religion, that of the Savior of mankind. If they do not establish and perpetuate the best systems of government on earth, it will be their own fault, for nature has given them every advantage they could desire.

In the next place, an equal distribution of landed property is a singular advantage as being the foundation of republican governments and the security of freedom. The New England states are peculiarly happy in this respect. Lands descend equally to all the heirs of the deceased possessor and perpetuities are entirely barred. In Connecticut the eldest male heir inherits two shares; this is a relic of ancient prejudices in favor of the rights of primogeniture, which the wisdom of succeeding legislatures will undoubtedly abolish. An act passed the legislature of New York a few years past, destroying and barring entailments and ordering that all intestate estates should descend to all the heirs in equal portions. No act was ever better timed or calculated to produce more salutary effects. The states of

Pennsylvania and North Carolina have made it an article in their constitutions that no estates shall be perpetual. I am not sufficiently acquainted with the constitutions of the other states to inform whether perpetuities are barred or not; but they may be avoided by a *common recovery,* a fiction often practised in the English courts of law.

But although the southern states possess too much of the aristocratic genius of European governments, yet it is probable that their future tendency will be toward republicanism. For if the African slave trade is prohibited, it must gradually diminish the large estates which are entirely cultivated by slaves, as these will probably decrease without recruits from Africa. And it is not probable that their place can be supplied by white people so long as vast tracts of valuable land are uncultivated, and poor people can purchase the fee of the soil.

But should the present possessors of lands continue to hold and cultivate them, still there is a new set of men springing up in the back parts of those states more hardy and independent than the peasants of the low countries and more averse to aristocracy. The unhealthiness of the climate in the flatlands is a circumstance that will contribute to the rapid population of the mountains where the air is more salubrious.

The idea, therefore, that the genius of the southern states is verging towards republicanism, appears to be supported by substantial reasons. It is much to be wished that such an idea might be well grounded, for nature knows no distinctions, and government ought to know none, but such as are merited by personal virtues.

The confiscation of many large estates in every part of the union is another circumstance favorable to an equal distribution of property. The local situation of all the states and the genius of the inhabitants in most of them tend to destroy all the aristocratic ideas which were introduced from our parent country.

Necessarily connected with an equal distribution of landed property is the annihilation of all hereditary distinctions of rank. Such distinctions are inconsistent with the nature of popular governments. Whatever pretensions some states have made to the name of *republics;* yet those that have permitted perpetual distinctions of property and hereditary titles of honor with a right of legislation annexed certainly never deserved the name of popular governments; and they have never been able to preserve their freedom. Wherever two or more orders of men have been established with hereditary privileges of rank, they have always quarreled till the power or intrigues of the superior orders have divested the people of all their civil liberties. In some countries they retain a show of freedom sufficient to amuse them into obedience; but in most states, they have lost even the appearance of civil rights.

Congress, aware of the tendency of an unequal division of property and the evils of an aristocracy or a mixed form of government, have inserted a clause in the Articles of Confederation forever barring all titles of nobility in the American states; a precaution evincive equally of the foresight, the integrity, and the republican principles of that august body.

Another circumstance favorable to liberty and peculiar to America is a most liberal plan of ecclesiastical policy. Dr. Price has anticipated most of my observations on this head. If sound sense is to be found on earth, it is in his reasoning on this subject. The American constitutions are the most liberal in this particular of any on earth; and yet some of them have retained some badges of bigotry. A profession of the Christian religion is necessary in the states to entitle a man to office. In some states, it is requisite to subscribe [to] certain articles of faith. These requisitions are the effect of the same abominable prejudices that have enslaved the human mind in all countries;

which alone have supported error and all absurdities in religion. If there are any human means of promoting a millennial state of society, the only means are a general diffusion of knowledge and a free unlimited indulgence given to religious persuasions, without distinction and without preference. When this event takes place, and I believe it certainly will, the best religion will have the most advocates. Nothing checks the progress of truth like human establishments. Christianity spread with rapidity before the temporal powers interfered; but when the civil magistrate undertook to guard the truth from error, its progress was obstructed, the simplicity of the gospel was corrupted with human inventions, and the efforts of Christendom have not yet been able to bring it back to its primitive purity.

The American states have gone far in assisting the progress of truth; but they have stopped short of perfection. They ought to have given every honest citizen an equal right to enjoy his religion and an equal title to all civil emoluments without obliging him to tell his religion. Every interference of the civil power in regulating opinion is an impious attempt to take the business of the Deity out of His own hands; and every preference given to any religious denomination is so far slavery and bigotry. This is a blemish in our constitutions, reproachful in proportion to the light and knowledge of our legislators.

The general education of youth is an article in which the American states are superior to all nations. In Great Britain the arts and sciences are cultivated to perfection; but the instruction of the lowest classes of people is by no means equal to the American yeomanry. The institution of schools, particularly in the New England states, where the poorest children are instructed in reading, writing, and arithmetic at the public expense, is a noble regulation, calculated to dignify the human species.

This institution is the necessary conse-quence of the genius of our governments; at the same time, it forms the firmest security of our liberties. It is scarcely possible to reduce an enlightened people to civil or ecclesiastical tyranny. Deprive them of knowledge, and they sink almost insensibly in vassalage. Ignorance cramps the powers of the mind at the same time that it blinds men to all their natural rights. Knowledge enlarges the understanding, and at the same time it gives a spring to all the intellectual faculties which direct the deliberations of the cabinet and the enterprises of the field. A general diffusion of science is our best guard against the approaches of corruption, the prevalence of religious error, the intrigues of ambition, and against the open assaults of external foes.

In the southern states education is not so general. Gentlemen of fortune give their children a most liberal education; and no part of America produces greater lawyers, statesmen, and divines; but the body of the people are indifferently educated. In New England it is rare to find a person who cannot read and write; but if I am rightly informed, the case is different in the southern states. The education, however, of the common people in every part of America is equal to that of any nation; and the southern states, where schools have been much neglected, are giving more encouragement to literature.

It is not my design to enumerate all the political and commercial advantages of this country; but only to mention some of the characteristic circumstances which distinguish America from all the kingdoms and states of which we have any knowledge.

One further remark, however, which I cannot omit is that the people in America are necessitated by their local situation to be more sensible and discerning than nations which are limited in territory and confined to the arts of manufacture. In a populous country where arts are carried to great perfection, the mechanics are obliged to la-

bor constantly upon a single article. Every
art has its several branches, one of which
employs a man all his life. A man who
makes heads of pins or springs of watches
spends his days in that manufacture and
never looks beyond it. This manner of fabricating things for the use and convenience
of life is the means of perfecting the arts;
but it cramps the human mind by confining
all its faculties to a point. In countries thinly inhabited, or where people live principally by agriculture as in America, every man
is in some measure an artist: he makes a
variety of utensils, rough indeed, but such
as will answer his purpose; he is a husband-
man in summer and a mechanic in winter;
he travels about the country; he converses
with a variety of professions; he reads public papers; he has access to a parish library
and thus becomes acquainted with history
and politics, and every man in New England is a theologian. This will always be
the case in America, so long as there is a
vast tract of fertile land to be cultivated
which will occasion emigrations from the
states already settled. Knowledge is diffused
and genius roused by the very situation of
America.

I have already mentioned three principles
which have generally operated in combining
the members of society under some supreme power: a standing army, religion,
and fear of an external force. A standing
army is necessary in all despotic governments. Religion, by which I mean superstition, or human systems of absurdity, is an
engine used in almost all governments, and
has a powerful effect where people are kept
in ignorance. The fear of conquest is an infallible bond of union where states are surrounded by martial enemies. After people
have been long accustomed to obey, whatever be the first motive of their obedience,
there is formed a habit of subordination
which has an almost irresistible influence,
and which will preserve the tranquillity of
government, even when coercion or the first

principle of obedience has ceased to operate.

None of the foregoing principles can be
the bond of union among the American
states. A standing army will probably never
exist in America. It is the instrument of tyranny and ought to be forever banished from
free governments. Religion will have little
or no influence in preserving the union of
the states. The Christian religion is calculated to cherish a spirit of peace and harmony
in society, but will not balance the influence
of jarring interests in different governments.
As to neighboring foes, we have none to
fear; and European nations are too wise or
have too much business at home to think of
conquering these states.

We must therefore search for new principles in modeling our political system. The
American constitutions are founded on principles different from those of all nations,
and we must find new bonds of union to
perpetuate the confederation.

In the first place, there must be a supreme power at the head of the Union,
vested with authority to make laws that respect the states in general and to compel
obedience to those laws. Such a power
must exist in every society or no man is
safe.

In order to understand the nature of such
a power, we must recur to the principles
explained under the first head of these observations.

All power is vested in the people. That
this is their natural and unalienable right is
a position that will not be disputed. The
only question is how this power shall be
exerted to effect the ends of government. If
the people retain the power of executing
laws, we have seen how this division will
destroy all its effect. Let us apply the definition of a perfect system of government to
the American states. "The right of making
laws for the United States should be vested
in all their inhabitants by legal and equal
representation, and the right of executing
those laws committed to the smallest possi-

ble number of magistrates, chosen annually by Congress and responsible to them for their administration." Such a system of continental government is perfect — it is practicable — and may be rendered permanent. I will even venture to assert that such a system may have, in legislation, all the security of republican circumspection; and in administration, all the energy and decision of a monarchy.

But must the powers of Congress be increased? This question implies gross ignorance of the nature of government. The question ought to be, must the American states be united? And if this question is decided in the affirmative, the next question is whether the states can be said to be united without a legislative head? Or in other words, whether thirteen states can be said to be united in government when each state reserves to itself the sole powers of legislation? The answer to all such questions is extremely easy. If the states propose to form and preserve a confederacy, there must be a supreme head in which the power of all the states is united.

There must be a supreme head, clothed with the same power to make and enforce laws respecting the general policy of all the states as the legislatures of the respective states have to make laws binding on those states respecting their own internal police. The truth of this is taught by the principles of government, and confirmed by the experience of America. Without such a head, the states cannot be *united;* and all attempts to conduct the measures of the continent will prove but governmental farces. So long as any individual state has power to defeat the measures of the other twelve, our pretended union is but a name, and our confederation a cobweb.

What, it will be asked, must the states relinquish their sovereignty and independence, and give Congress their rights of legislation? I beg to know what we mean by *United States?* If, after Congress have passed a resolution of a general tenor, the states are still at liberty to comply or refuse, I must insist that they are not *united;* they are as separate as they ever were, and Congress is merely an advisory body. If people imagine that Congress ought to be merely a council of advice, they will some time or other discover their most egregious mistake. If 3,000,000 people united under thirteen different heads are to be governed or brought to act in concert by a *Resolve, that it be recommended,* I confess myself a stranger to history and to human nature. The very idea of uniting discordant interests and restraining the selfish and the wicked principles of men by advisory resolutions is too absurd to have advocates even among illiterate peasants. The resolves of Congress are always treated with respect, and during the late war they were efficacious. But their efficacy proceeded from a principle of common safety which united the interests of all the states; but peace has removed that principle, and the states comply with or refuse the requisitions of Congress just as they please.

The idea of each state preserving its sovereignty and independence in their full latitude, and yet holding up the appearance of a confederacy and a concert of measures, is a solecism in politics that will sooner or later dissolve the pretended union, or work other mischiefs sufficient to bear conviction to every mind.

But what shall be done? What system of government shall be framed to guard our rights, to cement our union, and give energy to public measures? The answers to these questions are obvious and a plan of confederacy extremely easy. Let the government of the United States be formed upon the general plan of government in each of the several states. Let us examine the constitution of Connecticut.

The inhabitants of Connecticut form one body politic, under the name of the Governor and Company of the State of Connecticut. The whole body of freemen, in their collective capacity, is the supreme power of the state. By consent and firm compact or constitution, this supreme power is delegated to representatives chosen in a legal manner and duly qualified. These representatives, properly assembled, make laws binding on the whole state; that is, the supreme power or state makes laws binding on itself. The supreme power and the subjects of that supreme power are the same body of men. As a collective body, the citizens are all an individual; as separate individuals, they are subjects as numerous as the citizens.

When laws are enacted they are of a general tenor; they respect the whole state and cannot be abrogated but by the whole state. But the whole state does not attempt to execute the laws. The state elects a governor or supreme magistrate and clothes him with the power of the whole state to enforce the laws. Under him a number of subordinate magistrates, such as judges of courts, justices of the peace, sheriffs, etc., are appointed to administer the laws in their respective departments. These are commissioned by the governor or supreme magistrate. Thus the whole power of the state is brought to a single point; it is united in one person.

If the representation of the freemen is equal and the elections frequent, if the magistrates are constitutionally chosen and responsible for their administration, such a government is of all others the most free and safe. The form is the most perfect on earth. While bills are depending before the supreme power, every citizen has a right to oppose them. A perfect freedom of debate is essential to a free government. But when a bill has been formally debated and is enacted into a law, it is the act of the whole state, and no individual has a right to resist it.

But, as it has been before observed, the acts of the supreme power must be general; it has therefore by a general law delegated full authority to certain inferior corporations to make bylaws for the convenience of small districts and not repugnant to the laws of the state. Thus every town in Connecticut is a supreme power for certain purposes and the cities are invested with extensive privileges. These corporations, for certain purposes, are independent of the legislature; they make laws, appoint officers, and exercise jurisdiction within their own limits. As bodies politic, they are sovereign and independent; as members of a large community, they are mere subjects. In the same manner, the head of a family is sovereign in his domestic economy, but as a part of the state, he is a subject.

Let a similar system of government be extended to the United States. As towns and cities are, as to their small matters, sovereign and independent, and as to their general concerns, mere subjects of the state; so let the several states, as to their own police, be sovereign and independent, but as to the common concerns of all, let them be mere subjects of the federal head. If the necessity of a union is admitted, such a system is the only means of effecting it. However independent each state may be and ought to be in things that relate to itself merely, yet as a part of a greater body it must be a subject of that body in matters that relate to the whole. A system of continental government, thus organized, may establish and perpetuate the confederation without infringing the rights of any particular state. But the power of all the states must be reduced to a narrow compass; it must center in a single body of men; and it must not be liable to be controlled or defeated by an individual state. The states assembled in Congress must have the same compulsory power in matters that concern the whole as a man has in his own family, as a city has within the limits of the corporation, and as the legislature of a state has in the limits of that state, respecting matters that fall within their several jurisdictions.

I beg to know how otherwise the states will be governed as a collective body? Every man knows by his own experience that even families are not to be kept in subordination by recommendations and advice. How much less then will such flimsy things command the obedience of a whole continent? They will not — they do not. A single state, by noncompliance with resolves of Congress, has repeatedly defeated the most salutary measures of the states proposed by Congress and acceded to by twelve out of thirteen.

I will suppose for the present that a measure recommended by Congress and adopted by a majority of the legislatures should be really repugnant to the interest of a single state, considered in its separate capacity. Would it be right for that state to oppose it? While the measure is in agitation it is the undoubted privilege of every state to oppose it by every argument. But when it is passed by the concurrence of a legal majority, it is the duty of every state to acquiesce. So far from resisting the measure, those very individuals who opposed it in debate ought to support it in execution. The reason is very plain: society and government can be supported on no other principles. The interest of individuals must always give place to the interest of the whole community. This principle of government is not perfect, but it is as perfect as any principle that can be carried into effect on this side [of] heaven.

It is for the interest of the American states either to be united or not. If their union is unnecessary, let Congress be annihilated, or let them be denominated a council of advice and considered as such. They must then be stripped of their power of making peace and war and of a variety of prerogatives given them by the Articles of Confederation. In this case we ourselves and the states of Europe should know what kind of a being Congress is; what dependence can be placed on their resolves; what is the nature of the treaties which they have made and the debts they have contracted.

But if the states are all serious in a design to establish a permanent *union,* let their sincerity be evinced by their public conduct.

Suppose the legislature of Rhode Island had no power to compel obedience to its laws, but any town in that state had power to defeat every public measure. Could any laws be rendered effectual? Could it with propriety be called a state? Could it be said that there was any supreme power, or any government? Certainly not. Suppose the smallest town in Connecticut had power to defeat the most salutary measures of the state; would not every other town rise in arms against any attempt to exert such a power? They certainly would. The truth of the case is, where the power of a people is not united in some individual or small body of individuals, but continues divided among the members of a society, that power is nothing at all. This fact is clearly proved under the first head of these observations, and more clearly felt by our fatal experience.

The American states, as to their general internal police, are *not united;* there is no supreme power at their head; they are in a perfect state of nature and independence as to each other; each is at liberty to fight its neighbor and there is no sovereign to call forth the power of the continent to quell the dispute or punish the aggressor. It is not in the power of the Congress — they have no command over the militia of the states — each state commands its own, and should any one be disposed for civil war, the sword must settle the contest and the weakest be sacrificed to the strongest.

It is now in the power of the states to form a continental government as efficacious as the interior government of any particular state.

The general concerns of the continent may be reduced to a few heads; but in all the affairs that respect the whole, Congress must have the same power to enact laws and compel obedience throughout the continent as the legislatures of the several states have in their respective jurisdictions. If Congress have any power, they must have the whole power of the continent. Such a power would not abridge the sovereignty of each state in any article relating to its own government. The internal police of each state would be still under the sole superintendence of its legislature. But in a matter that equally respects all the states, no individual state has more than a thirteenth part of the legislative authority, and consequently has no right to decide what measure shall or shall not take place on the continent. A majority of the states *must* decide; our confederation cannot be permanent unless founded on that principle; nay more, the states cannot be said to be *united* till such a principle is adopted in its utmost latitude. If a single town or precinct could counteract the will of a whole state, would there be any government in that state? It is an established principle in government that the will of the minority must submit to that of the majority; and a single state or a minority of states ought to be disabled to resist the will of the majority, as much as a town or county in any state is disabled to prevent the execution of a statute law of the legislature.

It is on this principle and *this alone* that a free state can be governed; it is on this principle alone that the American states can exist as a confederacy of republics. Either the several states must continue separate, totally independent of each other, and liable to all the evils of jealousy, dispute, and civil dissension — nay, liable to a civil war upon any clashing of interests — or they must constitute a general head, composed of representatives from all the states, and vested with the power of the whole continent to enforce their decisions. There is no other alternative. One of these events must inevitably take place, and the revolution of a few years will verify the prediction.

I know the objections that have been urged by the supporters of faction, and perhaps by some honest men, against such a power at the head of the states. But the objections all arise from false notions of government or from a willful design to embroil the states. Many people, I doubt not, really suppose that such power in Congress would be dangerous to the liberties of the states. Such ought to be enlightened.

There are two fundamental errors, very common in the reasonings which I have heard on the powers of Congress. The first arises from the idea that our American constitutions are founded on principles similar to those of the European governments which have been called *free*. Hence people are led into a second error, which is that Congress are a body independent of their constituents and under the influence of a distinct interest.

But we have seen before that our systems of civil government are different from all others, founded on different principles, more favorable to freedom, and more secure against corruption.

We have no perpetual distinctions of property which might raise one class of men above another and create powerful family connections and combinations against our liberties. We suffer no hereditary offices or titles which might breed insolence and pride and give their possessors an opportunity to oppress their fellowmen. We are not under the direction of a bigoted clergy who might rob us of the means of knowledge and then inculcate on credulous minds what sentiments they please. Not a single office or emolument in America is held by prescription or hereditary right; but all at the disposal of the people, and not a man on the continent but drones and villains who has not the privilege of frequently choosing his legislators and impeaching his magistrates for maladministration. Such principles form the basis of our American governments — the first and only governments on earth that are founded on the true principles of equal liberty and properly guarded from corruption.

The legislatures of the American states are the only legislatures on earth which are *wholly* dependent on the people at large; and Congress is as dependent on the several states as the legislatures are on their constituents. The members of Congress are chosen by the legislatures, removable by them at pleasure, dependent on them for subsistence, and responsible to their constituents for their conduct. But this is not all. After having been delegated three years, the confederation renders them ineligible for the term of three years more, when they must return, mingle with the people, and become private citizens. At the same time, their interest is the same with that of the people; for enjoying no exclusive privileges but what are temporary they cannot knowingly enact oppressive laws, because they involve themselves, their families, and estates in all the mischiefs that result from such laws.

People, therefore, who attempt to terrify us with apprehensions of losing our liberties because other states have lost theirs, betray an ignorance of history and of the principles of our confederation. I will not undertake to say that the government of the American states will not be corrupted or degenerate into tyranny. But I venture to assert that if it should, it will be the fault of the people. If the people continue to choose their representatives annually and the choice of delegates to Congress should remain upon its present footing, that body can never become tyrants. A measure partially oppressive may be resolved upon, but while the principles of representation, which are always in the power of the people, remain uncorrupted, such a measure can be of no long continuance. The best constitution of government may degenerate from its purity through a variety of causes; but the confederation of these states is better secured than

any government on earth, and less liable to corruption from any quarter.

There is the same danger that the constitutions of the several states will become tyrannical as that the principles of federal government will be corrupted. The states in their collective capacity have no more reason to dread an uncontrollable power in Congress than they have, in their individual capacity, to dread the uncontrollable power of their own legislatures. Their security in both instances is an equal representation, the dependence, the responsibility, and the rotation of their representatives. These articles constitute the basis of our liberties, and will be an effectual security, so long as the people are wise enough to maintain the principles of the confederation.

I beg leave here to observe that a state was never yet destroyed by a corrupt or a wicked administration. Weakness and wickedness in the executive department may produce innumerable evils; but so long as the principles of a constitution remain uncorrupted, their vigor will always restore good order. Every stride of tyranny in the best governments in Europe has been effected by breaking over some constitutional barriers. But where a constitution is formed by the people and unchangeable but by their authority, the progress of corruption must be extremely slow, and perhaps tyranny can never be established in such government, except upon a general habit of indolence and vice.

What do the states obtain by reserving to themselves the right of deciding on the propriety of the resolutions of Congress? The great advantage of having every measure defeated, our frontiers exposed to savages, the debts of the states unpaid and accumulating, national faith violated, commerce restricted and insulted, one state filching some interest from another, and the whole body linked together by cobwebs and shadows, the jest and the ridicule of the world. This is not a chimerical description; it is a literal representation of facts as they now exist. One state found it could make some advantages by refusing the impost. Congress have reasoned with their legislature, and by incontrovertible proofs have pointed out the impropriety of the refusal, but all to no purpose. Thus one-fiftieth part of the states counteracts a measure that the other states suppose not only beneficial but necessary; a measure on which the discharge of our public debt and our national faith most obviously depend. Can a government thus feeble and disjointed answer any valuable purpose? Can commutative justice between the states ever be obtained? Can public debts be discharged and credit supported? Can America ever be respected by her enemies when one of her own states can, year after year, abuse her weakness with impunity? No, the American states, so celebrated for their wisdom and valor in the late struggle for freedom and empire, will be the contempt of nations unless they can unite their force and carry into effect all the constitutional measures of Congress, whether those measures respect themselves or foreign nations.

The Articles of Confederation ordain that the public expenses shall be defrayed out of a common treasury. But where is this treasury? Congress prescribe a measure for supplying this treasury; but the states do not approve of the measure; each state will take its own way and its own time, and perhaps not supply its contingent of money at all. Is this an adherence to the Articles of our Union? It certainly is not; and the states that refuse a compliance with the general measures of the continent would, under a good government, be considered as rebels. Such a conduct amounts to treason, for it strikes at the foundation of government.

Permit me to ask every candid American how society could exist if every man assumed the right of sacrificing his neighbor's property to his own interest? Are there no rights to be relinquished, no sacrifices to be made for the sake of enjoying the benefits

of civil government? If every town in Rhode Island, even the smallest, could annihilate every act of the legislature, could that state exist? Were such a selfish system to prevail generally, there would be an end of government and civil society would become a curse. A social state would be less eligible than a savage state, in proportion as knowledge would be increased and knaves multiplied. Local inconveniences and local interests never ought to disappoint a measure of general utility. If there is not power enough in government to remedy these evils by obliging private interests to give way to public, discord will pervade the state, and terminate in a revolution. Such a power must exist somewhere, and if people will quarrel with good government, there are innumerable opportunities for some daring ambitious genius to erect a monarchy on civil dissensions. In America there is no danger of an aristocracy; but the transition from popular anarchy to monarchy is very natural and often very easy. If these states have any change of government to fear, it is a monarchy. Nothing but the creation of a sovereign power over the whole, with authority to compel obedience to legal measures, can ever prevent a revolution in favor of one monarchy or more. This event may be distant, but is not the less certain. America has it now in her power to create a supreme power over the whole continent sufficient to answer all the ends of government without abridging the rights or destroying the sovereignty of a single state. But should the extreme jealousy of the states prevent the lodgment of such a power in a body of men chosen by themselves and removable at pleasure, such a power will inevitably create itself in the course of events.

The confederation has sketched out a most excellent form of continental government. The ninth article recites the powers of Congress, which are perhaps nearly sufficient to answer the ends of our Union, were there any method of enforcing their resolutions. It is there said what powers shall be exercised by Congress; but no penalty is annexed to disobedience. What purpose would the laws of a state answer if they might be evaded with impunity? And if there were no penalty annexed to a breach of them? A law without a penalty is mere *advice;* a magistrate without the power of punishing is a *cipher.* Here is the *great defect* in the articles of our federal government. Unless Congress can be vested with the same authority to compel obedience to their resolutions that a legislature in any state has to enforce obedience to the laws of that state, the existence of such a body is entirely needless and will not be of long duration. I repeat what I have before said. The idea of governing thirteen states and uniting their interests by mere resolves and recommendations, without any penalty annexed to a noncompliance, is a ridiculous farce, a burlesque on government, and a reproach to America.

Let Congress be empowered to call forth the force of the continent, if necessary, to carry into effect those measures which they have a right to frame. Let the president be, *ex officio,* supreme magistrate, clothed with authority to execute the laws of Congress, in the same manner as the governors of the states are to execute the laws of the states.

Let the superintendent of finance have the power of receiving the public monies and issuing warrants for collection in the manner the treasurer has in Connecticut. Let every executive officer have power to enforce the laws which fall within his province. At the same time, let them be accountable for their administration. Let penalties be annexed to every species of maladministration and exacted with such rigor as is due to justice and the public safety. In short, let the whole system of legislation be the peculiar right of the delegates in Congress who are always under the control of the people; and let the whole administration be vested in magistrates as few as possible in number, and subject to the control of Congress only. Let every precaution be used in *framing* laws, but let no part of the subjects be able to resist the execution. Let the people keep, and *forever keep*, the sole right of legislation in their own representatives, but divest themselves wholly of any right to the administration. Let every state reserve its sovereign right of directing its own internal affairs, but give to Congress the sole right of conducting the general affairs of the continent. Such a plan of government is practicable; and, I believe, the only plan that will preserve the faith, the dignity, and the union of these American states.

Thomas Jefferson: The Good Sense of the People

Many Americans felt Shays's Rebellion threatened their lives and property and warranted efforts for a stronger central government. Jefferson believed the real issue raised by the rebellion was not whether the people should be denied the right of independent political action but whether they needed to be better informed on public affairs. A free and vital press would enable them to form opinions and act more responsibly. The following letter was written to Edward Carrington from Paris on January 16, 1787.

Source: Ford, IV, pp. 357-361.

THE TUMULTS IN AMERICA I expected would have produced in Europe an unfavorable opinion of our political state. But it has not. On the contrary, the small effect of these tumults seems to have given more confidence in the firmness of our governments. The interposition of the people themselves on the side of government has had a great effect on the opinion here. I am persuaded myself that the good sense of the people will always be found to be the best army. They may be led astray for a moment, but will soon correct themselves.

The people are the only censors of their governors; and even their errors will tend to keep these to the true principles of their institution. To punish these errors too severely would be to suppress the only safeguard of the public liberty. The way to prevent these irregular interpositions of the people is to give them full information of their affairs through the channel of the public papers, and to contrive that those papers should penetrate the whole mass of the people. The basis of our governments being the opinion of the people, the very first object should be to keep that right; and were it left to me to decide whether we should have a government without newspapers, or newspapers without a government, I should

not hesitate a moment to prefer the latter. But I should mean that every man should receive those papers, and be capable of reading them.

I am convinced that those societies (as the Indians) which live without government enjoy in their general mass an infinitely greater degree of happiness than those who live under the European governments. Among the former, public opinion is in the place of law, and restrains morals as powerfully as laws ever did anywhere. Among the latter, under pretense of governing, they have divided their nations into two classes, wolves and sheep. I do not exaggerate.

This is a true picture of Europe. Cherish, therefore, the spirit of our people, and keep alive their intention. Do not be too severe upon their errors, but reclaim them by enlightening them. If once they become inattentive to the public affairs, you and I, and Congress and assemblies, judges and governors shall all become wolves. It seems to be the law of our general nature, in spite of individual exceptions; and experience declares that man is the only animal which devours his own kind; for I can apply no milder term to the governments of Europe, and to the general prey of the rich on the poor.

CONVENTION OF 1787

By September 1786 the infant confederation was in deep trouble. "Not worth a continental" was the stock phrase for the devalued currency of the Continental Congress: it seemed to reflect the prospects of the republic, too. Only in name were the United States united; in practice each state did what it pleased — or dared. There was no separation of powers: what little federal power existed was vested in the Congress. States ignored federal calls for revenue. The depression that began in 1785 had deepened, and Daniel Shays led Massachusetts farmers in armed rebellion. The weak central government could obtain little foreign credit. States refused to comply with terms of the peace treaty, giving Britain an excuse to continue to hold the forts at Detroit and other western points. One major achievement was the passing of the land ordinances of 1785 and 1787 (Northwest Ordinance), outlawing slavery in the Northwest Territory, and providing for the sale of western lands, for public schools, and for eventual statehood. But even this forward step was undertaken under pressure from lobbying speculators who stood to gain from ownership of large tracts of land. Farsighted Americans voiced the need for a more unified government.

By the UNITED STATES in CONGRESS Assembled,

A PROCLAMATION

WHEREAS definitive articles of peace and friendship, between the United States of America, and his Britannic majesty, were concluded and signed at Paris, on the 3d day of September, 1783, by the plenipotentiaries of the said United States, and of his said Britannic Majesty, duly and respectively authorized for that purpose; which definitive articles are in the words following.

In the Name of the Most Holy and Undivided
TRINITY.

IT having pleased the Divine Providence to dispose the hearts of the most serene and most potent Prince George the Third, by the Grace of God, King of Great-Britain, France and Ireland, Defender of the Faith, Duke of Brunswick and Lunenburg, Arch-Treasurer and Prince Elector of the Holy Roman Empire, &c. and of the United States of America, to forget all past misunderstandings and differences, that have unhappily interrupted the good correspondence and friendship which they mutually wish to restore; and to establish such a beneficial and satisfactory intercourse between the two countries, upon the ground of reciprocal advantages and mutual convenience, as may promote and secure to both perpetual peace and harmony; And having for this desirable end, already laid the foundation of peace and reconciliation, by the provisional articles, signed at Paris, on the 30th of November, 1782, by the commissioners empowered on each part, which articles were agreed to be inserted in, and to constitute the treaty of peace proposed to be concluded between the crown of Great-Britain and the said United States, but which treaty was not to be concluded until terms of peace should be agreed upon between Great-Britain and France, and his Britannic majesty should be ready to conclude such treaty accordingly; and the treaty between Great-Britain and France, having since been concluded, his Britannic majesty and the United States of America, in order to carry into full effect the provisional articles abovementioned, according to the tenor thereof, have constituted and appointed, that is to say, His Britannic majesty on his part, David Hartley, esquire, member of the parliament of Great-Britain, and the said United States on their part, John Adams, esquire, late a commissioner of the United States of America at the court

long lake and the water communication between it and the lake of the Woods, to the said lake of the Woods; thence through the said lake to the most north-western point thereof, and from thence on a due west course to the river Mississippi; thence by a line to be drawn along the middle of the said river Mississippi, until it shall intersect the northernmost part of the thirty-first degree of north latitude. South by a line to be drawn due east from the determination of the line last mentioned, in the latitude of thirty-one degrees north of the equator, to the middle of the river Apalachicola or Catahouche; thence along the middle thereof to its junction with the Flint river; thence straight to the head of Saint Mary's river; and thence down along the middle of Saint Mary's river to the Atlantic Ocean. East by a line to be drawn along the middle of the river Saint-Croix, from its mouth in the bay of Fundy to its source, and from its source directly north to the aforesaid Highlands which divide the rivers that fall into the Atlantic Ocean from those which fall into the river Saint Lawrence; comprehending all islands within twenty leagues of any part of the shores of the United States, and lying between lines to be drawn due east from the points where the aforesaid boundaries between Nova-Scotia on the one part, and East Florida on the other, shall respectively touch the bay of Fundy, and the Atlantic Ocean; excepting such islands as now are or heretofore have been within the limits of the said province of Nova Scotia.

ARTICLE 3d. It is agreed that the people of the United States shall continue to enjoy unmolested the right to take fish of every kind on the Grand Bank, and on all the other banks of Newfoundland; also in the gulph of Saint Lawrence, and at all other places in the sea, where the inhabitants of both countries used at any time heretofore to fish; and also that the inhabitants of the United States shall have liberty to take fish of every kind on such part of the coast of Newfoundland as British fishermen shall use, (but not to dry or cure the same on that Island) and also on the coasts, bays and creeks of all other of his Britannic Majesty's dominions in America; and that the American fishermen shall have liberty to dry and cure fish in any of the unsettled bays, harbours and creeks of Nova-Scotia, Magdalen islands, and Labradore, so long as the same shall remain unsettled, but so soon as the same or either of them shall be settled, it shall not be lawful for the

and between the subjects of the one, and the citizens of the other, wherefore all hostilities both by sea and land shall from henceforth cease; all prisoners on both sides shall be set at liberty, and his Britannic Majesty shall with all convenient speed, and without causing any destruction, or carrying away any negroes or other property of the American inhabitants, withdraw all his armies, garrisons and fleets from the said United States, and from every post place and harbour within the same, leaving in all fortifications the American artillery that may be therein, and shall also order and cause all archives, records deeds and papers, belonging to any of the said states, or their citizens, which in the course of the war may have fallen into the hands of his officers, to be forthwith restored and delivered to the proper states and persons to whom they belong.

ARTICLE 8th. The navigation of the river Mississippi, from its source to the Ocean, shall forever remain free and open to the subjects of Great-Britain and the citizens of the United States.

ARTICLE 9th. In case it should so happen that any place or territory belonging to Great-Britain or to the United States, should have been conquered by the arms of either from the other, before the arrival of the said provisional articles in America, it is agreed, that the same shall be restored without difficulty, and without requiring any compensation.

ARTICLE 10th. The solemn ratifications of the present treaty, expedited in good and due form, shall be exchanged between the contracting parties, in the space of six months, or sooner if possible, to be computed from the day of the signature of the present treaty. In witness whereof, we the undersigned, their ministers plenipotentiary, have in their name and in virtue of our full powers, signed with our hands the present definitive treaty, and caused the seals of our arms to be affixed thereto.

DONE at Paris, this third day of September

Thomas Mifflin

(Above) Proclamation issued by Congress telling the terms of the peace treaty signed by Britain and the United States in 1783; (below) Mr. and Mrs. Thomas Mifflin in a portrait by Copley; Mifflin was president of Congress prior to the Constitutional Convention

Congress Governs The Nation

Although named the United States, the government always acted as the "United States in Congress assembled." The chief executive was the president of Congress. For long periods no quorum could be mustered to transact business. The British spurned John Adams' efforts at a commercial treaty with the "disunited states," citing the need for thirteen treaties. The first real step toward interstate cooperation was a series of meetings in 1785 between Maryland and Virginia on navigation of the Potomac and other waterways important for opening up the West. James Madison led in calling for a meeting of all states in Annapolis.

(Left) George Read, Delaware representative at Annapolis and Philadelphia and (right) James Monroe

The Annapolis Convention

From September 11 to 14, 1786, twelve men representing five states met in Maryland's Old State House to attempt to resolve interstate conflicts. Four states ignored the convention, and delegates elected by four states did not attend. But three of the four most important commercial states were represented: New York, Pennsylvania, and Virginia (the Massachusetts delegates did not appear). Connecticut and New Jersey were also represented. James Madison and Alexander Hamilton took the lead in urging another meeting in Philadelphia the following spring, to include all thirteen states and to "devise such further provisions as shall appear to them necessary to render the constitution of the Federal Government adequate." New Jersey alone had empowered its delegates to act on matters beyond those of commerce.

State House, Annapolis, site of the brief convention, 1786

The Philadelphia Convention

The Philadelphia Convention opened May 25, 1787, at Independence Hall (the State House), eleven days behind schedule because of the tardiness of many delegates. Rhode Island boycotted the assembly. The political leaders of twelve states were the shapers of the new Constitution, although Congress had invited them only to consider amendments to the Articles of Confederation. In the one unanimous action of the Convention (it lasted all through the summer to Sept. 17), George Washington was elected to preside. Dean of the delegates was Dr. Franklin, aged 81. After much debate, each state was given one vote, regardless of size. To ensure freedom of debate, the Convention agreed to keep proceedings confidential. The first major issue of debate was introduced by Edmund Randolph on the third day of the Convention. The Virginia plan, a "big state" plan, called for a bicameral Congress, with states electing representatives in proportion to population or to financial contribution to the federal government. Some delegates claimed the plan went far beyond the authority of Congress, but the demand for a new Constitution prevailed.

(Top left) George Washington, convention chairman; (top right) Benjamin Franklin, head of the Pennsylvania delegation and oldest representative; (right) Elbridge Gerry, an early advocate of strong central government, refused to sign the final document

WE the People of the States of New-Hampshire, Massachusetts, Rhode-Island and Providence Plantations, Connecticut, New-York, New-Jersey, Pennsylvania, Delaware, Maryland, Virginia, North-Carolina, South-Carolina, and Georgia, do ordain, declare and establish the following Constitution for the Government of Ourselves and our Posterity.

ARTICLE

The Stile of this Government shall be, The United States of America.

II.

The Government shall consist of supreme legislative, executive and judicial powers.

III.

The legislative power shall be vested in a Congress, to consist of two separate and distinct bodies of men, a House of Representatives, and a Senate; each of which shall, in all cases, have a negative on the other. The Legislature shall meet on the first Monday in December in every year.

Legislature shall meet twice in every year, and shall assemble on the [...] Monday in December unless a different day shall be appointed by law.

Sect. 1. The Members of the House of Representatives shall be chosen every second year, by the people of the several States comprehended within this Union. The qualifications of the electors shall be the same, from time to time, as those of the electors in the several States, of the most numerous branch of their own legislatures.

Sect. 2. Every Member of the House of Representatives shall be of the age of twenty-five years at least; shall have been a citizen of the United States for at least three years before his election; and shall be, at the time of his election, a resident of the State in which he shall be chosen.

Sect. 3. The House of Representatives shall, at its first formation, and until the number of citizens and inhabitants shall be taken in the manner herein after described, consist of sixty-five Members, of whom three shall be chosen in New-Hampshire, eight in Massachusetts, one in Rhode Island and Providence Plantations, five in Connecticut, six in New-York, four in New-Jersey, eight in Pennsylvania, one in Delaware, six in Maryland, ten in Virginia, five in North-Carolina, five in South-Carolina, and three in Georgia.

Sect. 4. As the proportions of numbers in the different States will alter from time to time; as some of the States may hereafter be divided; as others may be enlarged by addition of territory; as two or more States may be united; as new States will be erected within the limits of the United States, the Legislature shall, in each of these cases, regulate the number of representatives by the number of inhabitants, according to the [...]

struck out { drawn from the public Treasury, but in pursuance of appropriations that shall originate in the House of Representatives.

Sect. 6. The House of Representatives shall have the sole power of impeachment. It shall choose its Speaker and other officers.

Sect. 7. Vacancies in the House of Representatives shall be supplied by writs of election from the executive authority of the State, in the representation from which they shall happen.

V.

(Above) Nathaniel Gorham, delegate from Massachusetts who served as chairman of the committee of the whole; (left) Washington's draft copy of the Constitution; (below) William Johnson, delegate from Connecticut, who broke a major deadlock with a proposal for dividing the legislative branch

Resolution . . .

The Virginia Plan was debated for two weeks, and on June 13 an amended version containing nineteen resolutions was reported out. The plan called for some separation of powers between legislative, executive, and judicial branches of government, but the executive was to be elected by the legislature, and a council consisting of the executive and several members of the judiciary would have the veto power. Madison and George Mason were the Virginia delegates who carried on the fight for Randolph's plan. On June 15 William Paterson introduced the New Jersey Plan, a "small state" plan amending the Articles of Confederation by giving the Congress some added powers.

State of the resolutions submitted to the consideration of the House by the honorable Mr Randolph, as agreed to in a Committee of the whole House

Resolved that it is the opinion of this Committee that a national government ought to be established, consisting of

a Supreme Legislative, Judiciary and Executive.

Resolved that the national Legislature ought to consist of two branches.

Resolved that the members of the first branch of the national Legislature ought to be elected by the people of the several States.

Resolved that the members of the second branch of the national legislature ought to be chosen by the individual Legislatures.

Resolved that each branch ought to possess the right of originating acts.

Resolved. That the national legislature ought to be empowered

to enjoy the legislative rights vested in Congress by the confederation; and moreover

to legislate in all cases to which the separate States are incompetent, or in which the harmony of the United States may be interrupted by the exercise of individual legislation.

to negative all laws passed by the several States contravening, in the opinion of the national legislature, the articles of union; or any treaties subsisting under the authority of the Union

and Compromise

After three more days of debate the delegates voted in favor of the fundamental changes envisioned by the Virginia Plan. The issues were sharply drawn: large states wanted proportional representation in the legislature; small states wanted equal representation. The Connecticut Compromise, offered by Roger Sherman and backed by William Johnson, broke the deadlock: representation would be by population in the lower house and each state would have an equal vote in the upper house. Franklin, too, called for compromise. Of fifty-five delegates, only forty-two were present Sept. 17, when the Constitution was signed. No one voted against the document, but three delegates refused to sign it.

Baltimore Courthouse Coll.; photo, Frick

National Archives

(Above) Luther Martin, member of the Maryland delegation; OPPOSITE PAGE: (top) Roger Sherman, delegate from Connecticut; detail of portrait by Ralph Earl; (left) Excerpts from the Virginia Plan as amended by the Philadelphia Convention; copy dated 1796; both Sherman and Martin opposed much of this plan and Martin walked out on the convention

The Constitution

(Above) Charles Cotesworth Pinckney, South Carolina, proposed giving the Senate the power to ratify treaties; (below) Caleb Strong, Massachusetts, favored having money bills originate in the House

The Constitution hammered out in the hot summer of 1787 represented a long series of compromises: two legislative houses, one elected on the basis of population, the other not; a president elected for a four-year term (Gouverneur Morris had fought for a lifetime president); separation of powers among legislative, executive, and judicial instead of complete Congressional domination. Franklin told the delegates on the last day of the Convention that the government they had shaped "can only end in despotism, as other forms have done before, when the people shall become so corrupted as to need despotic government, being incapable of any other."

There were few precedents for this written frame of government: the English constitution was not a written document; the interests of the delegates were divergent. Attitudes to the Constitution familiar to the late 20th century were not yet formulated. The doctrine that the Supreme Court had power to declare an act of Congress unconstitutional (judicial review) was unknown in 1787. Not until 1803 did Chief Justice John Marshall state the idea, and then it was for the political advantage of the Federalists in their battle against Jeffersonian democracy. Charles Evans Hughes later said, while governor of New York, "the Constitution is what the judges say it is."

(Above) Hugh Williamson, North Carolina, active in representation compromise but frequently changed his mind during debates; (below) George Clymer, Pennsylvania, served on the financial committee

(Above) James McHenry, Federalist from Maryland, kept private record of debate; (below) William Richardson Davie, North Carolina, swung his delegation to support Connecticut's representation compromise

James Madison: On the Balance of National and Local Authority

One of the men who would be heading for Philadelphia for the Convention of 1787 was James Madison. This man, who has come to be called the Father of the Constitution, was much concerned with what the assembly would try to do. Would it attempt to revamp the Articles of Confederation to make them workable, or would an entirely new constitution be the product of debate? In the following letter to Edmund Randolph, written April 8, 1787, Madison explained his views on the problems that confronted the nation and suggested the kind of government that he felt the United States needed. Many of these ideas were eventually incorporated into the Virginia Plan, presented to the Convention in its first month.

Source: *The Writings of James Madison*, Gaillard Hunt, ed., Vol. II, New York, 1901.

I AM GLAD TO FIND that you are turning your thoughts toward the business of May next. My despair of your finding the necessary leisure, as signified in one of your letters, with the probability that some leading propositions at least would be expected from Virginia, had engaged me in a closer attention to the subject than I should otherwise have given. I will just hint the ideas that have occurred, leaving explanations for our interview.

I think with you that it will be well to retain as much as possible of the old Confederation, though I doubt whether it may not be best to work the valuable Articles into the new system, instead of engrafting the latter on the former. I am also perfectly of your opinion that, in framing a system, no material sacrifices ought to be made to local or temporary prejudices. An explanatory address must of necessity accompany the result of the Convention on the main object. I am not sure that it will be practicable to present the several parts of the reform in so detached a manner to the states as that a partial adoption will be binding. Particular states may view different Articles as conditions of each other, and would only ratify them as such. Others might ratify them as independent propositions. The consequence would be that the ratifications of both would go for nothing. I have not, however, examined this point thoroughly. In truth, my ideas of a reform strike so deeply at the old Confederation, and lead to such a systematic change, that they scarcely admit of the expedient.

I hold it for a fundamental point that an individual independence of the states is utterly irreconcilable with the idea of an aggregate sovereignty. I think, at the same time, that a consolidation of the states into one simple republic is not less unattainable than it would be inexpedient. Let it be tried, then, whether any middle ground can be taken which will at once support a due supremacy of the national authority, and leave in force the local authorities so far as they can be subordinately useful.

The first step to be taken is, I think, a change in the principle of representation. According to the present form of the Union, an equality of suffrage, if not just toward the larger members of it, is at least safe to them, as the liberty they exercise of rejecting or executing the acts of Congress is uncontrollable by the nominal sovereignty of Congress. Under a system which would operate without the intervention of the states, the case would be materially altered.

A vote from Delaware would have the same effect as one from Massachusetts or Virginia.

Let the national government be armed with a positive and complete authority in all cases where uniform measures are necessary, as in trade, etc. Let it also retain the powers which it now possesses.

Let it have a negative, in all cases whatsoever, on the legislative acts of the states, as the King of Great Britain heretofore had. This I conceive to be essential and the least possible abridgment of the state sovereignties. Without such a defensive power, every positive power that can be given on paper will be unavailing. It will also give internal stability to the states. There has been no moment since the peace at which the federal assent would have been given to paper money, etc.

Let this national supremacy be extended also to the judiciary department. If the judges in the last resort depend on the states, and are bound by their oaths to them and not to the Union, the intention of the law and the interests of the nation may be defeated by the obsequiousness of the tribunals to the policy or prejudices of the states. It seems at least essential that an appeal should lie to some national tribunals in all cases which concern foreigners or inhabitants of other states. The admiralty jurisdiction may be fully submitted to the national government.

A government formed of such extensive powers ought to be well organized. The legislative department may be divided into two branches — one of them to be chosen every ——— years by the legislatures or the people at large; the other to consist of a more select number, holding their appointments for a longer term and going out in rotation. Perhaps the negative on the state laws may be most conveniently lodged in this branch. A council of revision may be superadded, including the great ministerial officers.

A national executive will also be necessary. I have scarcely ventured to form my own opinion yet, either of the manner in which it ought to be constituted or of the authorities with which it ought to be clothed.

An article ought to be inserted expressly guaranteeing the tranquillity of the states against internal as well as external dangers.

To give the new system its proper energy, it will be desirable to have it ratified by the authority of the people and not merely by that of the legislatures.

I am afraid you will think this project, if not extravagant, absolutely unattainable and unworthy of being attempted. Conceiving it myself to go no further than is essential, the objections drawn from this source are to be laid aside. I flatter myself, however, that they may be less formidable on trial than in contemplation. The change in the principle of representation will be relished by a majority of the states, and those too of most influence. The Northern states will be reconciled to it by the actual superiority of their populousness; the Southern by their expected superiority on this point. This principle established, the repugnance of the large states to part with power will in a great degree subside, and the smaller states must ultimately yield to the predominant will. It is also already seen by many, and must by degrees be seen by all, that unless the Union be organized efficiently on republican principles, innovations of a much more objectionable form may be obtruded, or, in the most favorable event, the partition of the empire into rival and hostile confederacies will ensue.

Joel Barlow: The Unfinished Revolution

Despite his conservative upbringing, Joel Barlow, statesman and poet, became one of the most liberal thinkers of his time. On the eleventh anniversary of the Declaration of Independence, he addressed the Society of the Cincinnati at Hartford, Connecticut. He eulogized the goals of the Revolution but warned that "the Revolution is but half completed." With independence won, the next great challenge was to constitute an effective government.

Source: Niles: "An Oration Delivered by Mr. Joel Barlow, at Hartford, Conn., to the Society of the Cincinnati, July 4, 1787."

On the anniversary of so great an event as the birth of the empire in which we live, none will question the propriety of passing a few moments in contemplating the various objects suggested to the mind by the important occasion. But at the present period, while the blessings claimed by the sword of victory and promised in the voice of peace remain to be confirmed by our future exertions — while the nourishment, the growth, and even the existence of our empire depend upon the united efforts of an extensive and divided people — the duties of this day ascend from amusement and congratulation to a serious patriotic employment.

We are assembled, my friends, not to boast but to realize — not to inflate our national vanity by a pompous relation of past achievements in the council or in the field but, from a modest retrospect of the truly dignified part already acted by our countrymen, from an accurate view of our present situation, and from an anticipation of the scenes that remain to be unfolded, to discern and familiarize the duties that still await us, as citizens, as soldiers, and as men. . . .

It would be wandering from the objects which ought to occupy our present attention again to recount the numerous acts of the British Parliament which composed that system of tyranny designed for the subjuga-tion of America. Neither can we indulge in the detail of those memorable events which marked our various stages of resistance, from the glooms of unsuccessful supplication to the splendor of victory and acknowledged sovereignty. The former were the theme of senatorial eloquence, producing miracles of union and exertion in every part of the continent, till we find them preserved for everlasting remembrance in that declaratory act of independence which gave being to an empire and dignified the day we now commemorate. The latter are fresh in the memory of every person of the least information. It would be impertinence, if not a breach of delicacy, to attempt a recital of those glorious achievements, especially before an audience, part of whom have been distinguished actors in the scene, others the anxious and applauding spectators. To the faithful historian we resign the task — the historian, whom it is hoped the present age will deem it their duty as well as their interest to furnish, encourage, and support.

Whatever praise is due for the task already performed, it is certain that much remains to be done. The Revolution is but half completed. Independence and government were the two objects contended for, and but one is yet obtained. To the glory of the present age and the admiration of the future, our severance from the British Empire was conducted upon principles as noble as they were new and unprecedented in the history of human actions. Could the same generous principles, the same wisdom and unanimity be exerted in effecting the establishment of a permanent federal system, what an additional luster would it pour upon the present age! A luster hitherto unequaled; a display of magnanimity for which mankind may never behold another opportunity.

Without an efficient government, our independence will cease to be a blessing. Shall that glow of patriotism and unshaken perseverance which has been so long conspicuous in the American character desert us at our utmost need? Shall we lose sight of our own happiness because it has grown familiar by a near approach? Shall thy labors, O Washington, have been bestowed in vain? Hast thou conducted us to independence and peace, and shall we not receive the blessings at thy hands? Where are the shades of our fallen friends? and what is their language on this occasion? Warren, Montgomery, Mercer, Wooster, Scammel, and Laurens, all ye hosts of departed heroes! rich is the treasure you have lavished in the cause, and prevalent the price you have paid for our freedom. Shall the purchase be neglected? the fair inheritance lie without improvement, exposed to every daring invader? Forbid it, honor; forbid it, gratitude; and oh, may heaven avert the impending evil.

In contemplating the price of our independence, it will never be forgotten that it was not entirely the work of our own hands; nor could it probably have been established, in the same term of time, by all the blood and treasure that America, unassisted, was able to furnish for the contest. Much of the merit is due, and our warmest acknowledgments shall ever flow to that illustrious monarch, the father of nations and friend of the distressed — the monarch who, by his early assistance, taught us not to despair; and who, when we had given a sufficient proof of our military virtue and perseverance, joined us in alliance, upon terms of equality; gave us a rank and credit among the maritime nations of Europe; and furnished fleets and armies, money and military stores, to put a splendid period to the important conflict. . . .

Unite in a permanent federal government; put your commerce upon a respectable footing; your arts and manufactures, your population, your wealth and glory will increase; and when a hundred millions of people are comprised within your territory,

New York Historical Society

Engraving of Joel Barlow by A. B. Durand after portrait by Robert Fulton

and made happy by your sway, then shall it be known that the hand of that monarch assisted in planting the vine from which so great a harvest is produced. . . .

Here shall that pride of the military character, the gallant Fayette, find his compensation for a life of disinterested service; whose toils have not ceased with the termination of the war; and whose successful endeavors to promote our interest in commercial and political arrangements can only be equaled by his achievements in the field. How will the posterity of that nobleman, and that of the other brave officers of his nation who have fought by your sides, on reviewing the American history, rejoice in the fame of their fathers; nor even regret the fate of those who bled in so glorious a field! . . .

The present is justly considered an alarming crisis, perhaps the most alarming that America ever saw. We have contended with the most powerful nation, and subdued the bravest and best appointed armies; but now we have to contend with ourselves, and encounter passions and prejudices more powerful than armies, and more dangerous to our peace. It is not for glory, it is for existence that we contend.

Much is expected from the Federal Convention now sitting at Philadelphia, and it is a happy circumstance that so general a confidence from all parts of the country is centered in that respectable body. Their former services, as individuals, command it, and our situation requires it. But although much is expected from them, yet more is demanded from ourselves.

The first great object is to convince the people of the importance of their present situation; for the majority of a great people, on a subject which they understand, will never act wrong. If ever there was a time in any age or nation when the fate of millions depended on the voice of one, it is the present period in these states. Every free citizen of the American empire ought now to consider himself as the legislator of half mankind. When he views the amazing extent of territory, settled and to be settled under the operation of his laws; when, like a wise politician, he contemplates the population of future ages, the changes to be wrought by the possible progress of arts in agriculture, commerce, and manufactures, the increasing connection and intercourse of nations, and the effect of one rational political system upon the general happiness of mankind — his mind, dilated with the great idea, will realize a liberality of feeling which leads to a rectitude of conduct. He will see that the system to be established by his suffrage is calculated for the great benevolent purposes of extending peace, happiness, and progressive improvement to a large proportion of his fellow creatures. As there is a probability that the system to be proposed by the Convention may answer this description, there is some reason to hope it will be viewed by the people with that candor and dispassionate respect which is due to the importance of the subject. . . .

Those who are possessed of abilities or information in any degree above the common rank of their fellow citizens are called upon by every principle of humanity to diffuse a spirit of candor and rational inquiry upon these important subjects.

Adams, to his immortal honor and the timely assistance of his country, has set the great example. His treatise in defense of the constitutions, though confined to the state republics, is calculated to do infinite service by correcting thousands of erroneous sentiments arising from our inexperience; sentiments which, if uncorrected in this early stage of our political existence, will be the source of calamities without measure and without end. Should that venerable philosopher and statesman be induced to continue his inquiries, by tracing the history of confederacies, and, with his usual energy and perspicuity, delineate and defend a system adapted to the circumstances of the United States — I will not say he could deserve more from his distressed country, but he would crown a life of patriotic labors and render an essential additional service to the world.

While America enjoys the peculiar felicity of seeing those who have conducted her councils and her battles, retire, like Cincinnatus, to the humble labors of the plow, it must be remembered that she there expects a continuance of their patriotic exertions. The Society of the Cincinnati, established upon the most benevolent principles, will never lose sight of their duty, in rendering every possible aid, as citizens, to that community which they have defended as soldiers. . . .

The present is an age of philosophy, and America the empire of reason. Here neither the pageantry of courts nor the glooms of superstition have dazzled or beclouded the mind. Our duty calls us to act worthy of the age and the country that gave us birth. Though inexperience may have betrayed us into errors, yet they have not been fatal; and our own discernment will point us to their proper remedy.

However defective the present confederated system may appear, yet a due consideration of the circumstances under which it was framed will teach us rather to admire its wisdom than to murmur at its faults. The same political abilities which were displayed in that institution, united with the experience we have had of its operation, will doubtless produce a system which will stand the test of ages in forming a powerful and happy people.

Elevated with the extensive prospect, we may consider present inconveniences as unworthy of regret. At the close of the war, an uncommon plenty of circulating specie and a universal passion for trade tempted many individuals to involve themselves in ruin and injure the credit of their country.

But these are evils which work their own remedy. The paroxysm is already over. Industry is increasing faster than ever it declined; and, with some exceptions, where legislative authority has sanctioned fraud, the people are honestly discharging their private debts and increasing the resources of their wealth.

Every possible encouragement for great and generous exertions is now presented before us. Under the idea of a permanent and happy government, every point of view in which the future situation of America can be placed fills the mind with peculiar dignity and opens an unbounded field of thought. The natural resources of the country are inconceivably various and great. The enterprising genius of the people promises a most rapid improvement in all the arts that embellish human nature. The blessings of a rational government will invite emigrations from the rest of the world and fill the empire with the worthiest and happiest of mankind; while the example of political wisdom and felicity, here to be displayed, will excite emulation through the kingdoms of the earth and meliorate the condition of the human race.

JOHN ADAMS: The Meaning of the American Revolution

John Adams sent the following lucid essay to Hezekiah Niles, editor of the Weekly
Register, *on February 13, 1818, and Niles praised it three weeks later. "Those who
delight to trace the early dawnings of the American Revolution," wrote Niles in an
editorial note, ". . . will be grateful for this tribute to the memory of the illustrious dead,
from the pen of such a distinguished co-adjutor and co-patriot, as John Adams." The
essay may have produced more than gratitude; it is thought that it inspired Niles to collect
and publish his monumental* Principles and Acts of the Revolution in America *(1822),
a leading source of our knowledge of the period.*

Source: *Niles' Weekly Register*, March 7, 1818.

THE AMERICAN REVOLUTION was not a common event. Its effects and consequences have already been awful over a great part of the globe. And when and where are they to cease?

But what do we mean by the American Revolution? Do we mean the American War? The Revolution was effected before the War commenced. The Revolution was in the minds and hearts of the people, a change in their religious sentiments of their duties and obligations. While the king, and all in authority under him, were believed to govern in justice and mercy according to the laws and constitution derived to them from the God of nature, and transmitted to them by their ancestors, they thought themselves bound to pray for the king and queen and all the royal family, and all in authority under them, as ministers ordained of God

for their good. But when they saw those powers renouncing all the principles of authority, and bent upon the destruction of all the securities of their lives, liberties, and properties, they thought it their duty to pray for the Continental Congress and all the thirteen state congresses, etc.

There might be, and there were, others who thought less about religion and conscience, but had certain habitual sentiments of allegiance and loyalty derived from their education; but believing allegiance and protection to be reciprocal, when protection was withdrawn, they thought allegiance was dissolved.

Another alteration was common to all. The people of America had been educated in a habitual affection for England as their mother country; and while they thought her a kind and tender parent (erroneously enough, however, for she never was such a mother) no affection could be more sincere. But when they found her a cruel beldam, willing, like Lady Macbeth, to "dash their brains out," it is no wonder if their filial affections ceased and were changed into indignation and horror.

This radical change in the principles, opinions, sentiments, and affections of the people was the real American Revolution.

By what means this great and important alteration in the religious, moral, political, and social character of the people of thirteen colonies, all distinct, unconnected, and independent of each other, was begun, pursued, and accomplished, it is surely interesting to humanity to investigate and perpetuate to posterity.

To this end it is greatly to be desired that young gentlemen of letters in all the states, especially in the thirteen original states, would undertake the laborious, but certainly interesting and amusing, task of searching and collecting all the records, pamphlets, newspapers, and even handbills which in any way contributed to change the temper and views of the people and compose them into an independent nation.

The colonies had grown up under constitutions of government so different; there was so great a variety of religions; they were composed of so many different nations; their customs, manners, and habits had so little resemblance; and their intercourse had been so rare and their knowledge of each other so imperfect that to unite them in the same principles in theory and the same system of action was certainly a very difficult enterprise. The complete accomplishment of it in so short a time and by such simple means was perhaps a singular example in the history of mankind. Thirteen clocks were made to strike together: a perfection of mechanism which no artist had ever before effected.

In this research, the glorioles of individual gentlemen and of separate states is of little consequence. The means and the measures are the proper objects of investigation. These may be of use to posterity, not only in this nation, but in South America and all other countries. They may teach mankind that revolutions are no trifles; that they ought never to be undertaken rashly; nor without deliberate consideration and sober reflection; nor without a solid, immutable, eternal foundation of justice and humanity; nor without a people possessed of intelligence, fortitude, and integrity sufficient to carry them with steadiness, patience, and perseverance through all the vicissitudes of fortune, the fiery trials, and melancholy disasters they may have to encounter.

The town of Boston early instituted an annual oration on the 4th of July, in commemoration of the principles and feelings which contributed to produce the Revolution. Many of those orations I have heard, and all that I could obtain I have read. Much ingenuity and eloquence appears upon every subject except those principles and feelings. That of my honest and amiable neighbor Josiah Quincy appeared to me the most directly to the purpose of the institution. Those principles and feelings ought to be traced back for 200 years and sought in the history of the country from the first plantations in America. Nor should the principles and feelings of the English and Scots toward the colonies through that whole period ever be forgotten. The perpetual discordance between British principles and feelings and those of America, the next year after the suppression of the French power in America, came to a crisis and produced an explosion.

It was not until after the annihilation of the French dominion in America that any British ministry had dared to gratify their own wishes, and the desire of the nation, by projecting a formal plan for raising a national revenue from America by parliamentary taxation. The first great manifestation of this design was by the order to carry into strict execution those acts of Parliament which were well-known by the appellation of the Acts of Trade, which had lain a dead letter, unexecuted for half a century — and some of them, I believe, for nearly a whole one.

This produced, in 1760 and 1761, an awakening and a revival of American principles and feelings, with an enthusiasm which went on increasing till in 1775 it burst out in open violence, hostility, and fury.

The characters the most conspicuous, the most ardent and influential in this revival, from 1760 to 1766, were first and foremost, before all and above all, James Otis; next to him was Oxenbridge Thatcher; next to him Samuel Adams; next to him John Hancock; then Dr. Mayhew; then Dr. Cooper and his brother. Of Mr. Hancock's life, character, generous nature, great and disinterested sacrifices, and important services, if I had forces, I should be glad to write a volume. But this I hope will be done by some younger and abler hand.

Mr. Thatcher, because his name and merits are less known, must not be wholly omitted. This gentleman was an eminent barrister at law, in as large practice as anyone in Boston. There was not a citizen of that town more universally beloved for his learning, ingenuity, every domestic and social virtue, and conscientious conduct in every relation of life. His patriotism was as ardent as his progenitors had been ancient and illustrious in this country. Hutchinson often said, "Thatcher was not born a plebeian, but he was determined to die one." In May 1768, I believe, he was chosen by the town of Boston one of their representatives in the legislature, a colleague with Mr. Otis, who had been a member from May 1761, and he continued to be reelected annually till his death in 1765, when Mr. Samuel Adams was elected to fill his place, in the absence of Mr. Otis then attending the congress at New York. Thatcher had long been jealous of the unbounded ambition of Mr.

Hutchinson, but when he found him not content with the office of lieutenant governor, the command of the castle and its emoluments, of judge of probate for the county of Suffolk, a seat in his Majesty's Council in the legislature, his brother-in-law secretary of state by the king's commission, a brother of that secretary of state a judge of the Supreme Court and a member of Council; now in 1760 and 1761 soliciting and accepting the office of chief justice of the Superior Court of Judicature, he concluded, as Mr. Otis did, and as every other enlightened friend of his country did, that he sought that office with the determined purpose of determining all causes in favor of the ministry at St. James's and their servile Parliament.

His indignation against him henceforward, to 1765 when he died, knew no bounds but truth. I speak from personal knowledge, for, from 1758 to 1765, I attended every superior and inferior court in Boston, and recollect not one in which he did not invite me home to spend evenings with him, when he made me converse with him as well as I could on all subjects of religion, morals, law, politics, history, philosophy, belle-lettres, theology, mythology, cosmogony, metaphysics (Locke, Clark, Leibniz, Bolingbroke, Berkeley), the preestablished harmony of the universe, the nature of matter and of spirit, and the eternal establishment of coincidences between their operations, fate, foreknowledge, absolute. We reasoned on such unfathomable subjects as high as Milton's gentry in pandemonium; and we understood them as well as they did, and no better. To such mighty mysteries he added the news of the day, and the tittle-tattle of the town.

But his favorite subject was politics, and the impending threatening system of parliamentary taxation and universal government over the colonies. On this subject he was so anxious and agitated that I have no doubt it occasioned his premature death. From the time when he argued the question of writs of assistance to his death, he considered the king, ministry, Parliament, and nation of Great Britain as determined to new-model the colonies from the foundation; to annul all their charters, to constitute them all royal governments; to raise a revenue in America by parliamentary taxation; to apply that revenue to pay the salaries of governors, judges, and all other Crown officers; and after all this, to raise as large a revenue as they pleased, to be applied to national purposes at the exchequer in England; and further to establish bishops and the whole system of the Church of England, tithes and all, throughout all British America. This system, he said, if it was suffered to prevail, would extinguish the flame of liberty all over the world; that America would be employed as an engine to batter down all the miserable remains of liberty in Great Britain and Ireland, where only any semblance of it was left in the world. To this system he considered Hutchinson, the Olivers, and all their connections, dependants, adherents, and shoelickers entirely devoted. He asserted that they were all engaged with all the Crown officers in America and the understrappers of the ministry in England in a deep and treasonable conspiracy to betray the liberties of their country for their own private, personal, and family aggrandizement.

His philippics against the unprincipled ambition and avarice of all of them, but especially of Hutchinson, were unbridled, not only in private, confidential conversations but in all companies and on all occasions. He gave Hutchinson the sobriquet of "Summa Potestatis," and rarely mentioned him but by the name of "Summa." His liberties of speech were no secrets to his enemies. I have sometimes wondered that they did not throw him over the bar, as they did soon afterwards Major Hawley. They hated him worse than they did James

Otis, or Samuel Adams, and they feared him more, because they had no revenge for a father's disappointment of a seat on the superior bench to impute to him, as they did to Otis; and Thatcher's character through life had been so modest, decent, unassuming, his morals so pure, and his religion so venerated that they dared not attack him. In his office were educated to the bar two eminent characters, the late Judge Lowell and Josiah Quincy, aptly called the Boston Cicero.

Mr. Thatcher's frame was slender, his constitution delicate; whether his physicians overstrained his vessels with mercury when he had the smallpox by inoculation at the castle, or whether he was overplied by public anxieties and exertions, the smallpox left him in a decline from which he never recovered. Not long before his death he sent for me to commit to my care some of his business at the bar. I asked him whether he had seen the Virginia Resolves:

> Oh yes, they are men! They are noble spirits! It kills me to think of the lethargy and stupidity that prevails here. I long to be out. I will go out. I will go out. I will go into court and make a speech which shall be read after my death as my dying testimony against this infernal tyranny they are bringing upon us.

Seeing the violent agitation into which it threw him, I changed the subject as soon as possible, and retired. He had been confined for some time. Had he been abroad among the people he would not have complained so pathetically of the "lethargy and stupidity that prevailed," for town and country were all alive, and in August became active enough and some of the people proceeded to unwarrantable excesses, which were more lamented by the patriots than by their enemies. Mr. Thatcher soon died, deeply lamented by all the friends of their country.

Another gentleman who had great influence in the commencement of the Revolution was Dr. Jonathan Mayhew, a descendant of the ancient governor of Martha's Vineyard. This divine had raised a great reputation both in Europe and America by the publication of a volume of seven sermons in the reign of King George II, 1749, and by many other writings, particularly a sermon in 1750 on January 30, on the subject of passive obedience and nonresistance, in which the saintship and martyrdom of King Charles I are considered, seasoned with wit and satire superior to any in Swift or Franklin. It was read by everybody, celebrated by friends, and abused by enemies.

During the reigns of King George I and King George II, the reigns of the Stuarts (the two Jameses and the two Charleses) were in general disgrace in England. In America they had always been held in abhorrence. The persecutions and cruelties suffered by their ancestors under those reigns had been transmitted by history and tradition, and Mayhew seemed to be raised up to revive all their animosity against tyranny in church and state, and at the same time to destroy their bigotry, fanaticism, and inconsistency. David Hume's plausible, elegant, fascinating, and fallacious apology, in which he varnished over the crimes of the Stuarts, had not then appeared.

To draw the character of Mayhew would be to transcribe a dozen volumes. This transcendent genius threw all the weight of his great fame into the scale of his country in 1761, and maintained it there with zeal and ardor till his death in 1766. In 1763 appeared the controversy between him and Mr. Apthorp, Mr. Caner, Dr. Johnson, and Archbishop Secker on the charter and conduct of the society for propagating the gospel in foreign parts. To form a judgment of this debate I beg leave to refer to a review of the whole, printed at the time and written by Samuel Adams, though by some very absurdly and erroneously ascribed to

Mr. Apthorp. If I am not mistaken, it will be found a model of candor, sagacity, impartiality, and close correct reasoning.

If any gentleman supposes this controversy to be nothing to the present purpose, he is grossly mistaken. It spread a universal alarm against the authority of Parliament. It excited a general and just apprehension that bishops and dioceses and churches and priests and tithes were to be imposed upon us by Parliament. It was known that neither king, nor ministry, nor archbishops could appoint bishops in America without an act of Parliament; and if Parliament could tax us they could establish the Church of England with all its creeds, articles, tests, ceremonies, and tithes, and prohibit all other churches as conventicles and schism shops.

Nor must Mr. Cushing be forgotten. His good sense and sound judgment, the urbanity of his manners, his universal good character, his numerous friends and connections, and his continual intercourse with all sorts of people, added to his constant attachment to the liberties of his country, gave him a great and salutary influence from the beginning in 1760.

Let me recommend these hints to the consideration of Mr. Wirt, whose life of Mr. Henry I have read with great delight. I think that after mature investigation he will be convinced that Mr. Henry did not "give the first impulse to the ball of independence," and that Otis, Thatcher, Samuel Adams, Mayhew, Hancock, Cushing, and thousands of others were laboring for several years at the wheel before the name of Mr. Henry was heard beyond the limits of Virginia.

If you print this, I will endeavor to send you something concerning Samuel Adams, who was destined to a longer career, and to act a more conspicuous and, perhaps, a more important part than any other man. But his life would require a volume.

John Quincy Adams: The Declaration and the Constitution

*To celebrate the fiftieth anniversary of Washington's inauguration, the New York
Historical Society invited John Quincy Adams, ex-President and now a congressman
from Massachusetts, to address it. Adams chose as his subject one that had been
discussed and debated since the nation's inception: the nature of federal government.
Against those who held that federalism meant a union of states, he argued that the
Constitution had been intended to fulfill the philosophy of the Declaration of Independence
by creating a union of the people. The speech, reprinted here in part, was delivered
on April 30, 1839.*

Source: *The Jubilee of the Constitution, A Discourse,* New York, 1839, pp. 13-118.

THE MOTIVE for the Declaration of Independence was on its face avowed to be "a decent respect for the opinions of mankind"; its *purpose* to declare the *causes* which impelled the people of the English colonies on the continent of North America to separate themselves from the political community of the British nation. They declare *only* the *causes* of their separation, but they announce at the same time their assumption of the separate and equal station to which the laws of nature and of nature's God entitle them among the powers of the earth. Thus their first movement is to recognize and appeal to the laws of nature and to nature's God for their *right* to assume the attributes of sovereign power as an independent nation. . . .

It is not immaterial to remark that the signers of the Declaration, though qualifying themselves as the representatives of the United States of America, in general Congress assembled, yet issue the Declaration *in the name and by the authority of the good people of the colonies;* and that they declare, *not* each of the separate colonies but the *united colonies,* free and independent states. The whole people declared the colonies *in their united condition* of RIGHT, free, and independent states.

The dissolution of allegiance to the British Crown, the severance of the colonies from the British Empire, and their actual existence as independent states, thus declared of *right,* were definitely established *in fact* by war and peace. The independence of each separate state had never been declared of *right.* It never existed *in fact.* Upon the principles of the Declaration of Independence, the dissolution of the ties of allegiance, the assumption of sovereign power, and the institution of civil government are all acts of transcendent authority which the people *alone* are competent to perform; and, accordingly, it is in the name and by the authority of the people that two of these acts — the dissolution of allegiance, with the severance from the British Empire, and the declaration of the united colonies as free and independent states — were performed by that instrument.

But there still remained the last and crowning act, which the *people* of the Union alone were competent to perform — the institution of civil government for that compound nation, the United States of America.

At this day it cannot but strike us as extraordinary that it does not appear to have occurred to any one member of that assembly, which had laid down in terms so clear, so explicit, so unequivocal the foundation of all just government, in the imprescriptible rights of man, and the transcendent sovereignty of the people, and who, in those principles, had set forth their only personal vindication from the charges of rebellion against their king and of treason to their country, that their last crowning act was still to be performed upon the same principles — that is, the institution by the *people* of the United States, of a civil government, to guard and protect and defend them all. On the contrary, that same assembly which issued the Declaration of Independence, instead of continuing to act in the name and by the authority of the good people of the United States, had immediately, after the appointment of the committee to prepare the Declaration, appointed another committee of one member from each colony to prepare and digest the form of confederation to be entered into between the colonies.

That committee reported on the 12th of July, eight days after the Declaration of Independence had been issued, a draft of Articles of Confederation between the colonies. This draft was prepared by John Dickinson, then a delegate from Pennsylvania, who voted against the Declaration of Independence and never signed it — having been superseded by a new election of delegates from that state eight days after his draft was reported.

There was thus no congeniality of principle between the Declaration of Independence and the Articles of Confederation.

The foundation of the former were a superintending Providence — the rights of man and the constituent revolutionary power of the people. That of the latter was the sovereignty of organized power and the independence of the separate or disunited states. The fabric of the Declaration and that of the Confederation were each consistent with its own foundation, but they could not form one consistent, symmetrical edifice. They were the productions of different minds and of adverse passions — one, ascending for the foundation of human government to the laws of nature and of God, written upon the heart of man; the other, resting upon the basis of human institutions, and prescriptive law and colonial charters. The cornerstone of the one was *right;* that of the other was *power.*

The work of the founders of our independence was thus but half done. Absorbed in that more than herculean task of maintaining that independence and its principles, by one of the most cruel wars that ever glutted the furies with human woe, they marched undaunted and steadfast through that fiery ordeal, and consistent in their principles to the end, concluded, as an acknowledged sovereignty of the United States, proclaimed by their people in 1776, a peace with that same monarch whose sovereignty over them they had abjured in obedience to the laws of nature and of nature's God.

But for these United States, they had formed no constitution. Instead of resorting to the source of all constituted power, they had wasted their time, their talents, and their persevering, untiring toils in erecting and roofing and buttressing a frail and temporary shed to shelter the nation from the storm, or rather a mere baseless scaffolding on which to stand, when they should raise the marble palace of the people to stand the test of time.

Five years were consumed by Congress and the state legislatures in debating and altercating and adjusting these Articles of Confederation. The first of which was:

"Each state *retains* its sovereignty, freedom, and independence, and every power, jurisdiction, and right which is not by this Confederation expressly delegated to the United States, in Congress assembled."

Observe the departure from the language, and the consequent contrast of principles, with those of the Declaration of Independence. Each state RETAINS its sovereignty, etc. Where did each state get the sovereignty which it *retains?*

In the Declaration of Independence, the delegates of the colonies, in Congress assembled, *in the name and by the authority of the good people of the colonies,* declare, not each colony but the *united* colonies, in fact and of right, not *sovereign* but free and independent states. And why did they make this declaration in the name and by the authority of the one people of all the colonies? Because, by the principles before laid down in the Declaration, the people, and the people alone, as the rightful source of all legitimate government, were competent to dissolve the bands of subjection of all the colonies to the nation of Great Britain, and to constitute them free and independent states.

Now the people of the colonies, speaking by their delegates in Congress, had not declared *each* colony a sovereign, free, and independent state; nor had the people of each colony so declared the colony itself, nor could they so declare it, because each was already bound in union with all the rest — a union formed *de facto* by the spontaneous revolutionary movement of the whole people, and organized by the meeting of the first Congress, in 1774, a year and ten months before the Declaration of Independence.

Where, then, did *each* state get the sovereignty, freedom, and independence which the Articles of Confederation declare it *retains?* Not from the whole people of the whole Union; not from the Declaration of Independence; not from the people of the state itself. It was assumed by agreement between the legislatures of the several states and their delegates in Congress, without authority from or consultation of the people at all.

In the Declaration of Independence, the enacting and constituent party dispensing and delegating sovereign power is the whole *people* of the united colonies. The recipient party, invested with power, is the united colonies, declared United States.

In the Articles of Confederation, this order of agency is inverted. Each state is the constituent and enacting party, and the United States, in Congress assembled, the recipient of delegated power — and that power, delegated with such a penurious and carking hand, that it had more the aspect of a revocation of the Declaration of Independence than an instrument to carry it into effect. . . .

Washington, though in retirement, was brooding over the cruel injustice suffered by his associates in arms, the warriors of the Revolution; over the prostration of the public credit and the faith of the nation in the neglect to provide for the payment even of the interest upon the public debt; over the disappointed hopes of the friends of freedom; in the language of the address from Congress to the states of the 18th of April, 1783 — "the pride and boast of America, that the rights for which she contended were the rights of human nature."

At his residence of Mount Vernon, in March 1785, the first idea was started of a revisal of the Articles of Confederation by an organization of means differing from that of a compact between the state legislatures and their own delegates in Congress. A convention of delegates from the state legislatures, independent of the Congress itself, was the expedient which presented itself for effecting the purpose, and an augmentation of the powers of Congress for the regulation of commerce as the object for which this assembly was to be convened. In January 1786, the proposal was made and adopted in the legislature of Virginia and communicated to the other state legislatures.

The convention was held at Annapolis in September of that year. It was attended by delegates from only five of the central states, who, on comparing their restricted powers, with the glaring and universally acknowledged defects of the Confederation, reported only a recommendation for the assemblage of another convention of delegates to meet at Philadelphia, in May 1787, from all the states and with enlarged powers.

The Constitution of the United States was the work of this Convention. But in its construction the Convention immediately perceived that they must retrace their steps and fall back from a league of friendship between sovereign states to the constituent sovereignty of the *people;* from *power* to *right;* from the irresponsible despotism of state sovereignty to the self-evident truths of the Declaration of Independence. In that instrument, the right to institute and to alter governments among men was ascribed exclusively to the *people;* the ends of government were declared to be to *secure* the natural rights of man; and that *when* the government degenerates from the promotion to the destruction of that end, the right and the duty accrues to the people to dissolve this degenerate government and to institute another.

The signers of the Declaration further averred that the one people of the *united colonies* were then precisely in that situation — with a government degenerated into tyranny and called upon by the laws of nature and of nature's God to dissolve that government and to institute another. Then, in the name and by the authority of the good people of the colonies, they pronounced the dissolution of their allegiance to the King and their eternal separation from the nation

of Great Britain, and declared the united colonies independent states. And here, as the representatives of the one people, they had stopped. They did not require the confirmation of this act, for the power to make the Declaration had already been conferred upon them by the people; delegating the power, indeed, separately in the separate colonies, not by colonial authority but by the spontaneous revolutionary movement of the people in them all.

From the day of that Declaration, the constituent power of the people had never been called into action. A confederacy had been substituted in the place of a government; and state sovereignty had usurped the constituent sovereignty of the people.

The Convention assembled at Philadelphia had themselves no direct authority from the people. Their authority was all derived from the state legislatures. But they had the Articles of Confederation before them, and they saw and felt the wretched condition into which they had brought the whole people, and that the Union itself was in the agonies of death. They soon perceived that the indispensably needed powers were such as no state government, no combination of them was, by the principles of the Declaration of Independence, competent to bestow. They could emanate only from the people. A highly respectable portion of the assembly, still clinging to the confederacy of states, proposed as a substitute for the Constitution a mere revival of the Articles of Confederation, with a grant of additional powers to the Congress. Their plan was respectfully and thoroughly discussed, but the want of a government and of the sanction of the people to the delegation of powers happily prevailed.

A constitution for the people and the distribution of legislative, executive, and judicial powers was prepared. It announced itself as the work of the people themselves; and as this was unquestionably a power assumed by the Convention not delegated to them by the people, they religiously confined it to a simple power to propose, and carefully provided that it should be no more than a proposal until sanctioned by the confederation Congress, by the state legislatures, and by the people of the several states, in conventions specially assembled by authority of their legislatures for the single purpose of examining and passing upon it.

And thus was consummated the work commenced by the Declaration of Independence — a work in which the people of the North American Union, acting under the deepest sense of responsibility to the Supreme Ruler of the universe, had achieved the most transcendent act of power that social man in his mortal condition can perform. Even that of dissolving the ties of allegiance which he is bound to his country, of renouncing that country itself, of demolishing its government, of instituting another government, and of making for himself another country in its stead.

And on that day, of which you now commemorate the fiftieth anniversary — on that 30th day of April, 1789 — was this mighty revolution, not only in the affairs of our own country but in the principles of government over civilized man, accomplished.

The Revolution itself was a work of thirteen years — and had never been completed until that day. The Declaration of Independence and the Constitution of the United States are parts of one consistent whole, founded upon one and the same theory of government, then new, not as a theory, for it had been working itself into the mind of man for many ages, and been especially expounded in the writings of Locke, but had never before been adopted by a great nation in practice.

There are yet, even at this day, many speculative objections to this theory. Even in our own country there are still philosophers who deny the principles asserted in the Declaration as self-evident truths; who deny the natural equality and inalienable

John Quincy Adams; daguerreotype by Brady

rights of man; who deny that the people are the only legitimate source of power; who deny that all just powers of government are derived from the *consent* of the governed. Neither your time, nor perhaps the cheerful nature of this occasion, permit me here to enter upon the examination of this antirevolutionary theory which arrays state sovereignty against the constituent sovereignty of the people, and distorts the Constitution of the United States into a league of friendship between confederate corporations.

I speak to matters of fact. There is the Declaration of Independence and there is the Constitution of the United States — let them speak for themselves. The grossly immoral and dishonest doctrine of despotic state sovereignty, the exclusive judge of its own obligations, and responsible to no power on earth or in Heaven, for the violation of them, is not there. The Declaration says it is not in me. The Constitution says it is not in me. . . .

The signers of the Declaration of Independence themselves were the persons who had first fallen into the error of believing that a confederacy of independent states would serve as a substitute for the repudiated government of Great Britain. Experience had demonstrated their mistake, and the condition of the country was a shriek of terror at its awful magnitude. They did retrace their steps, not to extinguish the federative feature in which their union had been formed — nothing could be wider from their intention — but to restore the order of things conformably to the principles of the Declaration of Independence and as they had been arranged in the first plans for a confederation — to make the people of the Union the constituent body and the reservation of the rights of the states subordinate to the Constitution. Hence the delegation of power was not from each state retaining its sovereignty, and all rights not expressly delegated by the states, but from the people of each and of all the states to the United States, in Congress assembled, representing at once the whole people and all the states of the Union.

They retained the federative feature preeminently in the constitution of the Senate, and in the complication of its great powers — legislative, executive, and judicial — making that body a participant in all the great departments of constituted power. They preserved the federative principle and combined it with the constituent power of the people in the mode of electing the President of the United States, whether by the electoral colleges or by the House of Representatives voting by states. They preserved it even in the constitution of the House, the popular branch of the legislature, by giving separate delegations to the people of each state. But they expressly made the Constitution and constitutional laws of the United States paramount not only to the laws but to the constitutions of the separate states inconsistent with them.

I have traced step by step, in minute and tedious detail, the departure from the principles of the Declaration of Independence in the process of organizing the Confederation — the disastrous and lamentable consequences of that departure and the admirable temper and spirit with which the Convention at Philadelphia returned to those principles in the preparation and composition of the Constitution of the United States.

That this work was still imperfect, candor will compel us all to admit; though in specifying its imperfections, the purest minds and the most patriotic hearts differ widely from each other in their conclusions. Distrustful as it becomes me to be of my own judgment, but authorized by the experience of a full half century, during which I have been variously and almost uninterruptedly engaged in both branches of the legislature and in the executive departments of this government, and released, by my own rapid approach to the closing scene of life, from all possible influence of personal interest or ambition, I may perhaps be permitted to remark that the omission of a clear and explicit Declaration of Rights was a great defect in the Constitution as presented by the Convention to the people, and that it has been imperfectly remedied by the ten articles of amendment proposed by the first Congress under the Constitution, and now incorporated with it.

A Declaration of Rights would have marked in a more emphatic manner the return from the derivative sovereignty of the states to the constituent sovereignty of the people for the basis of the federal Union than was done by the words, "We the people of the United States," in the Preamble to the Constitution. A Declaration of Rights, also, systematically drawn up, as a part of the Constitution, and adapted to it with the consummate skill displayed in the consistent adjustment of its mighty powers, would have made it more complete in its unity and in its symmetry than it now appears, an elegant edifice, but encumbered with superadditions, not always in keeping with the general character of the building itself.

A Declaration of Rights, reserved by the constituent body, the people, might and probably would have prevented many delicate and dangerous questions of conflicting jurisdictions which have arisen and may yet arise between the general and the separate state governments. The rights reserved by the people would have been exclusively their own rights, and they would have been protected from the encroachments not only of the general government but of the disunited states. . . .

The first object of the people declared by the Constitution as their motive for its establishment, *to form a more perfect Union,* had been attained by the establishment of the Constitution itself; but this was yet to be demonstrated by its practical operation in the establishment of justice, in the insurance of domestic tranquillity, in the provision for the common defense, in the promotion of the general welfare, and in securing the blessings of liberty to the people themselves, the authors of the Constitution, and to their posterity.

These are the great and transcendental objects of all legitimate government; the primary purposes of all human association. For these purposes the Confederation had been instituted, and had signally failed for their attainment. How far have they been attained under this new national organization?

It has abided the trial of time. This day, fifty years have passed away since the first impulse was given to the wheels of this political machine. The generation by which it was constructed has passed away. Not one member of the Convention who gave this Constitution to their country survives. They have enjoyed its blessings so far as they were secured by their labors. They have been gathered to their fathers. That posteri-

ty for whom they toiled, not less anxiously than for themselves, has arisen to occupy their places and is rapidly passing away in its turn. A third generation, unborn upon the day which you commemorate, forms a vast majority of the assembly who now honor me with their attention.

Your city, which then numbered scarcely 30,000 inhabitants, now counts its numbers by hundreds of thousands. Your state, then numbering less than double the population of your city at this day, now tells its children by millions. The thirteen primitive states of the Revolution, painfully rallied by this Constitution to the fold from which the impotence and disuniting character of the Confederacy was already leading them astray, now reinforced by an equal number of younger sisters, and all swarming with an active, industrious, and hardy population, have penetrated from the Atlantic to the Rocky Mountains, and opened a paradise upon the wilds watered by the father of the floods. The Union, which at the first census, ordained by this Constitution, returned a people of less than 4 million of souls; at the next census, already commanded by law, the semi-central enumeration since that day, is about to exhibit a return of 17 million. Never, since the first assemblage of men in social union, has there been such a scene of continued prosperity recorded upon the annals of time.

How much of this prosperity is justly attributable to the Constitution, then first put upon its trial, may perhaps be differently estimated by speculative minds. Never was a form of government so obstinately, so pertinaciously contested before its establishment; and never was human foresight and sagacity more disconcerted and refuted by the event than those of the opposers of the Constitution. On the other hand, its results have surpassed the most sanguine anticipations of its friends. Neither Washington, nor Madison, nor Hamilton dared to hope that this new experiment of government would so triumphantly accomplish the purposes which the Confederation had so utterly failed to effect. . . .

The Constitution of the United States was republican and democratic; but the experience of all former ages had shown that, of all human governments, democracy was the most unstable, fluctuating, and short-lived; and it was obvious that if virtue — the virtue of the people — was the foundation of republican government, the stability and duration of the government must depend upon the stability and duration of the virtue by which it is sustained.

Now the *virtue* which had been infused into the Constitution of the United States, and was to give to its vital existence the stability and duration to which it was destined, was no other than the concretion of those abstract principles which had been first proclaimed in the Declaration of Independence; namely, the self-evident truths of the natural and unalienable rights of man, of the indefeasible constituent and dissolvent sovereignty of the people, always subordinate to a rule of right and wrong, and always responsible to the Supreme Ruler of the universe for the *rightful* exercise of that sovereign, constituent, and dissolvent power.

This was the platform upon which the Constitution of the United States had been erected. Its VIRTUES, its republican character consisted in its conformity to the principles proclaimed in the Declaration of Independence, and as its administration must necessarily be always pliable to the fluctuating varieties of public opinion; its stability and duration by a like overruling and irresistible necessity was to depend upon the stability and duration in the hearts and minds of the people of that *virtue*, or, in other words, of those principles proclaimed in the Declaration of Independence and embodied in the Constitution of the United States. . . .

Every change of a President of the United States has exhibited some variety of poli-

cy from that of his predecessor. In more than one case, the change has extended to political and even to moral principle; but the policy of the country has been fashioned far more by the influences of public opinion and the prevailing humors in the two houses of Congress than by the judgment, the will, or the principles of the President of the United States. The President himself is no more than a representative of public opinion at the time of his election; and as public opinion is subject to great and frequent fluctuations, he *must* accommodate his policy to them; or the people will speedily give him a successor; or either house of Congress will effectually control his power.

It is thus, and in no other sense, that the Constitution of the United States is democratic; for the government of our country, instead of a democracy the most simple, is the most complicated government on the face of the globe. From the immense extent of our territory, the difference of manners, habits, opinions, and, above all, the clashing interests of the North, South, East, and West, public opinion formed by the combination of numerous aggregates becomes itself a problem of compound arithmetic, which nothing but the result of the popular elections can solve.

It has been my purpose, fellow citizens, in this discourse to show:

1. That this Union was formed by spontaneous movement of the *people* of thirteen English colonies, all subjects of the King of Great Britain, bound to him in allegiance and to the British Empire as their country; that the first object of this Union was united resistance against oppression, and to obtain from the government of their country redress of their wrongs.

2. That failing in this object, their petitions having been spurned and the oppressions of which they complained aggravated beyond endurance, their delegates in Congress, *in their name and by their authority,*

issued the Declaration of Independence —
proclaiming them to the world as *one people*,
absolving them from their ties and oaths of
allegiance to their king and country, renouncing that country; declaring the UNITED
colonies, independent states, and announc-
ing that this ONE PEOPLE of thirteen united,
independent states, by that act, assumed
among the powers of the earth that separate
and equal station to which the laws of nature and of nature's God entitled them.

3. That in justification of themselves for
this act of transcendent power, they proclaimed the principles upon which they held
all lawful government upon earth to be
founded; which principles were the natural,
unalienable, imprescriptible rights of man,
specifying among them, life, liberty, and the
pursuit of happiness; that the institution of
government is to *secure* to men in society
the possession of those rights; that the institution, dissolution, and reinstitution of government belong exclusively to THE PEOPLE
under a moral responsibility to the Supreme
Ruler of the universe; and that all the *just*
powers of government are derived from the
consent of the governed.

4. That under this proclamation of principles, the dissolution of allegiance to the
British King, and the compatriot connection
with the people of the British Empire, were
accomplished; and the *one people* of the
United States of America became one separate, sovereign, independent power, assuming an equal station among the nations of
the earth.

5. That this one people did not immediately institute a government for themselves. But instead of it, their delegates in
Congress, by authority from their separate
state legislatures, without voice or consultation of the people, instituted a mere Confederacy.

6. That this Confederacy totally departed from the principles of the Declaration of
Independence, and substituted, instead of
the constituent power of the people, an assumed sovereignty of each separate state as
the source of all its authority.

7. That as a primitive source of power,
this separate state sovereignty was not only
a departure from the principles of the Declaration of Independence but directly contrary to and utterly incompatible with
them.

8. That the tree was made known by its
fruits; that after five years wasted in its
preparation, the Confederacy dragged out a
miserable existence of eight years more, and
expired like a candle in the socket, having
brought the Union itself to the verge of dissolution.

9. That the Constitution of the United
States was a *return* to the principles of the
Declaration of Independence, and the exclu-
sive constituent power of the people; that it
was the work of the ONE PEOPLE of the
United States; and that those United
States, though doubled in numbers, still
constitute as a nation but ONE PEOPLE.

10. That this Constitution, making due
allowance for the imperfections and errors
incident to all human affairs, has under all
the vicissitudes and changes of war and
peace been administered upon those same
principles during a career of fifty years.

11. That its fruits have been, still making
allowance for human imperfection, a more
perfect Union, established justice, domestic
tranquillity, provision for the common defense, promotion of the general welfare, and
the enjoyment of the blessings of liberty by
the constituent *people* and their posterity to
the present day.

And now the future is all before us, and
Providence our guide.

Index

Names of persons with an asterisk (*) are those of authors of selections in this book. In each case the selection (sometimes more than one) is the first entry following the name.

claration of t

human events it becomes necessary

which the Laws of Nature and of

We hold these

ty and the pursuit of Happiness.

of Government becomes destructi

ing its powers in such form, as

for light and transient causes s

to which they are accustomed.

right, it is their duty, to throw of

essity which constrains them to a